SUMMER

The Bartlett
School of
Architecture

Contents

BARTLETT

**SUMMER
2022**

Introduction

Returning to on-site learning over the course of this year has brought new energy and activity to the studios, classrooms, workshops and labs of The Bartlett School of Architecture. The joy of our student community coming together to share and collaborate within the creative spaces at 22 Gordon Street and Here East has been both inspiring and uplifting.

However, the 2021-22 academic year has also highlighted the need for the school to begin an overdue journey of self-reflection and to face up to some honest and difficult truths about our responsibilities as educators. We need to ensure that all students feel safe and valued. It is our responsibility to help shape a positive future for architecture, by nurturing the next generation to become thoughtful and conscientious practitioners. Our highest priority is to ensure this moment accelerates our school's journey of transformational change and acts as a springboard to support and celebrate our students more fully.

We are determined to remain focused on our students' remarkable ingenuity, their unique vision and their insightful creativity. This year's Summer Show book is a celebration of just that. Within its pages you will see the work of more than 700 of our 1,700 students, from five of our taught programmes: Architecture BSc, Architectural & Interdisciplinary Studies BSc, Engineering & Architectural Design MEng, Architecture MSci and Architecture MArch.

This year's show also marks the first time in two years that we have been able to bring our community together to display our students' work in a physical space. It is truly heart-warming and restorative for everyone to be able to welcome our guests in person to the school this year.

We are pleased that the digital innovations that were advanced so rapidly in response to the Covid-19 pandemic have not been set aside. Our online exhibition space has received hundreds of thousands of visitors over the past two years and will once again be showcasing our students' thought-provoking projects.

A big thank you needs to be said to our professional services and academic staff at The Bartlett School of Architecture, The Bartlett Faculty and across the UCL campus. Teams of dedicated administrators, technicians, librarians, tutors, lecturers, professors, security, facilities, communications and events staff have worked incredibly hard throughout the year. Thank you also for the contributions of our many guests and supporters, including alumni, practitioners and researchers. Your guidance, friendship and support have a value beyond measure to everyone in the Bartlett community.

We are so proud of the work our students have produced, and even just a brief glance through the pages of this book shows why. We are also deeply proud of who they are – curious, socially conscious and informed. As The Bartlett School of Architecture moves forward – under the guidance of our new Director, Amy Kulper, who will be joining us in September 2022 – we will do so with renewed purpose to help our students feel as proud of us as we are of them.

Professor Jacqui Glass
Interim Director of The Bartlett School of Architecture

Professor Christoph Lindner
Dean of The Bartlett Faculty of the Built Environment

Architecture BSc
(ARB/RIBA Part 1)

Architecture BSc (ARB/RIBA Part 1)

Programme Directors:
Ana Monrabal-Cook, Luke Pearson

Architecture BSc establishes primary knowledge and understanding about the core principles of the discipline, providing a platform from which experimental and challenging design work can emerge.

The programme teaches students the fundamentals of architecture, developing their critical ability to consider what it means to synthesise architectural designs and what methods they can utilise to do so. This year the programme continued to introduce students to new and diverse methods and research themes across three years and 16 design units. From participatory practices to advanced simulations, to studies of material life cycles or experimental drawings and digital animations, units and their students continue to push the boundaries of design thinking at undergraduate level. Experimentation is tied to a rigorous approach to design – not only in spatial planning but also in technology, social engagement, environmental design and computation. This allows our students to produce complex and layered buildings.

Our Year 1 cohort is organised as a single group before a design unit system begins in Year 2. The first year is contextual, through which architectural expertise is developed using diverse experimentation and exploration. Through modules such as 'The History of Cities and their Architecture' and 'Making Cities', students are introduced to different disciplines, developing an understanding of the architect's historical and social role. In design, students experience the collaborative and iterative nature of architectural design as a year group through both individual and group projects.

In Years 2 and 3 our design units offer unique expertise and a broad range of approaches, allowing students to connect their studies to their developing interests. The 16 units explore diverse themes and agendas, including the relationship between architecture and landscape; digital simulation and fabrication; and the role of narrative and the political context of design, from working with housing associations in the UK to the contextual study of architecture in the Global South. Each unit establishes a methodology that builds core skills and expands students' work in new directions, providing three diverse experiences over the course of their degree.

Following tailored research briefs, students are encouraged to contextualise their projects by carrying out in-depth studies into urban and rural conditions. Through these they gain an understanding of the complexities of producing architecture in radically different environments. Throughout the degree, students relate their design projects to all other taught modules. This culminates in Year 3, in which design and technology are developed in synthesis, complemented by self-selected thematic interests in history and theory. By the end of their undergraduate studies, our students are equipped to engage with the design of architecture in a sophisticated manner, placing their own practice and research into wider socio-political, historical and environmental contexts.

This year the varied and ambitious design projects all showed a desire to tackle the complexities of our built environment and the pressing issues it faces. Students addressed ecology through bioreceptive materials, analyses of sites through deep time and new ways of understanding natural processes through advanced computation. The social potential of architecture was explored in work examining circular material economies, the architecture of Haiti and collaborative projects with a university in Kigali, Rwanda. Architecture as spatial storytelling assumed a renewed purpose as a way of connecting people, with students exploring innovative techniques using digital animation and game engines to explore alternative futures and suggest new ways of living.

While we became accustomed to using digital platforms during the pandemic, this year has seen a return to studio culture through hybridised ways of learning and designing. We have found ways to augment traditional design methods using the new digital tools and communications platforms that have become ubiquitous over the last two years. In this context students have continued to create projects that are both rigorous and imaginative, and that demonstrate not only great accomplishment, but also a desire to question the discipline of architecture. The designs produced by our undergraduate students point towards a future that is both experimental and inclusive, in which radical new ways of working can be used for social change, serving to question both the roles and boundaries of the architectural profession.

Many thanks to our Programme Senior Administrator, Kim van Poeteren; our Teaching and Learning Administrator, Beth Barnett-Sanders; and all of our Programme Postgraduate Teaching Assistant team – Jatiphak Boonmun, Stephannie Contreras-Fell, Tea Marta, Carlota Nuñez-Barranco Vallejo, Petra Seitz, Eva Tisnikar and Tom Ushakov – for all their dedication and energy.

Year 1 Students

Ariel Alper, Alexandra Audas, Lucy Ayres, Beau Beames, Salima Begum, Siya Bhandari, Charlotte Burden, Clive Burgess, Thomas Butterworth, Mason Cameron, Diego Carreras, Nathan Cartwright, Joshua-Jefferson Celada Flordeliz, Yufei Cheng, Chi (Jenna) Ching, Lok Chiu, Ifsah Chowdhery, Jaewoong (Justin) Chung, Shu (Sarah) Chuwa, Rosa Crossley-Furse, Pacharamon (Myla) Danwachira, Natania De-Marro, Laura Dietzold, Sammy Doublet, Josiah Elleston-Burell, Hsiang-Yu (Sean) Fan, Wentong (Iris) Feng, Delphi Fothergill, Jessica Georgelin, Beatriz Goodwins Banuelos, Kiran Gosal, Harshal Gulabchandre, Serena Haddon, Thomas Henly, Aocheng Huang, Holly Hunt, Vladut Iacob, Dahui Im, Kai Jackson, Hye (Helen) Joung, Aryan Kaul, Hashaam Khan, Nadiya Khan, Libby Ko, Beulah Kuku, To (Marcus) Lam, Yiwen (Yuna) Lee, Lihui (Lily) Lin, Laura Maczik, Jillian Mak, Duncan McAllister, Caitlin McHale, Junjie Mei, Allyah Mitra Nandy, Kullaphat Ngamprasertpong, Lily Nguyen, Laura Noble, Tilly Ollerenshaw, Sean Ow, Kai Pentecost, Alex Perez Escamilla, Bryan Png Yiliang, Akif Rahman, Adam Raymond, Iolo Rees, Regan Reser, Jessica Richard, Arthur Ritchie, Jio Ryu, Mattia Salvadori, Andrew Seah, Ryhan Sheik, Hannah Simon, Soph Siney, Nikhita Sivakumar, Charles Smare, Jodie Spencer, Pasathorn Srichaiyongphanich, Sofie Stiekema, Chunyi (Sally) Sun, Hossain Takir, Aleksandra Tarnowska, Alessandra Villanueva, An Vu, Shuheng Wang; Lola Wilson, Theodor Wolf, Zhi (Tina) Wu, Hiu (Amy) Yam, Min Yoo, Yaowen Zhang, Jingwen (Michaelia) Zheng, Deqing (Rachel) Zhou, Peiyan Zou

Y1.1

Materials for Change

Year 1

Directors: Max Dewdney, Frosso Pimenides

This year, in returning to physical teaching, we also expanded the territory of the studio outwards across a series of London sites. Shifting the learning environment to both inside and outside the studio allowed us to spread out and slow down the pace of production. By slowing down, we encouraged students to find their own voices and seek inspiration from their own cultural backgrounds to cultivate confidence and resilience.

The first part of the year was structured around two projects: individual research and a collective installation across six London squares. These projects allowed students to explore architecture, a practice which relies hugely upon the collective ethos of working together with colleagues, tutors, craftspeople and clients.

Students designed, fabricated, installed and performed interventions that emerged from their readings of these sites – the hidden stories and qualities of a place, forgotten events or even the imagined alternative realities. If a place were a person, how would you listen to their feelings and memories? A square is a place that can enable, encourage and host all sorts of unplanned, unforeseen experiences for a group or an individual. We therefore explored ways to connect people together.

The main building project of the year, 'Materials for Change', continued the year's investigations over three scales: body, building and city. Students were asked to examine whether the built structures – buildings and their surroundings that form 'the city' – as well as the clothes, actions and identities that surround and are expressed by our bodies, are tailored to our needs. The first phase helped to understand the scale of the city and the building in relation to the body. In the second phase students were asked to design a micro-building, while connecting their vision to the larger area. Students were encouraged to imagine radical possibilities for how the city could be, with new ways of building enabling new ways of living.

During this year's field trip to Glasgow, we witnessed and were inspired by a resilient city with a strong urbanity and cultural materiality.

Associate
Gavin Robotham

Tutors
Alastair Browning, Ivan Tsz Long Chan, Zachary Fluker, Maria Fulford, Jack Hardy, Ashley Hinchcliffe, Tahmineh Hooshyar Emami, Vasilis Ilchuk, Fergus Knox, Stefan Lengen, Siraaj Mitha, Isaac Simpson, Colin Smith

Departmental Tutor
Sabina Andron

Thank you to our guest review panellists: Laura Allen, Aurore Baulier, Matthew Butcher, Nat Chard, Nikhil Cherian, Edward Denison, Julika Gittner, Tamsin Hanke, Colin Herperger, Ajmona Hoxha, Edwin Hu, Steve Johnson, Paul Kohlhaussen, Kit Lee-Smith, Marilia Lezou, Tim Lucas, Jaqlin Lyon, Jacob Meyers, Ana Monrabal-Cook, Tim Norman, Colin O'Sullivan, Francisca Lopez Pani, Thomas Parker, Jolanta Piotrowska, Emily Priest, Sophia Psarra, Danielle Purkiss, Rahesh Ram, Lizzie Ruinard, Martin Sagar, Narinder Sagoo, Ellie Sampson, Eoin Shaw, Bob Sheil, Sarah Smith, Mark Smout, Luke Topping, Oliver Wilton, Simon Withers, Yeena Yoon

Thanks to photographers: Jason Brooks, Robert Newcombe, Jatin Naru

Thanks to Sabina Andron, Niamh Grace, James Green, Tom Davies & the B-made team and to our Terrace Club guest speakers Alastair Browning, Christoph Linder, Aeli Roberts. Special thanks to Abigail Tan (St Giles Hotel)

Glasgow field trip: thanks Stuart and Ally Cotton (Kilmahew Trust), Katherine Lee (GSA), Andy Summers, Graeme Sutherland

Y1.1, Y1.3, Y1.5, Y1.6 Guildhall Yard: Diego Carreras, Laura Dietzold, Josiah Elleston-Burell, Jessica Georgelin, Thomas Henly, Aocheng Huang, Holly Hunt, Hye (Helen) Joung, Libby Ko, Beulah Kuku, Yiwen (Yuna) Lee, Laura Maczik, Pasathorn Srichaiyongphanich, Theodor Wolf, Zhi (Tina) Wu 'Gestures/Exchange: A Performance of Memories'. Guildhall Yard, a historic civic space which lies empty most of the time, is temporarily filled with performance and sound to re-enact memories of its past. Theatre, costume and sound are intrinsic to Guildhall Yard, which was built upon a Roman amphitheatre as the ceremonial centre of the livery companies of London. The yard is a *tabula rasa* ready for imprinting. Through performance, movement of the body, costume and sound are united and enable the memories of the yard and its history to resurface.

Y1.2 Site Context Studies: All Students 'Catalysts, Edges & [Un]Stable Elements: A Study of London Squares'. A public square can be seen as a void or *tabula rasa*; often they are contested spaces and not in public ownership. The project recorded fragments across a series of study sites in 2D and 3D. These took the form of scaled models, castings of details and edge conditions and translations of elements from the site into another material or form.

Y1.4, Y1.7, Y1.8 Peckham Square: Ifsah Chowdhery, Natania De-Marro, Sammy Doublet, Serena Haddon, Dahui Im, Lily Nguyen, Sylvia Ninh, Sean Ow, Adam Raymond, Iolo Rees, Mattia Salvadori, Andrew Seah, Hossain Takir, An Vu, Deqing (Rachel) Zhou 'Gestures/Exchange: Balk – Reimaging Peckham's Trading History'. Built on the site of the Peckham branch of the Grand Surrey Canal, Peckham Square was crucial in handling cargo brought to London via canal in the 19th and early 20th centuries. Boats would deliver raw timber ready to be processed and squared for construction. These beams were carried by canal workers (lumpers), who transported wood from the barges to the timber warehouses, which have since been replaced by a modern leisure centre and drama school. The performance brings the movements of the canal workers to life through the physicality of the connection to the timbers at the forefront of the choreographed movements. The actors carry timber planks gusseted by concertina fabric. By way of these movements the surfaces expand and contract, accentuating the postures, rhythms and struggles of the lumpers as they haul the unprocessed timber through the docks.

Y1.9, Y1.11, Y1.12 Queen Square: Jaewoong (Justin) Chung, Aryan Kaul, Hashaam Khan, Laura Noble, Tilly Ollerenshaw, Kai Pentecost, Bryan Png Yiliang, Regan Reser, Jessica Richard, Jio Ryu, Ryhan Sheik, Soph Siney, Sofie Stiekema, Chunyi (Sally) Sun, Alessandra Villanueva, Shuheng Wang, Yaowen Zhang 'Gestures/Exchange: The Queen's Journey'. Queen Square commemorates Queen Charlotte, whose statue overlooks the surrounding hospitals where she would visit her husband, George III. The installation reinvigorates the historic remnants of the square, returning the focus of the site back to the Queen herself. Through the use of forced perspective on a prescribed bench in the square, the royal procession interacts with a small region of the square, reinforcing the intimacy the Queen and her husband shared. An armrest, foot stool and ergonomic cushion come together to direct the viewers towards the statue of Queen Charlotte. In the procession, actors enter two by two and set up installation pieces, as well as three fabric screens that frame and dress the statue in a fitting makeover of royal blue.

Y1.10, Y1.13, Y1.14 Arnold Circus: Alexandra Audas, Lucy Ayres, Beau Beames, Siya Bhandari, Clive Burgess, Thomas Butterworth, Nathan Cartwright, Yufei Cheng, Lok Chiu, Delphi Fothergill, Beatriz Goodwins Banuelos, Nadiya Khan, Caitlin McHale, Nikhita Sivakumar, Aleksandra Tarnowska, Lola Wilson 'Gestures/Exchange: Resurfacing the Buried'. Arnold Circus stands on the site of the Old Nichol slum, demolished in the 19th century. The installation uncovers long-buried structures by reimagining the architectural and domestic elements in the Victorian slum. Even in the present day, Arnold Circus is a contested space challenged with protecting its heritage. The community is invited to enjoy this window into the past, remembering the collective memories of what was there before.

Y1.15, Y1.17, Y1.18 Neal's Yard: Chi (Jenna) Ching, Wentong (Iris) Feng, Kiran Gosal, Vladut Iacob, To (Marcus) Lam, Lihui (Lily) Lin, Jillian Mak, Duncan McAllister, Junjie Mei, Allyah Mitra Nandy, Kullaphat Ngamprasertpong, Alex Perez Escamilla, Arthur Ritchie, Hannah Simon, Min Yoo, Jingwen (Michaelia) Zheng 'Gestures/Exchange: The Lover, the Barista, the Botanist and the Gatekeeper'. Neal's Yard sits tucked away in a corner of Seven Dials, London. Historically a site for warehouses, it is now a theme park for tourists to explore. Despite its small size, the yard juggles public, commercial and residential activities, leaving little space or need for new interventions. Instead of adding to the packed space, the installation reflects upon its existing qualities. Due to its similarity to a stage set, the performance directs attention to the highly curated nature of the space. Drawing on existing characteristics, four mechanisms are created – the gatekeeper, the barista, the botanist and the lovers – each exploring the gestures and exchanges of the yard. Each prop encourages participation, with one leading to the next, taking the causal passer-by from a passive member of the audience to an active contributor. By putting on a performance in the existing 'stage', the project looks beyond the theatrical façade, encouraging people to critically reflect upon their environment and their movement through it.

Y1.16, Y1.19, Y1.20 South End Green: Salima Begum, Charlotte Burden, Mason Cameron, Joshua-Jefferson Celada Flordeliz, Shu (Sarah) Chuwa, Rosa Crossley-Furse, Pacharamon (Myla) Danwachira, Hsiang-Yu (Sean) Fan, Emma Greaves, Harshal Gulabchandre, Kai Jackson, Akif Rahman, Charles Smare, Jodie Spencer, Hiu (Amy) Yam, Peiyan Zou 'Gestures/Exchange: A Cloud in South End Green'. The fountain of South End Green is a reminder of the River Fleet that used to flow down from Hampstead Heath. A collection of found, temporary objects – cans, bottles, lighters and canisters – are displayed underneath a cloud of fabric draped around the fountain. The ghost of the river rises above, illuminated by the torches beneath.

Y1.21 Building Proposal Models: All Students 'Re-Imagined Realities'. Architectural designers have to understand place, location and area. The essence of a place, made up of magic, memories and ideas, must be personally interrogated. Over the course of the year, students learn to listen to sites, identifying key aspects that will be heightened, changed or reconfigured through design. Personal experience – whether that be cultural heritage, family roots or individual identity – is key to designing a building. It is how we understand and interpret daily habits, enabling us to invent new ways of inhabiting a room, place or location. The resulting architecture acts as a catalyst for existing sites. They could be set in the now or in the distant future, adding to and enhancing the life that is there.

Y1.3

Y1.4

Y1.5

Y1.6

Y1.7

Y1.8

Y1.9

Y1.10

Y1.11

Y1.12

Y1.13

Y1.14

Y1.15

Y1.16

Y1.17

Y1.18

Y1.19

Y1.20

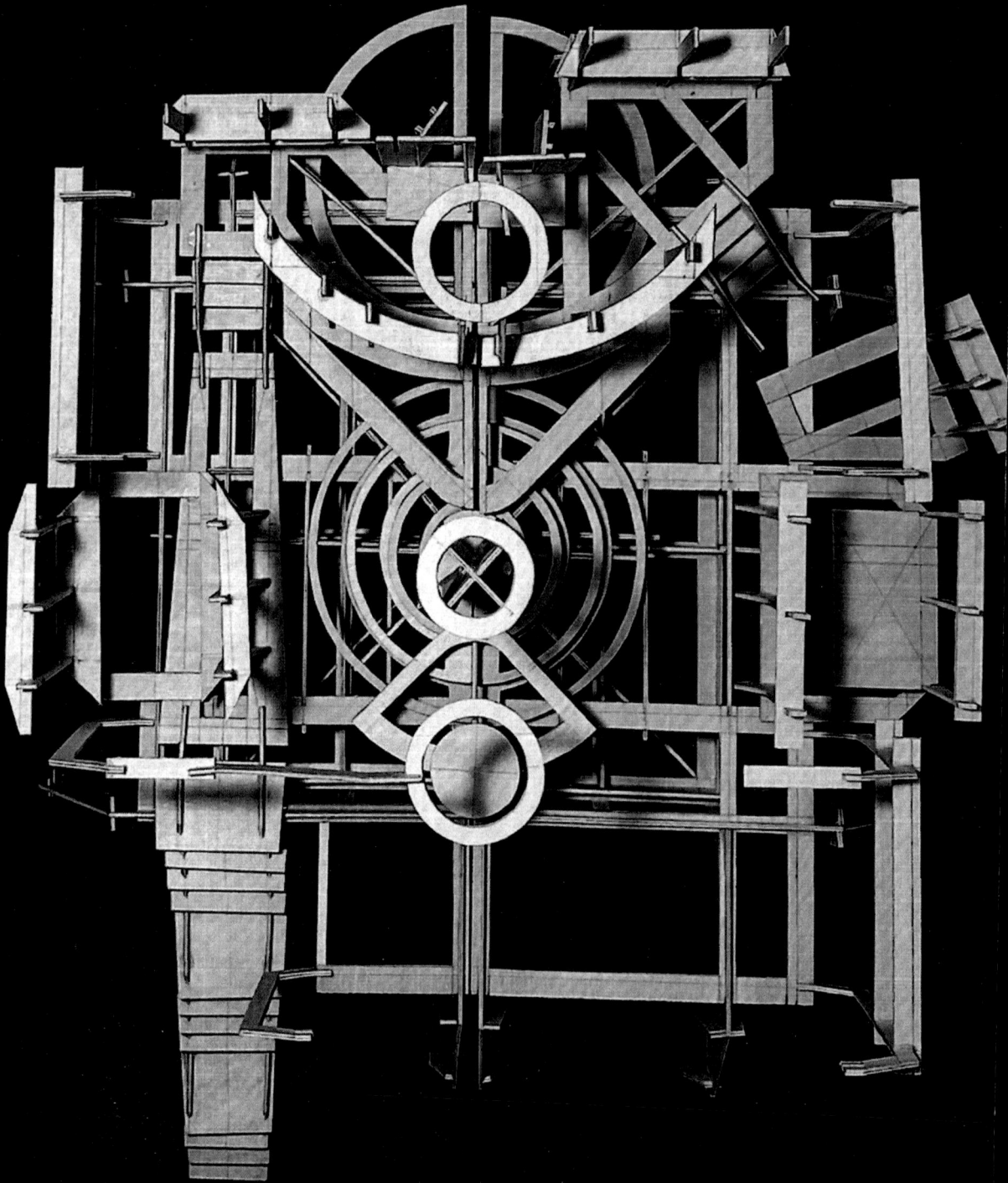

Reformulating Practice UG0

Murray Fraser, Michiko Sumi

In recent years UG0 have explored social and environmental sustainability in an inventive and sensuous manner, with projects tackling issues such as energy consumption, environmental damage, everyday ecosystems and urban biodiversity. While these urgent matters continue to inform the unit's creative direction, this year students also reflected on what they will be doing in their future careers and were asked to think of potential ways to reformulate how architects practice today.

Architectural practice need not be as it is now, yet what else might it become? Taking London as the location for projects, while also studying key examples of alternative forms of practice from around the world, the unit examined issues of ethics, justice, inclusivity and cultural identity.

An obvious question to ask is why is this issue important to architectural students? In the main part, many people study architecture because they want to make a real difference to society, primarily through the act of designing higher quality and more sustainable built environments. Yet, within a condition of neoliberal capitalism, there are extremely powerful socio-economic forces that make social improvement difficult. Most architectural practices opt to operate within the limits set by neoliberal capitalism, arguing that it is impossible to do much if one tries to escape the system and that it is better to tackle matters from within. In contrast, however, some contemporary architects have explicitly tried to find new ways of practice in the belief that a resistant, even revolutionary stance is required.

With this in mind, this year's field trip was to Bristol, where UG0 met with artists, architects and environmental researchers, among others. They also visited the collective art studios in Spike Island where different forms of creative practice are being forged.

Year 2
David Abi Ghanem, Ani Begaj, Esin Gumus, Rabiyya Huseynova, Fahad Zafar Janjua, Tran (Thu) Lai, Milen Purewal

Year 3
Luke (Taro) Bean, Vanessa Chew, Maria Garrido Regalado, Wei Lim, Joseph Russell, Shannon Townsend, Nathan Verrier, Yeung (Julie) Yeung

Technical tutors and consultants: Nicholas Jewell, Ewa Hasla (Atelier One Engineers), John I'Anson (Atelier One Engineers), Tea Marta, Matei Mitrache

Critics: Anthony Boulanger, Eva Branscome, Pedro Geddes, Ifigeneia Liangi, Ana Monrabal-Cook, Thomas Parker, Luke Pearson, Stuart Piercy, Neba Sere, Ben Stringer, Dan Wilkinson

Sponsors: Bean Buro, KPF Architects

0.1 Maria Garrido Regalado, Y3 'The Rituals of Architecture'. Model. This close-up shot gives a roof plan view of a small timber-framed baldachin where a solitary, obsessive architect works. In the various spatial pockets of this tiny structure, the architect can enact the ten key rituals of their everyday routine as a practitioner of this ancient yet modern profession.

0.2 Luke (Taro) Bean, Y3 'Waterworks Baths and Studios'. City Road Basin, EC1. Exploded axonometric. This diagrammatic drawing shows the servicing system for a building that includes three medium-sized architectural studios intermixed with a suite of public and semi-public baths. It outlines the different networks for recycling water from the adjacent Regent's Canal or from the aquifer below, as well as for filtered water collected by the building's roof.

0.3–0.4 Shannon Townsend, Y3 'The Euston Sanatorium'. Euston Road, NW1. Isometric section; plan. Sitting on one of the most polluted roads in London, this scheme improves urban air quality and human health by adopting a bio-reactive façade and a series of internal filtering systems which will naturally cleanse the flow of air through the building. As an action to tackle the climate crisis, this will help improve our chances of reaching pollution targets that seem out of reach.

0.5 Luke (Taro) Bean, Y3 'Waterworks Baths and Studios'. City Road Basin, EC1. Sketch plans. This is one of the early iterations of the building's possible spatial arrangements and was fundamental in coming up with a subtle mix of architectural offices and swimming pools. Stressed employees, as well as members of the wider public, can luxuriate in these pools as a retreat from the busy city around them.

0.6 Nathan Verrier, Y3 'Deptford Creek'. Convoy's Wharf, SE8. Bird's-eye perspective. Convoy's Wharf is one of London's most significant historical sites but it has lain abandoned and a new development plan threatens to swamp it with luxury housing. Adopting a different approach entirely, this scheme envisages a rewilded forest with a new forestry commission building that also includes community spaces for residents. The wider purpose is to enable coexistence between humans and nature.

0.7 Vanessa Chew, Y3 'Proposal for an Intergenerational Amalgam'. Dalston, E8. Interior renders. The project uses colour theory and natural materials to enhance user experience and promote intergenerational interaction within a new type of architectural office. A series of interior spaces encourage the architects to engage with the building's other occupants. This in turn enables them to design more meaningful and thoughtful projects for children and the elderly alike.

0.8 Joseph Russell, Y3 'Tightening the Green Belt: Oakwood Mews'. Enfield, N14. Roof plan. This design for new housing and associated community facilities in a woodland setting tackles the current housing shortage in the UK, and particularly London, by rethinking the concept of the Green Belt. The chosen site is in Enfield, opposite Oakwood Underground Station, designed by Charles Holden along with several other stations on the Piccadilly Line. The proposal is for a more ecological, sustainable form of suburban development.

0.9–0.10 Vanessa Chew, Y3 'Proposal for an Intergenerational Amalgam'. Dalston, E8. Model; planometric drawing. Given its location in the heart of Dalston, the building's programme imagines an intergenerational architectural practice that is an antithesis to the mainstream projects which exclude minority age groups, notably absent from Dalston's recent gentrification. Instead, there are a range of buildings for old, middle-aged and young people within a lively, colourful and playful landscape.

0.11–0.14 Wei Lim, Y3 'The Aylesbury "Renewal" Initiative'. Walworth, SE17. Isometric view; elevation; perspective section; view of walkway in the sky. The project situates itself in the Aylesbury Estate to propose an alternative, slow-paced refurbishment strategy for the estate's recovery. It proposes to blur the boundaries of the construction site – its processes, builders and council-house tenants – reconceiving them so that existing residents are not displaced while refurbishment takes place, in a coexistence of inhabitation and construction.

0.15–0.17 Yeung (Julie) Yeung, Y3 'Reimagining Bermondsey through Craft'. Bermondsey, SE1. Interior perspectives; technical prototypes. An arts-and-crafts community centre that fuses two interrelated processes: coffee brewing and the manufacture of 'coffee leather' from waste coffee grounds. It builds on Bermondsey's lost history of leather tanneries, while the architecture, as a living automaton, reveals workshops, archives, a theatre and café chambers, where walls become the canvas and instruments become the walls.

0.18 Luke (Taro) Bean, Y3 'Waterworks Baths and Studios'. City Road Basin, EC1. Elevation. For the exterior design of the new architectural offices combined with public and semi-public baths, the building wears its woven cladding panels like the armour of a samurai. This enables its skin to breathe in summer and winter alike, with the hot water steaming into the air on chilly days after being released via the chimneys and cowls on the rooftop.

0.19–0.20 Joseph Russell, Y3 'Tightening the Green Belt: Oakwood Mews'. Enfield, N14. Aerial perspective; elevations. Cockfosters London Underground depots are set to be demolished. The building materials, such as bricks and steel, can be repurposed to build housing and community facilities nearby. The scheme also adopts a hyper-local approach to harvested materials: adjacent arable land can provide straw for insulation and thatched roofs, while pine trees can provide timber. This localised sourcing significantly reduces the project's carbon footprint.

0.3

0.4

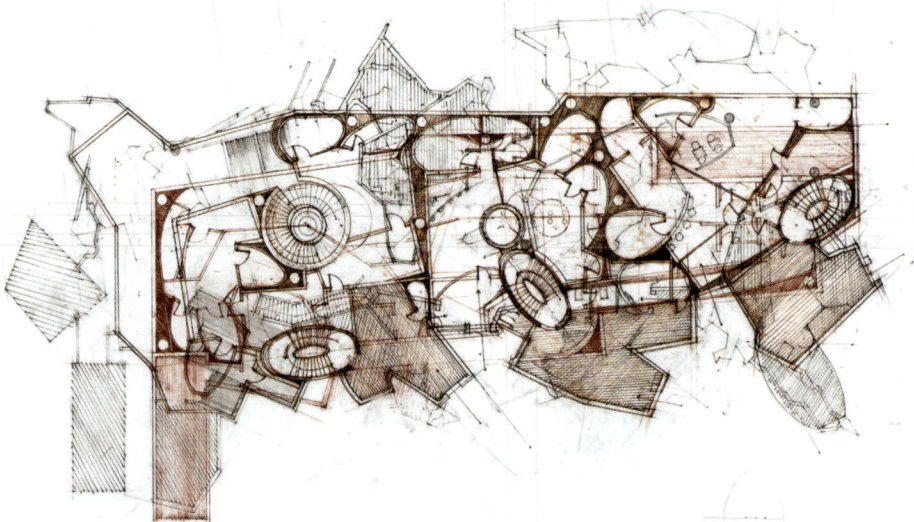

0.5

0.6

0.7

0.8

0.9

0.10

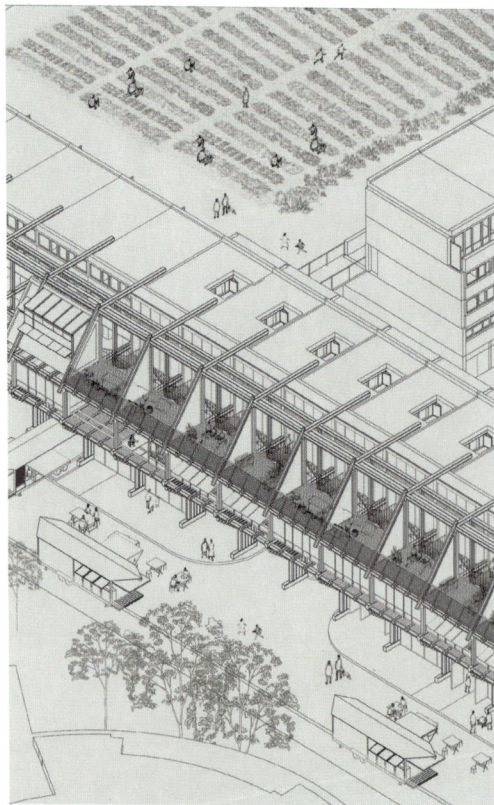

0.11

0.12

0.13

0.14

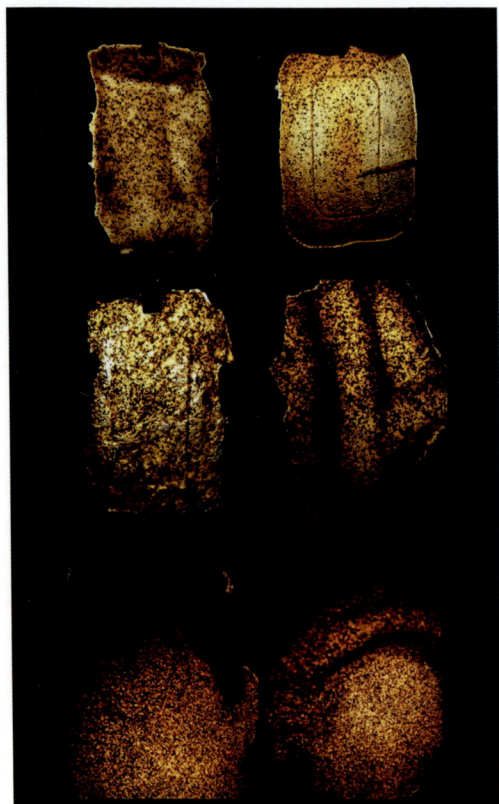

0.17

0.18

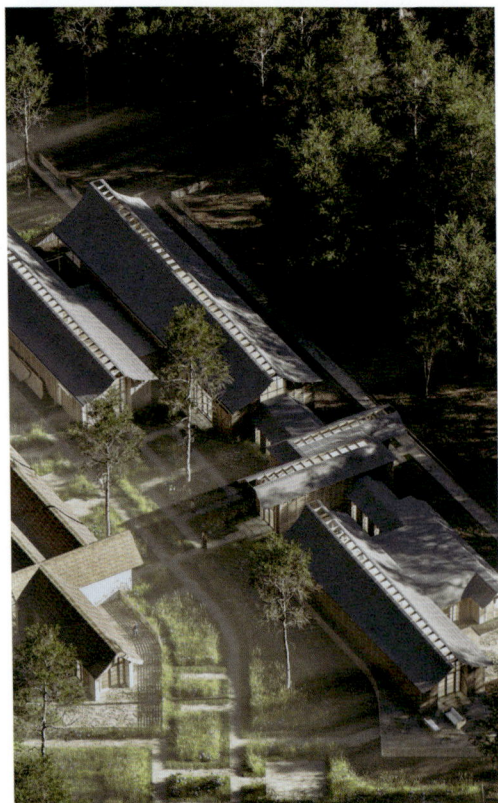

0.19

0.20

Common Ground

Rosie Hervey, Margit Kraft, Toby O'Connor

By the 2080s London's sea level is expected to have risen by between approximately 45cm and 1m. In the meantime many of our current flood water management assets are ageing or already at capacity. Simultaneously there is huge pressure on local authorities across London to provide more space for housing and commerce.

How do we embrace environmental issues such as fluvial and surface water flooding? How do we balance the needs of wildlife habitats, industrial estates and residential communities?

This year UG1 has been practising how to design for change over time. Exploring architecture as a process rather than as a product, we experimented with guiding and framing change across a wide range of physical and temporal scales.

Now more than ever, architects need training to work with confidence in situations of deep uncertainty. Together we questioned what it means to build with resilience and generosity, designing a locally integrated landscape vision that unlocks, shapes and preserves a piece of land in the Lea Valley for the next 150 years or more.

We moved through six chapters: Relief, Ground Up, Resilience, Generosity, Comfort and Narrative. In the process we considered proposals from the extraction of raw materials with which projects are made to the wider ecosystems and economies in which they are and will be situated. We developed designs both through landscape and structural strategies and material and interior studies. In each case we thought through the perspectives of imagined users and established a dialogue between our proposed landscape vision and the comfort of a good room.

Our investigations have been informed by seminars and workshops led by architects, planners, scientists and local stakeholders, including a field trip to the Centre for Alternative Technology in Wales. These events have encouraged students to engage with the need for diverse and inventive collaboration to tackle the climate emergency.

Across three sites in the Lea Valley, shared with a parallel set of third-year Cambridge University undergraduates, students developed individual briefs and responded with grounded and ambitious design proposals. They investigated intelligent relationships between factories and workspaces, urban wetlands and willow plantations, testing the resilience of their proposals through potential future scenarios at a variety of scales.

Year 2
Fatemah (Sean) Abkhou, Arnold Freund-Williams, Zuzanna Jastrzebska, Shouryan Kapoor, Mikaella Konia, Riya Mamtora, Elina Seyed Nikkhou, Jerzy (George) Szczerba, Amelia Teigen, Yerkin Wilbrandt

Year 3
Yu (Colin) Cheng, Rupert Rochford, Barbara Sawko, Yuqi (Sunny) Wang

Technical tutors and consultants: Paul Allen, Joe Barton, Dieter Brandstatter, Aurimas Bukauskas, Philip Christou, Jonathan Cook, Emaad Damda, Deborah Eastwood-Hancock, Nigel Gervis, Lee Heykoop, George Horne, Oskar Johanson, Gemma Manache, Quentin Martin, Christine McLennan, Simon Myers, Jez Ralph, Ian Russell, Patrick Shannon, Sarah Thomas, Tom Ushakov, Chris Watson, Paul Wood

With special thanks to Cody Dock and Margent Farm

Critics: Julia Backhaus, Alice Edgerly, Anastasia Glover, Ben Hayes, Stefan Lengen, William Marr-Heenan, Jane Wong

With thanks to UG5, UG6 and Cambridge University Y3S3 students

1.1–1.2 Zuzanna Jastrzebska, Y2 'Grain Valley'. How can a compromise be struck between industrial development, nature and human settlements? The project answers this question with a factory that is designed to be part of the ecosystem, rather than an individual object. Instead of taking the form of a production building, the factory is designed as a thatch mountain, a harmonious and permanent installation on the site's hilly landscape, uniting the area's industry with the contours of the Lea Valley.

1.3–1.5 Rupert Rochford, Y3 'Conversing with Wetlands'. Setting a precedent for the wider Lea catchment, the project proposes the selective removal of a concrete flood relief channel, embracing flooding to generate wetland creation and rewilding, which the architecture both frames and adapts to over time. This landscape strategy offers a more sustainable approach to flood defence within the valley, seeking to protect metropolitan sites along the course of the river as the climate emergency worsens. This goes hand in hand with a phased building strategy which integrates rewilding with the migration and evolution of human use, in this case converting a plastics factory to a conservation and education facility.

1.6, 1.11 Arnold Freund-Williams, Y2 'Arts and Crafts in the Lea'. The Lea Valley is a landscape that has been shaped over time by natural and human forces. As a place of rich biodiversity and deep industrial heritage, the project invokes the spirit of the Arts and Crafts movement, investigating William Morris's statement that 'Wherever nature works there will be beauty.' The project sets out a series of small-scale artisanal workshops which enable and encourage flexibility between indoor and outdoor spaces. The buildings themselves are designed to be embedded within the natural world, with a structure and material palette directly shaped by nature.

1.7 Yu (Colin) Cheng, Y3 'Undulation, a Vista'. The project focuses on achieving the optimal design solution for a sustainable glass-processing factory. A carbon calculator and a customised script are the main design tools. The embodied carbon of the structure was monitored carefully and its subsequent design iterations were evaluated before finalising the proposal. Relying on sustainable and locally sourced materials such as UK-grown timber and rammed earth, the core ambition of the project is to imagine a new relationship between human society and the natural world, starting from the present and specific industrial context.

1.8, 1.16 Riya Mamtora, Y2 'Natural Soap Factory'. Based in an area heavily damaged by its past and current industrial activities, the project applies a socio-bio-centric vision of *buen vivir*, investigating a reciprocal relationship between our health and the environment we live in. The building, whose function is to clean the surrounding soil, water and air while manufacturing soaps, will encourage a new way of production: one which considers its environment and sees making as a community activity and not something driven by money or individuality. The philosophy can also be applied more broadly to encompass more than factories and more than production. Design investigations examine how the building's function might develop through its conversion into a food hall which also values local production and care for the environment.

1.9 Amelia Teigen, Y2 'The Glass Compass'. The project considers adaptation over time, shifting from a recycling centre to a dance college over a 150-year timeframe. A central glass tower provides a landmark or 'compass' for the community in Enfield, guiding people towards the River Lea to appreciate its presence and not just pass it by. Public and private spaces are intertwined through generous circulation spaces, allowing both the

community and the private users of the building to enjoy the internal atmosphere. The landscape strategy within which the building is integrated includes new bodies of water, extending the depth of the river edge into the industrial urban grain and working sensitively with the existing topography and light industrial urban grain.

1.10, 1.18 Mikaella Konia, Y2 'What if the Earth Runs Out?' Initially occupying and adapting an existing brick warehouse, the project investigates the slow excavation and subsequent densification of the area, using earth from the site to develop a rammed earth factory. The project anticipates that space above the industrial sheds will eventually be used for residential units. As a showcase for how rammed earth could be used for large multi-storey buildings, the project tests the construction methods and details required for resilience in shifting weather conditions.

1.12, 1.20 Shouryan Kapoor, Y2 'Common Ground: Tools of Porosity'. The project addresses the underlying issues affecting the Lea Valley on a wider scale: extreme land prices, overwhelming housing needs, threats of flooding and the economic squeeze on small-scale businesses. Set in a flood-receptive landscape strategy which broadens and encourages movement across the river, the proposed rammed earth structure accommodates both housing and workspaces, with generously top-lit workshops filling the centre of the deep plan and housing occupying the perimeter, capitalising on the beautiful views of the valley.

1.13 Jerzy (George) Szczerba, Y2 'Plant Factory'. Acting as a spatial filter, the project uses materiality and building orientation to gently control the internal conditions of temperature, humidity and light to make an ideal environment for growing orchids. The plants travel slowly through a sequence of spaces in the linear plan, with public cafes and viewing stations allowing people to observe different stages of the orchids' growth as they meander between internal and external spaces. The longer-term strategy includes the gradual accumulation of residential edge buildings, hand in hand with the phasing of orchid production into a communal garden.

1.14 Fatemeh (Sean) Abkhou, Y2 'Stacking CLT'. The project provides a new piece of landscape infrastructure that enables the growth of the area and ensures that residential development is carried out sustainably. Occupying the tidal mudflats, a new willow plantation provides the bank with stability while providing raw materials for the fabrication of cross-laminated timber (CLT) structures using materials sourced on-site.

1.15, 1.19 Elina Seyed Nikkhou, Y2 'Poplar Boat Yard'. Located in the lower River Lea, the project encourages London's reconnection to its industrial history and its waterways, as well as providing much-needed infrastructure for those living on the waters. Since the decline in industry, London's waterways have become home to many; however, these boaters have long been neglected and mistreated. The project gives a public face to the boating community and provides communal space for the maintenance and upkeep of their boats.

1.17 Yuqi (Sunny) Wang, Y3 'Dye in the Lea'. The project addresses the vast amounts of pollution caused by the fashion industry. A programme of phytoremediation is initially employed to eliminate existing industrial soil contaminants. These plants then form the ingredients for natural fabric dyes that are created on the premises and subsequently filtered, before re-entering the surrounding waterways. Instead of creating entirely new structures, the project utilises the existing bricks found on-site, developing wrap-around façades that capture the sun's ultra-violet rays to aid the factory's dyeing and drying processes, while also forming an infrastructure of industrial-scale display.

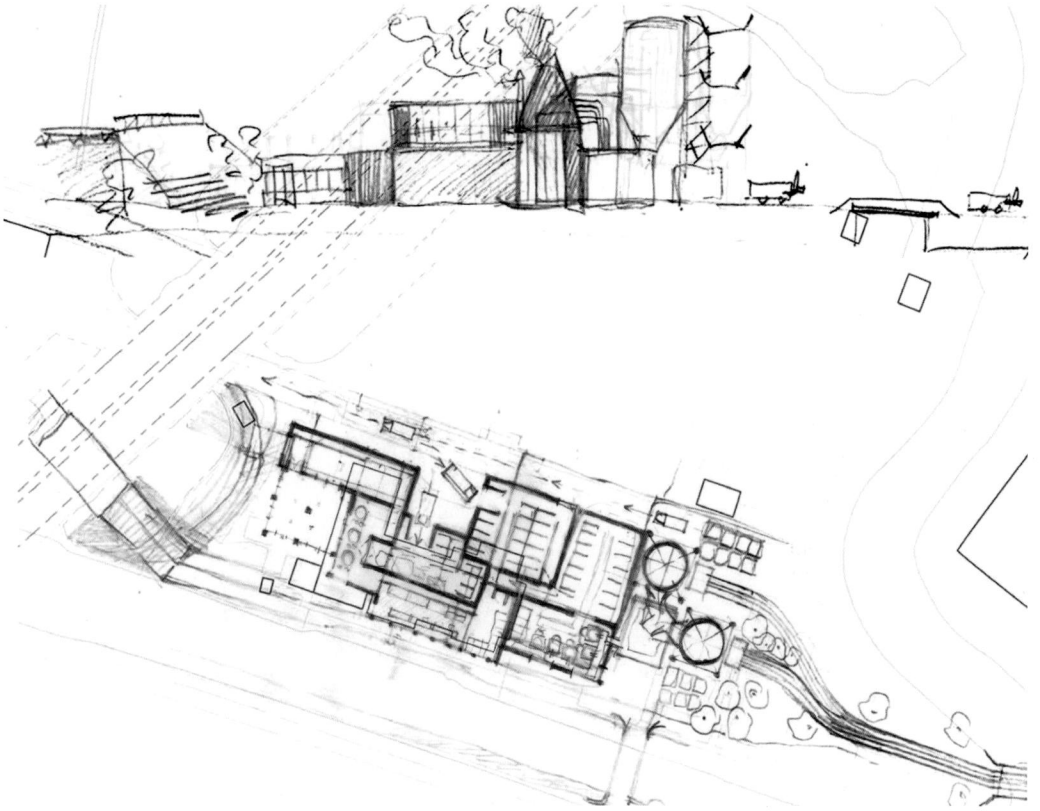

1.2

1.3

1.5

1.6

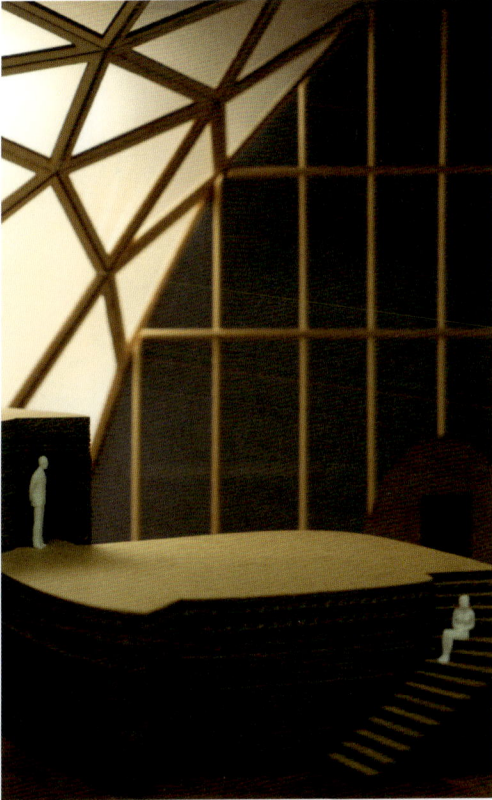

1.7

1.8

1.9

1.10

1.11

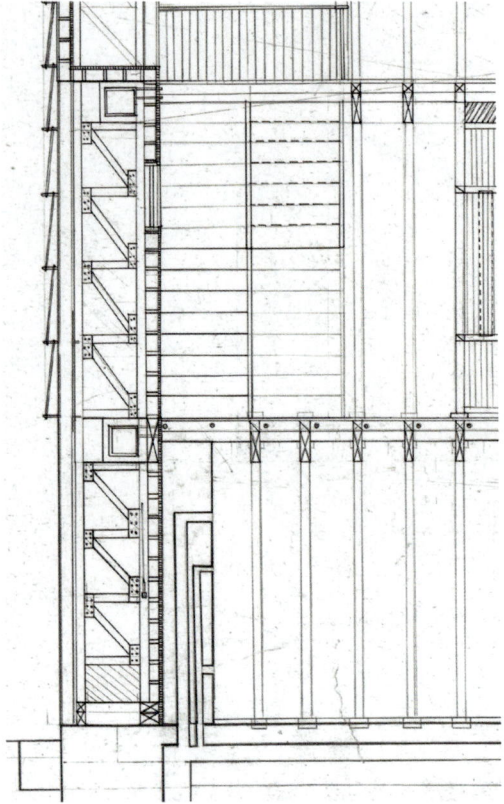

1.12

1.13

1.14

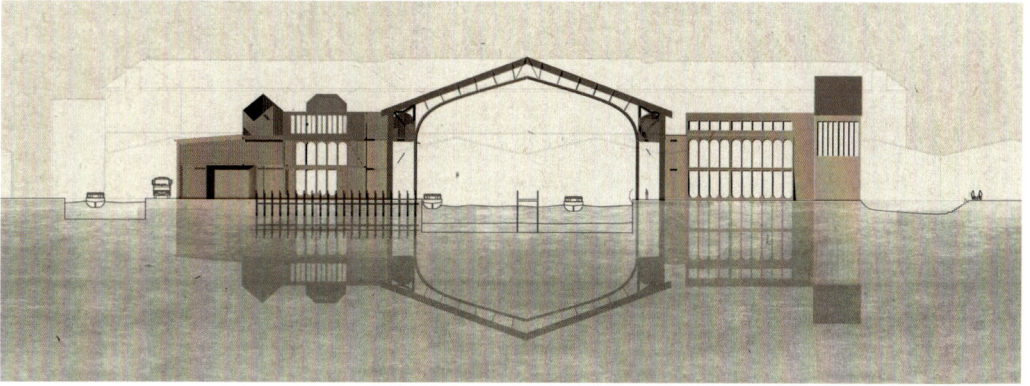

1.15

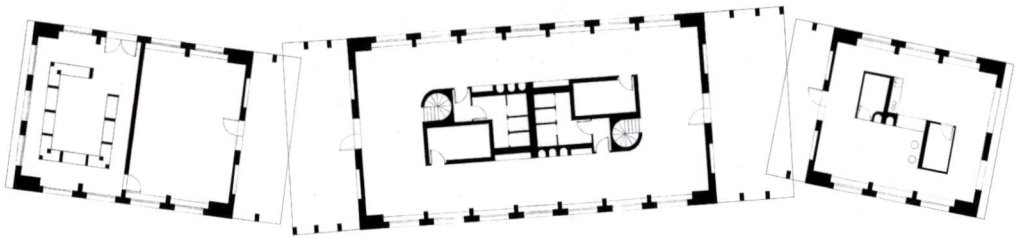

1.16

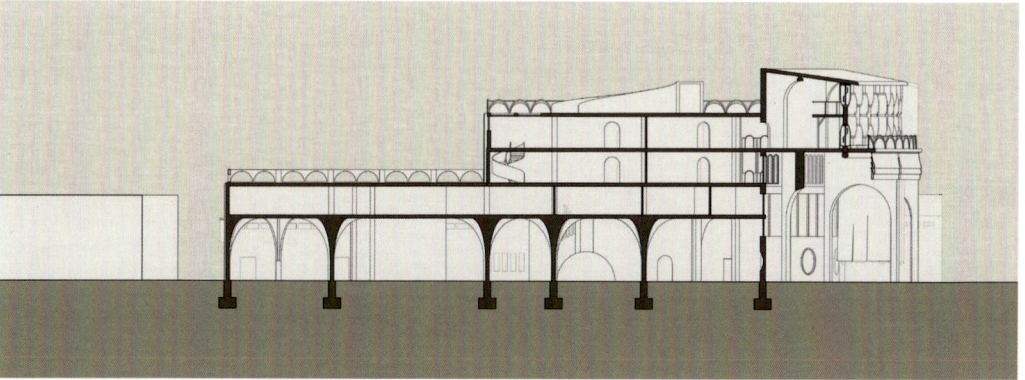

1.17

1.18

1.20

Eco-Promethean

UG2

Maria Knutsson-Hall, Barry Wark

In Greek mythology, Prometheus was a Titan who moulded man from clay and stole fire from the Gods to give to humanity. He was so inventive that in Western classical traditions he became a figure who represented the quest for innovation. In giving fire to the humans, Prometheus had disobeyed Zeus and was severely punished; thus his name has also become associated with the unintended consequences of our actions and mass suffering.

In a more contemporary sense, Prometheanism is a term popularised by theorist John Dryzek. It describes an environmental orientation that views the Earth as a resource whose utility is determined primarily by human needs and interests, and whose environmental problems are overcome through human innovation. The unintended consequences of this anthropocentric world view have leveraged technology to accelerate productivity beyond sustainable levels and led to the exploitation of natural resources, creating the so-called Anthropocene age. We are presented on a daily basis with the devasting impact of human activity on the planet, revealing how our actions (predominantly in the Global North) are creating seemingly irreversible, ultimately horrific changes.

A monumental shift in how we perceive our relationship to the natural world is needed. We can no longer view humans and our artefacts as privileged, separate and impervious to everything on the planet, but must rather understand that all things on earth are enmeshed in a global ecology. Ecocentrism is an ontological and ethical belief that refutes existential privileges or divisions between human and non-human beings and could help to redefine how we see our place within the biosphere.

This year UG2 reinvigorated the environmental project in architecture with a sense of hopefulness, asking how ecocentric values might redirect Prometheanism towards creating buildings that could mitigate or even reverse environmental destruction. Students focused on innovation and lateral thinking, harnessing various technologies across design, simulation and fabrication. Projects were undertaken in Glasgow, the year the city hosted COP26, with proposals ranging from carbon capture facilities to refurbishment and reuse of derelict buildings and to new forms of spaces that help us connect with the environment.

Year 2
Magdalena Herman, Sophie Hoet, Jazzlyn Jansen, Arushi Kulshreshtha, Sze Chun Liu, Rauf Sharifov, Annika Siamwalla, Yong (Benedict) Siow, Besim Smakiq, Pasut Sudlabha

Year 3
Blenard Ademaj, Yuto Ikeda, Zahra Parhizi, Elijah Ramsay, Zuzanna Sienczyk, Elise Wehowski

Many thanks to our technical tutors and consultants: James Palmer, Levent Ozruh, Tony Le

2.1, 2.11–2.12 Yuto Ikeda, Y3 'The Clyde C: Urban Carbon Capture'. Inadequate progress in reducing carbon dioxide emissions has only aggravated advancing climate change. The project mitigates this from an architectural perspective, with a large-scale installation of carbon capture technology. 'The Clyde C' is a project that integrates carbon removal within a residential programme. The site is situated on an abandoned dock in Govan, Glasgow, providing its industrial history of shipbuilding as a contextual background. The developed procedural system which generates computational aggregations helps optimise carbon capture performance and the integration of programmes. In addition, a stable carbon sink of biochar is introduced as an acoustic buffer between domestic and technical spaces, as well as for interstitial growth enhanced by its fertile characteristic.

2.2–2.4 Zuzanna Sienczyk, Y3 'Wool Experience'. Nearly 80% of building insulation is made from synthetic fibres whose production is a major contributor to climate change. This project examines the possibility of turning back to the use of a natural, often forgotten resource – wool. Through the use of a water jet machine, wool fibres can be embedded into timber, offering a level of insulation comparable to the synthetic alternative, while decreasing its environmental impact and reviving British industry. The main scope of the project is focused on designing an insulation system that will allow for the refurbishment of old buildings that currently lack insulation. Fleece as an insulator would not only benefit the environment, but also the Scottish economy, where the wool market experienced an unprecedented downturn during the pandemic, forcing numerous shepherds to burn their harvests to avoid rising costs.

2.5, 2.13 Jazzlyn Janssen, Y2 'Rewilding the City: New Botanical Gardens'. Inspired by the natural vegetation scattered around the edges of Glasgow's historical façades, a bioreceptive building celebrates the too often discarded foliage. Focusing on the overlooked beauty of moss, the public open-air theatre on the west side of Glasgow embraces and designs for the effects of the natural environment on the architecture, encouraging biodiversity and coexistence. The controlled rewilding of its walls and the varying filtration of light play foundational roles in activating these spaces as flourishing human and non-human zones. This new method of engaging, experiencing and interacting with the environment balances the urban and the wild, allowing for ecological restoration and reconnection in a new form of botanical garden.

2.6 Sze Chun Liu, Y2 'High Rise'. The project speculates on an alternative future for the now demolished concrete Whitevale Towers in Glasgow's east end. The project considers the anonymity of high-rise living and looks to foster community between residents through rezoning the tower into vertical neighbourhoods. The project is also driven by the importance of building reuse, with a particular focus on 20th-century residential towers, which are ubiquitous across the city of Glasgow.

2.7 Zahra Parhizi, Y3 'Living Claycelium'. This project uses mycelium as a bonding agent for clay, with 3D-printed 'claycelium' creating an active multilayer wall system with exceptional structural integrity and cladding properties. The architecture's wall allows mycelium to continue to grow inside the clay, strengthening the building over time.

2.8–2.10 Elise Wehowski, Y3 'Carbon Building'. A new eco-conscious structure to unite the neighbourhood of Haghill, Glasgow, with a sheltered public plaza serving as a central meeting point. Biochar is produced by heating biomass and can store up to 70% of carbon present in the original material. The project integrates as much biochar as possible to help create a reusable carbon sink. The component-based design allows for quick disassembly and can be reused many times. The designs are also cast in part-based moulds that can be assembled in any shape.

2.14–2.15 Blenard Ademaj, Y3 'The Scottish Multi-Faith Society'. Grottos occupy a space between architecture and garden, allowing humans and non-humans to coexist within a single environment. The project takes this notion of grottos and uses the unmaintained conditions of the site to create a language within the building, blurring the barrier between architecture and nature to enable us to bring forth new methods of construction.

2.16 Elijah Ramsay, Y3 'Eco Anxiety Retreat'. As awareness around the environmental crisis increases, many people are left filled with anxiety, hopelessness and a sense of nihilism. The building creates a space for users to experience the therapeutic and biophilic properties of natural landscapes and simultaneously witness the role of technology at work in mitigating environmental degradation. The project uses maerl, a natural entity similar to coral that sequesters carbon. Through environmental analysis, the spa is designed to propagate maerl in increasing amounts. The project is seen as a prototypical condition that could be replicated along the Scottish coast.

2.17 Arushi Kulshreshtha, Y2 'Clydeside CPA'. Located along the north bank of the River Clyde, the project transforms the Clyde riverside into an inclusive performance space and proposes Glasgow's first external covered public space.

2.18 Magdalena Herman, Y2 'MycoClinic'. The MycoClinic provides biodegradable 3D-printed roofs made of mycelium and soil. After the myco-roof cladding decays and falls onto the ground, the process of mycoremediation begins to positively impact the environment.

2.19 Besim Smakiq, Y2 'Museum of the Glasgow Style'. The project explores ideas around camouflage and context through the use of neural-network style-transfer algorithms.

2.20 Yong (Benedict) Siow, Y2 'Co-Space'. The project speculates upon a series of structures for both humans and non-humans within the Scottish landscape.

2.2

2.3

51

2.5

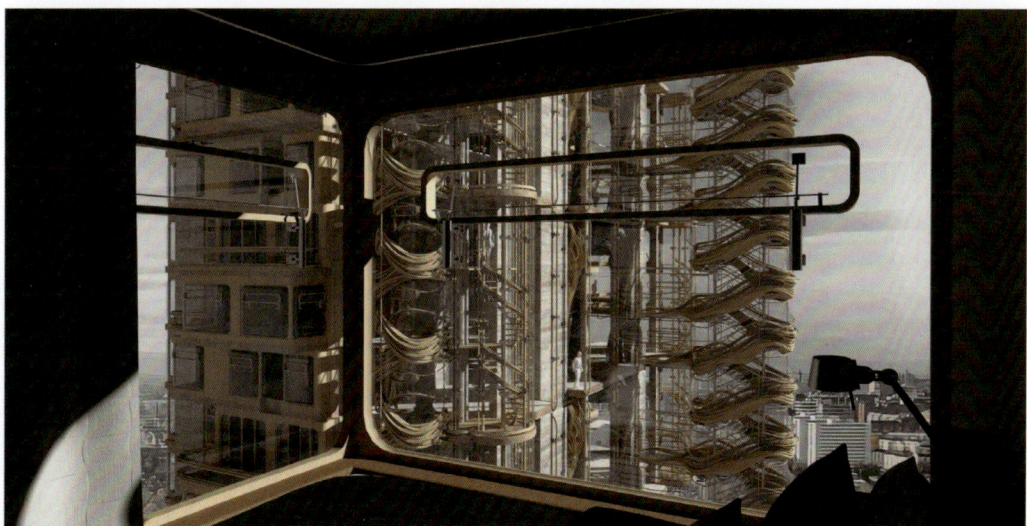

2.6

2.7

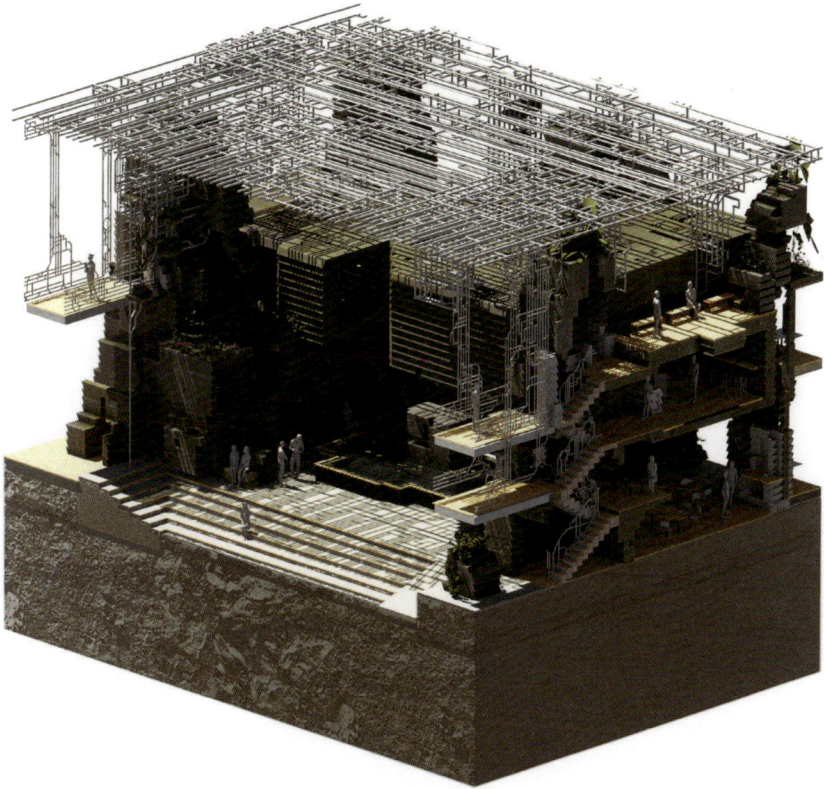

2.9

2.10

2.11

2.12

2.14

2.15

2.16

2.17

2.18

2.19

2.20

The Year of Magical Thinking

Ifigeneia Liangi, Daniel Wilkinson

UG3 addresses personal and political issues with nuanced and characterful proposals. Having a hand in the practical and a foot in the magical, our unit style is a work in progress, with each year's students contributing towards its future. We have a history of addressing issues of the feminine, the polychromatic, the sensual and the figurative. Within this, we discuss questions of identity and are fascinated by forgotten histories and alternative realities.

This year we considered the relationship between architecture and its authors. The tone of this was defined by the desires and personalities of our students, fuelled by questions of whether architecture can be autobiographical or take the form of a diary: while an autobiography tells a story according to a single moment in time, a diary is made up of daily entries. As an extension of this personal approach our students chose their own sites, which spread across the world.

All portfolios tell stories, whether they come from a storytelling unit or not – they ask us to suspend our disbelief and to imagine. This year our students became characters in their projects. Through buildings that blur the line between design and construction, they questioned when the occupation of a project actually begins and how the activities of living and learning can contribute to processes of assembly.

Each year we welcome the tweaking and adjusting of our brief by our students. This might involve amplifying one particular aspect at the expense of another or using its suggestions to embark on an even wilder flight of fantasy. The projects we design are magical and critical: magical in the surprising and unexpected poetic stance they take with the world and critical in the way they engage intellectually with social and political awareness.

Year 2
Laura Maxine Diekmann, Sophie Du Ry Van Beest Holle, Scarlet Fernandes, Phoebe Hampson, Mayling Ly, Natalia Michalowska, Barbara (Basia) Nohr, Kateryna Skiba, Ziyan Zhao, Yanyu (Cici) Zhou

Year 3
Anna Arzumanyan, Christian Coackley, Andrew Cowie, Yi (Glory) Kuk, Evgeniya (Eugene) Kulakova, Alexander Pozen, Joanna Van Son, Jiahui Zhang

Technical tutor and consultant: Martin Reynolds

Critics: Adam Bell, Amy Bodiam, Lola Haines, Vasilis Ilchuk, Laura A Keay, Vsevolod Kondratiev-Popov, Martin Reynolds, Sayan Skandarajah

3.1, 3.14 Joanna Van Son, Y3 'The School of Painter-Architecture'. The building is formulated around the idea of squatting on commercial land in Hackney Wick as a commentary on intellectualised labour within architectural education. Through the lens of the painter-architect, studios are designed, plotted and constructed using experimental manipulations of light, stroke and colour. Paint will not only envelop the architecture, but will also be tested as a process of design, its results being ingrained within the lifetime of the building.

3.2–3.3 Christian Coackley, Y3 'Architectural Education: The Age of Belonging'. In light of the enduring issues we are facing, such as a climate and ecological emergency, Britain must nurture a culture of collaboration in architectural education to meaningfully address them. This project proposes a third iteration of The Bartlett School of Architecture. In contrast to the building's two previous iterations, Wates House (1975) and 22 Gordon Street (2016), the next version of the school will be constructed over the course of a thousand years by its students and tutors.

3.4 Alexander Pozen, Y3 'The Soviet Split'. Russian culture can be seen as destructively oscillating between anarchy and dictatorship. The Ministry of Animation seeks a compromise between the two: democracy. This conflict between order and chaos is manifested through fire, which burns part of the building down every few years, encouraging a renewal of the political agenda.

3.5 Mayling Ly, Y2 'The School of Ancestral Worship'. Vietnamese culture and traditions have been forgotten by the children of Vietnamese immigrants in Hackney. The school is a response to this, and specifically the significance of ancestral worship. In Vietnam, there is a common belief in the afterlife, a separate realm in which deceased ancestors live. Through ritualistic acts of making, the students are taught by the spirits of these ancestors.

3.6 Scarlet Fernandes, Y2 'A Watchmaking Factory, Museum and Shop in Clerkenwell'. As a response to Clerkenwell's overlooked history of watchmaking and the organisation of labour in ant colonies, the project imagines a tyrannical queen ant who takes credit for the making of the watches in her factory. The design draws attention to the performance of watchmaking, encouraging conversation around the craft, to bring about its revival in the area.

3.7 Natalia Michalowska, Y2 'Oasis'. As well as accommodating conventional therapeutic facilities such as psychotherapy rooms, the clinic incorporates hydro, plant and physical therapy spaces. Rainwater is collected at the heart of the clinic, revealing itself while people travel through the building. Located in Kentish Town, the ground floor is open to the neighbourhood so that residents can enjoy the garden and use facilities such as the teashop or access ad-hoc mental health help.

3.8 Barbara (Basia) Nohr, Y2 'Worshipping the Ordinary: A Shrine for the Overlooked'. The project explores an architectural prototype of the wayside shrines in rural Poland and the life circulating around them. It highlights the pressures and divisions forced on ordinary families by religious and political institutions. By reclaiming the space as somewhere humble and peaceful life can be worshipped, a sense of belonging and wellbeing is fostered.

3.9 Kateryna Skiba, Y2 'An Animistic Approach to Architecture: The Living Temple'. The project is a celebration of Ukrainian beliefs and folk traditions in pre-Christian times, when it was believed that everything has a spirit: each plant, animal and household object. Located in one of Dnipro's most spiritual areas, ordinary objects like doors, candles, chandeliers, trees and ovens are transformed, as if inhabited and animated by supernatural forces, creating a living temple.

3.10 Phoebe Hampson, Y2 'The Vinegar Mother's Parliament of Pickling'. The project is set in a pickling factory in the picturesque town of Aldeburgh, Suffolk. The Golden Galleon, a famous fish and chip shop, operates from the building and produces pickled goods, as well as hosting a weekly opera. This temporarily resolves Aldeburgh's small-village syndrome, as depicted in Benjamin Britten's *Peter Grimes*, drawing parallels between a misunderstood outsider and modern-day Londoners.

3.11–3.12 Yi (Glory) Kuk, Y3 'A Garden of Rebirth'. The relationship between psyches and gardens, the wild and the curated, comes together in this project, captured through a laborious but healing process of drawing and flow state, a spiritual discipline in itself. In Aokigahara, Japan, known for its unusual geography and abandoned objects, a garden of rebirth is constructed, transforming the forest into a growing garden of the everyday. As a hybrid between a garden, a monastery and a hotel, the building records the passing of time as it continues to grow.

3.13 Sophie Du Ry Van Beest Holle, Y2 'Shygirl's Hyperpop Factory'. Situated in Canning Town, the building acts as a space for local artists to explore the microgenre of 'hyperpop'. Containing both art and music studios, the factory encourages collaboration across mediums, with a nightclub to test out these ideas. Inspired by Shygirl's London-based hyperpop collective, the project's focus lies in encouraging more women to produce music by providing a space to push the boundaries of pop music, art and fashion.

3.15 Yanyu (Cici) Zhou, Y2 'The Clinic of Light Elves'. A paediatric dental clinic located on Gray's Inn Road, London, a neighbourhood that has a history of clinical dentistry that can be dated back to the barber-surgeons of medieval times. To ease the anxiety and fear of seeing the dentist, the building uses the language of dental tools in its details, which function as fairy tale storytelling elements.

3.16 Ziyan Zhao, Y2 'Facing the Sea with Spring Blossom'. This project is an unconventional Montessori school for autistic students. It recreates the house described in the poem 'Facing the Sea with Spring Blossoms' by the Chinese poet Haizi, whose own autism informed his work. Located in a coastal village in Shenzhen, the school encourages children to make their own learning choices.

3.17 Jiahui Zhang, Y3 'School of Poetry'. The school of poetry defies traditional hierarchies in education by promoting collaboration between teachers and students. Its architecture embraces the historical Chinese poem 'The Land of Peach Blossom', with its curriculum being designed around traditional techniques for making tea oil. The language of the architecture is taken from studies of traditional Chinese structures, materials and decoration.

3.18 Anna Arzumanyan, Y3 'Humanimality'. By recognising the history overshadowed by George Washington's legacy, the building redirects people's attention from the Mount Vernon estate in Virginia, USA, towards those who suffered for its creation. The site is a reminder of a hierarchy built on perpetuating 'otherness' and its grim consequences. The programme of an indigenous community centre allows for an alternative reading of history. This provides an opportunity for visitors to familiarise themselves with a culture that interacts with the natural world in a harmonious manner.

3.2

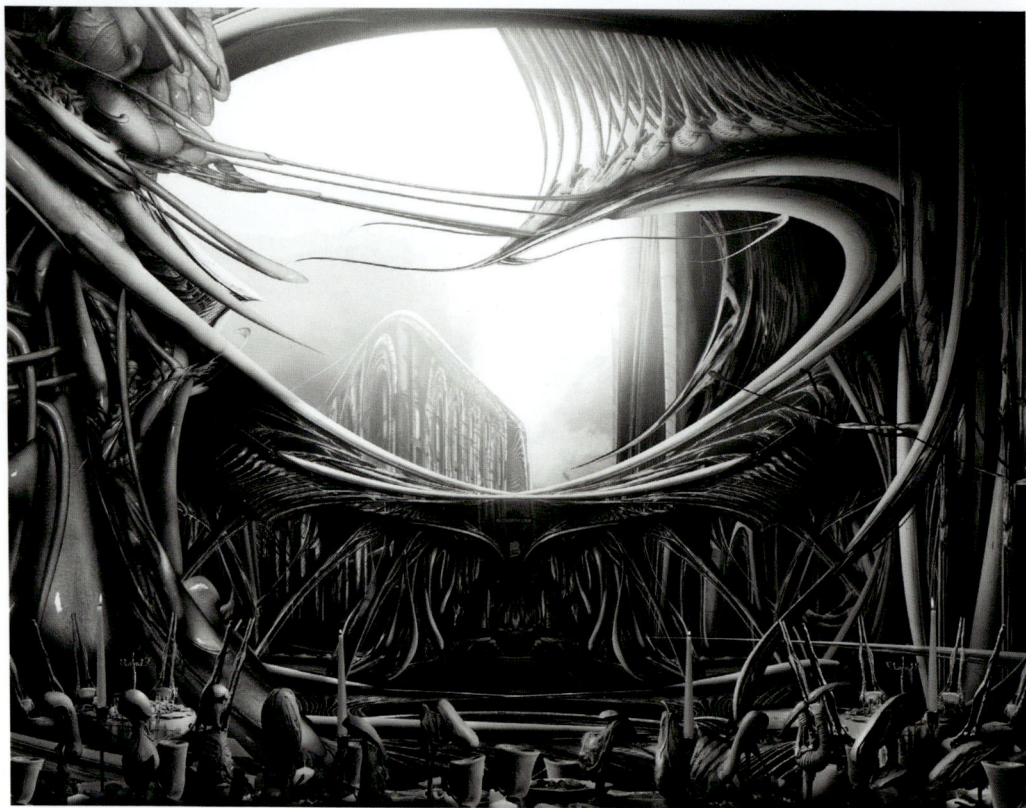

3.3

3.4

3.5

3.6

3.7

3.8

3.9

3.10

3.11

3.12

3.13

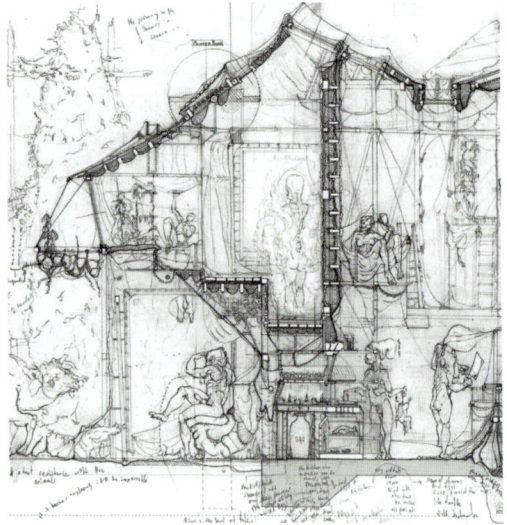

3.14

3.15

3.16

3.17

4.1

Anamnesis

Katerina Dionysopoulou, Billy Mavropoulos

As a fallout of the pandemic, self-isolation has inevitably altered the defining archetype of spaces, our homes metamorphosing into the city. Our place of rest now serves as an office and studio, classroom and gym, restaurant and cinema. The threshold between interior and exterior is inverted, the park now serving as a vast common room, enclosed only by trees and foliage that form screens between porous pockets of space.

In the process of exiting the pandemic, we enter an age of spatial revolution and ambiguity, with a continuing dissolution of architectural and historical typologies.

This year UG4 interrogated the theme of anamnesis, reconstructing memories of space to reconfigure a future that is unexpected yet familiar. We employed memories as a design tool, a conceptual and methodological contraption to construct constellations of forms, narratives and information. Our deconstruction of memory revealed opportunities for discourse on shifting paradigms and architecture's response to it. The familiar yet foreign city of London acted as our testbed, where the fabric of the capital supplied us with incentives to design new interventions within the present. Its history provided unconventional opportunities for the city to leverage conditions of impermanence to act as catalysts for change.

The built environment is not stagnant; it evolves alongside humanity to be harmonious with the region and socio-cultural community. An increasingly important issue is the treatment and disposal of construction materials. Within the UK, the construction industry is the largest consumer of resources, requiring more than 400 million tonnes of material a year: 32% of landfill waste comes from the construction and demolition of buildings. Waste is simply material without an identity. Value for these materials can be recreated by extracting embedded memories, while also introducing and preparing for new ones. Consideration of transiency and permanency became part of our design methodology.

We prepared our interventions for potential unpredicted shifts, both physically and programmatically. To do so required both a radical approach and a deep understanding of materials and how to reimagine them in new contexts. Our design is informed by, but not limited to, past architectural contributions, reassigned to a contemporary context.

Year 2
Marco Carraro, Shuhao Guo, Sally Kemp, Hoi (Derek) Lee, Gabriella Peixouto Bandeira Da Silva, George Perks, Keeleigh Pham, Eden Robertson, Adriana Rodriguez-Villa Lario, Caitlin Wong

Year 3
Fangxingchi (Brendan) Du, Max Hubbard, Kyra Johnston, Gaeul Kim, Moe Kojima, Daniel Langstaff, Siqi Ouyang, Hei (Leo) Tse

Technical tutors and consultants: Kacper Chmielewski, Simon Pierce, Tom Ushakov

Thanks to our critics: Kacper Chmielewski, Maria Knutsson-Hall, Cameron Overy, Simon Pierce, Matt Pratt, Caitlin Tobias Kenessey, Barry Wark

4.1, 4.11 Marco Carraro, Y2 'The Electrical Complexity'. The project responds to the ever-increasing issue of e-waste, serving as a catalyst for change in the current model of production, consumption and disposal of e-goods. The proposal reappropriates the Interchange Warehouse, dividing it into four elements: an e-waste disassembly hub; a storage area for retrieved components; a dynamic display that archives the sorted and disassembled items; and a small electrical workshop which aims to empower people to repair and engage with electronics.

4.2–4.3, 4.26 Hei (Leo) Tse, Y3 'The Arches at Nine Elms'. The project proposes a boxing gym in Nine Elms, addressing the complex issue of class discrimination through a multidimensional programme. The programme centres around a communal boxing gym enriched with a social space and a physiotherapy clinic to address the high injury rate of the intensive combat sport.

4.4, 4.27 Keeleigh Pham, Y2 'Limehouse Textiles and Fashion Workshop'. The project proposes a series of artists' workshops in Limehouse, reinhabiting the now abandoned and derelict sailmaking workshops with the aim of supporting East London's burgeoning fashion industry. The proposal provides spaces for young designers to develop alternative textiles and garments, as well as runway show events to exhibit their work.

4.5, 4.9, 4.21 Moe Kojima, Y3 'The Bridge'. Prior to gentrification, Vyner Street, adjacent to Regent's Canal, was the heart of the art scene in East London. The project proposes an open studio for artists and aims to bridge different communities, serving as a social condenser. The site's forgotten craft of silk weaving informs the roof tile design, reflecting the local climate while suggesting the thousands of strings that come together to form cloth.

4.6 Fangxingchi (Brendan) Du, Y3 'Silo-D'. The project proposes a space for people to release and escape urban stress in Silvertown, East London. It contains private tea houses, skywalks, a watchtower and a club. Timber serves as the structure's main material, creating a fragile and delicate form above ground which is juxtaposed with the robust underground palette of concrete and granite.

4.7, 4.15 Caitlin Wong, Y2 'Floating Playground'. Located on top of Pollock's Toy Museum, the project proposes a museum inspired by the materiality and mechanics of vintage toys. As well as having playrooms, programmes include the pre-existing toy shop, a workshop, a toy library and a café. The proposal focuses on the experiential aspect of play and embodies architectural playfulness and vibrancy.

4.8, 4.10 Maxwell Hubbard, Y3 'Areopagitica'. Sitting adjacent to the House of Lords, Abingdon Green is frequently utilised by broadcasting companies for news reports, with the Houses of Parliament featuring prominently in the background. Due to its semi-permanent and unregulated usage, the site is confused and under-employed. The historical precedents of Thorney Island, the Cottonian Library and Doulton Pottery feed into the architecture to create transparency in the murky world of political broadcasting.

4.12–4.13 Gabriella Peixouto Bandeira Da Silva, Y2 'The House Above'. The project proposes a space for miniature filmmaking on Berwick Street, Soho, responding to the site's rich history of film production and light manufacturing. The building is extended, providing film studios and community space. The perforated tile façade allows sunlight to penetrate the building and rotates to ensure there is a constant supply of light throughout the day.

4.14, 4.25 Gaeul Kim, Y3 'Therapeutic Herbal Playtower'. The former public baths, gymnasium and playtower in Ladywell, once an exuberant venue and second home to generations of Lewisham locals, has been derelict since 2004. The project proposes to rejuvenate the site and bridge generations, responding to the site's urban grain. Therapeutic herbs are sourced from the adjacent St Mary's churchyard and interweave with the aromatic water canal, celebrating the revival of old medicinal springs and fountains that were once an important resource.

4.16 Eden Robertson, Y2 'Chambers of Primordial Water'. This project interrogates the role of water within Jewish practice and how it can be incorporated into secular society. Jewish religious texts place importance on the construction and use of the 'mikvah', a man-made pool of spring water used for purification purposes. The proposal explores the themes of birth, life and water, serving as a water birthing facility and hydrotherapy centre for ante- and post-natal care.

4.17 Hoi (Derek) Lee, Y2 'The Whittington Inn'. Highgate historically served as a gateway to London, and many travellers used its inns for overnight stays. With the development of railways, theatres and music halls, these local inns entered a state of decline. The project proposes an inn and multi-use venue that ensures a steady stream of visitors, keeping the inn viable on an indefinite basis.

4.18, 4.23 Siqi Ouyang, Y3 'Sound in Haggerston'. Haggerston Baths has been derelict since 2000, and current redevelopment plans go against the wishes of locals, who would prefer to restore the original swimming pool. The project responds to these demands by preserving the main façade of the existing building, with a new roof structure interpolated from the neighbouring architectural identities. Curves representing waves, arches and elements developed from Victorian bath interiors are reflected through the spatial layout.

4.19 Sally Kemp, Y2 'Finsbury Park Reservoir'. During the 18th century, Finsbury Park and its reservoir were notorious hotspots for promiscuous behaviour. To discourage this behaviour, the government converted the space into a park. This new proposal plans to open the historic underground reservoir and transform it into a community space, while preserving its original layout, creating a labyrinth of arches with interwinding paths and gardens.

4.20, 4.22 Daniel Langstaff, Y3 'Launch Point Congreve'. In the early 1870s on a former factory site next to the River Lea in Bromley-by-Bow, construction began on a large new gasworks. The project uses principles taken from archaeoastronomy to stir the primally existential relationship humans had with the cosmos. These manifest as walls that gradually erode to mark the solar eclipses of the next thousand years, and an opening to view the rotation of the stars around Polaris in the night sky.

4.24, 4.28 Kyra Johnston, Y3 'The Strange Palace Hotel'. The project is a journey back in time, merging the past and present of central London's Strand Palace Hotel. It seeks to reinterpret the hotel's central courtyard, navigating human relationships with animals through augmented reality and highlighting the changes over time through immersive museum exhibits. The use of augmented reality challenges the need for real-life animals and provides a futuristic alternative to combat the abuse prevalent in zoos and circuses.

4.29 Shuhao Guo, Y2 'A Stage Performing Gin's Memory'. A gin palace and distillery located in an abandoned tram tunnel under Kingsway in central London. The proposal links the history of theatre in Covent Garden with gin culture in Holborn, mirroring the way in which trams once physically linked the two areas. Inside, visitors can view the whole manufacturing process before enjoying a drink, while outside, pedestrians can see these visitors from above.

4.2

4.3

4.4

4.5

4.6

4.7

4.8

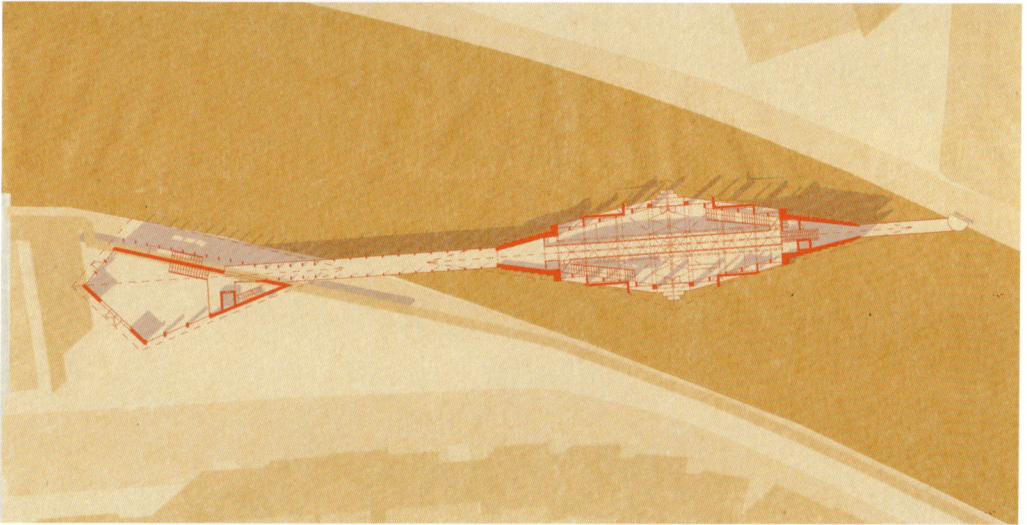

4.9

4.10

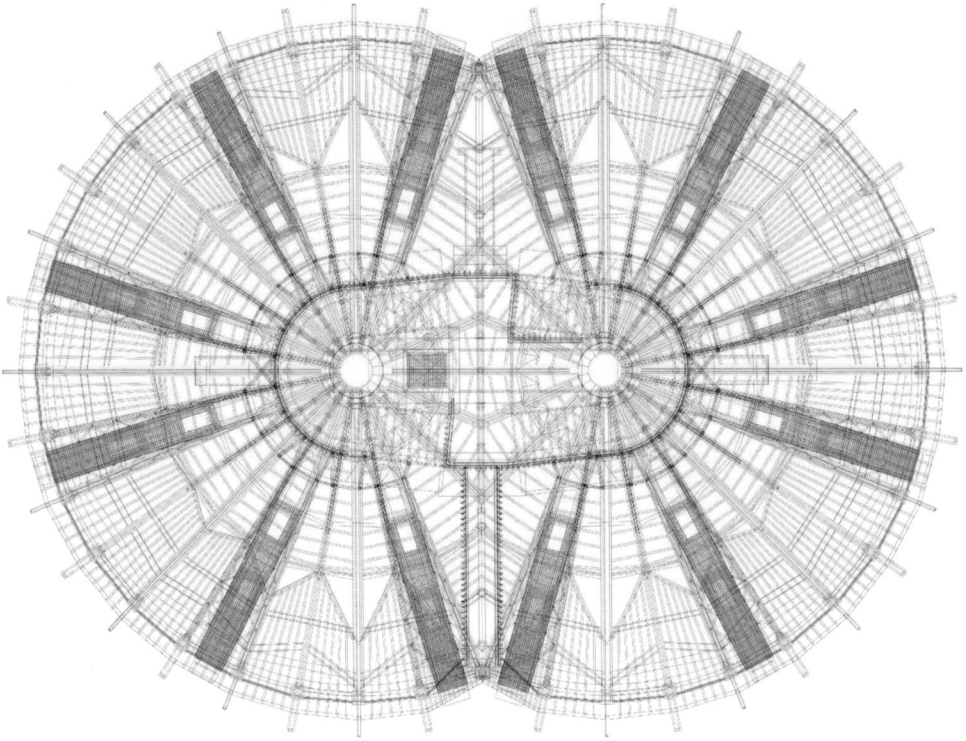

4.11

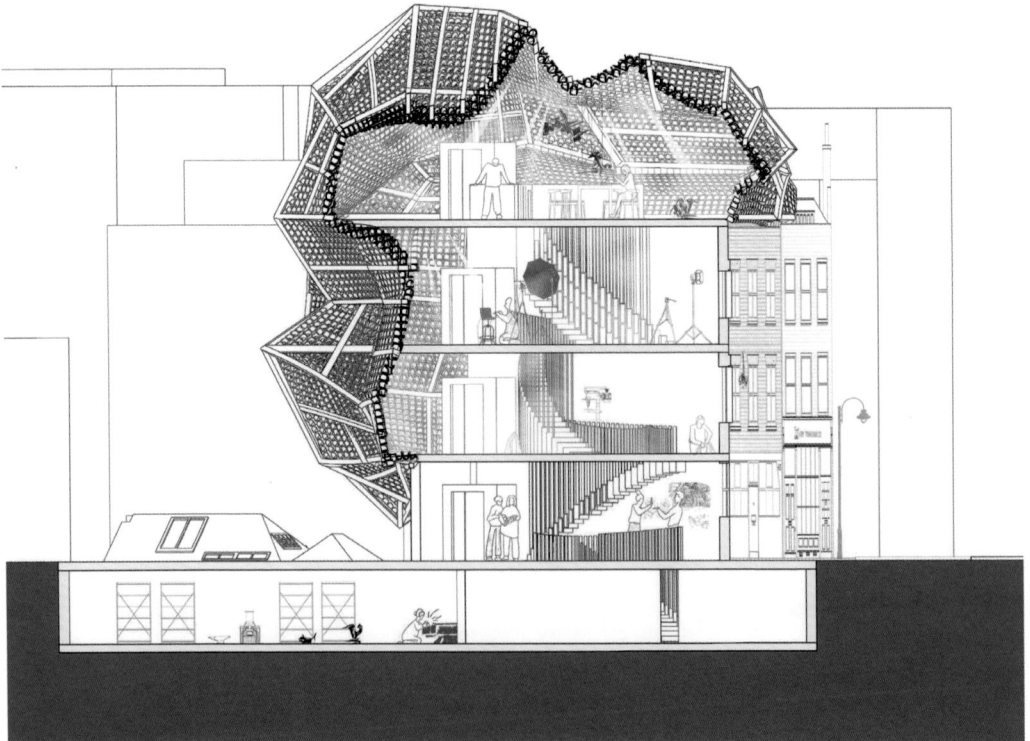

4.12

4.13

4.14

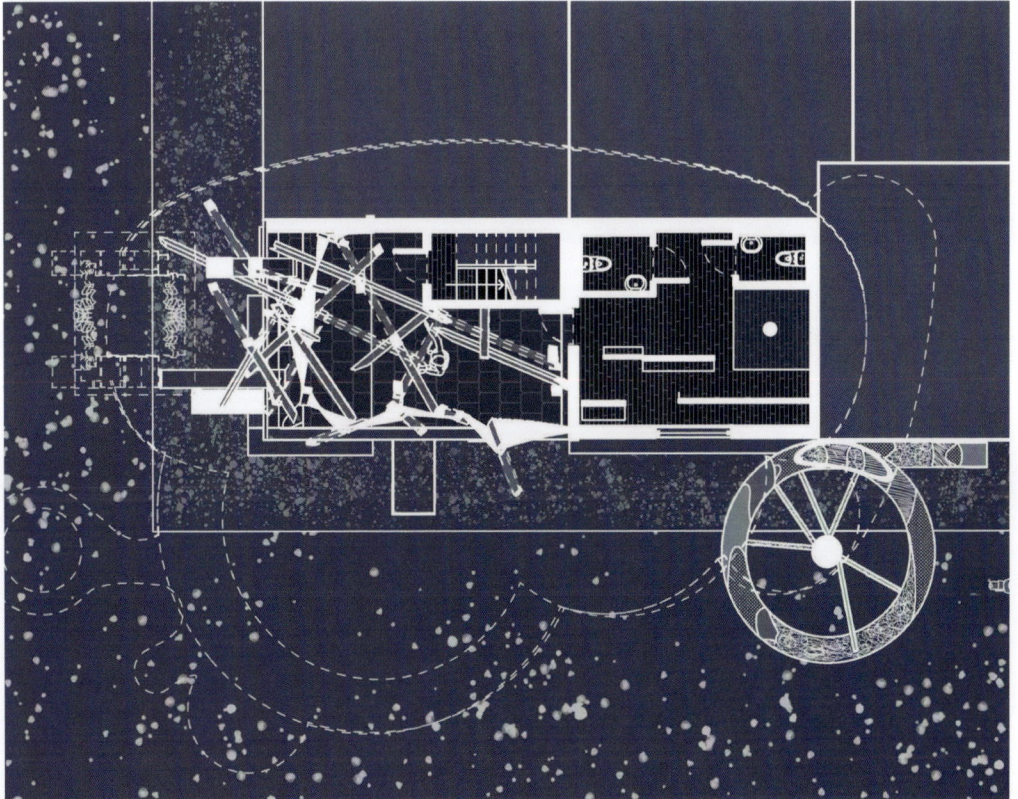

4.15

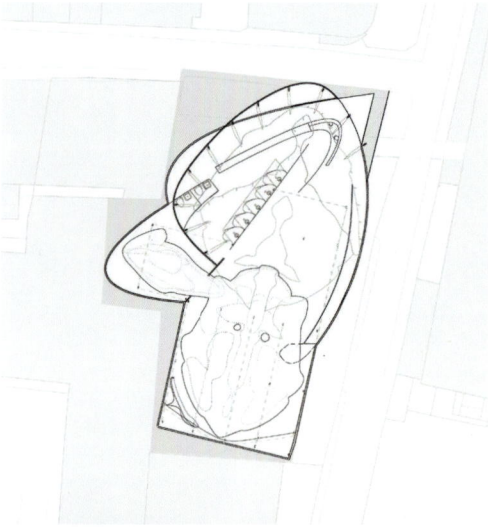

4.16

4.17

4.18

4.19

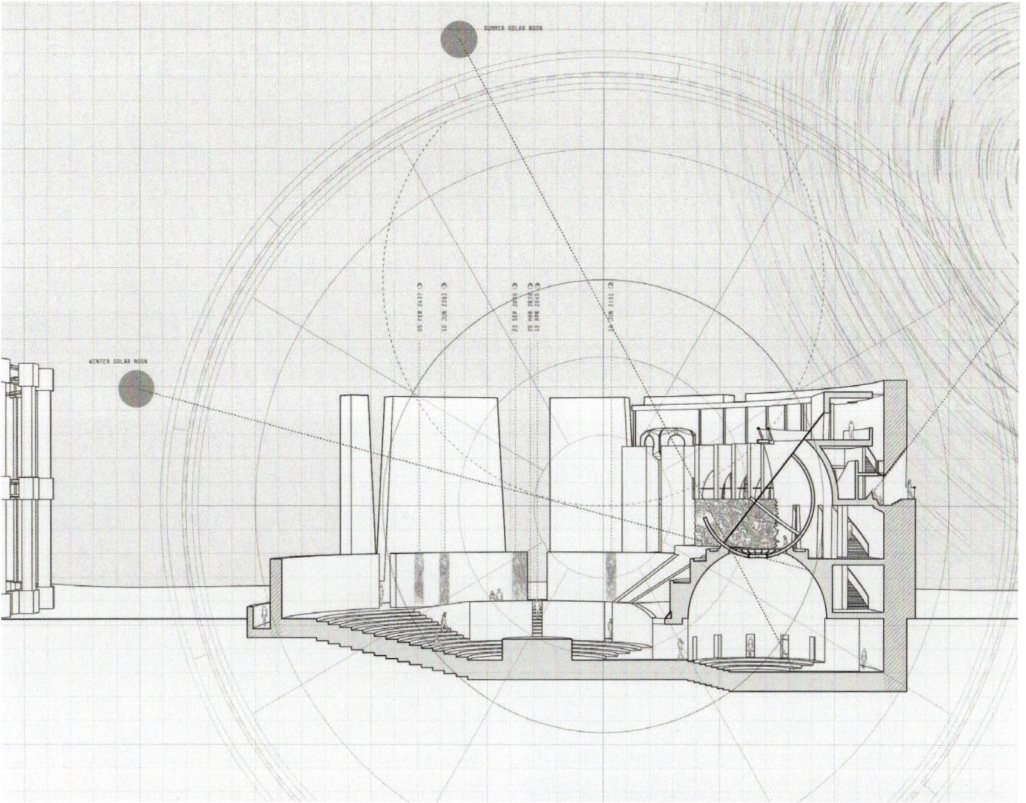

4.20

4.21

4.22

4.23

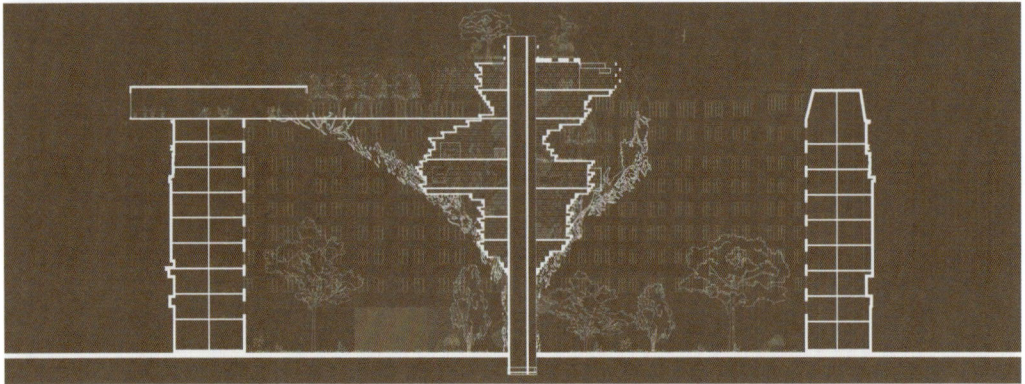

4.24

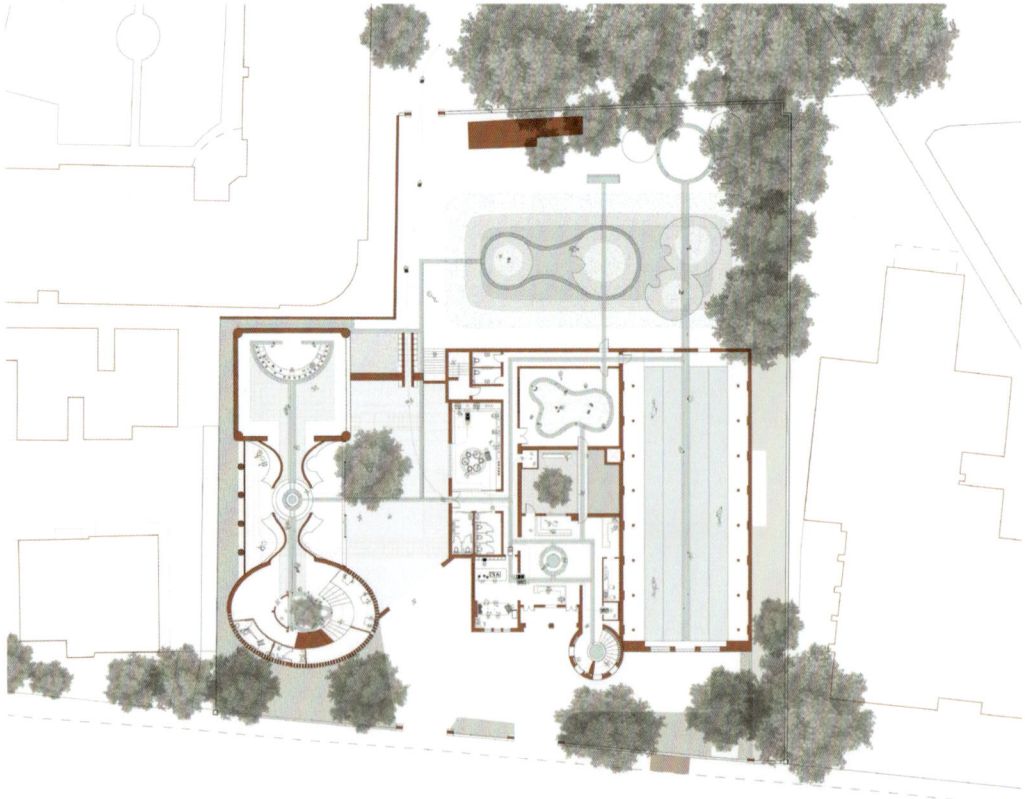

4.25

4.26

4.27

4.28

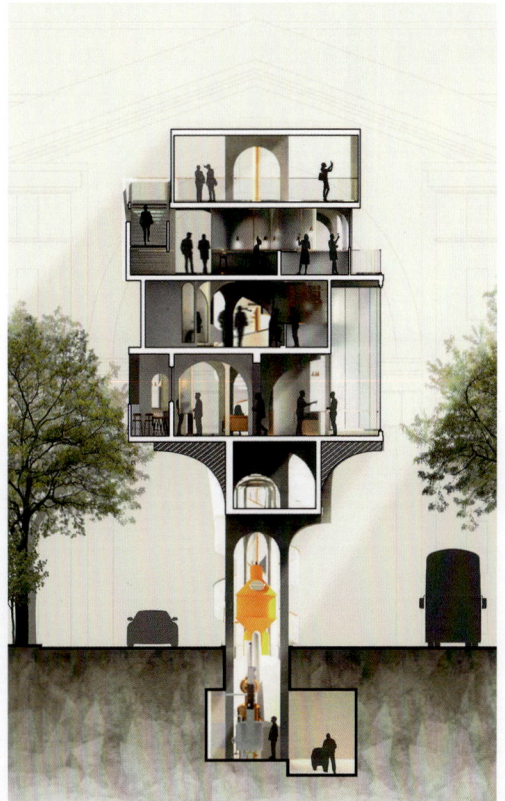

4.29

Feedback Loops

Julia Backhaus, Ben Hayes

Circular design is about creating an architecture that no longer has a life cycle with a beginning, middle or end. As the architecture collective Rotor states, a circular economy promises an endless cycle of reusable resources. With regards to the construction industry, the concept often centres around the metaphor of the urban mine, which understands the city as an accumulation of valuable materials and reusable elements. If the circular economy is more about a mindset than complex technical solutions, however, it is likely that many African countries, such as Rwanda, with indigenous and ingenious approaches to keeping scarce materials in circulation, are already more circular than the industrialised North.

This year we worked as archipreneurs, collaborators, integrators and spatial activists to develop a creative understanding of feedback loops, both as a design strategy and as a working practice. The focus of the unit's investigation was Rwanda, 'the land of the thousand hills', a tropical landlocked country in East Central Africa. Rwanda has taken a proactive approach and put climate resilience at the heart of its policies. It was one of the first countries to ban single-use plastic bags, has the largest Green Fund in Africa and is often a testbed for pioneering and innovative approaches in sustainability. As one of the most densely populated countries in Africa, Rwanda has created model villages across the country, providing housing to people in rural areas and relocating others from areas prone to flooding and landslides. We used the term 'village' as a tool to find alternative architectural strategies and started the year by exploring the terminology of 'local' through the prism of technology and with circularity in mind.

In collaboration with the University of Rwanda, local communities and expert African and Western consultants, we shared lived experiences and ideas and studied Rwanda's village models as a testbed for productive experimentation. We explored the artistic potential of circularity as a point of departure for meaningful, imaginative and site-specific architecture. Our areas of interrogation reached from micro-mining to edible homes, from social cohesion to local narratives, from ancient traditions to cutting-edge technologies.

Year 2
Maria Bystronska, Ana-Maria Cazan, Fasai Chainuvati, Marike Jungk, Ioana Oprescu, Teshan Seneviratne, Yingqi (Izzy) Shen, Ilinca-Maria Stanescu, Shiyan Zhu

Year 3
Samuel Field, Holly Griffiths, Adam Lynes, Kun (Anna) Pang, Tharadol (Robin) Sangmitr, Hanlin (Finn) Shi

Technical tutors:
Anja Kempa, Jack Newton, Jack Spence

Thank you to our critics: Pedro Font, Theo Games, Kaowen Ho, Bruce Irwin, Anja Kempa, CJ Lim, Ana Monrabal-Cook, Josephine Mwongeli, Jack Newton, Luke Pearson, Vincent Rwigamba, Kit Lee-Smith, Jack Spence and the students from the School of Architecture and Built Environment (SABE), University of Rwanda

5.1 Samuel Field, Y3 'Uncertain Ground'. This project addresses the future of hostile landscapes, speculating on the safety of vulnerable sites and looking holistically at strategies for landslide resilience. A recent fatal landslide location is rehabilitated. Emerging within a phased masterplan, a disaster-mitigating village typology connects to a village hub and safe-houses, responding to a set risk framework. Resisting and retreating spaces are proposed. These combine to create a resilient landscape – one which resists, retreats and adapts to the uncertain ground.

5.2 Adam Lynes, Y3 'Unearthing Rwanda's Expression through Excavation'. The project is a symphony of performance, carving and construction, exploring the relationship between stone and wood. It articulates a micro-quarrying strategy which highlights the art of traditional excavation, transportation and construction techniques. Across Rwanda, the performing arts are valued practices of entertainment and expression. The theatre expands the facilities of Komera and integrates their current practices, such as weaving, into the building's function and materiality.

5.3 Teshan Seneviratne, Y2 'Well-Grounded'. An agricultural training centre for workers on Rwandan coffee plantations which allows them to enjoy the product of their hard work. The building rethinks current typologies of agricultural production. By reflecting the cascading landscape of the site through its form, spaces such as the rooftop are reappropriated into productive surfaces. The project supports the workers throughout the year by creating centralised and productive spaces where teaching and production can coexist.

5.4–5.5, 5.7 Hanlin (Finn) Shi, Y3 'Earth Institute'. This project explores how the use of local soil can be innovatively used as a construction material to aid displaced communities in Kigali. It investigates the circularity of soil construction, utilising traditional methods in parallel with high-tech manufacturing technologies. The proposal is a critique of the current policies towards informal housing and forced relocation. The project acts as a catalyst and educational tool for developing new, accessible and low-cost village house typologies.

5.6 Marike Jungk, Y2 'Kubu-Gutegura'. Drawing inspiration from Kinyarwanda words for playing and planning, the project utilises the board of the popular game Igisoro to develop a collaborative planning approach for a new village square. While socialising over a round of Igisoro, players negotiate a layout of activities and spatial qualities to strengthen the inhabitants' agency in their built environments.

5.8 Ilinca-Maria Stanescu, Y2 'The CommuniTEA Museum'. With a key research topic focusing on the closely linked issues of tea production and water availability, the project creates a gathering space for the people of Gihombo where they can grow, process, consume and celebrate tea, while at the same time learning about efficient water strategies.

5.9–5.10 Holly Griffiths, Y3 'Soft School'. This project takes an approach to education that considers environmental conditions at the heart of child development following the 1994 Rwandan genocide. Sited just outside the capital Kigali, the school uses the materiality of light to create positive and enriching learning environments. Through investigating light, colour and emotion, lighting systems that support students struggling with their mental health are implemented in the school, highlighting the need for specific learning typologies to aid the next generation.

5.11 Fasai Chainuvati, Y2 'The Water Balance'. Rwanda faces a water crisis where 31% of the population has no clean water access and approximately 3,000 children pass away annually from a lack of water sanitation. Sitting on the water's edge and floating on Lake Kivu, the proposal creates an internal water-dependent environment. By welcoming local fishing communities and commemorating and filtering the water source, an equilibrium between water and life is created.

5.12–5.13 Ana-Maria Cazan, Y2 'Wild House'. What if our settlements were designed to allow a greater diversity of species to live alongside humans? This project addresses the idea of synanthropic cohabitation through the creation of a community centre designed for all its surrounding residents, human and non-human. The house invites these species to take part in mundane day-to-day activities in order to examine the comfort and suitability of its different occupants.

5.14–5.16 Yingqi (Izzy) Shen, Y2 'The Clayground'. Based in Gihombo, the proposal is a clay sanctuary where locals pass on their cultural heritage through methods of making, maintaining and most importantly playing within fragmented spaces. Through the building's circulation, issues of scarcity in social spaces and drinking water are addressed. The building acts as a test ground for clay experiments, exhibiting methods of construction to reinforce the creative potential, leading locals to reimagine innovative possibilities within a vernacular context.

5.17–5.18 Tharadol (Robin) Sangmitr, Y3 'The Maker's Yard'. This project is a material exploration scheme whereby the architecture of the yard acts as a 1:1 testbed for the fragments and components innovated and analysed on-site. The yard also acts as a catalyst and node of departure for future settlement developments in rural western Rwanda.

5.19 Shiyan Zhu, Y2 'Kivu Fulfilment Centre'. This project is part of a proposed decentralised social infrastructure situated on the shore of Lake Kivu. Local drone technologies are used to deliver fish parcels and emergency medicines and enhance food security in the region. The project challenges the Western distribution model under which enormous homogeneous buildings solely designed for industrial activities sterilise their immediate surroundings.

5.20 Ioana Oprescu, Y2 'The Edible House'. Climate change, drought and natural disasters are damaging food production in Rwanda. Around 90% of the country depends solely on agriculture, exposing Rwanda's vulnerability to food insecurity. This project functions as an emergency kit. In the event of isolated crop damage, the house can nutritionally sustain three families throughout the year. During other times, it provides a community garden and a safe water source for the village.

5.21–5.22 Kun (Anna) Pang, Y3 'Ghosts of Atomgrad 9'. The world today is littered with a new typology of site: the nuclear wastelands of the Anthropocene. These sites are often left abandoned and forgotten, along with the mistakes which were made to create them and the people that suffered. In this project, Pripyat, the *atomgrad* designed to serve Chernobyl, is explored as a site of the Symbiocene. The design acknowledges the tragic events of 1986 and, through the process of casting mycelium ghosts, grows a palimpsest of memories.

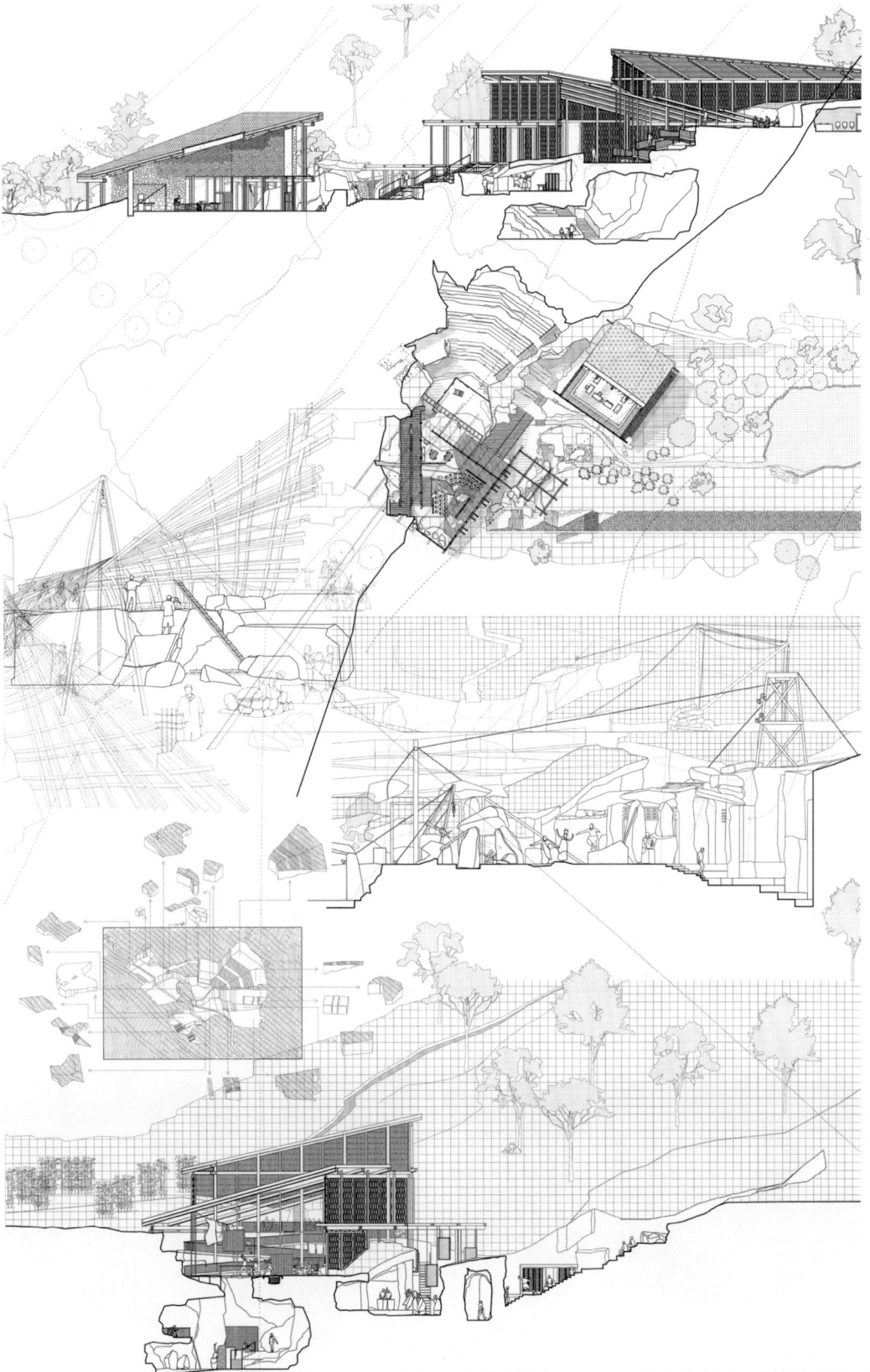

5.3

5.4

5.5

5.6

5.7

5.8

5.9

5.10

5.11

5.12

5.13

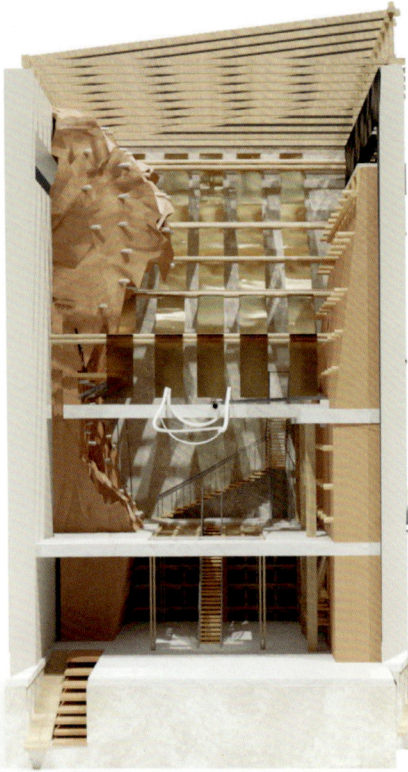

5.14

5.15

5.16

5.17

5.18

University Of Kigali, KG 5dr St   Colline Wagaba Village   Hope Apartment KG 796 St, Kigali   Rutsiro Health Centre

5.19

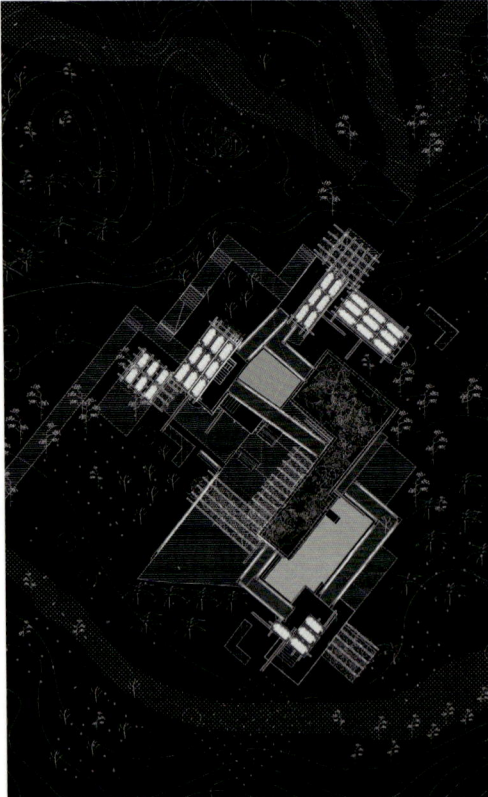

5.20

5.21

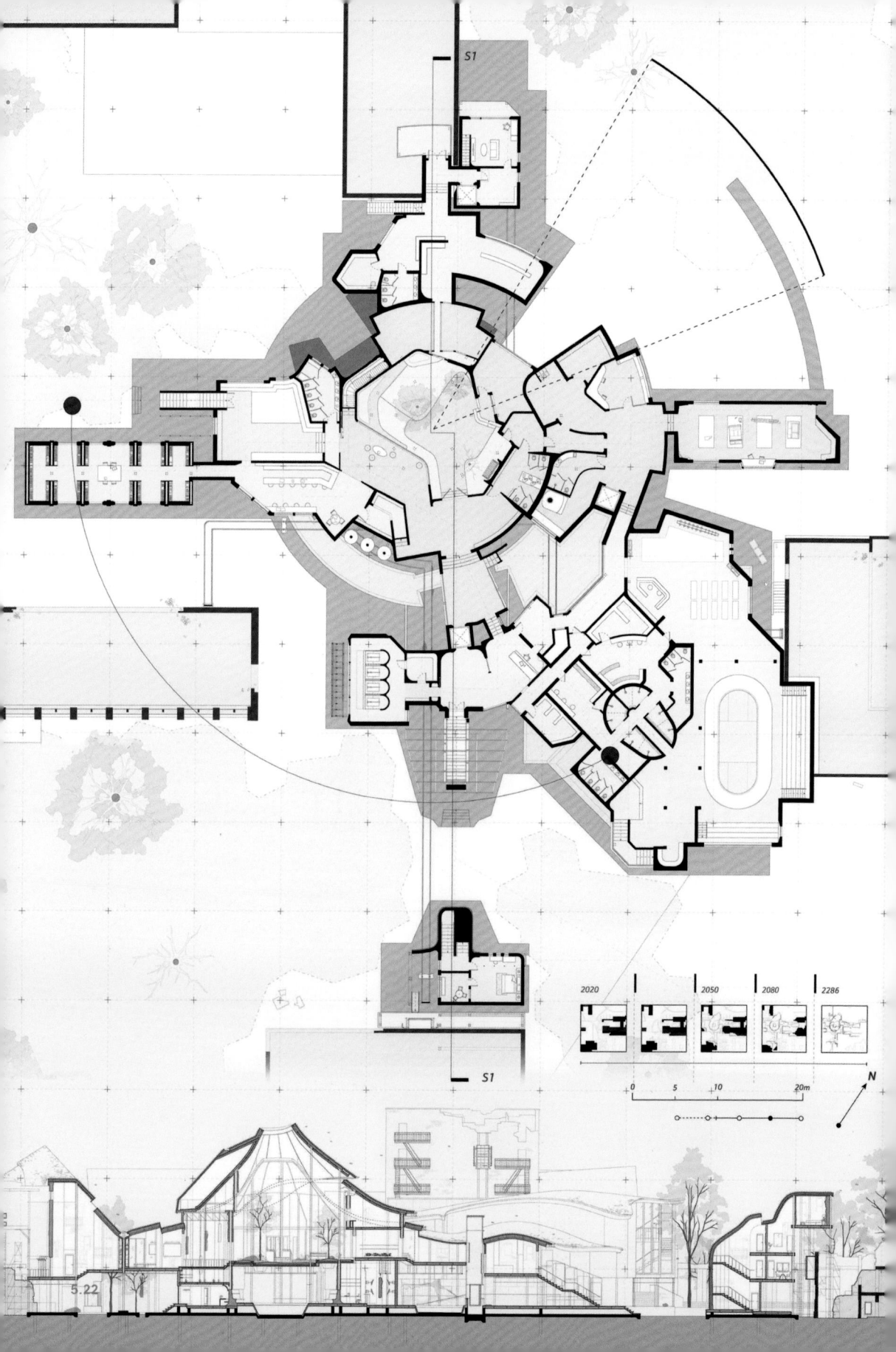

S1

S1

2020　2050　2080　2286

0　5　10　20m

N

5.22

The Gravel is the Place for Me

UG6

Stefan Lengen, Jane Wong

UG6 conceives new spatial experiences and experimental typologies. We encourage rigorous dialogue between drawing and making, the real and the fantastical. This year we sought 'third landscapes' across the British Isles and beyond as sites for a year-long research and design enquiry. The notion of the 'third landscape', first coined by the French designer, botanist and writer Gilles Clément, was articulated largely in the context of urbanism and ecology, referring to the liminal spatial conditions in the built environment and the exceptionally diverse biological communities they harbour.

UG6 posits that when these 'third landscapes' are understood in relation to the conditions of their abandonment – whether this be political, economic or social – they can be reimagined as spaces for new forms of use and exchange that challenge the market-driven processes shaping much of the built environment.

From the fragile peatlands of the Flow Country, Scotland to the abandoned salt pans of Molentargius, Sardinia, sites were selected by each student based on a deep and personal interest.

Building upon precise site analysis, students speculated on a new reading of these 'third landscapes', reimagining human and non-human relationships with respect to history, culture and contemporary networks of communities, infrastructure and public amenities.

These manifested as spatial strategies and imaginative, site-specific programmes such as new post-contamination social infrastructures, the repurposing of salt production ruins for a new bathing culture and the introduction of cradle-to-cradle grazing settlements for marshland rehabilitation.

Through experimentations in making, digital fabrication and testing, projects were developed through intuitive design and tacit knowledge. These informed alternative architectural visions, creating precise spatial armatures and an architectural presence that celebrates the idiosyncrasies of each place while responding to precise environmental conditions, from open-air boggy courtyards to typhoon-adaptive kinetic roofs.

Based on rigorous investigations and a field trip to Flimwell Park and Dungeness, UG6 students discovered and experienced a plethora of experimental construction methodologies. These sparked an array of projects, from reframing views of an at-risk habitat to relocating the first UK climate refugees, all serving to reveal, augment and cherish neglected qualities and communities. Together they reimagine 'third landscapes' as sites of alternative ecological and socio-political relationships.

Year 2
Shujian (Bob) Bao, Adam Butcher, Sofia Forni, Magdalena Gauden, Luke Gifford, Claudiu-Liciniu Horsia, Julia Rzaca, Julia Specht, Sidre Sulevani, Nicole Zhao

Year 3
Pui (Benson) Chan, Rhiannon Howes, Minhe Li, Mufeng Shi, Henry Williams

Thanks to all the structural and environmental consultants who have worked with individual students to realise their projects. Special thanks to Maria Fulford and Sal Wilson

Thanks to our workshop tutors for their remarkable commitment and dedication: Carlota Nuñez-Barranco Vallejo, Ben Spong, William Victor Camilleri

Critics: Nat Chard, Zachary Fluker, Ocian Hamel-Smith, Steve Johnson, Margit Kraft, Perry Kulper, Ifigeneia Liangi, Ana Monrabal-Cook, Toby O'Connor, Luke Pearson, Joel Saldeck, Daniel Wilkinson, Ivana Wingham

6.1 Julia Specht, Y2 'History Is in the Mud: A Community Research Centre for Tollesbury Wick'. The project addresses and negotiates the tensions between archaeological activities, habitat preservation and public access at Tollesbury. It proposes a community research centre that treads and rests lightly on the ground, providing space for multidisciplinary research that engages the local community and visitors in active fieldwork, nurturing a wider cultural consciousness of the environmental and historical value of the territory.

6.2–6.3 Adam Butcher, Y2 'The Dance between Land and Sea: Residence for a Coastal Custodian'. The project challenges the notion of defence in the context of erosion and rising sea levels, and poses an alternative approach to negotiating the constant state of flux found along the littoral edge of Benacre Broad. It puts forward the character of a coastal custodian who develops a deep understanding of and engagement with nature.

6.4 Luke Gifford, Y2 'The Natural Museum: A Peatland Rehabilitation Centre for the Flow Country'. The project investigates the fragile ecosystem of the Flow Country in Scotland and its rich archaeology. It addresses the misguided perception of peatscape as wasteland and highlights its significance as a major carbon sink. The project proposes a new reading of the territory as a natural museum. A research facility is envisioned for scientific fieldwork and peat rehabilitation, engendering a new form of care and appreciation for the region

6.5–6.6 Minhe Li, Y3 'Mining Culture: A Cultural Park for Wheal Coates Mine'. The project speculates an alternative post-industrial vision for the mining district of St Agnes to transform the industrial ensemble into a park with cultural programming. Architectural fragments are repurposed and reinterpreted for projections, animation and other forms of cultural activity. Through these interventions, a conservation strategy is developed to stabilise the industry's remains while facilitating new use.

6.7 Claudiu-Liciniu Horsia, Y2 'Harvesting at the Delta: Poetics and Functions of the Danube'. Throughout the centuries, the Danube Delta has been a place for those seeking refuge from hostile social and political conditions elsewhere. The project focuses on the Dobrogea region of Romania and responds to Lipovan traditions, beliefs and ways of living. The project proposes a design that focuses on the Lipovans' main trades in reeds, grains, fish and clay as a network of resources that is continually evolving.

6.8–6.9 Nicole Zhao, Y2 'The World It Comes From: A Tidal Boat-to-Plate Restaurant'. The project develops an analysis and reinterpretation of landscape devices created by humans – from fish traps to oyster pits – based on deep knowledge of the local conditions of the Blackwater Estuary. Reflecting on the environmental consciousness embedded in those devices, a restaurant is proposed to celebrate the gifts of the estuary and embrace the forces and cycles of nature.

6.10 Shujian (Bob) Bao, Y2 'Carving an Inhabitable Landscape: An Excavated House and Workplace'. The project proposes a post-industrial vision for the remaining terraces of Shoreham Cement Quarry to nurture the emerging 'third landscape' and provide a home for a gardener and a sculptor, so as to slowly rejuvenate the entire quarry over decades.

6.11–6.12 Mufeng Shi, Y3 'Negotiating Precarity: A Communal Typhoon Refuge for Yantian'. The project investigates the topographical and environmental conditions that transformed Yantian into one of the most productive landscapes in the world. These same conditions render the port and its community vulnerable to forceful typhoons, extreme weather conditions and flooding. Recognising the precarious conditions of port

workers and the lack of community infrastructure, the project proposes a reactive typhoon refuge for the local community.

6.13 Pui (Benson) Chan, Y3 'Gruinard's Redemption: Rehabilitating Contaminated Landscapes'. The project investigates the processes of contamination of Gruinard Island in Scotland. It challenges the exclusionary nature of conventional decontamination operations, and puts forward an alternative strategy of rehabilitating the territory through a socially inclusive process of construction. The project proposes a community research centre that embodies the contaminated earth, which over time neutralises and transforms into a memorial to the island's history.

6.14–6.15 Julia Rzaca, Y2 'Out There in the Darkness: New Landscape Rituals for Dartmoor'. The building proposes a revival of the ancient Dartmoor druidical myths and their relationship to territory at large. With a dual programme, it revolves around two main ideas of reclaiming the landscape: the physical act of walking and the ritual of potion-making.

6.16, 6.18 Henry Williams, Y3 'A Village Being Abandoned: A Socially Inclusive Spatial Strategy for Fairbourne'. Against the imminent threat of sea-level rise and acceleration of coastal erosion, the project analyses and critiques the UK's decommissioning process for the village of Fairbourne. It speculates a nuanced and inclusive strategy that negotiates the tensions between resistance and retreat, and creates new conditions for an intergenerational community.

6.17 Sidre Sulevani, Y2 'The Afterlife of the Royal Docks'. The project charts the transformation of the site of the Royal Docks from marshland to the service yard of the British Empire, and speculates alternative visions for its post-empire future. Responding to the lack of community amenities and leisure facilities for the inhabitants of the neighbourhood, it proposes a kayaking leisure centre with spaces for all ages and abilities.

6.19–6.20 Sofia Forni, Y2 'Choreographies in Bodies of Salt Water: A Communal Bathhouse for Molentargius'. The project develops a careful analysis of Molentargius' relationship to salt, from its history of prolific salt production to its modern-day recreational use and tourism in the salt works. Addressing the contemporary social gap between locals and visitors, the project reimagines the vestiges of salt basins as a communal bathhouse, where the boundaries of public and private life blur, providing space for social exchange and relaxation.

6.21 Rhiannon Howes, Y3 'Nationalising Saltmarshes: A Spatial and Political Strategy for the Estuaries of the South-East'. The project challenges the political shortsightedness and ecological illiteracy that have led to the misunderstanding and mismanagement of the UK's estuaries and their intertidal marshes. These habitats have been gradually disappearing due to human terraforming of the shoreline, accelerated by climate change and rising sea levels in what has become known as the 'coastal squeeze'. Stretching across the coastline between the Thames and Orwell rivers, the project reframes the saltmarsh as a national infrastructure.

6.22–6.23 Magdalena Gauden, Y2 'Cradle to Cradle: Regenerative Futures for Toruń's Fortified Landscapes'. The project develops a radical reading of Toruń through the analysis of its ground conditions, which were dramatically transformed by geomorphological and human forces. Focusing on one of the city's fortresses, the project proposes a permaculture centre that harnesses the lay of the land and its associated ecological and social networks. It nurtures a circular economy of production that reconnects the local community with its unique ecosystem and topography.

6.3

6.4

6.5

6.6

6.7

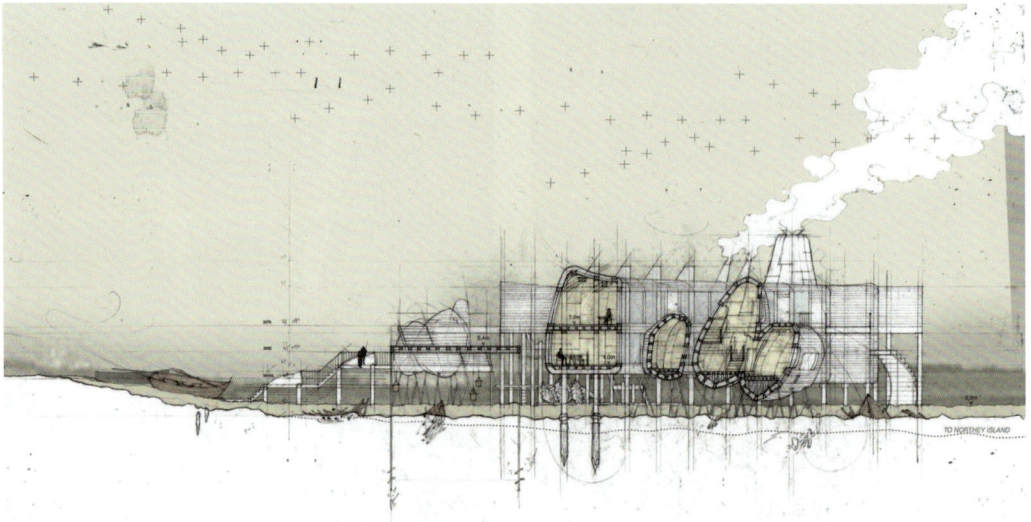

6.8

6.9

6.10

6.11

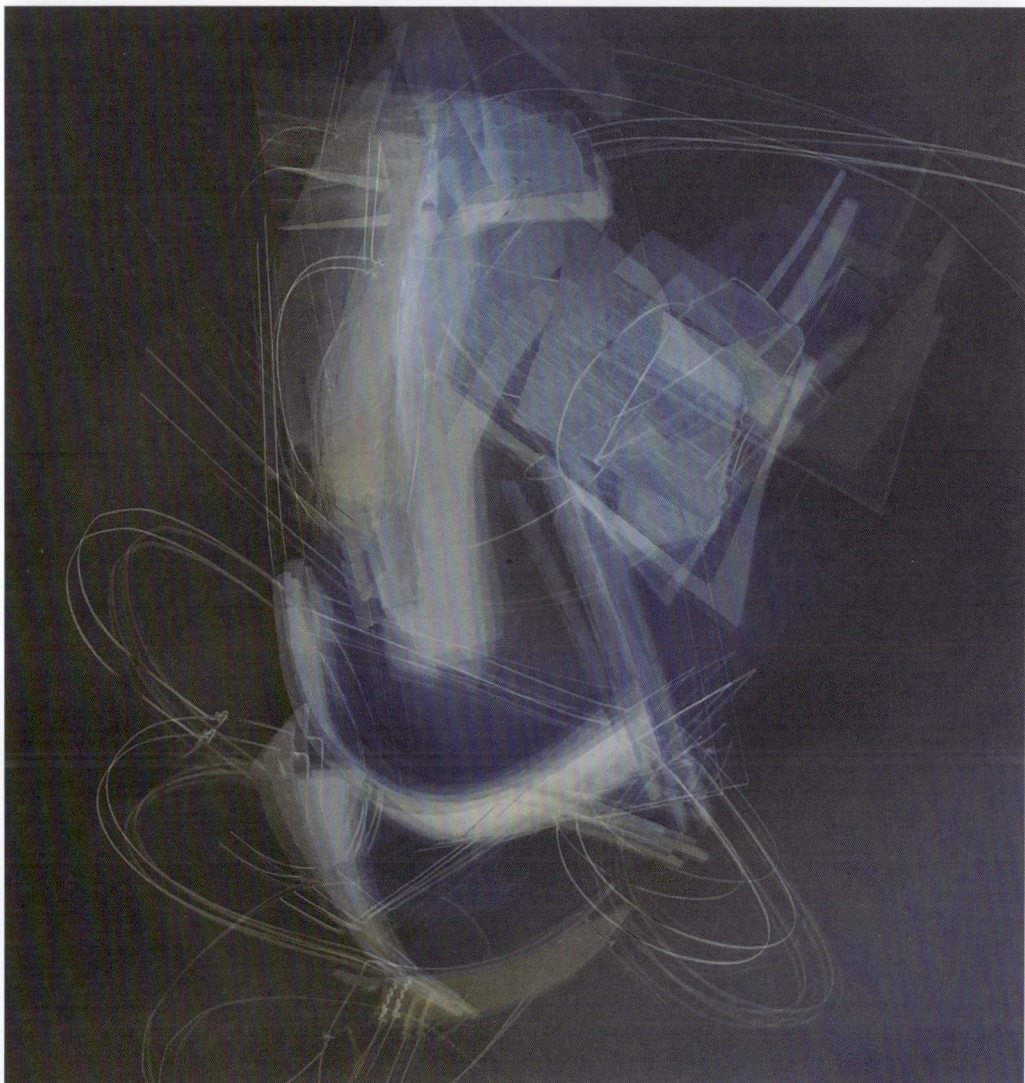

6.12

6.13

6.14

6.15

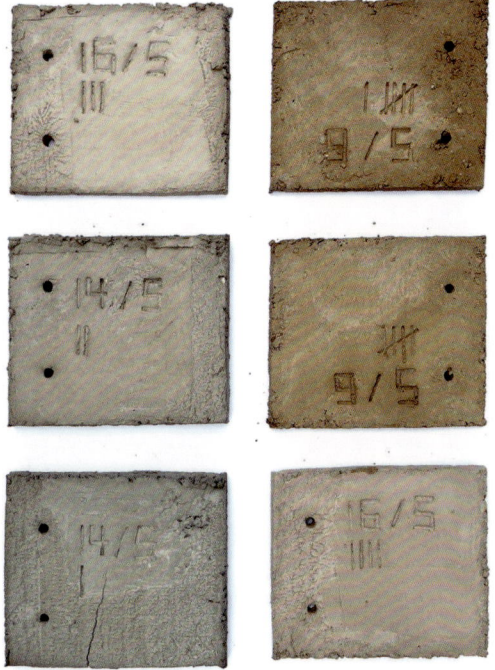

6.16

6.17

6.18

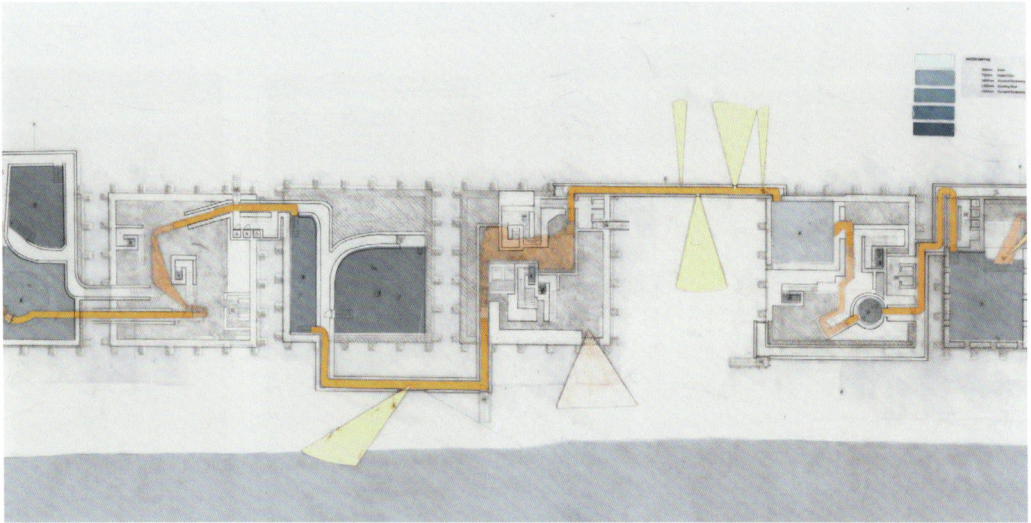

6.19

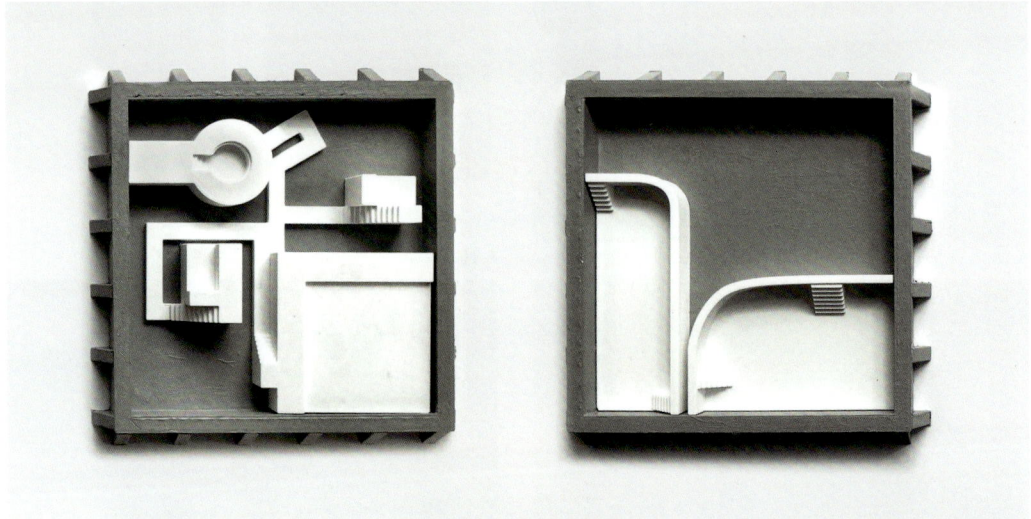

6.20

6.21

6.22

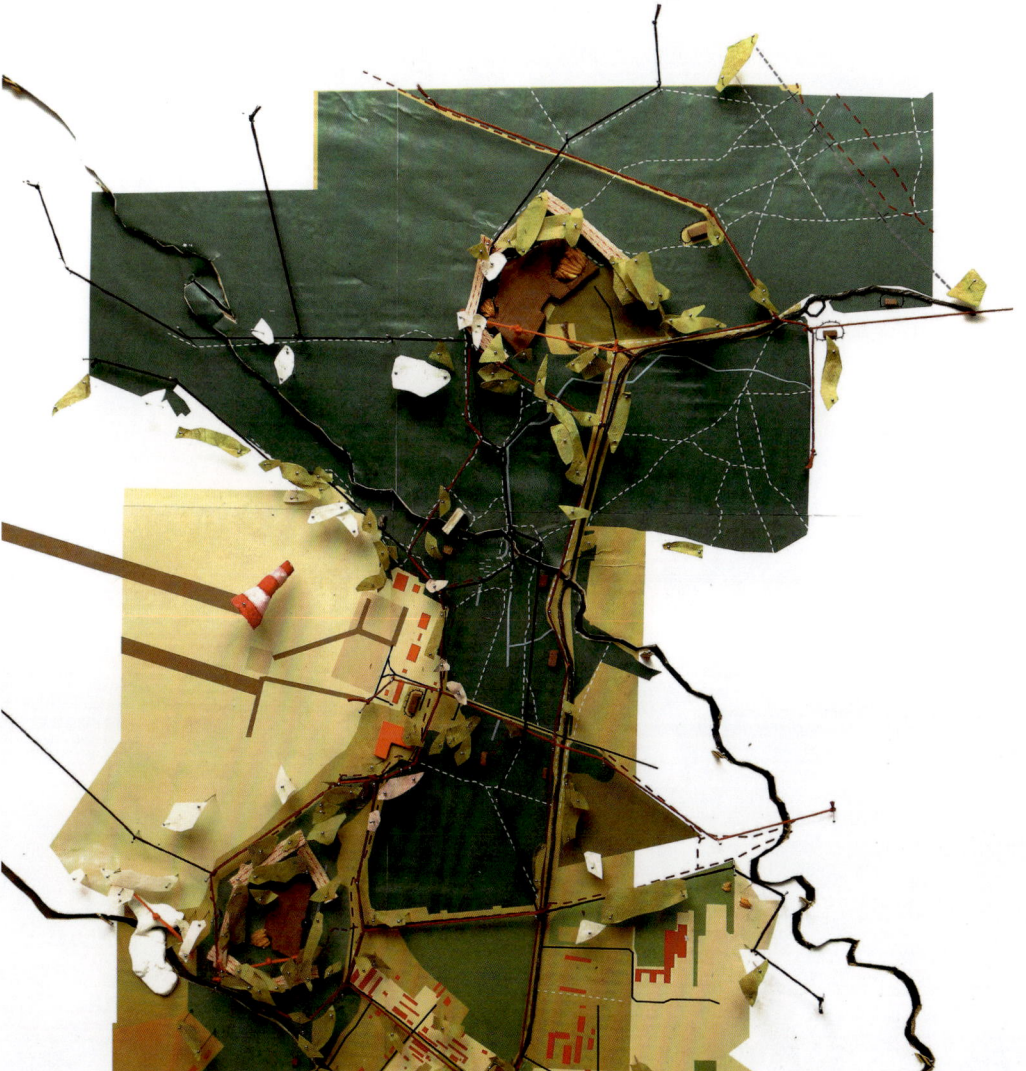

6.23

Taking Stock

UG7

Joseph Augustin, Christopher Burman, Luke Jones

This year UG7 explored the production of building materials and its role in architectural form-making. The unit understands that this relationship exists across incompatible scales. Commodity supply chains and sites of production form planetary-scale networks of logistics, trade and finance. 'Architecture', at the scale of building, space and inhabitation, is innately local, anthropometric and part of everyday life. The relationship between one scale and another is itself a design problem.

We began the year working with a set of design methods, mapping scenarios of material flows and future material cultures alongside tectonic studies of building elements and spaces, to create an immediate connection between global environmental impacts and architectural fundamentals. Each student selected a material and mapped its supply chain and environmental impacts, then developed an agenda for a specific 'tectonic' form of construction, based around its innate capacities.

In term two the unit moved its focus to Peterborough. Situated on the northern fringe of London's commuter rail network, it is home to about 200,000 people and is the UK's fastest growing city, despite simultaneously being regularly voted as the 'worst place to live'.

A medieval town transformed by its nodal position in transport networks, Peterborough is a former centre of brick production with abundant local stone resources. Set on the edge of a Fenland landscape – waterlogged, flat and vulnerable to flooding – it is also prosperous, connected and historic. Our field trip to the city included visits to several local material producers, limestone quarries and stone businesses. Its centre exhibits all the deficiencies of 20th-century UK urban planning; a ring road, endless car parks, a huge shopping centre, suburbs and multiple supermarkets. It has significant social issues, as well as enormous energy, diversity and potential.

As such, the city provides a model for thinking through how architecture might reconstruct itself as an agent of environmental transition. The year culminated in projects exploring the notion of the 'basic building', challenging students to develop an architecture that renegotiates the technical complexity and impact of the contemporary construction industry, reprioritising materiality and reconsidering the civic identity that might emerge.

Year 2
Sarah Bibby, Shing (Bertha) Ho, Fatim Kamara, Hui-Shun Low, Esma Onur, Alexandria Pattison, Gabriela Sawicka, Emily To, Jade Wong, Zaynah Younus

Year 3
Nasser Al-Khereiji, Monika Buranasetkul, Anna Dixon, Alannah Fowler, Marten Hall, Natthasha (Ying) Jintarasamee, Yan (Johnson) Lam

Technical tutors and consultants: Simon Beames, Oliver Houchell

Critics: Alina Kvirkvelia, James Green, Tom Ushakov

Special thanks to Daniel Wilson and the team at Stamford Stone and Alexandre Bertrand at The Stone Masonry Company

109

7.1–7.2 Sarah Bibby, Y2 'A Round Town'. The project presents an urban strategy to be implemented in the city of Peterborough by 2066. To reconnect the city to natural material cycles, a masterplan is created through a system of round-wood components which redefine civic space. The design favours small personal infrastructures that can be quickly assembled and deployed to promote the continuous circulation of civic life at different levels within the city.

7.3–7.4 Nasser Al-Khereiji, Y3 'Solar Mosque of Peterborough'. In consideration of the 2066 demographic projections for Peterborough and the UK as a whole, the project proposes the introduction of a new civic building of religious significance in the form of a mosque. Like the nearby cathedral, the new central mosque is constructed predominantly of stone from the surrounding quarries, exploring contemporary production methods.

7.5, 7.12 Monika Buranasetkul, Y3 'Architecture of Waste'. A culinary school provides the site for investigations into how different types of local food waste could influence the spatial design of a building. Experimenting with the production of bio-based materials using different binders, a series of building components such as wall panels, tiles or windows sit alongside temporary pavilions, demonstrating the reuse of seasonal waste.

7.6, 7.13 Anna Dixon, Y3 'Technopera 2066'. In the year 2066, Peterborough is dominated by the industrial coalition. The coalition, led by the self-titled 12 Monks, grew the industrial outskirts from barren edges to an overwhelming sprawl towards Peterborough's medieval heart. This unceasing growth disaggregated the community and culture of the city, and now threatens its last vestige of history and heritage, Peterborough Cathedral.

7.7, 7.9 Alannah Fowler, Y3 'Artichokey Yard'. The yard is a social housing programme for the more vulnerable inhabitants of Peterborough, to help tackle the issue of homelessness and heal the community after the effects of the closure of the Warming Rooms homeless shelter and the Covid-19 pandemic. Integral to the project is its application of clay and ceramic features throughout the building's design and structure. Extruded clay blocks are used as the main building component, with additional features that demonstrate the possibilities of extrusion as a primary method of fabrication.

7.8, 7.17 Yan (Johnson) Lam, Y3 'Recycling Tyres into Architecture'. Every year large volumes of rubber tyres are wasted without being recycled, polluting and damaging our environment. This project uses recycled rubber crumb from rubber tyres as an architectural material. Proposals seek to address issues of energy use which are intensified by the UK's poorly insulated building stock, by proposing an alternative rubber wall build-up with structural and thermal qualities.

7.10, 7.24–7.25 Alexandria Pattison, Y2 'The Eco-Hub'. A community resource centre provides a place for hands-on agricultural education, grow spaces, greenhouses, workshops and a tool library. Panelised and volumetric hempcrete modules are designed to be produced off-site and quickly assembled in place. Since the Covid-19 pandemic, many people have realised that access to clean air and the ability to socialise are important factors of life that had previously been taken for granted.

7.11 Shing (Bertha) Ho, Y2 'Nene Railway Museum'. Located along the south bank of the River Nene, the scheme is situated between the East Coast Mainline and the Nene Valley Railway, a steam-hobbyist line. The project adds onto the current museum and terminus and utilises engineered timber, drawing inspiration from neighbouring half-timbered buildings and historical steel structures.

7.14 Gabriela Sawicka, Y2 'International Language Cinema'. A new cultural site is proposed at the heart of Peterborough, showcasing international cinema as a starting point for language and cultural exchange. A timber frame construction with locally sourced stone and large mycelium infill panels provides an acoustic environment optimised for speech and performance.

7.15 Natthasha (Ying) Jintarasamee, Y3 'The Olfactory Sensory Experience of the Making of Gin'. Through the creation of a gin distillery and infusion bar, the project commits to the development of 'vibrant Peterborough' as in the 2016–2036 development plan. A programme of microdistilleries and infusion labs is created in addition to private accommodation and facilities to provide a complete weekend learning experience for gin lovers.

7.16 Fatim Kamara, Y2 'Three Saints Village'. The project provides refuge to flood victims in Peterborough. In 2066, the east of the city is seasonally flooded due to its proximity to the River Nene. The cathedral grounds are predicted to escape regular flooding, as its land level is slightly higher and natural vegetation reduces surface run-off. The grid is responsive to needs and provides supportive communal areas for both short and longer-term residents to gather and live comfortably within the safety of the cathedral walls.

7.18–17.21 Marten Hall, Y3 'The Total Spoliation of Whitworth Mill, 2022–2066'. This project approaches existing disused buildings as valuable building stock. The entirety of the building's fabric is treated as *spolia*, with total reuse enforced. This is an opportunity for a carbon-neutral design and construction, with a closed cycle of deconstruction and construction. The site is positioned as an urban quarry, with the extraction of segments of building approached as though they were quarry blocks. The choice of a decommissioned flour mill in Peterborough as both site and stock enables a proposal that labours over how a building is replaced, as well as how a new building is designed.

7.22 Esma Onur, Y2 'River Nene Inhabited Bridge'. The inhabited bridge across the River Nene creates a new kind of civic space within the city. The site is located at a distance from supermarkets and restaurants. The inhabitable bridge provides a mixture of food kiosks and dining areas as an alternative space for workers and residents, while its architecture explores composite clay construction methods.

7.23 Hui-Shan Low, Y2 'The Bamboo Bathhouse'. Thermal bathing rituals and modern hydrotherapy are understood to help cure and relieve physical and mental distress. In line with traditional therapies, the bathhouse creates a space for relaxation of the soul, the body and the mind. The design of the bathhouse showcases contemporary and traditional construction techniques associated with an emerging bamboo supply chain.

7.26 Emily To, Y2 'Boats of a Feather Flock Together'. The Boston to Peterborough wetland corridor will create greater connections between the North and South of the Fen District. Anticipating the completion of the new connection by 2066, the boaters' station accommodates an influx of leisure boats coming into Peterborough. The station acts as a rest stop and space for boaters to connect, offering key facilities, including a boat maintenance area that is central to the building. Integrated birdhouses provide a site for the cultivation of existing ecologies.

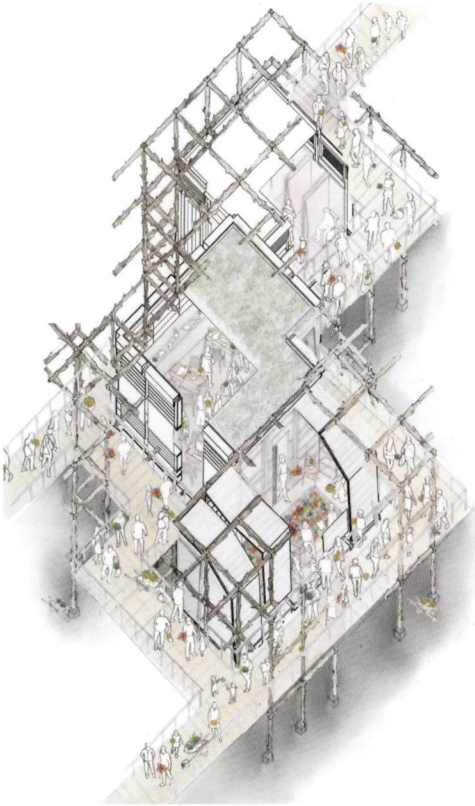

7.2

7.3

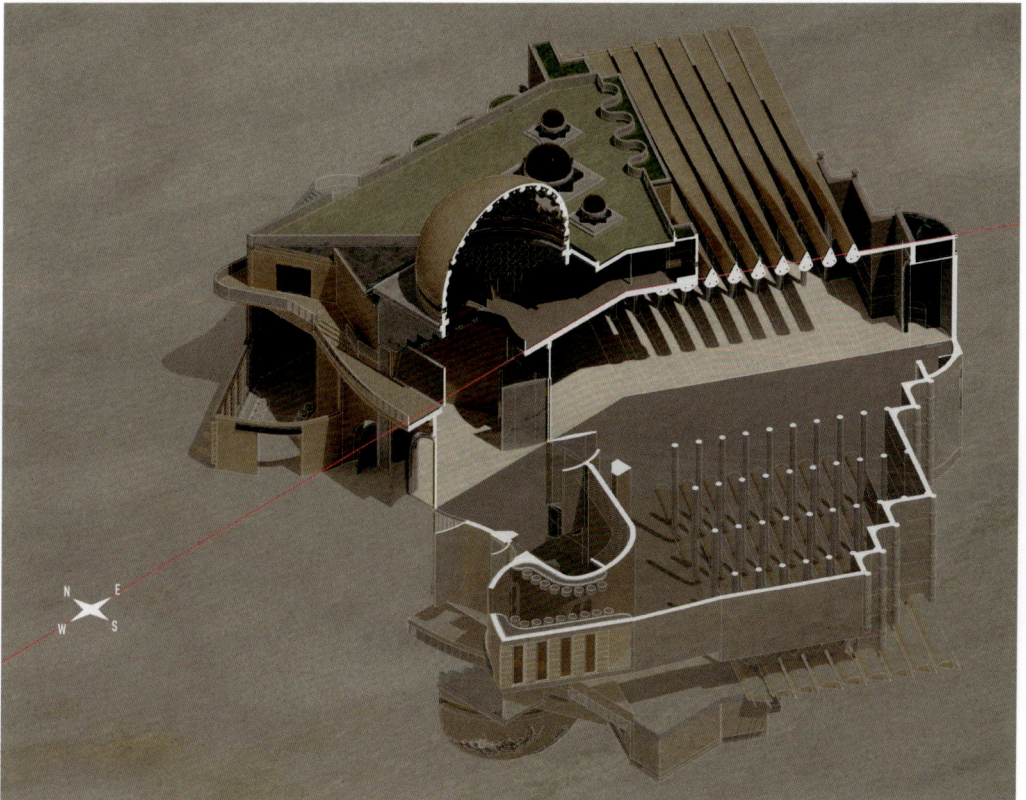

7.4

7.5

7.6

7.7

7.8

7.9

7.10

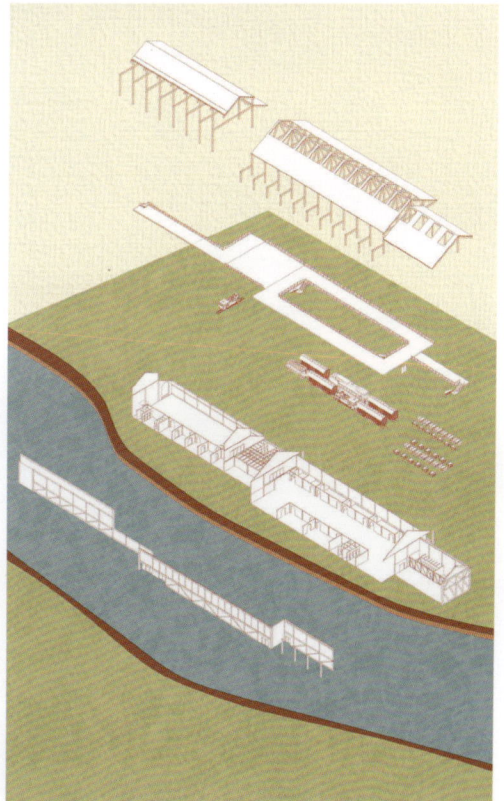

7.11

7.12

7.13

7.14

7.15

7.16

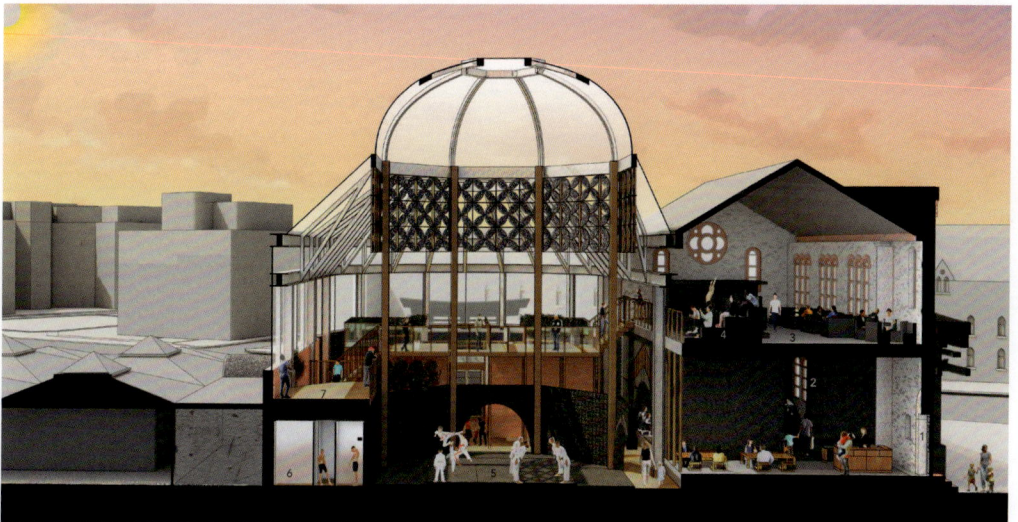

7.17

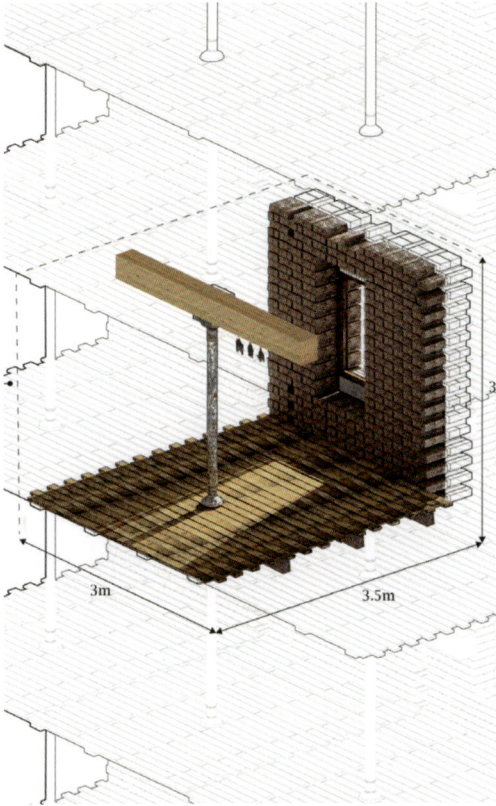

7.19

7.20

7.21

117

7.22

7.23

7.24

7.25

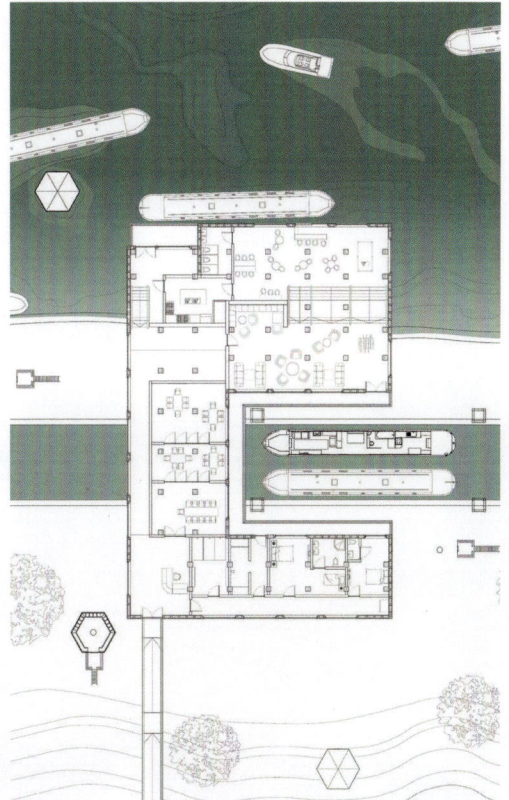

7.26

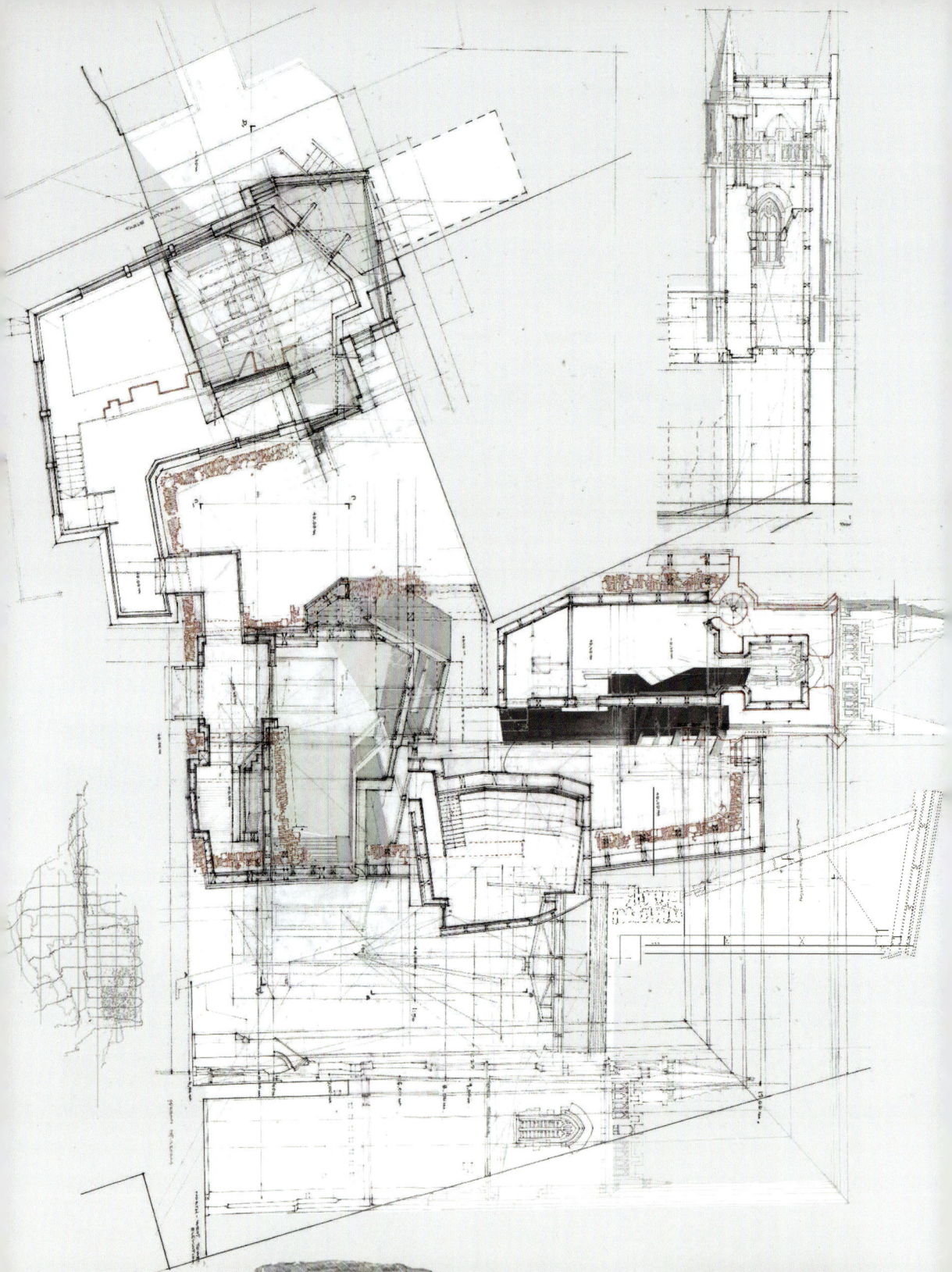

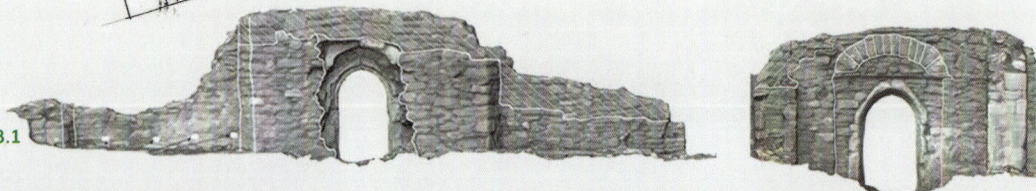

8.1

Prototypes for an Afterlife   UG8

Farlie Reynolds, Greg Storrar

UG8 welcomes curious students interested in prototypical materials, structures and technologies. We work between the drawn, the made and the moving image to champion innovative architectural strategies rooted in the environmental challenges of our time. As we rally to address the climate crisis and rethink the very fundamentals of how we live our lives, our collective gaze slowly shifts towards different visions of the world to come. This year the unit prototyped for an 'afterlife'. We explored the curiosities, idiosyncrasies and opportunities inherent in the working and re-working of architecture with a previous life.

Every 10 minutes a building in the UK is demolished. Our architectures are mortal – eternal sufferers of the relentless laws of gravity, destructive weather, disobedient tenants and the metronomic wrecking ball of the architectural press. Wiping the slate clean can be an aggressive act of social, cultural and material erasure, but to retain in some capacity – to lease new life – requires embracing and interfacing awkward or inconvenient fragments and memories.

Any radical act of retention, resurrection or reincarnation requires prototyping. We worked with and against materials, infrastructures, building fragments and technologies, borrowing and leaning on existing fabric to develop our own architectures of reinvention.

Our field trip was a journey through stone, from the deep mines of the Peak District, through the pennant stone city of Bristol, to the vast open quarries of the Isle of Portland. Along the way we discovered bold prototypes such as the Smithsons' Solar Pavilion and the work of Frei Otto in Hooke Park.

The year's first design project was a making-led residency in Flimwell. We constructed and deployed a series of prototypes to speculate upon how and why materials might adopt new uses and meaning in subsequent lives. These methodologies informed and evolved into the building projects that followed. Located in constrained urban sites in central Bristol, the projects include: a museum of contested histories built from the remains of cancelled buildings and monuments; a reinterpretation of the public house constructed in unfired clay; and a night school that reconfigures the ruin of a deconsecrated church.

Year 2
Lorenzo Angoli, Myles Green, Chanya (Miu) Ieosivikul, Jinyi (Athena) Li, Hannah Lingard, Luke Saito Koper, Cosmin Ticus, Mateusz Zwijacz

Year 3
Oi (Tiffany) Chin, Jacob Meyers, Krit Pichedvanichok, Oska Smith, Adam Stoddart, Luke Sturgeon, Yen Ting

Technical tutors and consultants: Tom Budd, Steve Johnson

Special thanks to Steve Johnson and all those at Flimwell Park and the Woodland Enterprise Centre whose support and dedication made 'The Flimwell Prototypes' such a success.

Thanks also to our critics and skills tutors: Luke Bowler, Theo Brader-Tan, Tom Budd, Barbara-Ann Campbell-Lange, Nat Chard, James Della Valle, Penelope Haralambidou, Steve Johnson, Tea Maria Marta, Ana Monrabal-Cook, Cira Oller Tovar, Ben Spong, Negar Taatizadeh

8.1, 8.10 Cosmin Ticus, Y2 'Negotiating the Wreckage'. An adult education centre for traditional crafts sits upon and within the ruined church of St Mary le Port in Bristol's Castle Park. Through a reappropriation of *l'art du trait* techniques in fabrication drawing, practices of woodworking, ceramics and stonemasonry reside within both the building and its design.

8.2, 8.5, 8.14–8.15, 8.18–8.19 Oska Smith, Y3 'Towards a New Public House'. A neglected church ruin in Bristol serves as the foundations for the recontextualisation of a public house. The pub's eroded function as an important civic space is re-established through the reframing of its material culture. A new ceramic architecture aims to be more expressive and inclusive, drawing inspiration from the diversity of traditional brick and glazed tiles, and recognising the aesthetic and social pluralism in the surrounding communities it serves.

8.3, 8.9, 8.11–8.13 Hannah Lingard, Y2 'The Bristol Institute of Oral Histories'. Stewarding and curating an intimate tradition of historical enquiry, this new museum for the spoken word collects, interprets and broadcasts every voice in the city. An architecture of stone, steel and softwood announces, amplifies and attenuates stories of the past, present and future.

8.4, 8.6, 8.27 Myles Green, Y2 'Do Pictures Talk of Mirrors?' A production studio and cinema reclaims a forgotten corner of Castle Park in the centre of Bristol. The architecture learns from the complex material make-up of projection, from the scale of the screen surface down to the chemical composition of the film strip. The appearance of everyday construction materials is transformed by oxygen-starved heating and other prototypical metamorphosis techniques, substituting unsustainable precious metals with waste by-products from the building industry.

8.7 Luke Saito Koper, Y2 'Hotwells Village Hall'. A campus of reconfigurable community spaces brings together residents and students in the historic residential neighbourhood of Clifton Village, Bristol. Incrementally shapeshifting through the day and over a term, the architecture actively and passively flexes to suit the cohabitation of two typically disparate communities.

8.8 Lorenzo Angoli, Y2 'Clifton's Acoustic Chamber Hall'. Musical performance and artist residencies come together in this hybridisation of two architectural typologies: the music hall and the hostel. Learning from the fabrication of traditional string instruments, the building's internal envelope is a series of crafted acoustic timber chambers, each tuned to the modes of rehearsal, recording and recital that they accommodate.

8.16–8.17 Jinyi (Athena) Li, Y2 'Recipes and the City: A New Reciprocity'. A cooperative food store and culinary kitchen for Bristol's Clifton Village. Perched on a steep urban site, this stepped architecture of processing, preserving, cooking and dining spaces seeks to support Bristolians in recultivating their interpersonal relationships in the post-pandemic world through a renewed understanding of food and the city.

8.20–8.21, 8.23–8.26 Jacob Meyers, Y3 'Centre for Bristol's Contested Histories'. A civic forum and archive for contested histories located in Bristol's historic Old City becomes a beacon of a new democratic order where citizens can rewrite their future. The building is a physical embodiment of its programme, constructed out of reclaimed stone and rubble-filled gabion bags, salvaged from the projected demolition of maligned nearby buildings with dark pasts – a cairn for a city.

8.22 Mateusz Zwijacz, Y2 'Finding a New Earth'. A community centre and shelter run by the LGBTQIA+ community offers a new home to accommodate, witness and share the queer stories and tales of Bristol past and present. Providing accommodation for youth in danger of homelessness and a headquarters for charity support organisations, the proposal is an intervention into the lost and forgotten identity of the city, drawing upon the stories of its segregated communities.

8.28 Oi (Tiffany) Chin, Y3 'Redressing Mary le Port: A New Clothing Market for the Circular Economy'. In this upcycled fashion studio and showroom negotiating the ruins of Mary le Port church, recycled household fabric is deployed as a building material. Combining traditional tailoring techniques with contemporary construction principles, the building is able to recycle and reconstitute itself over time, maintaining relevance as showrooms and fashion styles evolve.

8.29 Chanya (Miu) Ieosivikul, Y2 'Old City District Screening Rooms'. A gallery for the moving image seeks to rejuvenate the post-pandemic cinema experience by embracing alternative and unexpected ways of both screening and viewing film. In the District Cinema, space becomes image, and vice versa, through an exploration in projection, illumination and receptive architectural surfaces.

8.30 Yen Ting, Y3 'Dying for Dark, the Darker the Worse'. A new city theatre and cinema for avant-garde production, staging and screening sits at the intersection of medieval and modern Bristol. Exploring the prototypical use of wax as structure, light modulator and heat exchanger, the architecture seeks spectacle in the techniques of building performance.

8.31–8.32 Luke Sturgeon, Y3 'In the Corner – At the Edge'. A new harbour workshop and landmark at the edge of Bristol's Cumberland Basin and surrounding dock infrastructure. Constructed in stone, the building operates as a series of sculpted voids derived from physical and digital fluid dynamic simulations. The pressure differentials invoked by the architecture enable passive ventilation of workshop spaces, allowing a zero-carbon approach to a traditionally energy-intensive building programme.

8.2

8.3

8.4

8.5

8.6

8.7

8.8

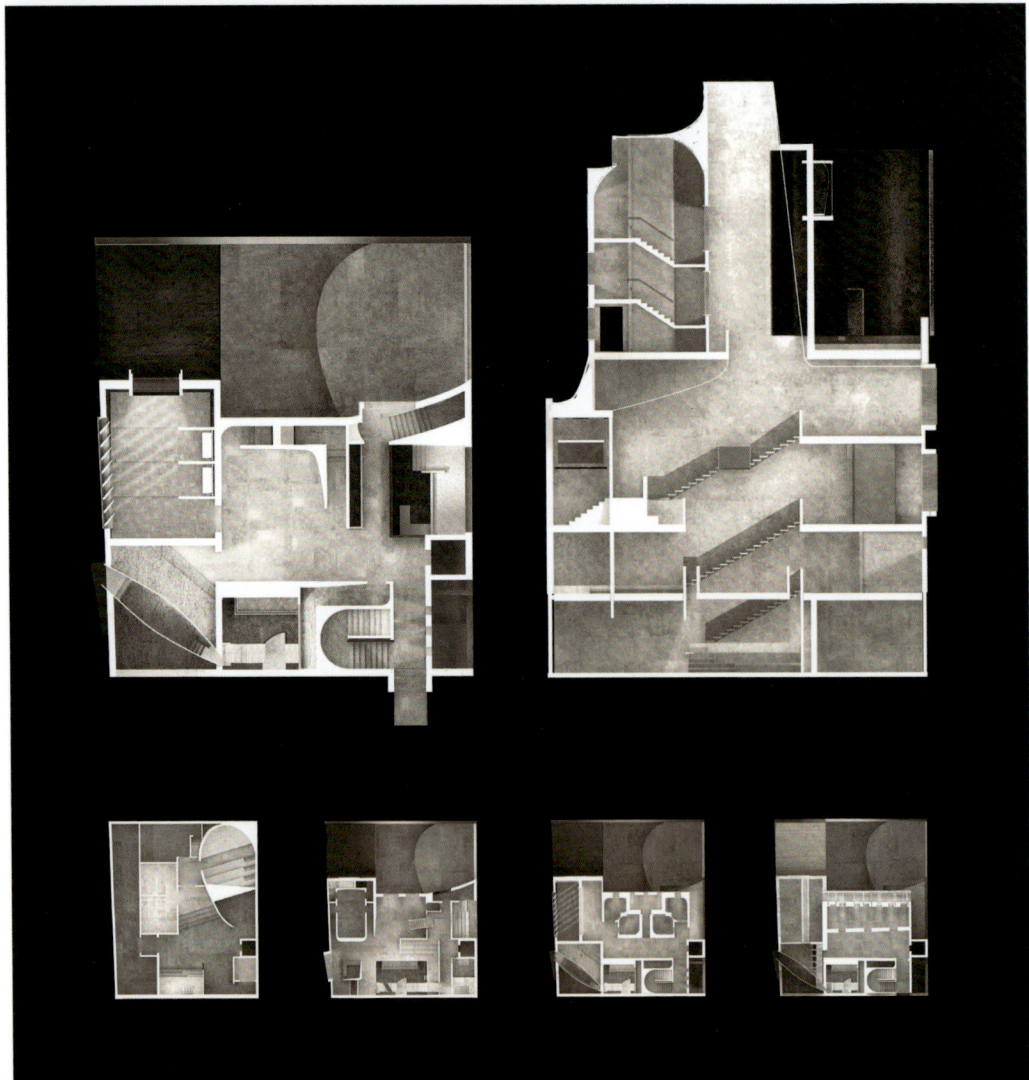

8.9

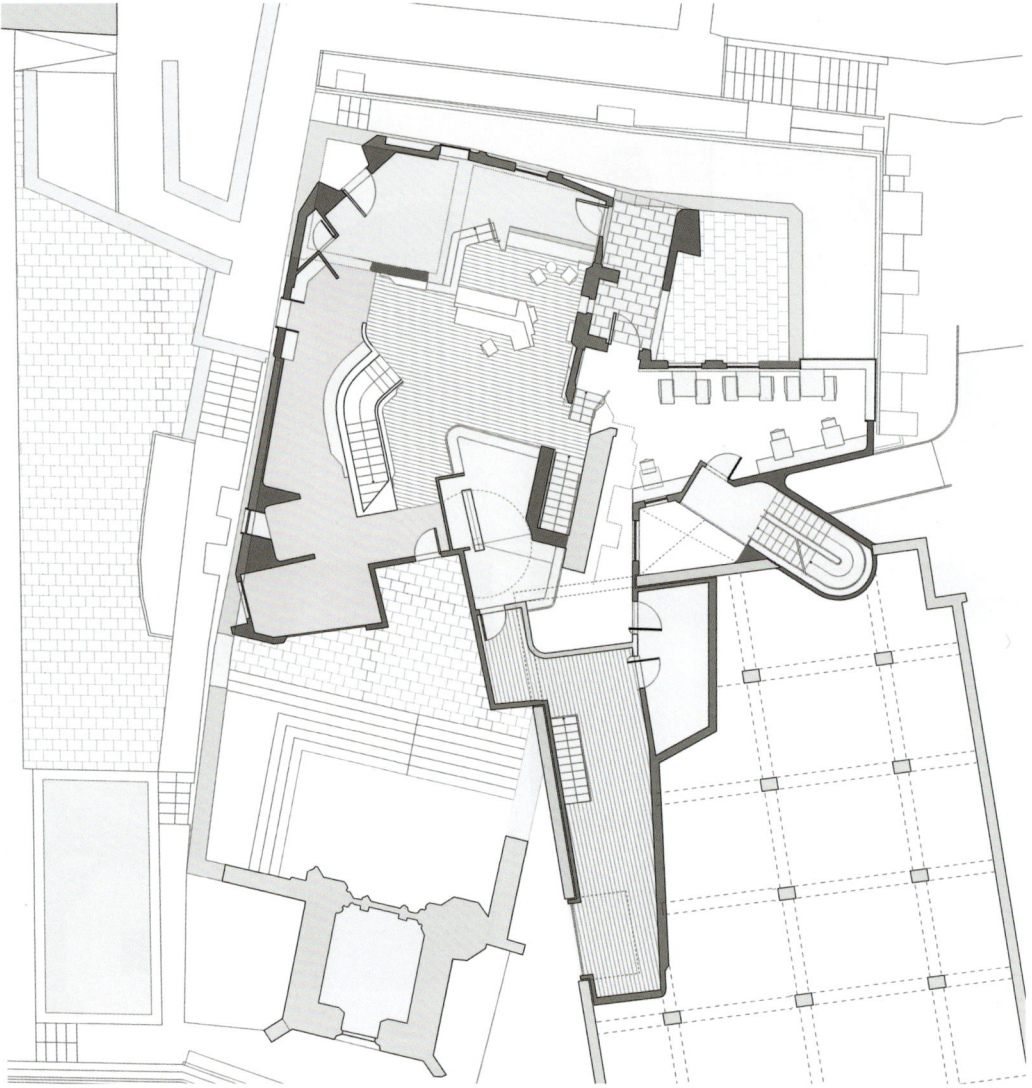

8.14

8.15

8.16

8.17

8.18

8.19

8.20

8.21

8.22

8.23

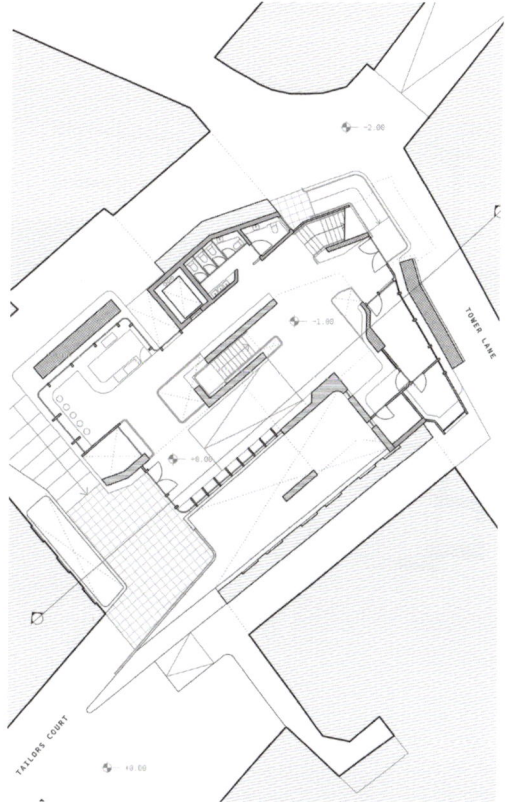

8.24

8.25

8.26

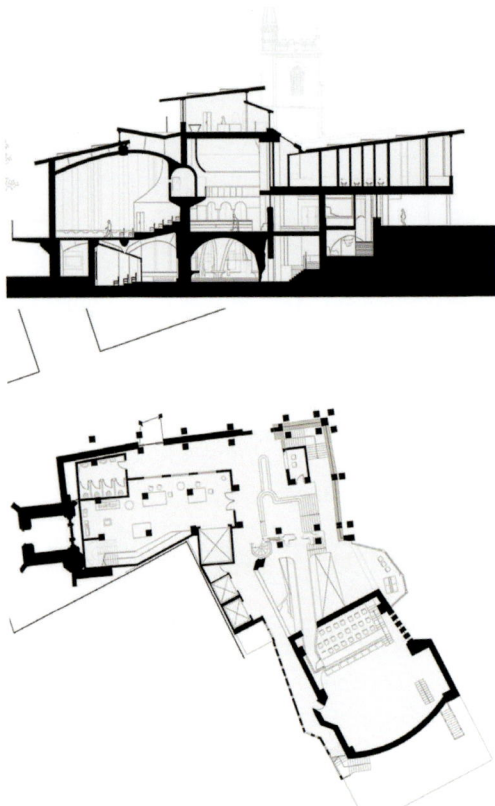

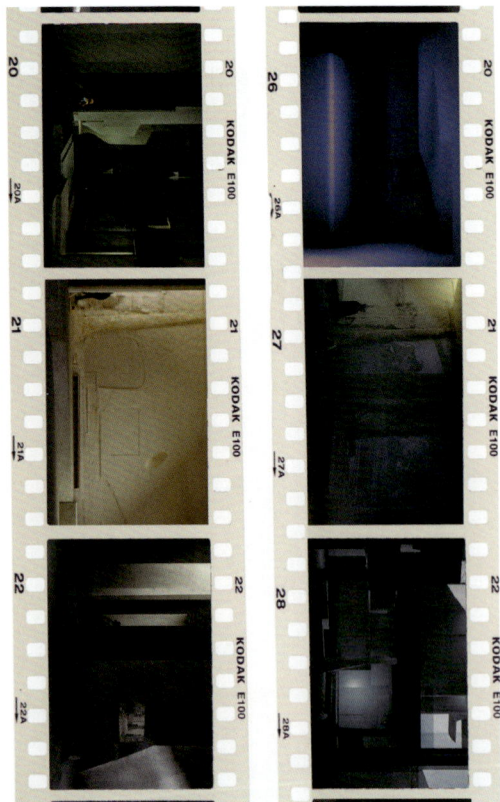

8.31

8.32

131

Among the Trees

UG9

Jessica In, Chee-Kit Lai

Concerns about our natural environment are not an exclusively contemporary issue. The impact of humans on the climate has been known and understood since antiquity. Theophrastus, a pupil of Aristotle and the 'father of botany', speculated that land became warmer when the clearing of forests exposed them to sunlight. The increasing degradation of our natural world and the effects of climate change have brought about a new urgency to an old, frequently ignored imbalance – how can we support nature alongside humankind?

This year UG9 considered the forest in its many forms, assessing both its practical and poetic elements as well their cultural and social influences. The unit explored the forest as storyteller and spectacle, as well as the potential future of the forest. It also considered the different physical and temporal scales of forests, from the local (Flimwell Park) to the national (Northern Forest project) and international (The Great Northern Forest).

Our field trip this year took us on a road trip through the proposed Northern Forest, travelling coast-to-coast via Liverpool, Manchester, Leeds and Hull. In addition to students researching the local context and selecting building sites, we visited historic and contemporary architecture, explored forest trails in the Peak District, took nature walks in the Kilnsea Wetlands and investigated the tidal island of Spurn Point.

Students developed their own architectural proposals, addressing issues around the climate crisis, landscape, ecologies, community, protest and legacy. Our final building proposals are sited in and around the Northern Forest. Here they address highly contextual issues concerning local histories, economies, energy production, cultural regeneration and landscape restoration.

Throughout the year we reviewed and discussed our work with a diverse group of guest critics, including those from outside of the architectural profession. We continue the unit's ambition to push the limits of architectural representation.

Year 2
Sara Abbod, Zhun Lyn Chang, Yongjun Choi, Rebecca Criste, Shiwei Lai, Maisy Liu, Rohini Mundey, Chi (Matthew) Wang

Year 3
Supitchaya (Praew) Anivat, Yiu (Raymond) Cham, Park Jin Chan, Hei (Eunice) Cheung, Wei (Keane) Chua, Eleanor Hollis, Ayaa Muhdar, Michalis Philiastidis

Technical tutors and consultants: Tom Budd, Thomas Parker, Donald Shillingburg

Critics: Bamidele Awoyemi, Alex Borrell, Theo Brader-Tan, Barbara-Ann Campbell-Lange, Nat Chard, Finbarr Charleson, Krina Christopoulou, Alex Fox, James Hampton, Rory Harmer, Kyriakos Katsaros, Ness Lafoy, Constance Lau, Doug Miller, Maxwell Mutanda, Giles Nartey, Thomas Parker, George Proud, Guang Yu Ren, Narinder Sagoo, Ellie Sampson, Sayan Skandarajah, Ben Spong, Sohanna Srinivasan, Manijeh Verghese, Viktoria Viktorija, Rain Wu, Fiona Zisch

Special thanks: Steve Johnson and Flimwell Park, Jason Coe, Amin Taha and Groupwork

9.1 Wei (Keane) Chua, Y3 'A Palimpsest of Vilified Rhododendrons'. This palimpsest model examines the contradictory relationship of the once sought after, but now vilified, *Rhododendron ponticum*, exploring the possibility of repurposing the existing plants as spatial beacons and mapping their chaotic spread and controlled removal.

9.2–9.4 Hei (Eunice) Cheung, Y3 'Reimagining Cohabitation: Offshore Energy Reskilling Centre'. Sited in St Andrew's Dock, Hull, the proposed programme offers the community the opportunity to join and transition to the renewable energy sector. The building embraces the natural rhythm of currents and sediment movement and introduces ways in which architectural foundations can be modified to encourage habitats for marine species, while simultaneously responding to the reskilling journey of the workers.

9.5, 9.7 Park Jin Chan, Y3 'Beyond Carbon'. The project speculates on the future of coal beyond energy production, as the UK plans to completely phase out its use by 2024. Sited in Maltby, a former coal mining town in South Yorkshire, The Carbon Fibre Institute will be a testbed for the transformation of redundant coal stockpiles into carbon fibre building components. Its form is driven by the material possibilities of carbon fibre, while also responding to the extraordinary landscape in which it is embedded.

9.6 Park Jin Chan, Y3 'Unstable Grounds'. Drawing device for recording the changing topography of Flimwell Park, East Sussex. The instrument is embedded into the woodland and attached onto the trunk of a sweet chestnut tree.

9.8 Shiwei Lai, Y2 'Cows Mouth Quarry'. Located in the South Pennine Moors in Lancashire, The Cows Mouth Theatre, built on an ex-quarry of the same name, allows audiences to enjoy acoustic experiences within a natural conservation area.

9.9 Yongjun Choi, Y2 'Hull Maritime Museum'. Located in Hull, near the River Humber Estuary, the proposed museum is a memorial to the lost elements of St Andrew's Dock. Its uneven hallway imitates a ship's hull and its interaction with changing tides.

9.10 Sara Abbod, Y2 'Sheffield Seed Archive'. Sited in Sheffield, a series of spaces allow for the meticulous process of preservation, cataloguing and storing, to support the restoration of local species and their propagation in future landscapes.

9.11, 9.14 Rohini Mundey, Y2 'The Woodland Hostel'. Located in the Peak District, Derbyshire, the hostel supports a culture of self-sufficiency through awareness of timber and food growing cycles. The building responds to the constantly shifting managed forest landscape by growing commercial crops on a sustainable basis over the next 50 years. Surrounding the hostel, five towers are placed in different felling sites and constructed slowly over this time frame. A timber catalogue is produced reflecting these individual environments. The towers are then assembled using the itemised tree forks to inform their structural concepts.

9.12 Rebecca Criste, Y2 'Salford Community Garden Centre'. A garden centre for Salford, Greater Manchester. The focus of the building is to engage its users in collaborative activities that encourage social interaction and help strengthen the sense of community in the local area.

9.13 Yiu (Raymond) Cham, Y3 'Kersal Wetland Flood Retreat Centre'. A centre for visitors to the Kersal Wetlands in Greater Manchester, providing shelter and relief during times of flood. Built of mudbricks of varying porosity and water absorption, the structure mitigates the effect of flooding on the ground while also collecting water from its blue roof.

9.15 Zhun Lyn Chang, Y2 'Lower Broughton Community Theatre'. The theatre provides locals with a new performing arts space and community centre. Designed to encourage multifunctional use of its spaces, the building is constructed from cork due to its excellent acoustic and insulation properties as well as its credentials as a carbon-negative material.

9.16 Michalis Philiastidis, Y3 'Selenophile'. A selenophile – person who loves the moon – partakes in the process of meditation in this wellness centre that uses reflected moonlight as its primary 'material'. Located in Derbyshire's Peak District, the building is spatially arranged according to the phases of the moon. Its light is used for the purposes of navigating the building but also to create spaces of contemplation.

9.17 Eleanor Hollis, Y3 'Inhabiting a Continuity for Dementia Respite'. As a respite centre for dementia patients and their carers, the project addresses the exponential rise of dementia within the local area and wider society. Situated within the evolving Humber region, the building rests on a fragile landscape affected by the devastating impacts of coastal erosion. Constructed of chalk, the building is designed to erode over time to stabilise the delicate landscape.

9.18 Chi (Matthew) Wang, Y2 'Swillington Museum'. The steeply sloping clay landscape, sited in Leeds on a former brickworks quarry, provides the setting and inspiration for a building constructed from the Earth. The museum celebrates the quarry, excavating the clay ground to form the base and key spaces. The building itself is an exhibit, demonstrating an innovative use of local material to visitors while also creating a carbon-neutral building.

9.19 Supitchaya (Praew) Anivat, Y3 'Museum for Trees of the Future'. Located in Hessle, East Yorkshire, the museum invites its visitors to experience the trees of our soon-to-be-warmer climate. By preserving a collection of trees from three biomes – tropical rainforests, savannah grasslands and deserts – the trees can be returned to their indigenous locations after they have recovered from overheating or rapid loss of greenspace through natural succession.

9.20, 9.21 Maisy Liu, Y2 'A Recipe for Waste Reinvention: The Biochar Centre'. A production and research centre in Beverley, East Yorkshire, the building illustrates the potential of biochar, a biomass-based material with innovative applications in construction and agriculture. The project demonstrates how biochar production and landscape development can support one another. Visitors are immersed in the process of biochar production through the kiln and skylit spaces. The heat generated during production supports the hypocaust flooring system and thermal baths, while a steam-filled walkway envelops visitors in the kiln's interior environment.

9.22–9.25 Wei (Keane) Chua, Y3 'The Under-Bog Revival'. Peatlands – commonly vilified as vague terrains and places of death and waste – are the most ecologically productive land-based carbon sinks, storing up to 25 times more carbon than trees. Sited in the Colliers Moss Common in Merseyside, the project proposes a symbiotic alliance of architecture and peat. By treating architecture as a plug-in device that augments the carbon sequestration prowess of the ecological peat, the proposed building is an evolutionary catalyst to preserve, restore and protect these significant peatlands. The architecture adopts a long-term approach in tandem with slow landscape recovery. Through three construction and programmatic phases over a 50-year period, the architecture grows slowly, just like peat. Over time it will become a beacon of hope for peatland restoration and awareness across the UK.

9.2

9.3

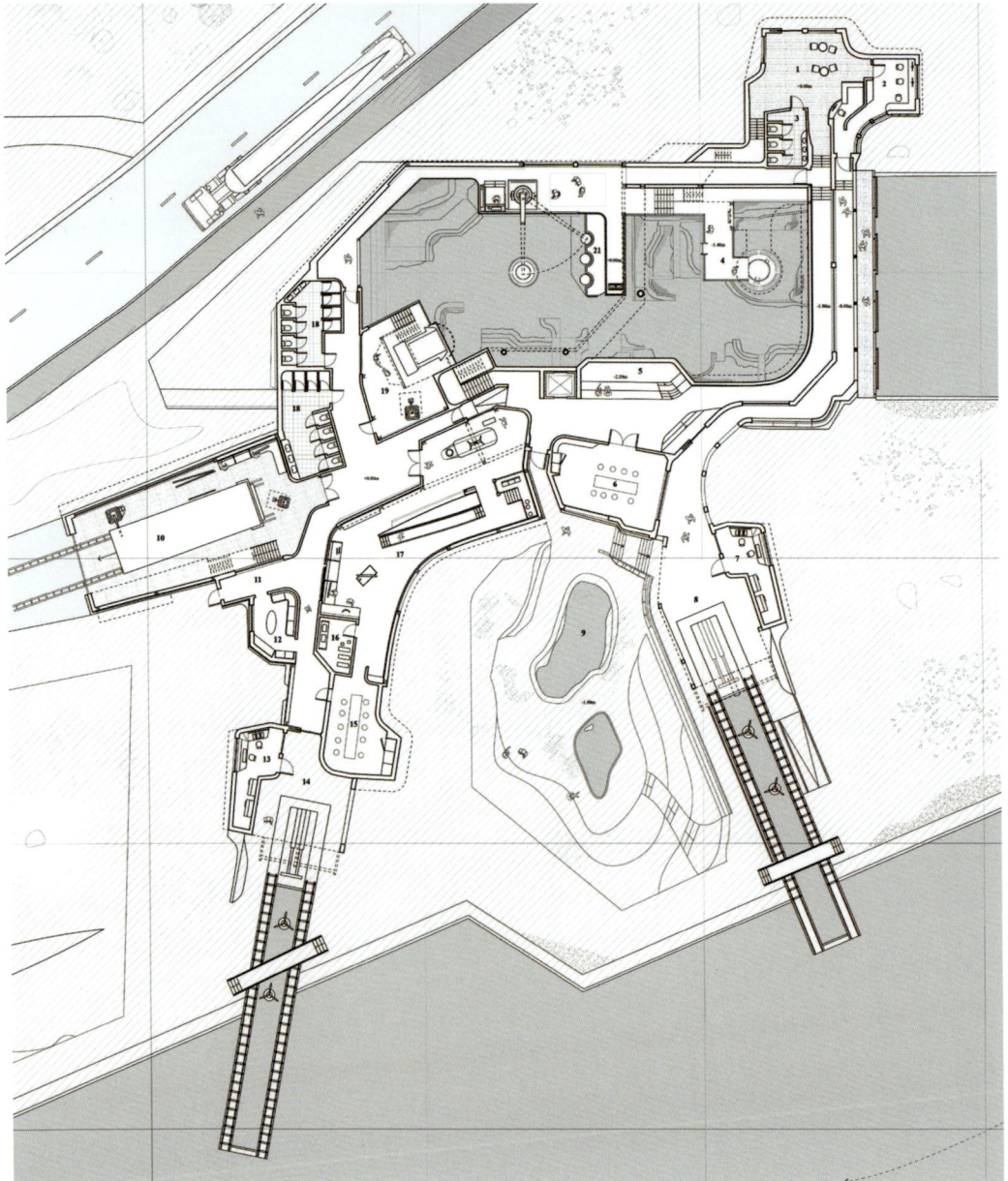

9.4

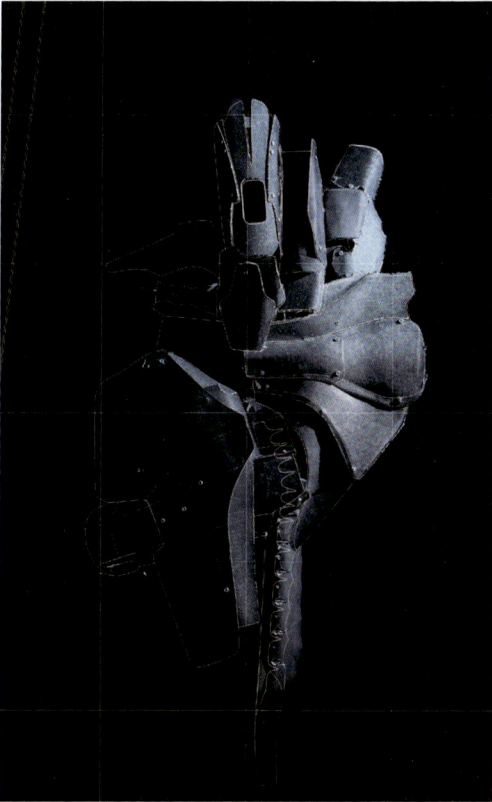

9.5

9.6

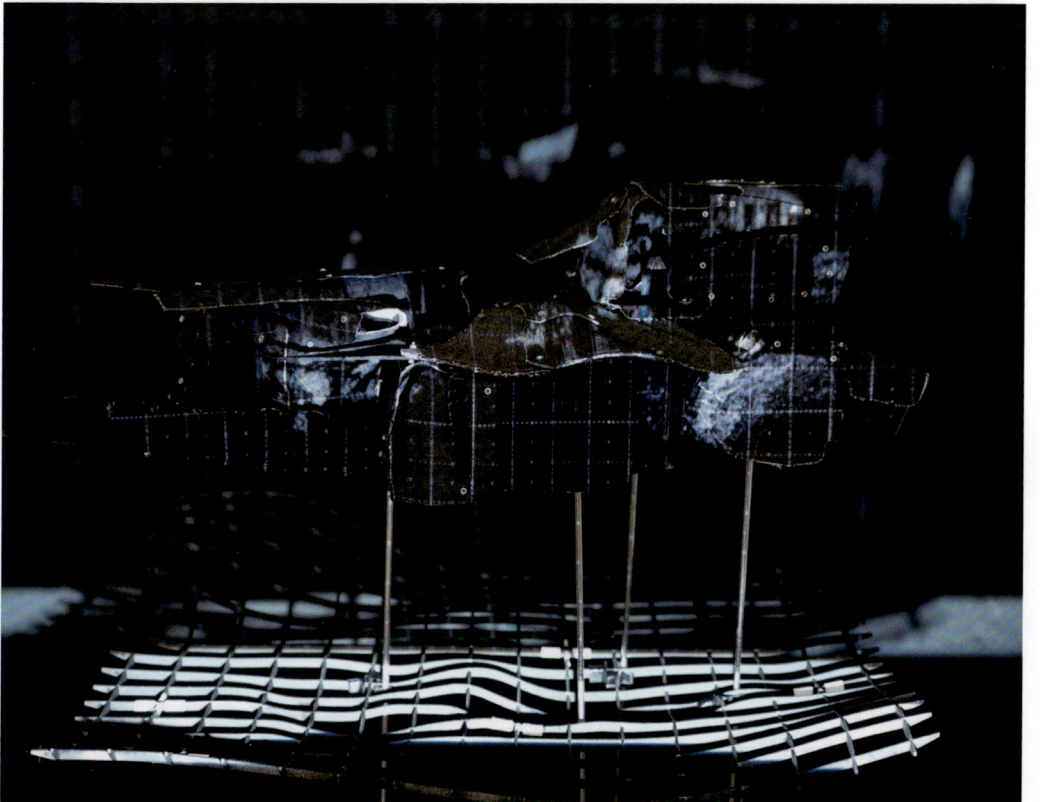

9.7

9.8

9.9

9.10

9.11

9.12

9.13

9.14

9.15

9.16

9.17

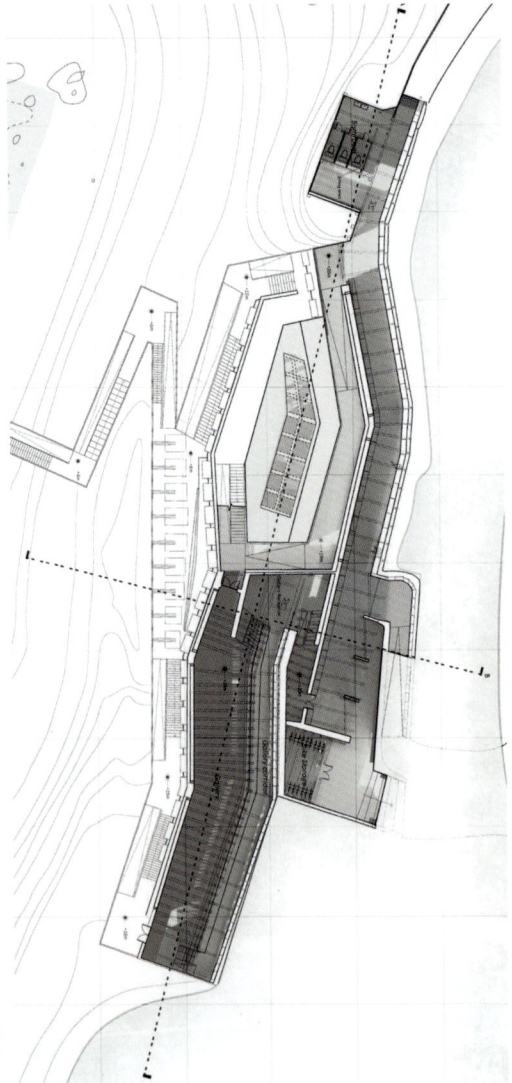

9.18

9.19

9.20

9.21

9.22

9.23

9.24

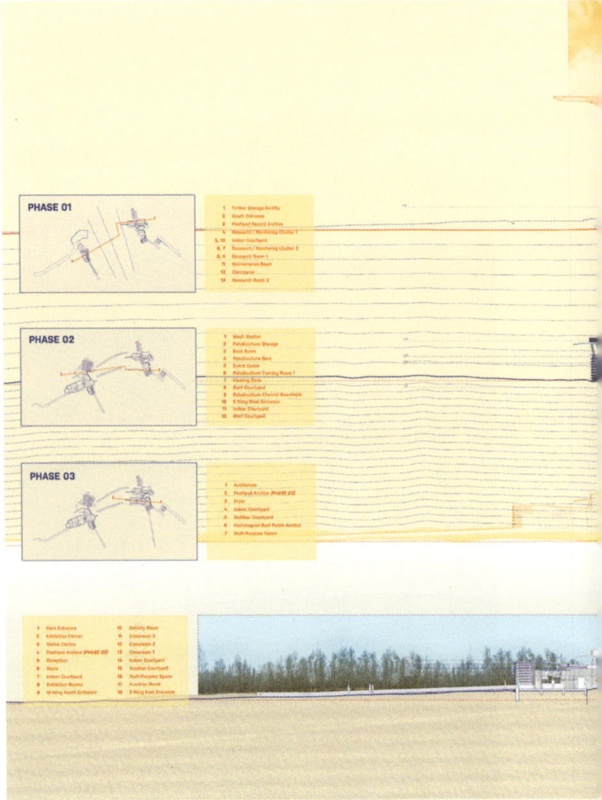

9.25

Future 2053 Landform Section

2022
2023
2024
2025
2026
2027
2028
2029
2030
2031
2032

Paludiculture Phase Initiation

2033
2034
2035
2036
2037
2038
2039
2040
2041
2042
2043
2044
2045
2046
2047
2048
2049
2050
2051
2052

Community Involvement Initiation

2053

Original 2022 Landform Section

Polyrhythms: Haiti

Pedro Gil-Quintero, Neba Sere

UG10 acknowledges the Global North/South paradigm and recognises residual tensions and paradoxes as methods to explore both contemporary and historical relationships between the UK and Latin America. The unit draws attention to the differing phenomena and cohabitations between these diverse contexts, exploring what has been borrowed, drawn upon and taken from either side of the Atlantic. We highlight what remains of those actions, dialogues and exchanges, in relation to migrant communities, architectures, visual arts, literature, music and ideas.

Architecture and architectural practitioners have a responsibility to understand the socio-economic context in which they are operating. In a city such as London, it is crucial that we understand how communities are impacted by regeneration and development. The effects are not always positive for everyone and marginalisation of the most disadvantaged in society happens through gentrification. Architecture is therefore always political.

Each year UG10 selects a Latin American region upon which to focus its investigations into typologies, including construction idioms and techniques, funding streams, design activism and material iterations. We promote speculations on radical ideas, design solutions, resilient futures and alternative visions. This year UG10 celebrated Haiti, Blackness and Afro-Latin American 'AfroLatinidad' culture through the lens of our London-based design projects.

Situated in the Caribbean, Haiti is one of the countries in Latin America with significant African heritage. It has a long and proud legacy of culture, history, art, literature and architecture. Its population is predominantly Black, with strong ethnic and ancestral links to Africa dating back to the 15th century. UG10 studied Haiti and its culture while looking for progressive lessons that can be applied to London and its rich multi-cultural setting. We are interested in Haiti and the erasure of Blackness in the (Latin-American) cultural context.

Design projects are situated in the London Borough of Enfield, the proud home to one of the highest populations of African and Caribbean diaspora in the city.

Year 2
Amy Bass, Zeynep Cam, Amy Daja, Fardous Khalafalla, Kah Miin Loh, Iga Najdeker, Maria Pop, Skylar Smith, Alara Taskin, Tsz (Vivianne) Wong

Year 3
Minh (Dominik) Do, Michela Morreale, Junyoung Myung, Natnicha (Amy) Ng, Thananan (Orm) Sivapiromrat

Technical tutor and consultant: Freya Cobbin

Critics: Shade Abdul, George Aboagye Williams, Prince Henry Ajene, Julia Backhaus, Umi Lovecraft BP, Remi Connolly-Taylor, Akua Danso, Murray Fraser, Jonathan Hagos, Ben Hayes, Fabrizio Matillana, Stephanie Poynts, Max Rengifo, Gurmeet Sian, Michiko Sumi, Jessica Tang

Sponsors: Adrem, Atelier Red, HOK

10.1–10.5 Minh (Dominik) Do, Y3 'Letters of Character'. The refurbishment and extension of an existing library to house a modern youth centre with the mission of decriminalising young people in public spaces. The project promises a safe environment which offers creative opportunities through literature. The programme allows young people to pass on their newly acquired understanding to the general public by holding regular exhibitions. The library is envisioned as an asset that serves the wider Ponders End community.

10.6–10.8 Kah Miin Loh, Y2 'The Connection between Nature and Living'. A housing project with regreening interventions brings the spirit of the Yanomami indigenous peoples' *shapono* (community housing) from Venezuela to Fitzrovia. The housing is designed for families or individuals who work in Fitzrovia and have an interest in taking part in collective climate action. It serves as a precedent for the regreening and rewilding of Fitzrovia and London on a wider urban scale.

10.9 Fardous Khalafalla, Y2 'The Instrument of Culture'. The project takes inspiration from the tradition of Haitian carnivals by celebrating the work of musicians and providing a platform for them to launch their careers through showcasing their work. The design is inspired by Haitian carnival floats, where artists perform above crowds who watch from the streets below. The project fulfils the need for a purpose-built structure that celebrates music as a cultural commodity in Enfield.

10.10 Tsz (Vivianne) Wong, Y2 'The Garden of Eden in Enfield'. Inspired by Haitian literature, the project adds nature to a busy high street in Enfield by introducing a lightweight timber frame structure that sits on top of existing roofs. Referencing the Mayor of London's aspiration to turn the capital into the first national park city in the world, the project creates a calm green space in the city for the local Enfield community.

10.11–10.12 Zeynep Cam, Y2 'Playschool for Enfield'. The project proposes an alternative nursery where children educate themselves via their senses and have fun while doing so. The design of a playscape empowers children to take initiative and learn freely. By giving younger generations a space for creative learning through play, the project builds a strong sense of community, with the hopes of inspiring children to contribute to their local area in the future.

10.13–10.14 Iga Najdeker, Y2 'FunTech Centre of Edmonton'. The project addresses the problem of digital exclusion and the limited access to learning, amplified during the pandemic, for young people from disadvantaged backgrounds. The proposed technology centre is a place where children between the ages of 10 and 16 can visit to participate in after-school activities. The project proposes several areas of emerging technology, creating future employment opportunities for children through skills and knowledge transfer while helping them to advance their digital abilities in a fun, innovative way.

10.15–10.16 Amy Bass, Y2 'F.I.G. (Female Integrated Gym)'. The gym is an urban oasis and a safe space for the women of Enfield and beyond. Inspired by Haitian martial arts, the design has four design principles: female empowerment, reuse, regreening and cultural sensitivity. The retrofit project serves as a framework for how post-pandemic, vacant buildings can be repurposed to create community spaces while educating and helping the wider society.

10.17–10.18 Amy Daja, Y2 'The Resident's Hounfor'. Vodou is an integral part of Haitian history and culture that is often misunderstood by the West. The pilgrimage to the grotto of St Francis de Assisi is an annual event for Haitian vodouists that can be traced back to religions from West Africa, where the Atlantic slave trade originated. The project proposes an extension of the new library as part of the Fore Street, Joyce Avenue and Snell's Park regeneration to create much-needed community space for the local tenants, and residents' association.

10.19–10.20 Junyoung Myung, Y3 'Shapes of Differentia'. The London Borough of Enfield has a diversity of ethnicities among its different communities. Religion is one of the aspects that can help unite people and bring them together. The project proposes a multi-faith festival centre that allows different religious communities to freely celebrate their traditional events, have festive meals and interact with one another. The design is inspired by Haiti's culture of recycling and repurposing, as well as the gingerbread timber frame construction prevalent in Haiti.

10.21 Skylar Smith, Y2 'Bamboo Hub for Enfield's Caribbean Community'. The project celebrates the way in which the local Caribbean community can become a part of the high street. By refurbishing the existing office building, the new multifunctional centre will include a bamboo recycling workshop, dance studios, kitchen areas for local food entrepreneurs and public spaces to host events and markets. The varied activities will foster the cultural exchange between Haiti and London.

10.22 Natnicha (Amy) Ng, Y3 'R.A.G.E. Academy of Music (Rap And Grime Entertainment)'. The project addresses the need to educate local working-class young people on the culture of Haitian hip hop music as a method to develop confidence, self-expression and a sense of belonging. In response to the lack of spaces celebrating Black music, the project decolonises the existing spaces of music performance, creating a new typology which represents Black music and allows it to thrive. The design is derived from sampling and mixing an amalgamation of coded forms, Haitian construction techniques and a material palette inspired by Haiti and Enfield.

10.2

10.3

10.4

10.5

10.6

10.7

10.8

10.9

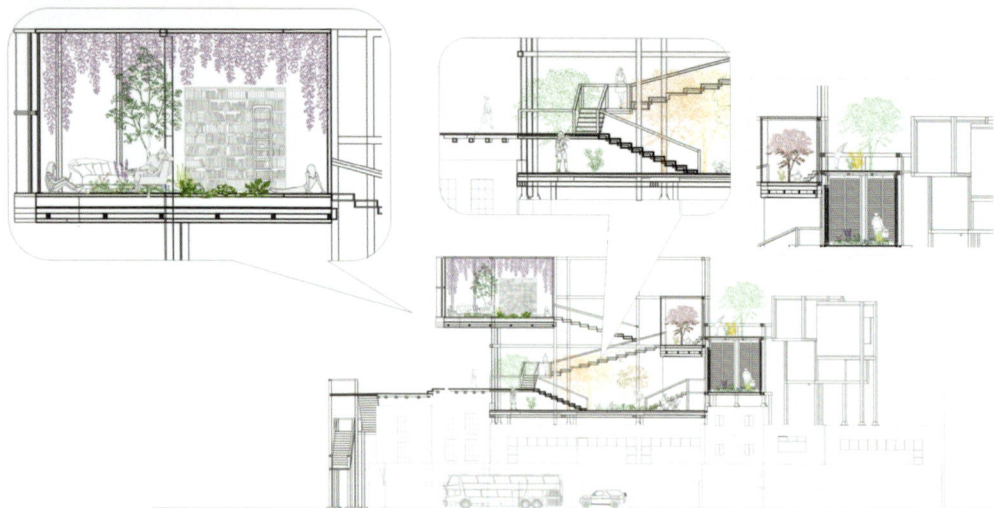

10.10

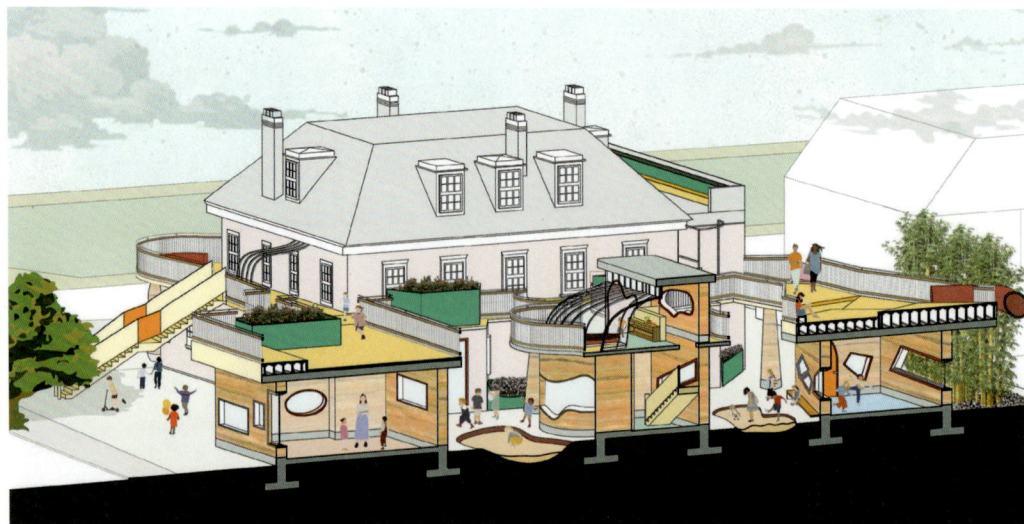

10.11

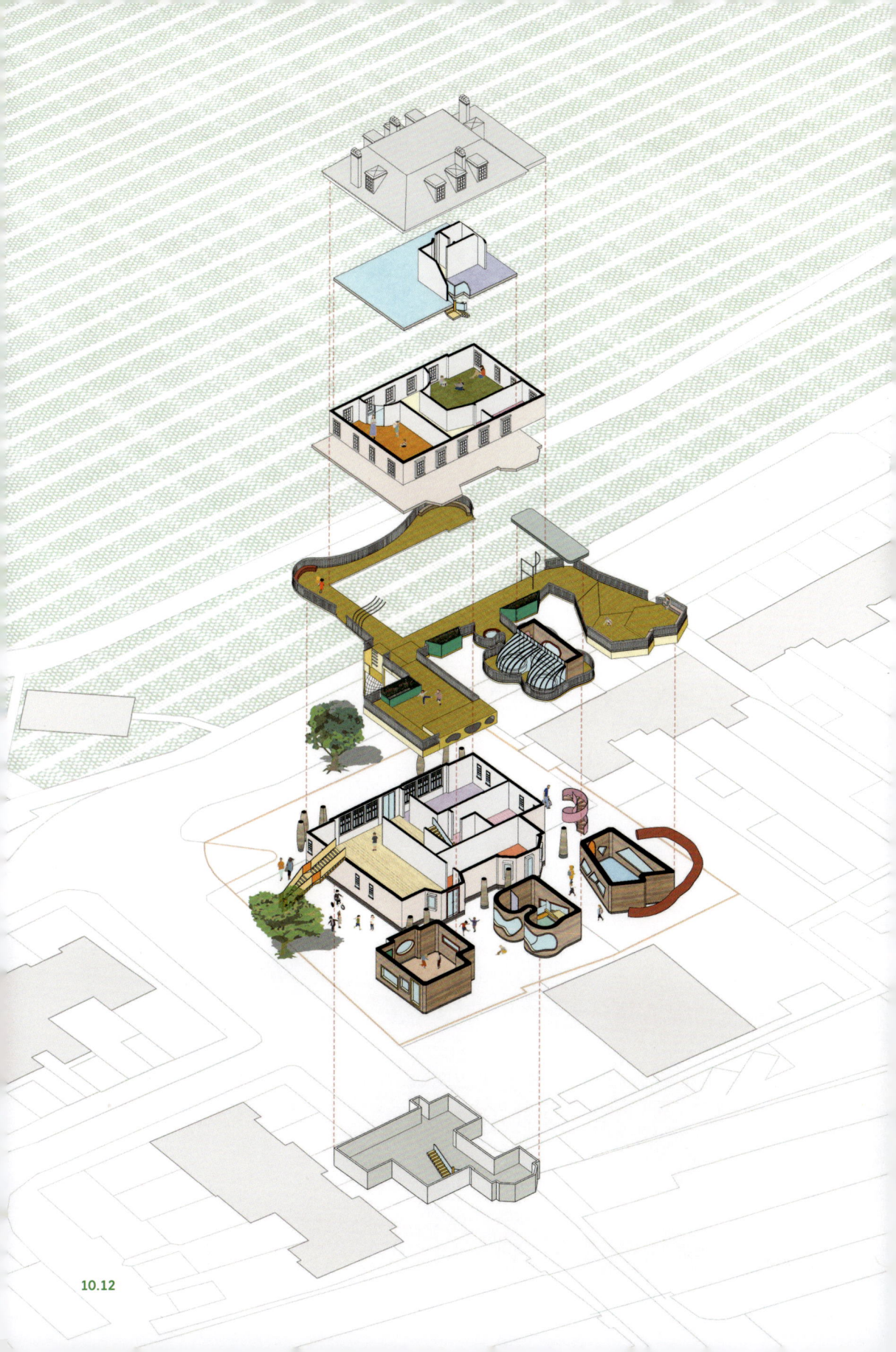

10.13

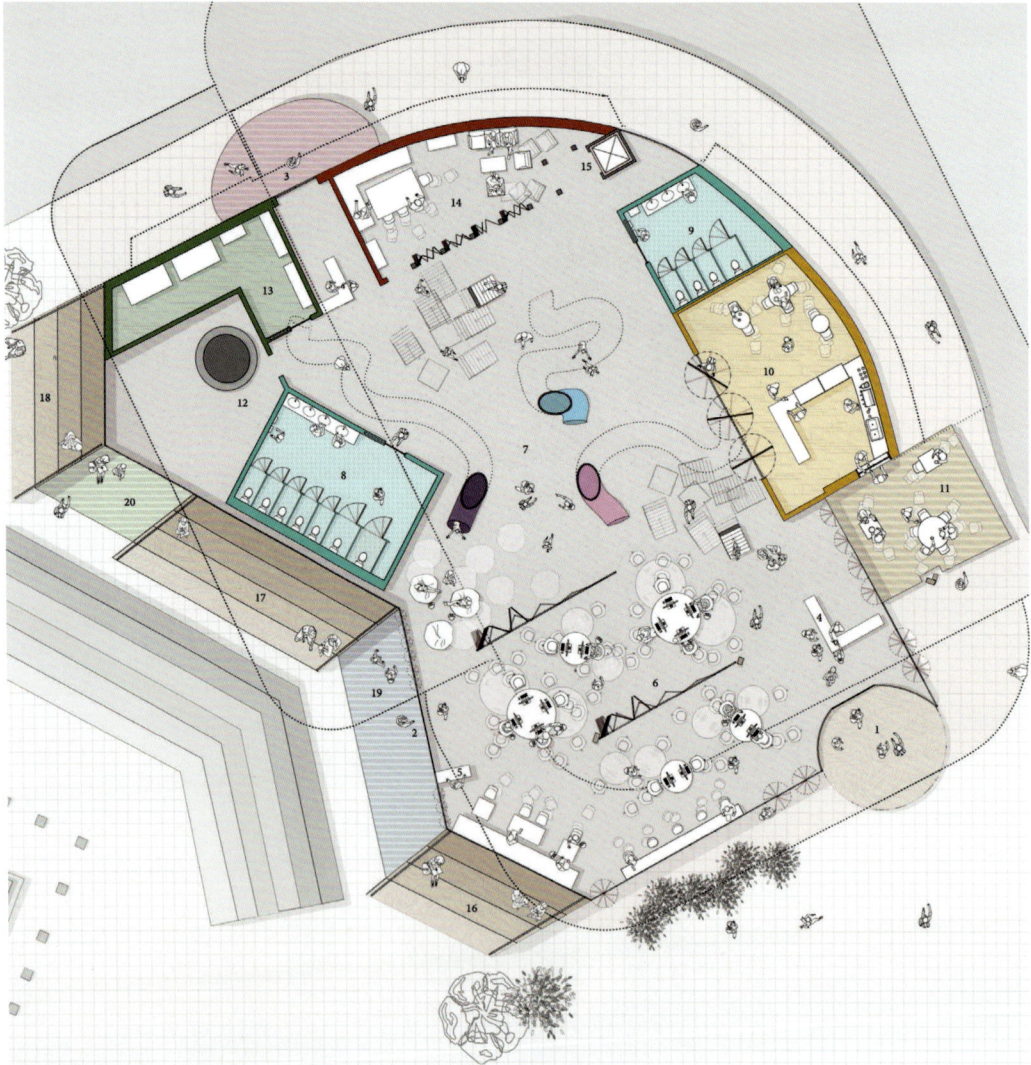

10.14

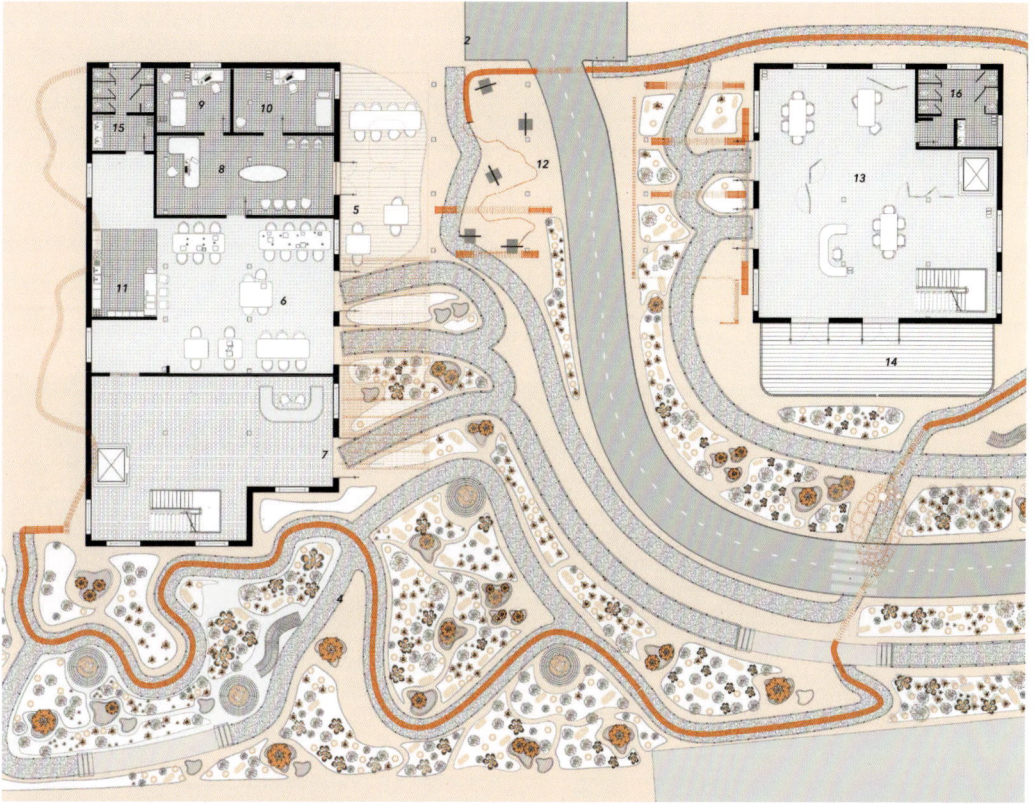

10.15

10.16

10.17

10.18

154

10.19

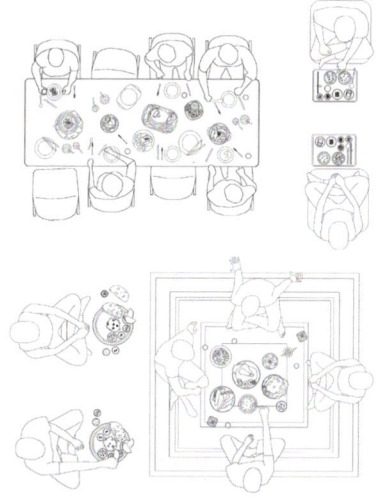

10.20

10.21

10.22

11.1

Alternate Endings

Haden Charbel, Déborah López Lobato

The history of our civilisation has largely been defined by the stability in weather patterns that is associated with specific geographic locations. Cities were often created and developed according to the ways in which agriculture, livestock, resources and habitable conditions intersected. In turn, these also shaped how our societies evolved, with social constructs that adhere to different systems of value and consequently to various forms of colonisation.

A new climate regime is currently playing out. There is no guarantee on the accuracy of climate predictions nor any precedent for how we, at local and global scales, will adapt to these possible scenarios. Current forecasts of existing trends point towards the forced relocation of communities, inundation of cities, mass desertification and the disparity of wealth as inevitable, with implications for economic, social, political and ecological spheres.

In fiction, an 'alternate ending' is one possible ending of a story that was considered, but ultimately discarded in favour of another resolution. This year UG11 used Climate-Fiction (Cli-Fi) and world building as vehicles to research, experiment with and project diverse scenarios, events and trends.

We conducted a field trip to Scotland, spending a total of seven days between Edinburgh and the Isle of Skye. Here we visited a spectrum of architectural sites, old and new, as well as viewing vast natural formations, landscapes and intense climatic conditions.

Collapsing the locality of specific sites in terms of materials, structure, environmental conditions and spatial design, our projects conceived spaces for communal public gathering, responding to human and non-human life, routines, rituals and protocols in constructing new possible futures. These 'alternate endings' were tested and experienced in the form of virtual walkable pilgrimages and narratives that portray the past and present of these potential scenarios.

Year 2
Emmanouil Konstantinou, George Sanger, Layla Stevens, Kwong (Christine) Wong

Year 3
Sebastian Bellavia, Natalia Da Silva Costa Dale, Adnan Demachkieh, Gabriel Fryer-Eccles, Jovan Jankovic, Luana Martins Rodrigues, Jackson Saez, Josef Slater, Benjamin Woodier

Technical tutors and consultants: Ruth Cuenca, Martin Reynolds

11.1–11.4 Sebastian Bellavia, Y3 'Post-Industrial Ecologies'. The project proposes a public facility which functions to promote the growth of the local ecosystem while fostering a new symbiotic relationship between industry and nature, preserving the collective memory of the local community. This also includes physical data storage within the fabric of the building itself. A new relationship with material reuse is developed through workshop facilities and teaching areas which promote the use of practical skills, fusing automation with craftsmanship to utilise and reinvent the industrial landscape. Parts of the building's growing façade are fabricated from scrap material to create a space that is visually reminiscent of industrial typologies, combined with religious and monolithic forms, to create an experiential space which reconstructs the area's collective memories.

11.5–11.9 Josef Slater, Y3 'Project C: Reinhabiting the Mexican Countryside'. In a future where closed borders coincide with extreme digital connectivity, non-state actors such as tech companies, NGOs and wealthy individuals hold more power than ever. As the south of the world faces climate-induced crises such as urban overpopulation and mass water and food shortages, these non-state actors have begun to see opportunity in tackling global issues. Project C has been created by a non-state player, FL Systems, to find ways of reinhabiting the now deserted Mexican countryside. The project is ambitious, hoping to overcome major issues surrounding the environmental and economic factors of living outside of megacities. Following the initial construction of a one-man home, a larger settlement is built. A system of cells, each hosting up to 40 people, connects across the desert and explores the relationship between the simultaneous facilitation of human lives and non-human information networks in an unforgiving environment.

11.10–11.13 Adnan Demachkieh, Y3 'The Sanctuary of Time'. Driven by the need to establish Foula, a remote Scottish archipelago, as a self-sustainable community capable of socio-economic development, the island's residents along with the Scottish government are increasingly capitalising on its natural and cultural heritage through tourism. These endeavours, however, are happening at a time of climate crisis in which human activity is the main contributor. The project plays on the dialogue between conservation and utopianism. The masterplan involves the creation of a nature reserve funded by the Scottish government to accommodate birdwatching tourism, incorporating multiple structures such as puffin watchtowers, islander and tourist accommodation, a wool mill and a souvenir shop. This highlights the inherent paradox in balancing the need for development with the need for conservation in light of climate change, a dilemma represented by changes in the architecture, reflecting the built environment's relationship with nature at three periods of time in the future. Such adaptation exhibits a desperate need to prolong the eventual self-collapse and lengthen the intrinsic temporality of the project through challenging resource availability and socio-economic conditions.

11.14–11.16 Gabriel Fryer-Eccles, Y3 'Caledonian 2.0: An Autonomous Forest Regeneration'. In 2050 an anonymous ecological entrepreneur initiates a regeneration project within a dying pine reserve in the valley of Glen Loyne in the Scottish Highlands. The initial structure is centred around six of the last surviving pines and provides a mainframe for data collection, with access points for human regulation of the project while in early development. These six pines are now at the centre of a regenerated pocket of the Caledonian ecosystem. By 2080, the artificial intelligence decentralised autonomous organisation that conducts the regeneration is embodied by a structure, built largely from native material, that sprawls throughout the forest protecting the physical attributes of the ecosystem. The project is an autonomous forest regeneration centre, accommodating human exploration but not prioritising it.

11.17–11.20 Benjamin Woodier, Y3 'Algocratic Resolutions'. In the modern political landscape, governmental systems are a key facet of what makes countries competitive at a global scale. Systems determine the organisation and internal logic of a body on social, political, environmental, economic and demographic scales. An example of an efficient modern system would be an algocracy, or algocratic capitalism. This is a system governed autocratically by advanced algorithms with large amounts of data, which can make informed decisions in place of humans. One of these systems could help to cope with high levels of migration, with data collection processes allowing algorithms to make quick decisions to create ideal migrant communities. The project looks at instituting an algocratic system within a housing project intended to mitigate issues around an influx of migration caused by climate crises within the next 100 years. The system would efficiently place migrants into homes based on their needs and backgrounds, adapting to necessity over time. While placed in a quarry to the south of Aberdeen, the project can be applied to any brownfield site, allowing for systematised reuse of land nationally or globally.

11.21–11.24 George Sanger, Y2 'Fairbourne Frontier'. Adopting the resilient and sentimental values of people from Fairbourne, Wales, this project creates an architecture that negotiates both displacement and climate change. With the complete devaluation of Fairbourne's properties, the project envisions that the residents will try to salvage their losses by deconstructing Fairbourne as they know it and rebuilding their community along the saltmarshes of the Mawddach Estuary.

11.25–11.26 Natalia Da Silva Costa Dale, Y3 'Zone 19'. The cultural centre, located in the Caribbean region of north Colombia, is combatting the inevitable difficulties of severe ecological change caused by increased pollution and rising sea levels over the next century. The programme sparks a renewed ecological consciousness using sound as a tool to stimulate the growth of bamboo. The cultural centre seeks to continue and expand Hernando Chindoy's educational ecosystem, allowing people from all societies to enter this neutral political zone despite political and ethnic conflict in the country. The centre functions symbiotically for humans and nature, as it caters for both the growing of bamboo and public entertainment events. This project creates an education and performance hub that draws attention to the importance of a sensitive relationship with the natural world.

11.27–11.29 Emmanouil Konstantinou, Y2 'Reverse Colonialism'. In a speculative scenario where marginalised and colonised people are equal to their oppressors, a monument is erected in celebration of their diverse identities. Structurally it restricts the encroaching growth of governmental bodies by encapsulating esoteric qualities. The visual language reflects a mystical and monastic aura, allowing the building to become a threshold between terrestrial and ethereal realms. Technology is used as a medium for the retelling of traditional cultures and practices suppressed through history. The spaces capture elements of traditional heterogeneity through geometric shapes and ornamentation, both of which serve to soften the two opposing styles, bridging futurism and historicism with the expression of modernism.

11.2

11.3

11.4

11.5

11.6

11.7

11.8

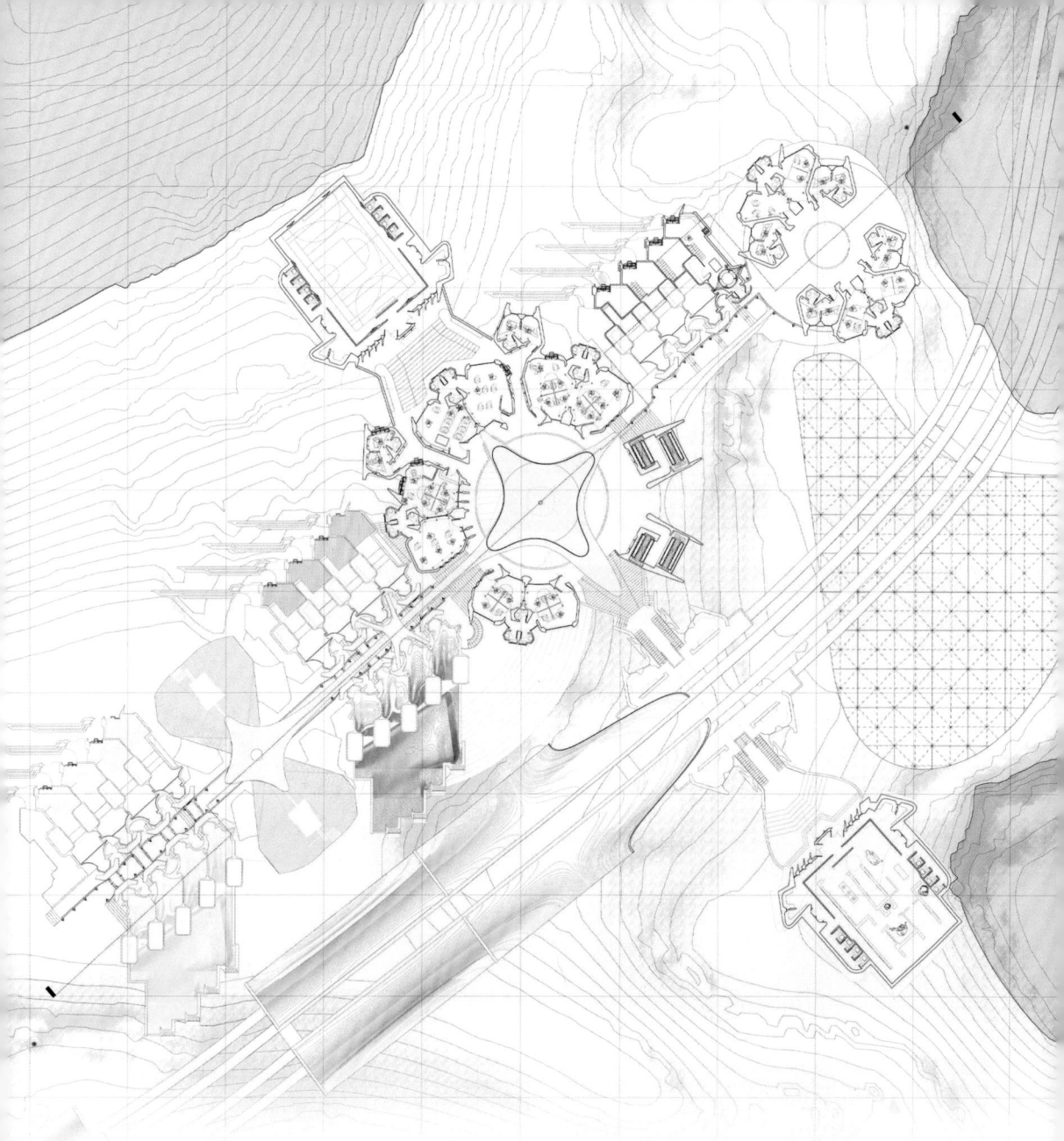

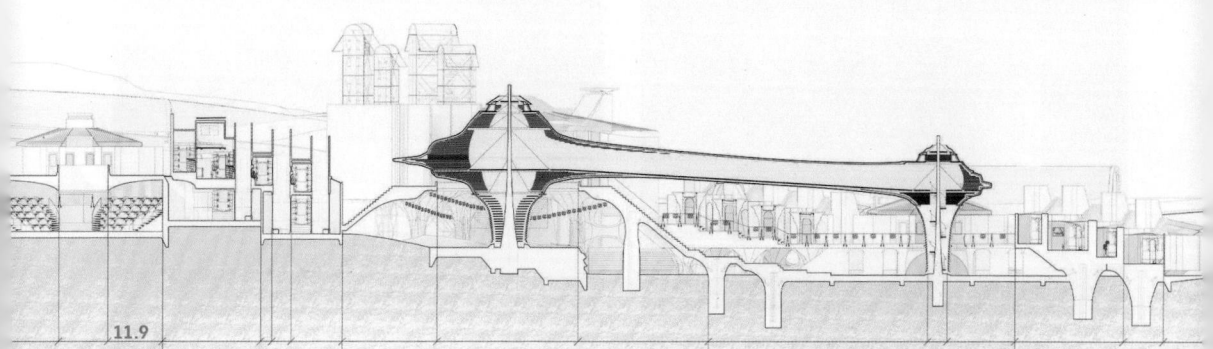

11.9

11.10

11.11

11.12

11.13

11.14

11.15

11.16

11.17

11.18

11.19

11.20

11.21

11.22

11.23

11.24

11.25

11.26

11.27

11.28

11.29

Settlement

Hannah Corlett, Níall McLaughlin

A settlement suggests a collection of buildings housing a community in a particular place. It might take its characteristics from the landscape, the environment, the work that people do or the materials available for building. We imagine it as a situation with its own origins which develops over time, creating a particular energy and attraction. It is probably linked to a hinterland of other places and settlements within a network of connection, rivalry and influence.

Another meaning for the word settlement is an agreement. It might be simple or complex, but the inference is that something once disputed or debated has been settled, in a way that is acceptable to all parties.

Both meanings of the word require each other. To live together we must share certain values and know how to cooperate, even in the face of disagreements.

To settle is to find a comfortable position. You look for your favourite place in a room, with the right aspect and sense of protection. You watch your cat prowling around until she has found the perfect place to curl up. This kind of settling belongs to our oldest animal intuitions and we suggest that it is at the heart of architectural experience. It is a sense of feeling at home. We become attached to places that nourish our physical and emotional needs. Good architects can create these places.

Finally, buildings themselves settle. They sink gradually into their sites; they wear and weather, requiring our attention and care. People develop habits around buildings: they acquire histories. Soon they become almost invisible, but they still have a profound impact on our sense of who we are and how we place ourselves in time.

This year UG12 were asked to design a settlement and the buildings within it, working together in cooperation and competition. After agreeing a set of understandings for the community and establishing a relationship with the landscape, it was necessary to respond to each other as individual buildings morphed, through design progression, inhabitation and wear. The year was one of continued negotiation. A journey with a process rather than an end.

Year 2
Dimitris Andritsogiannis, Jack Bowers, Yutong (Sabrina) Li, Jatin Naru, Nora Seferi, Oyku Sekulu, Ilya Tchevela, Haodi (Hardy) Wang

Year 3
Nana Boffah, Aaron Green, Eleanor Middleton, Leonids Osipovs, Clara Popescu, Flavia Scafella, Fergal Voorsanger-Brill, Joy You

Technical tutors and consultants: Matt Driscoll

Critics: Negin Amiri, Katerina Dionysopoulou, Matt Driscoll, Asif Kahn Architects, Billy Mavropoulos, Níall McLaughlin Architects, Farlie Reynolds, Adam Richards Studio, Greg Storrar, Threefold Architects, Steve Webb, Webb Yates Engineers

With thanks to Peter Scully and the team at B-made for the *Exploring Design Through Lenses: Making, Measuring, Modelling and Manipulation* workshops

12.1 All Students, Y2&3 'Settlement'. A 180 x 240cm communal site drawing of the Oare Marshes following a visit to Faversham, Kent. The drawing took place in advance of planning the settlement together via regular town hall meetings.

12.2–12.4 Jack Bowers, Y2 'The Faith Space'. A space for contemplation, divided into two parts: prayer room and courtyard. Greatly influenced by the idea of simplicity, the building is designed around Shinohara-inspired dialectics, with balance between the rigid structural grid, carved space, scale and use of light.

12.5 Eleanor Middleton, Y3 'The Children's Home'. Nestled between two town squares sits a home for unaccompanied minors fleeing persecution in their homelands. It provides a safe place for children to flourish, learn and imagine. The translucent, ordered exterior envelops an intricate and welcoming brick courtyard within.

12.6–12.8 Fergal Voorsanger-Brill, Y3 'The Avian Housing'. The project caters for clients that migrate: birds and human beings living seasonally as their Mesolithic ancestors once did. A weaving between printmaking, physical production and digital fabrication forms the warp and weft of the architecture, a calcification of behaviour in a place over time.

12.9–12.10 Jatin Naru, Y2 'The Jam Factory'. The site's prominent position at the border of the main town square mixes and promotes the importance of civic and industrial authority, as the owner of the factory is both a major businessperson and a landowner in the settlement. The tower allows them to overlook the community and their orchards beyond. A simple grid underpins the building's structure and the order of the process within.

12.11–12.12 Joy You, Y3 'The Research Centre'. The centre is used by scientists, researchers and students of climate change, and makes scientific research visible and legible to the public, while educating them about the climate emergency. To emphasise this transparency, the building focuses on the relationship between interior and exterior. Levels of transparency and privacy are achieved through the layering of different materials, including acrylic, polycarbonate and ethylene tetrafluoroethylene (ETFE). Living material (microalgae) within the ETFE visually articulates the imminence of climate change through the impact of atmospheric pollution.

12.13–12.15 Haodi (Hardy) Wang, Y2 'The Local Pool'. The pool embraces the natural water features of the Oare Marshes and translates them into a visual, audible and interactive environment. Three pools exist for the locals: wave, tidal and thermal. The wave pool is located in the natural marsh pond, with a wind-driven organ that generates music and waves to enhance children's play. The tidal pool responds to the ebb and flow of the moon, encouraging adults to exercise. The thermal pool allows the older generation to explore and relax within the reeds like marsh birds.

12.16–12.18 Nana Boffah, Y3 'The Boat Yard'. The project secures Faversham to its roots by providing training in the traditional crafts of boat and building construction. The architecture acts as a frame in which to experiment with different techniques and typologies, aiding the regeneration of the creek via a community resource. The yard is divided into three separate buildings: the main shed, ancillary area and public space. The forms of these buildings embody different stages of a boat's life – framing, planking and its afterlife (anchored).

12.19–12.21 Yutong (Sabrina) Li, Y2 'The Salt Marsh & Funeral Home'. A traditional salt marsh is returned to the easternmost promontory of Faversham. A factory is set up to process the salt to fuel the local economy.

In tandem, a contemporary funeral home questions the grieving process by actively encouraging mourners to participate in the burial preparations of their deceased. The salt provides a natural medium for the embalming process as well as informing the construction. The buildings create spaces for harvesting the salt, the treatment and burial of the dead, and a sensual experience for the living to help them negotiate the five stages of grief.

12.22–12.23 Flavia Scafella, Y3 'The Post Office'. The post office functions as a social bond for a new settlement. The building also acts as a cosmic device, amplifying the cycles of the community and the natural rural environment of the Oare Marshes with their subtle celestial movements. The architecture is the shell of its users and the environment it sits in. It follows the symmetry between the existing patterns of the sun, moon and tides, and the choice and application of local forms and materials.

12.24 Oyku Sekulu, Y2 'The Market Bridge'. The bridge connects the centre of the village in the east to new residences in the west. At low tide the two halves of the bridge remain connected, but as the water rises, the central platform opens and the outer skins slide back to enable boats to pass. The market interior houses kiosks and stalls run by those local to the marshes. The building's material is born of the Oare Creek's landscape. A bamboo garden sits centrally, out of which the building's frame is built and will be maintained.

12.25 Aaron Green, Y3 'The Retirement Home'. A cohousing project intended to adapt to the changing lifestyles of 12 retirees who live there. Their 12 apartments are split over two levels and joined by a winter garden, greenhouse and existing pub, all arranged around a central courtyard. Circulation provides opportunities for chance encounters. Layered levels of intimacy are explored in the buffer spaces between the public walkway and courtyard, and the private residences.

12.26 Dimitris Andritsogiannis, Y2 'The Ceramics Studio'. The project consists of twin studios divided by a kiln, placed upon the water's edge. The site swims in an abundance of mud brought in by the tide, which the building transforms into clay. When ready, the clay is formed, baked and glazed in the hot kiln, which also heats up the studios during the winter.

12.27–12.28 Ilya Tchevela, Y2 'The Gallery & Vault'. The project pays respect to the materialisation and protection of sentiment. Objects depict an unknown story, perhaps of migrating and settling, when only the small and irreplaceable could be accommodated. The monumental effect of the floor-to-ceiling walls draws attention to the objects on display and contrasts with the smaller vault, which anchors itself within the depths of the gallery space. The rigid horizontal and vertical walls are countered by corridors of light which seep through the building, helping to demarcate the space.

12.29 Nora Seferi, Y2 'The School'. The project is designed to encourage the children of the settlement to make the most of the land, integrating ecology and nature as fundamental parts of their education. They play, grow, interact, discover, navigate and swim. The spaces are built from the landscape and the programme flexes through the day, week and year.

12.30 Clara Popescu, Y3 'The Reed Housing'. Reed houses sit atop a timber stilt frame, ensuring a limited footprint to conserve the volatile Oare Marshes. The gridded superstructure is informed by the site's topography. The modular one-bed, two-bed and family units are unified by reed roofs and a reed-bed filtration system that purifies the wastewater to regenerate the marshes.

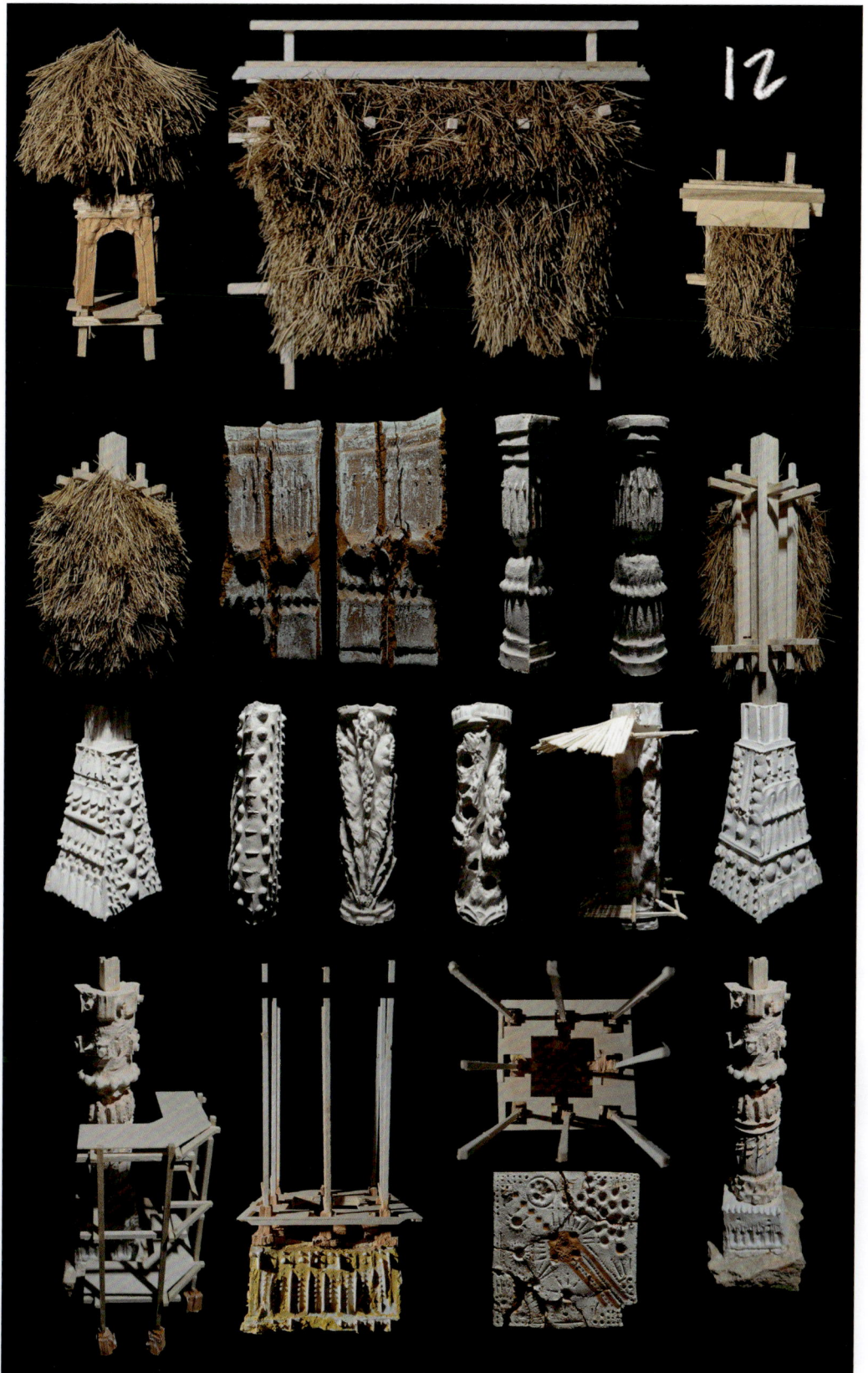

12.2

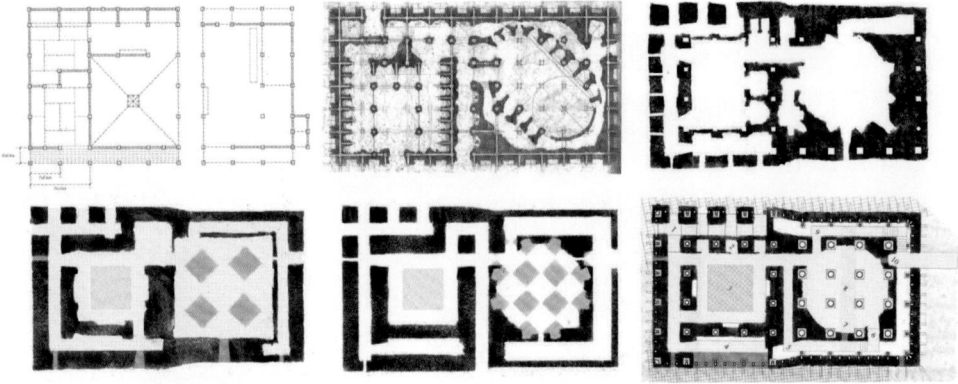

12.3

12.4

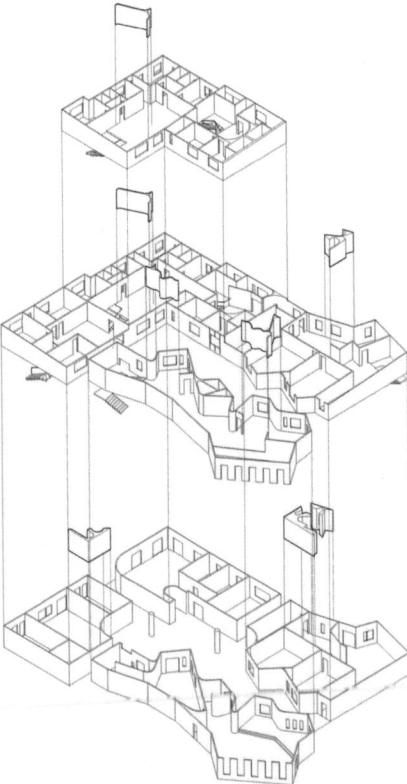

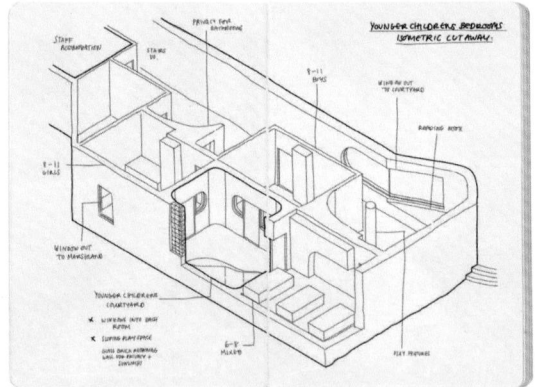

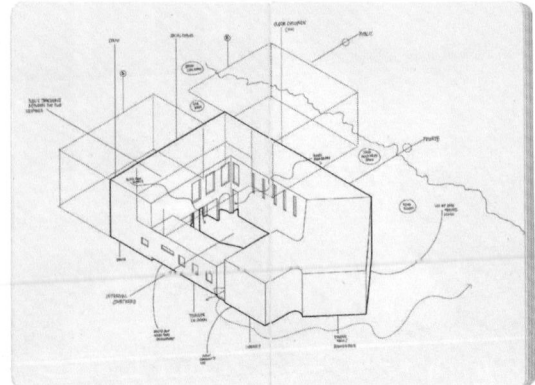

12.5

12.6

12.7

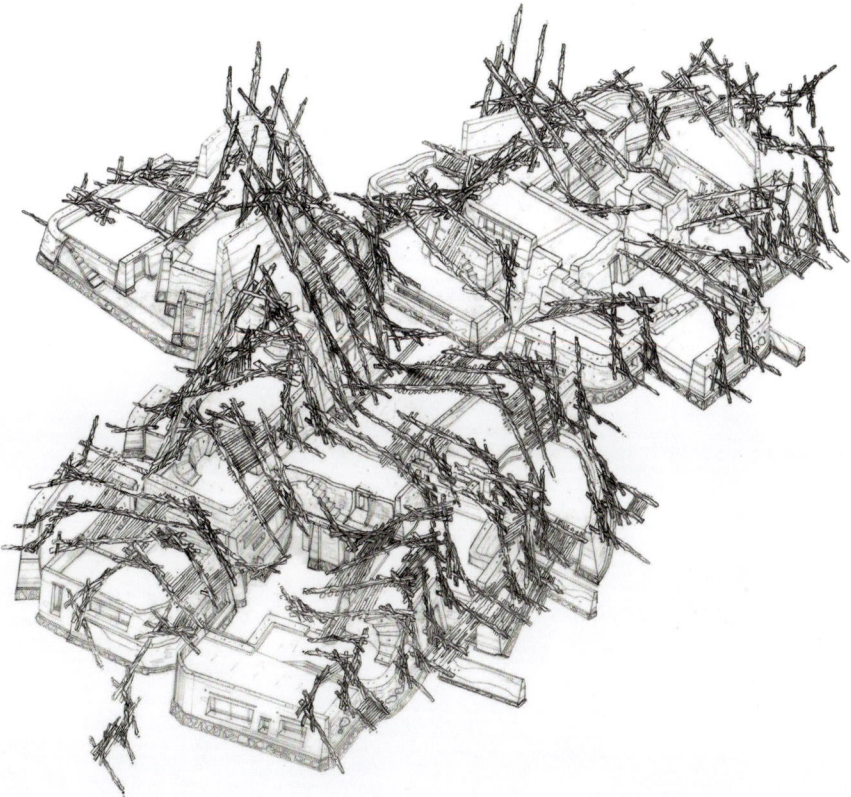

12.8

12.9

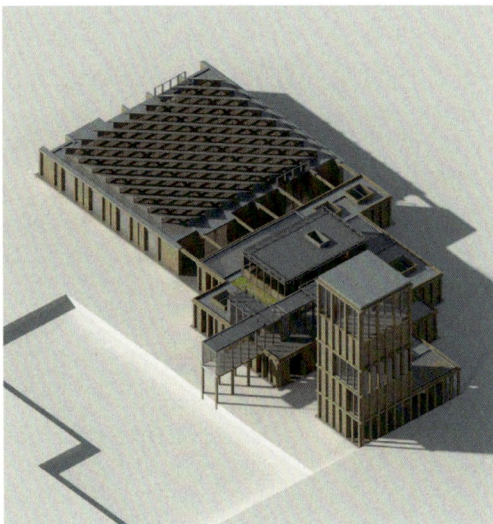

12.10

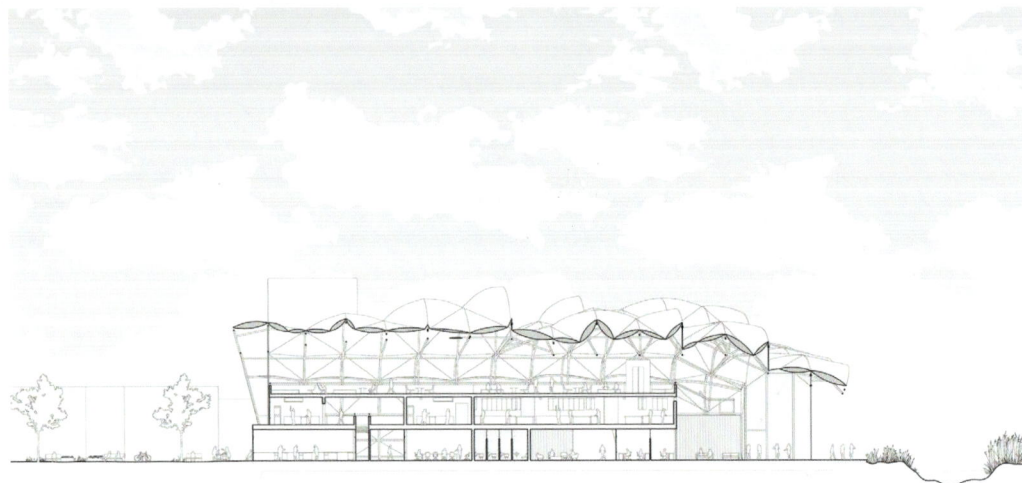

12.11

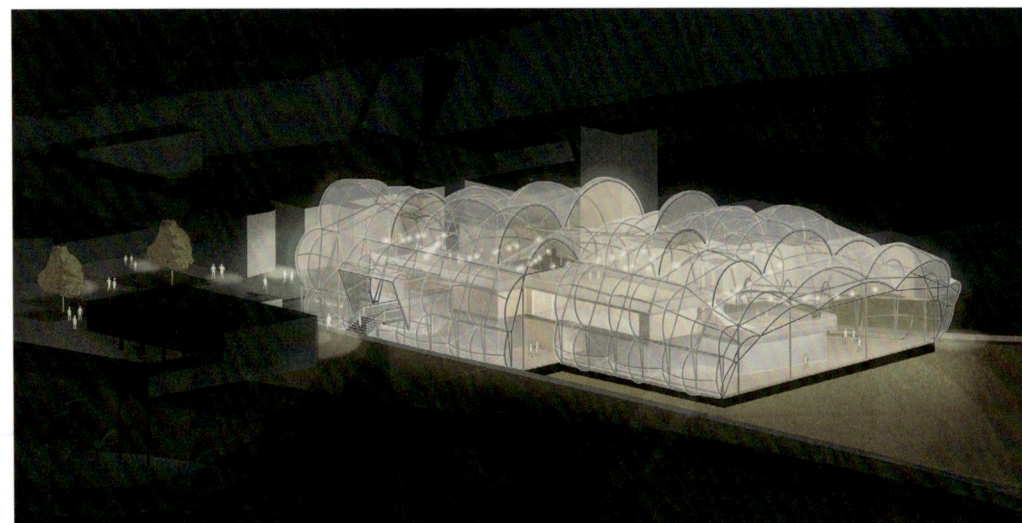

12.12

12.13

12.14

12.15

12.16

12.17

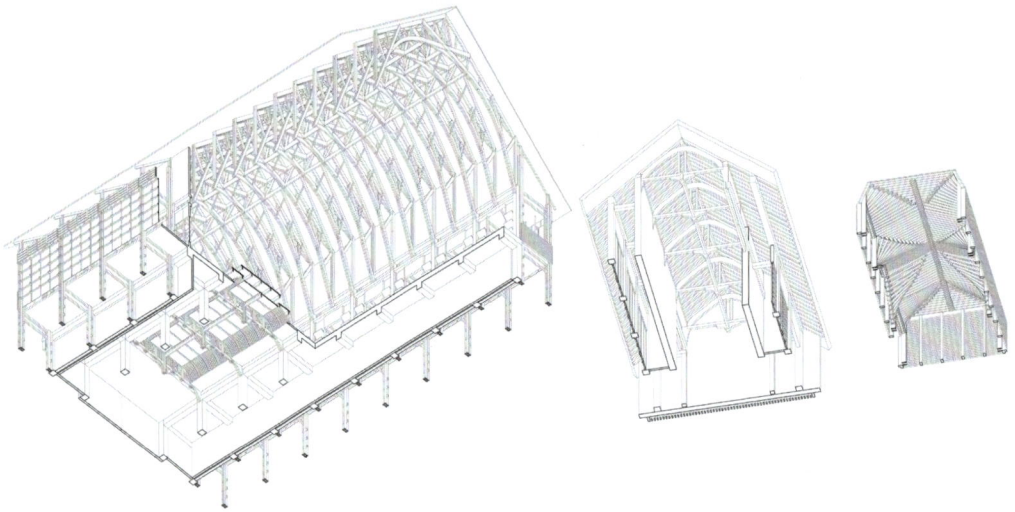

12.18

12.19

12.20

12.21

12.22

12.23

12.24

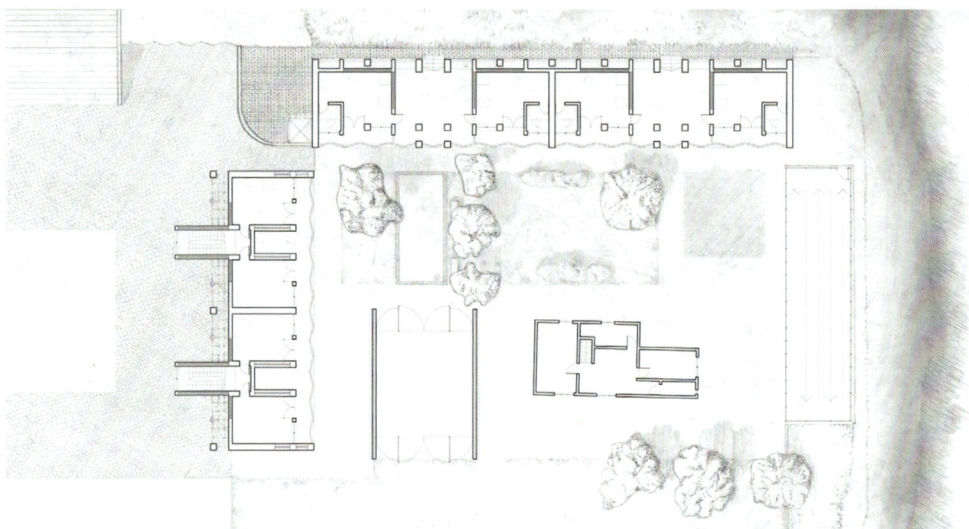

12.25

12.26

12.27

12.28

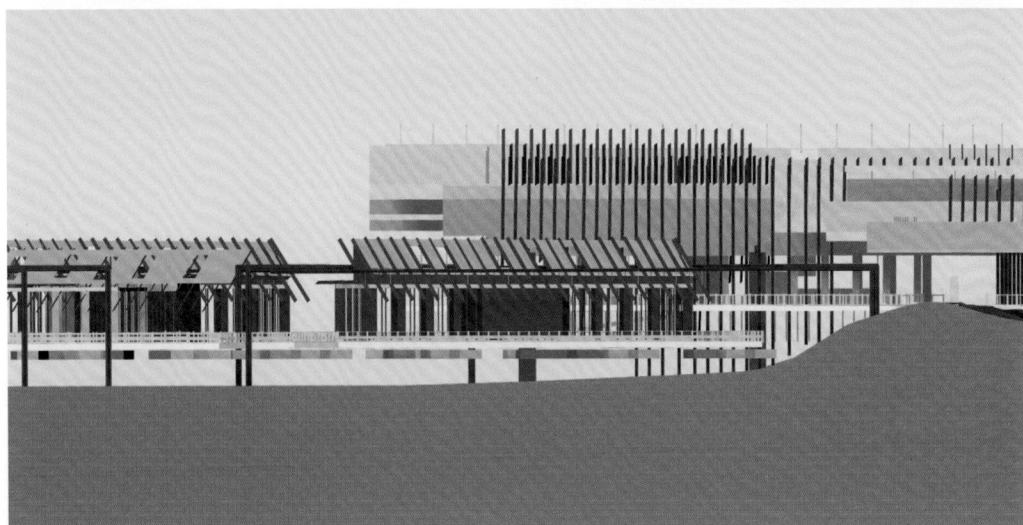

12.29

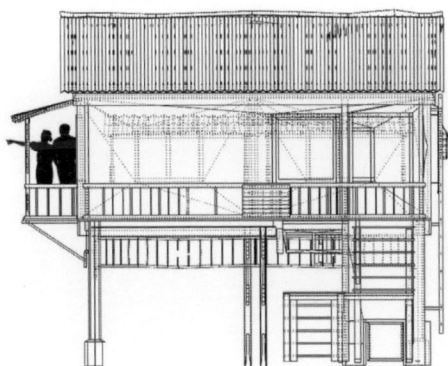

12.30

13.1

The Vibes Are About to Be Immaculate

Tamsin Hanke, Colin Herperger

This year UG13 learned from the disruptive creation of couture to develop a new process of architectural design.

Couture is the highest echelon of an industrial process. It offers a forum for goods beyond those which are wearable, saleable and practical and is set apart just sufficiently from the realm of the real world to exist entirely for the purposes of inspiration. Couture can interact with the cultural present in a way that is immediate, responsive and reciprocal, allowing it to benefit from advances in technology and cultural thinking.

Students were asked to research cultures of innovation – defining couture not as a contingent of fashion, but rather as a method of creative production that is present in all disciplines, from the sciences to landscape and across the arts. We are interested in the particularities of this mindset, including the people, their influences and contexts. We are also curious about how ideas around innovation are communicated through drawings, images and descriptions, as well as by the final pieces themselves.

For our field trip, UG13 travelled from York to Berwick-upon-Tweed via Lindisfarne. We explored a range of architectural projects and works of innovation including aviation, sculpture and landscape. Projects have been sited both in locations from the trip and from around London, varying in scales from the expanse of the flooding causeway at Lindisfarne to tight urban sites in Camden. Each project was developed with a rigorous respect towards architectural convention and an adventurous approach to spatial and aesthetic assumptions,

We see opportunity in the type of innovation which looks at where culture might be able to move towards, rather than remaining where it is. We are interested in the elements that go into making an environment of true innovation, driving culture forward and advancing our thinking on what is possible.

UG13 helps students to find a way of working that drives them as individuals – one that can be sustained beyond the limitations of a graded project. We encourage students to find agency through clear and confident decision-making, and to explore and communicate complex ideas of architecture and design through simple architectural programmes.

Year 2
Chuhan (Paris) Feng, Edmund (Flurry) Grierson, Veronika Khasapova, Adam Klestil, Po (Tate) Mok, Peter Moore, Luiza-Elisabeta Oruc, Roland Paczolay, Fangyi (Erica) Zhou

Year 3
Bogdan Botis, Daniel Collier, Shyem Ramsay, Zhelin (Simon) Sun, Ying (Sunny) Sun, Peixuan (Olivia) Xu, Chan (Antonio) Yang, Ron Zaum

Technical tutor and consultant: Syafiq Jubri

Critics: Sam Davies, Niki-Marie Jansson, Madhav Kidao, Patch Perez, Kevin Pollard, Dan Pope

13.1–13.4, 13.8–13.10 Peixuan (Olivia) Xu, Y3
'Sweet Simulacra'. A chocolate workshop and museum transforms York's confectionery history into sweet simulacra. Challenging Baudrillard's view that the hyperreality of digitalisation loses its original meaning, the building intends to create an architectural hybrid of digital fabrication and analogue crafting, bringing back the driving force of desire.

13.5–13.7 Po (Tate) Mok, Y2 'The Nautilus'. The project is intrigued by the form of bone structures and how nature is predicated on the idea of 'design' – the correlation of structure with function that lies at the heart of the molecular nature of life. Through continuous exploration of bone and skin, aesthetic and material implications begin to present themselves in a newfound awareness of transparency, translucency and the exposing of structure and backlit forms.

13.11–13.15 Daniel Collier, Y3 'Children/Factory'. This project explores the definition of the sublime as the perception of danger from a place of safety. A primary school acts as a safe environment through which the industrial processes that support us can be viewed by integrating factories directly into the school, separated from the pupils by a thin, semi-permeable membrane. The project also acknowledges England's transition from an industrial to a post-industrial economy for this new generation of children. Steiner schools were originally set up as a response to the industrial revolution and looked to reconnect with a way of life situated in the landscape sublime. In the post-industrial West, they now have the opportunity to reconnect children with both the landscape sublime and the industrial sublime.

13.16 Ron Zaum, Y3 '4 Orsman Road'. The project is situated at 4 Orsman Road, a creative hub located in Tuscany Wharf, overlooking Regent's Canal and surrounded by studios. The notion of scenography and creative spaces that reshape architecture's purpose allows for the development of stone shell housing and a variety of flexible spaces for lectures, galleries or shows.

13.17 Roland Paczolay, Y2 'Duality of Absence'. The project bridges the gap between the deceased and the living through the use of dualistic philosophy. Duality pertains to a view of life which accepts the tension and paradox of human existence. The union of opposing forces is translated into a monumental architectural language which invites mourners in while impressing on them the importance of life.

13.18 Peter Moore, Y2 'More than Just a Post Office'. The Royal Mail has its roots as a bespoke courier service for the monarchy. As it expanded, it held onto its royal origin in its design and aesthetic. The postal system was at the forefront of industrialisation, and during this time, through beautiful craftsmanship and engineering, the Royal Mail was in its prime as a cultural and political symbol. The project questions the current march towards efficiency by proposing a romanticised, ornamented post office that revels in the luxurious. It seeks to be more beautiful and more designed than it needs to be – placing great importance on aesthetic pleasure.

13.19 Chuhan (Paris) Feng, Y2 'An Invitation to See My New Nose'. The project – a consultation hub sited in Harley Street, London – is inspired by the history and surgical procedures of plastic surgery. The main design motif in the project is a building that pretends to be a landscape, interrogating the challenge of harmoniously merging natural and man-made together in the surgery. It treats the vast plain site by digging into the ground and building upon it to create a raised landscape that hugs the sunken building. It questions how architecture can be surgically constructed.

13.20 Shyem Ramsay, Y3 'The Urban Ecology Sanctum'. The project is located in Millwall Park on the Isle of Dogs, and consists of an ecotherapy centre with accommodation and public allotments. The construction of the timber truss structures explores the iterative design of the roof and the connections of timber joints, forming an organic appearance.

13.21 Ying (Sunny) Sun, Y3 'Slipping into Fantasy'. The project explores the intimate relationship between architectural features and their inhabitants. It proposes a water park and holiday centre for people to relax and unwind, providing visitors with the opportunity to explore their subconscious fantasies in an obscure, intimate and illusionary environment. Located in Brighton, the building sits along the seashore. Unique structural spaces are created to allow building inhabitants, architectural elements and the site's landscape to playfully engage with each other. This can be experienced through a series of designs, from the changing rooms to the water slides.

13.22 Fangyi (Erica) Zhou, Y2 'Breaking the Dogmatism of Learning'. The project, a new co-learning centre situated on the bank of the Lee Navigation in the vibrant neighbourhood of Hackney Wick, seeks to investigate future possibilities of learning by triggering constant curiosity in the learning process. The building provides a series of interrelated educational spaces, ranging from large lecture rooms to small individual studying units. The key motif of the design is to maximise the encounters between interdisciplinary activities by creating three tiers of discovery: looking at, looking through and looking past.

13.23 Luiza-Elisabeta Oruc, Y2 'The Repository of Childhood Imagination'. The project is an investigation into curiosity and imagination and looks at how adults can experience feelings of childlike excitement within architecture. Located next to the V&A Museum of Childhood, the building is an example of how embracing play can lead to unleashing creativity and imagination. The project invokes a sense of comfort and nostalgia, being equal parts familiar and fantastical, as well as a sense of discovery and curiosity in the unknown.

13.24 Edmund (Flurry) Grierson, Y2 'This is Going to Make Some Noise'. This project accommodates a new state-of-the-art wind tunnel testing facility in Middlesbrough, a post-industrial town in North Yorkshire. Middlesbrough is being simultaneously destroyed and rebuilt to enable the town's 'levelling up'. Wind sculpts the space, creating acoustic blocks between rooms that generate both privacy and intimacy. The architecture also considers complex team dynamics within elite sports, with the premise that not all teammates are team players.

13.25 Chan (Antonio) Yang, Y3 'Performing for the Surveillance Society'. As surveillance becomes more and more prevalent, inhabitants of the town hall continue to act out choreographed, regimented performances for the consumption of the observers nested within the voyeurs' corridors that circulate throughout the building. In contrast, inspired by the current counter-surveillance design movement and its material influences, the project also illustrates how the inhabitants of the public circuses would rebel against this dominant voyeuristic system.

13.2

13.3

13.4

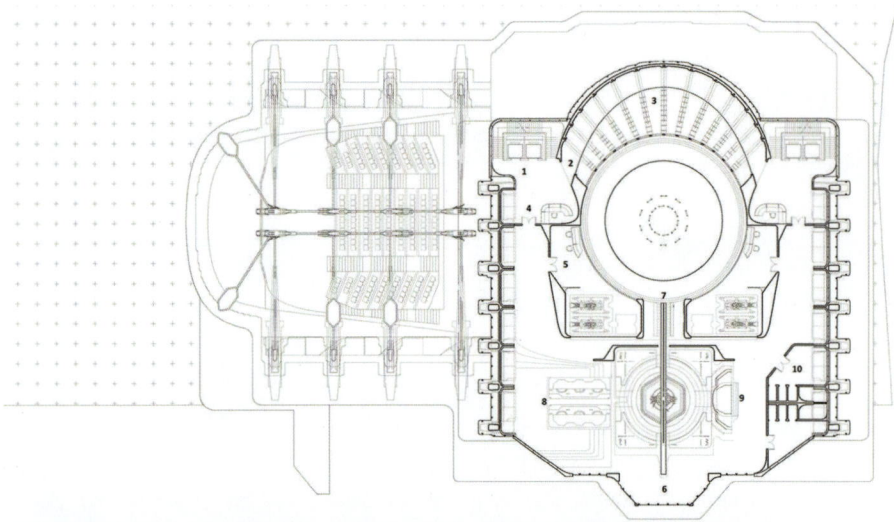

13.5

13.6

13.7

13.8

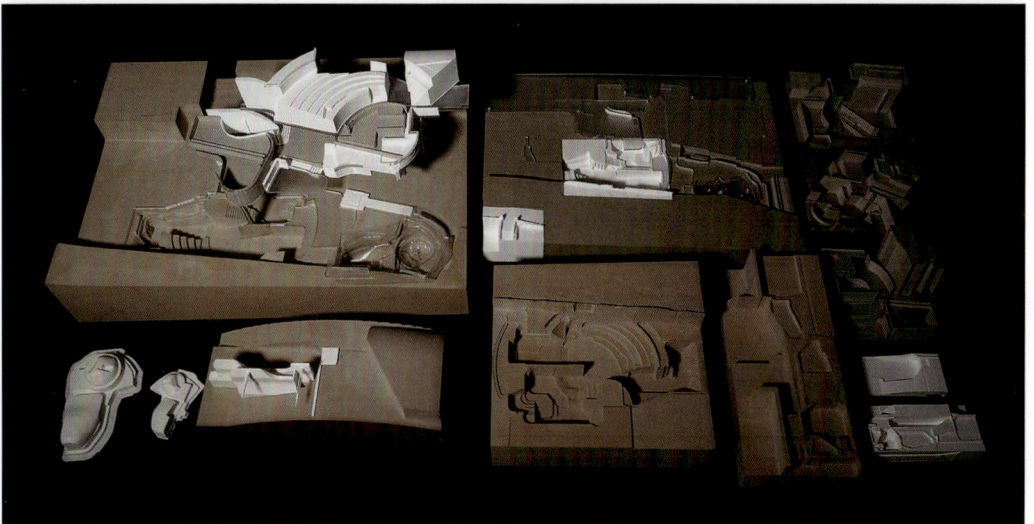

13.9

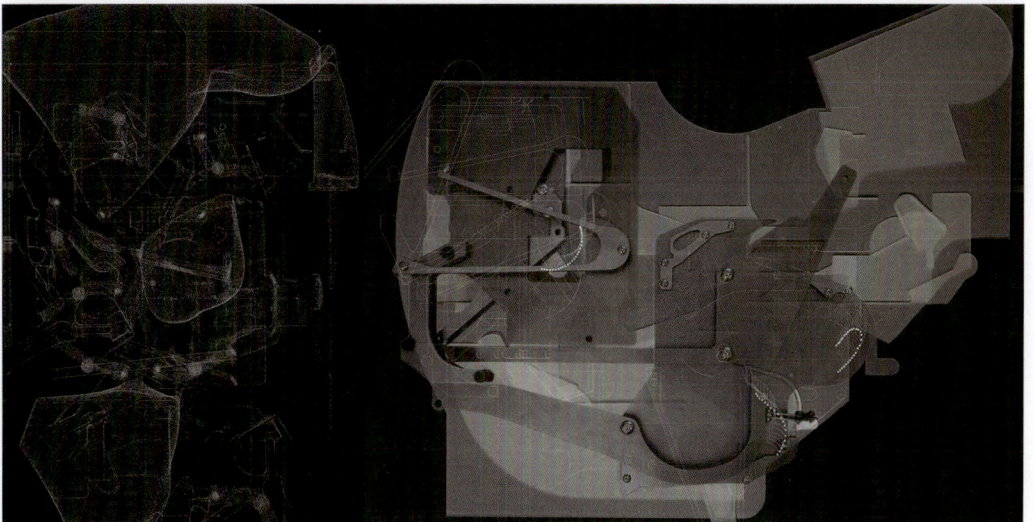

13.10

13.11

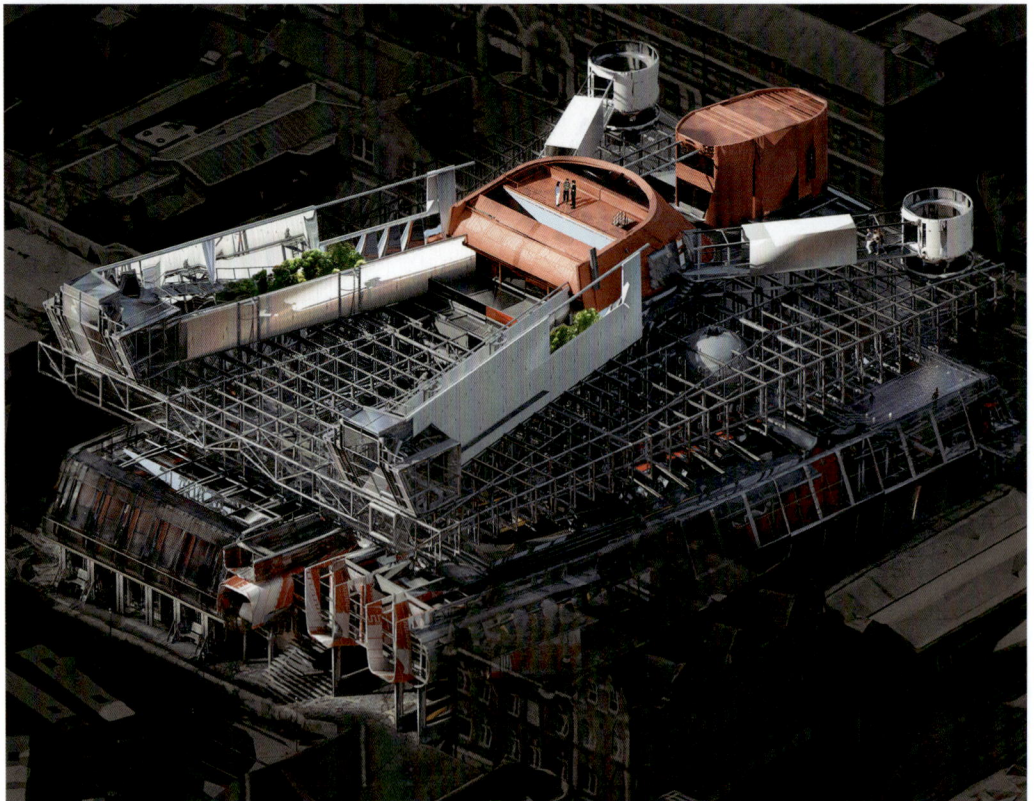

13.12

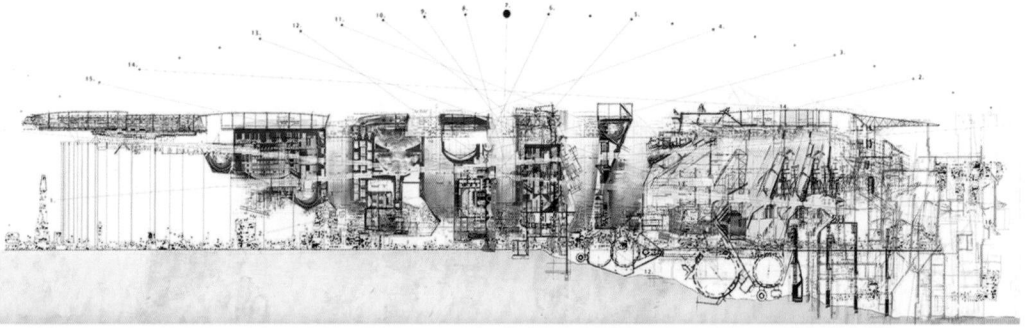

13.13

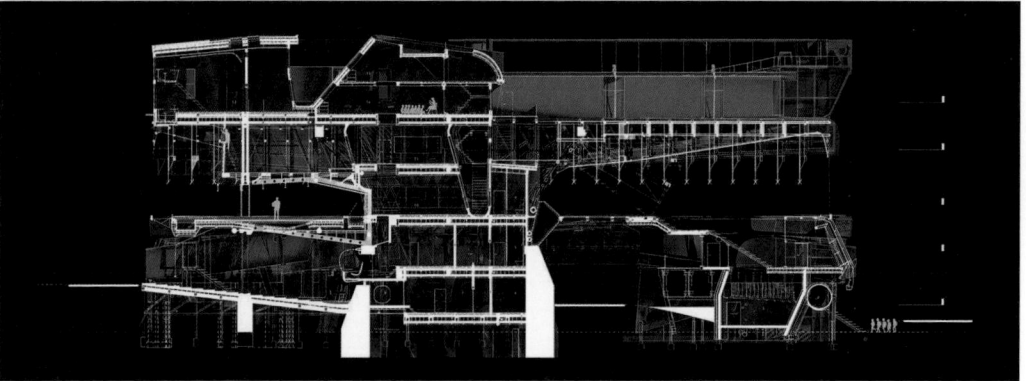

13.14

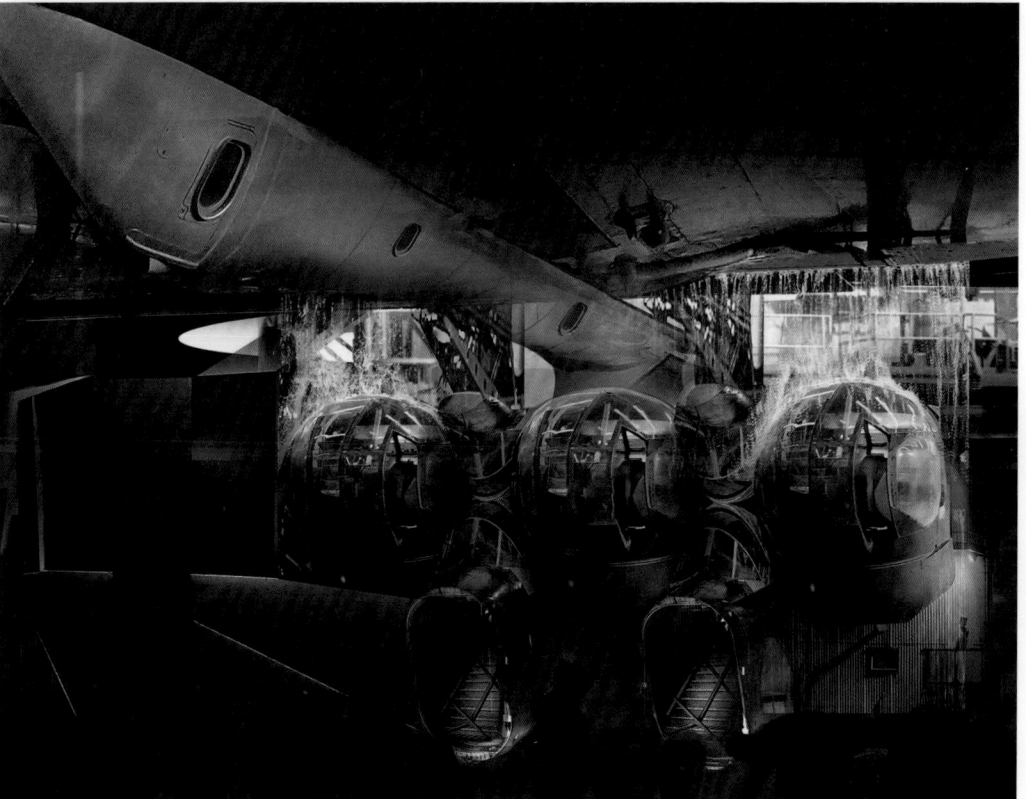

13.15

13.16

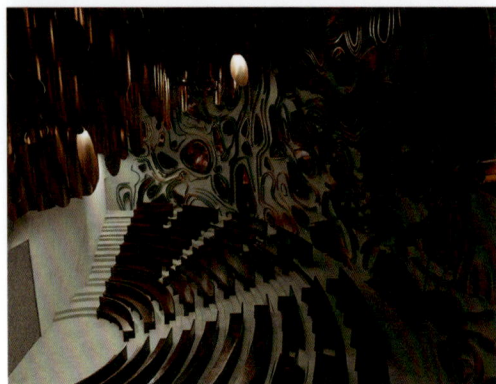

13.17

13.18

13.19

13.20

13.21

13.22

13.23

13.25

13.24

The Memory of Work

UG14

David Di Duca, Tetsuro Nagata

This year UG14 continued its studies into how societies remember and forget through collective rituals, commemorative monuments and the built environment. This year we focused on post-industrial UK to consider how places rich in heritage and social identity reframe their futures while continuing to celebrate their past.

For the past half-century information technology has transformed lives in the UK and encouraged economic growth. The country has witnessed a seismic shift from an economy reliant on manufacturing to one dominated by the service sector, leading to the decline of the industrial heartlands and a desperate need for adaptation. As the government reflects on a need to rebalance the economy following the pandemic and considers options to increase investment in manufacturing, UG14 examined how these post-industrial communities are moulded to forget, but still able to remember.

We visited The Potteries in the West Midlands, one of the most important historical industrial sites in the world. The geology and infrastructure of the area led it to become a flourishing global industry – a seam of clay and coal supplied the raw materials required to create ceramics, while canals provided an effective means of transportation. We marvelled at the ornate Victorian architecture and were dismayed to learn how it was being disregarded by the local council. We visited active and former factories and redundant collieries. We questioned the validity of these buildings and challenged ourselves to reimagine the abandoned spaces as stages to newly found events. In so doing we sought to design a layered architecture that sculpts new histories and identities.

We took part in a ceramics workshop to learn some of the techniques passed down through generations and communicate ideas to people – the creativity, skill and haptic knowledge that forms the collective memory of work. All human-made objects embody the processes that created them, representing a moment in time, both for the artist and for society. In an era when LiDAR scanning and 3D printing are digitally incorporated into architectural design, UG14 is simultaneously interested in the intentional and unintentional clues and messages we leave through our hands, for others to discover.

Year 2
Ibrahim Charafi, Maria Hussiani, Chin (Shirley) Lam, Giulia Mombello Perez, Chisom Odoemene, Zeynep Okur, Charize Orio, William Tindall

Year 3
Chantelle Chong, Dylan Duffy, Jack Kinsman, Ling (Stefanie) Leung, Xavier Simpson, Libby Sturgeon, Hau (Charmaine) Tang

Technical tutor and consultant: Danielle Purkiss

Critics: Sarah Firth, Stefana Gradinariu, Mads Hulsroy-Peterson, Kevin Kelly, Eleanor Lakin, Benjamin Mehigan

14.1, 14.16–14.18 Dylan Duffy, Y3 'Where the Giants Walked'. The project inserts itself into the now unused Chatterley Whitfield Colliery in Stoke-on-Trent. The programme responds to the need for funding to maintain the historic site by creating a giant puppet workshop which holds a bi-yearly event to attract vendors and visitors. The workshop houses a series of specialist designers and ateliers manufacturing elements of the giant around a central construction table to form a reconfigurable building. The project investigates methods of efficiency and recycling in the construction of giant marionette puppets and buildings by utilising methods of material transformation and designing for the disassembly of different components at varying scales of construction.

14.2 Xavier Simpson, Y3 'Exploring Terroir'. Sited at the heart of Stoke-on-Trent's 'mother town', the project reinhabits Burslem's disused indoor marketplace. In order to shed light on the abandoned but not forgotten site, the programme proposes a community kitchen and garden with a central focus on the Staffordshire dish, 'lobby' – a stew traditionally eaten by poorly paid potters. The project also explores the potential of reusing the waste materials produced by cooking lobby to generate a new materiality that is unique to Burslem and its community.

14.3–14.4 Chantelle Chong, Y3 'At First, There Lay a Swamp'. The project explores a community space and wellness destination that provides tranquil yet surreal peat baths to visitors of the derelict Chatterley Whitfield Colliery. The bathhouse initiates a political discussion on the mining industry's difficult relationship with public health and subverts ideas of dirt and preconceptions of coal, retelling its narrative as the product of fossilised plants being subjected to millions of years of heat and pressure, eventually leading to their decay.

14.5–14.6 Hau (Charmaine) Tang, Y3 'Non-Fungible Architecture'. In response to Stoke-on-Trent's history and declining economy, the project researches trends in community currency, cryptocurrency and non-fungible tokens (NFTs). The project proposes a minting facility to produce an alternative clay currency and house a pottery workshop for six artisans to collaborate on unique ceramic artworks to be sold as NFTs. The programme celebrates the uniqueness and imperfection of ceramic handcraft through architecture, questioning the dialectics of financial and craft value.

14.7–14.9 Jack Kinsman, Y3 'The Community of Brass'. In the abandoned Chatterley Whitfield Colliery, the project uses the local mineshafts as a supply for geothermal water, combining programmes of a traditional brass band music space with a geothermal energy plant. The building design is formulated through a mixture of ceramic and laser-etched steel to control airflow and heat circulation through the space. As the building's temperature increases, its bimetallic panel system causes the contortion and transformation of the generated sounds in the performance spaces. while alluding to the local historic steelwork culture of the potteries.

14.10 Chisom Odoemene, Y2 'Tintinnabulum'. The building programme is a handmade-bell and saggar factory and residency, which will revive Stoke-on-Trent's past by supporting its near-extinct handmade ceramics culture. Traditional apprenticeships will be reinstated, as the craftspeople live, work and learn from each other until they graduate. This revival will be celebrated by the chiming of handmade bone china bells, swinging from a carillon. The bell tower will act as a timekeeper for the different processes and rituals taking place in the building and beyond.

14.11, 14.14 Ling (Stefanie) Leung, Y3 'The Earth Beneath My Feet'. Once known as the 'Mother of Potteries', the town of Burslem has deteriorated into a ghost town marked by derelict bottle kilns. The project proposes a community centre including a ceramics studio and anagama kiln. In addition, a farm sustains the production of flour for the manufacture of the town's iconic delicacy, oatcakes, made in a communal kitchen. This project proposes an alternative approach to traditional clay-based construction methods by integrating 'cooking' and 'building' to promote sustainable construction knowledge in the wider community.

14.12 William Tindall, Y2 'Reiterating the Potter's Wheel'. A former pottery in Burslem is demolished and its parts used to construct the proposed building, imprinting the memories of the past onto the new. The building programme is a repair shop and gallery for the personal items of those heralding from Stoke. These objects will be repaired and curated into biannual exhibitions, telling the hidden story of those whose lives were drastically impacted by the decline in manufacturing in the region.

14.13, 14.15 Libby Sturgeon, Y3 'The Potter's Senate'. Despite the 1910 federation of Stoke-on-Trent that combined six towns into a single borough, one of the long-standing problems of the city is its 'six-town mentality' and internal rivalries. The proposal is to introduce a local parliament building that has performance at the heart of its design methodology – translating stories of the six towns into performance and subsequently into architecture. By capturing these stories in the building, ritual and tradition become firmly implanted in the parliament and rekindle a sense of collective identity.

14.2

14.3

14.4

14.5

14.6

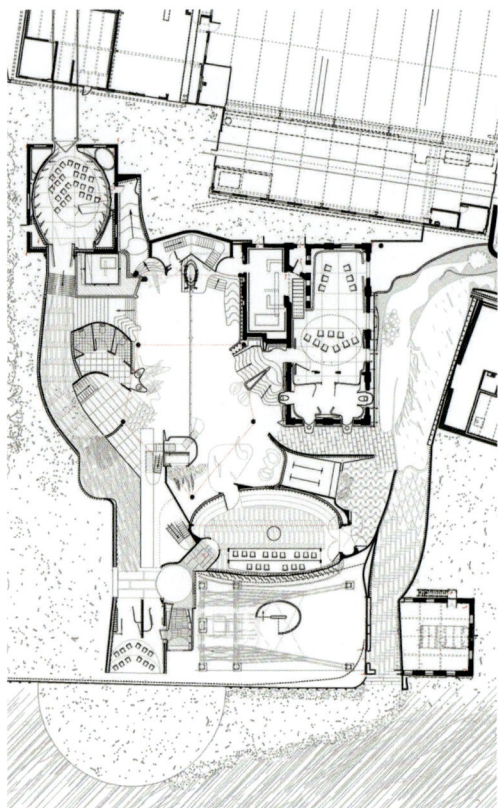

14.7

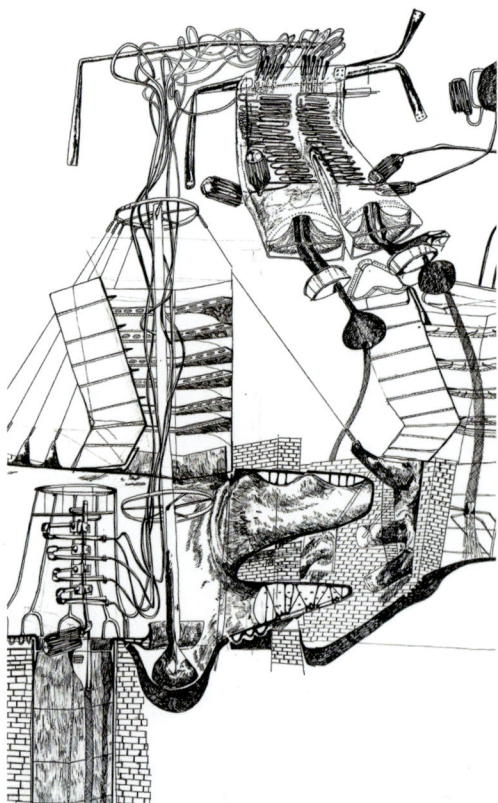

14.8

14.9

14.10

14.11

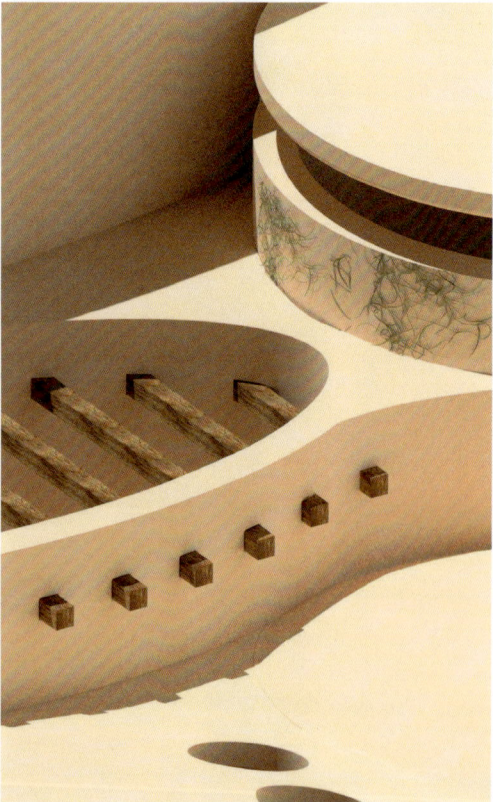

14.12

14.13

14.14

14.15

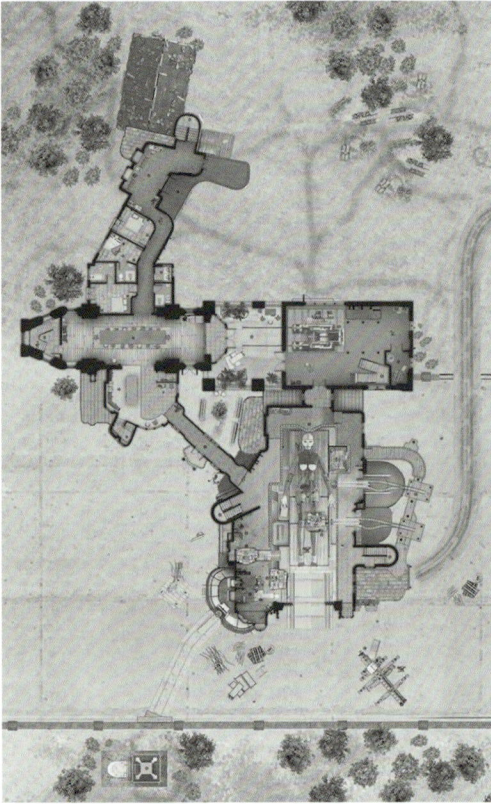

14.16

14.17

14.18

Finite

Abigail Ashton, Tom Holberton, Jasmin Sohi

This year UG21 considered the finite.

The past 18 months of accelerated digital development have tested what can be achieved with less material consumption and physical movement. As we return to a supposed 'normality', urgent questions remain unanswered. As of 2014, humanity's global ecological consumption is 1.7 times the Earth's capacity. Apocalyptic deadlines suggest the world will be running out of sand (20 years), fresh water (28 years), food (18 years) and iron (64 years). Architecture increasingly looks beyond one moment of design to influence material supply chains and consider the entire lifespan of a space.

UG21 were asked to consider different aspects of the finite and the infinite. Can we create inventive architecture by imposing a strict limit on a material, a boundary, on time or perception? When do we use infinite digital space and infinite change to augment the fixed and finite? When do society's rules create artificial limits and change the ways in which we design?

Architecture that values the finite needs to be created within time. Many systems around us operate as infinite games, with no ultimate outcome, measuring their value through incremental changes. New ways of drawing, modelling and filmmaking can consider architecture as a dynamic process of near infinite change and feedback. The Poincaré disk model, used by M. C. Escher, draws infinite space in a simple circle using hyperbolic geometry. Computer simulations and calculus quantify infinitesimal changes to provide certain predictions from many tiny moments of uncertainty. Fractal shapes contain never-ending patterns that resemble one another across different scales.

The students' research this year straddled the material and immaterial, the physical and the infinite. They developed inventive design processes that not only followed strict rules of resources, materials and making but also provided architecture that was dynamic, reflective and thoughtful – and made best use of the digital infinite.

We travelled to the Isle of Portland on the south coast of the UK, an area described by Jonathan Meades as a 'bulky chunk of geological, social, topographical and demographic weirdness'. Here students developed their own highly individual design processes and architectures.

Year 2
Ayisha Belgora, Nan-Hao Chen, Maria Gasparinatou, Ioi (Nicole) Ho, Ina-Stefana Ioan, Katie Karmara, Archie Koe, Zofia Lipowska

Year 3
Peter Cotton, Cosimo De Barry, Zeb Le Voi, George Neyroud, Jack Powell, Rafiq Sawyerr, Supawut Teerawatanachai, Walinnes (Air) Walanchanurak

Technical tutor and consultants: Jasmin Sohi with additional support from Julian Besems, Jatiphak Boonmun, Steve Webb

Critics: Julian Besems, Roberto Bottazzi, Naomi Gibson, Kostas Grigoriadis, Andrew Porter, Bethan Ring, Jasmin Sohi

21.1, 21.9 Cosimo De Barry, Y3 'Royal Academy of Music: Isle of Portland'. The project proposes a satellite facility for the Royal Academy of Music, based in London, on the Isle of Portland, in Dorset. The programme consists of a music studio complex for use by invited guests of the academy and for the local population to gain access to music equipment. The Portland stone façade of the building is resampled and remixed to create a colourful new face for the proposal which sits in a disused former Portland stone quarry.

21.2–21.8 George Neyroud, Y3 'A Chimeric Nursery'. In a disagreement over the preservation of Christ Church Spitalfields, a newly built nursery is now subject to demolition. The project introduces machine learning models that are derived from Nicholas Hawksmoor's architectural designs, which have the ability to produce bespoke church plans for a new site. As the building must also satisfy the inhabitants, the children become authors alongside the architect and mediator. By oscillating between hand drawing, clay fabrication and digital modelling, the building becomes a chimeric object of a brand-new language, with the blended information of the three authors now distilled into a new nursery within the empty church walls of St George-in-the-East.

21.10–21.11 Nan-Hao Chen, Y2 'Time-Erosion'. The programme is a series of leisure facilities that work as observatory spaces along the coastal path in Portland for hikers and tourists. The project's design is driven by the wave data of Portland, which informs how the geological features of Portland are shaped through time. With a combination of architectural elements generated by 3D modelling software and the composition of spaces inspired by the quarries, the project takes users on a journey to explore the geological features of the Portland Bill.

21.12–21.14 Ayisha Belgore, Y2 'Boundaries'. The project addresses the definition of architecture across administrative boundaries and questions how it changes as buildings develop and form. It focuses on the tangential relationship of boundaries and allows them to become an element in building design and construction. Materiality is fundamental to this project. The architecture, although functional, is at its heart a composition in, and a love letter to, stone. By being situated in the Isle of Portland, an area famous for its limestone quarries, the project remains true to this approach.

21.15–21.16 Walinnes (Air) Walanchanurak, Y3 'A Butterfly's Metamorphosis'. A butterfly conservatory that proposes to resurrect decayed and lost quarry grounds to bring back biodiversity through rewilding the landscape. By embracing a butterfly's lifecycle, the space will re-enact a butterfly's chronicle through its distinctive phrases: egg, caterpillar, chrysalis and butterfly. This is done by incorporating the ideology of time and space through its superior qualities and structural colour.

21.17–21.18 Archie Koe, Y2 'Skate on Kintsugi: Belonging on the Isle of Portland'. A multi-storey skatepark in a quarry on the Isle of Portland. The project provides the younger generation of Portland with a skatepark and gives them a place to belong. By supporting troubled youths and instilling a sense of community, the project will mitigate potential mental health problems. *Kintsugi*, the Japanese art of repair, informs the materiality and skate-inspired pseudo-parametric design language.

21.19 Ioi (Nicole) Ho, Y2 'Post-Covid Healing Hub'. The project is focused on helping patients who are chronically ill with Covid-19, as well as providing data for scientific research, by creating a therapeutic architecture that blends seamlessly with its surrounding environment. The building explores how architecture and aesthetics can create an environment conducive to the healing process. Plants serve as the healing centre of the building, promoting social interaction between residents and increasing physical, mental and physical wellbeing. The main feature of the building is a vertical perforated green-brick façade combining stone and plants, which challenges the idea of cohabitation and the coexistence of species. The Covid-19 pandemic is a turning point in human history. The new centre can provide a space for the public to enjoy a range of services such as counselling and physical therapy to help deal with issues before they develop into chronic health problems.

21.20 Ina-Stefana Ioan, Y2 'Resting in Myths'. The project brings together mythology and leisure in a storytelling environment buried deep inside a hill while also being lightly cantilevered off the ground. Its ambition is to create a dialogue on both sides of an existing hikers' path and to draw on Portland's rich culture by strategically presenting some of its long-lived legends in a mythology museum and resting area. These legends are told and represented through an image encryption algorithm that dictates the design when linked to the site's topographic curves. The design language borrows from illustrated stories relating to the surrounding area to fuel the script with data, further contextualising the design. High spatial interconnectivity introduces a seamless transition between under- and overground platforms. Using the area's topographic lines is at the core of the spatial arrangement, and the surrounding steep landscape is the dictator of the interior conditions.

21.21 Zofia Lipowska, Y2 'Dancing With the Landscape'. The relationship between cliffs, boulders and the human body provides the inspiration for a dance studio located between Bowers Quarry and Tout Quarry Sculpture Park. The experience of wandering among the stones, trying to stay in equilibrium on the uneven ground and feeling how the landscape influences movement are the main drivers for the project. The programme includes dance studio facilities, a kinetic sculpture park and a universal performance space that faces the English Channel.

21.22 Rafiq Sawyerr, Y3 'A Preserved Current'. A building project that asks how historic buildings that have been frozen in time through the listing process can be adapted to satisfy the needs of the current environment. The project interrogates whether a fixed form of preservation is the only way a building's architectural, programmatic and historical interests can remain intact. In response to these factors, the design proposes an offshore library close to Portland Harbour, restoring the use of the Mulberry Harbour Phoenix Caissons by repopulating them with redesigned caissons, to replace the many lost during the war.

21.2

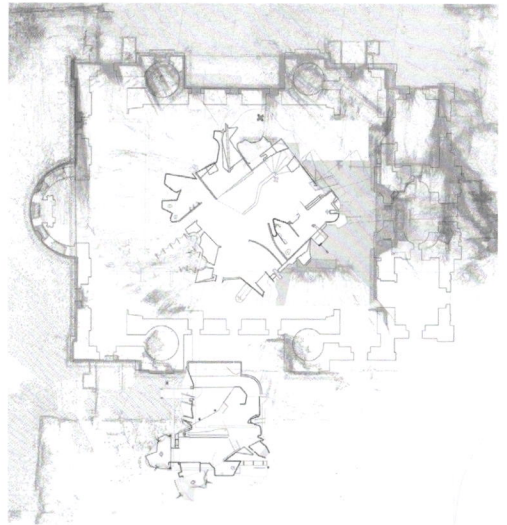
21.3

21.4

21.5

21.6

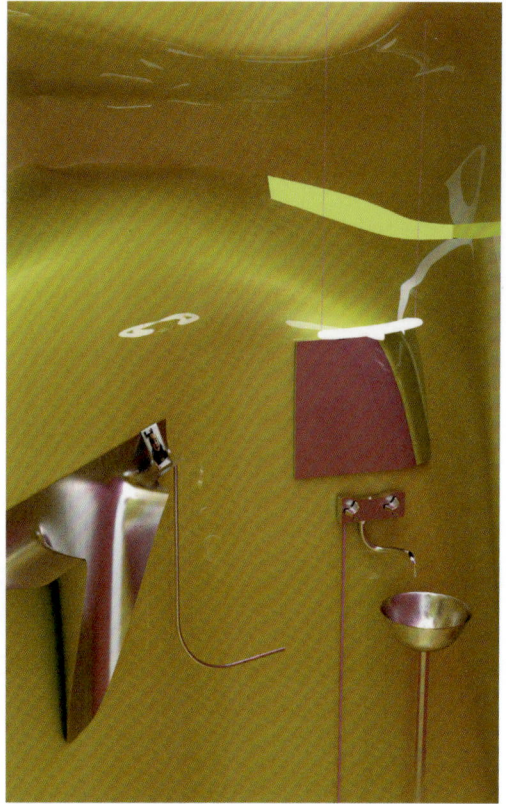

21.7

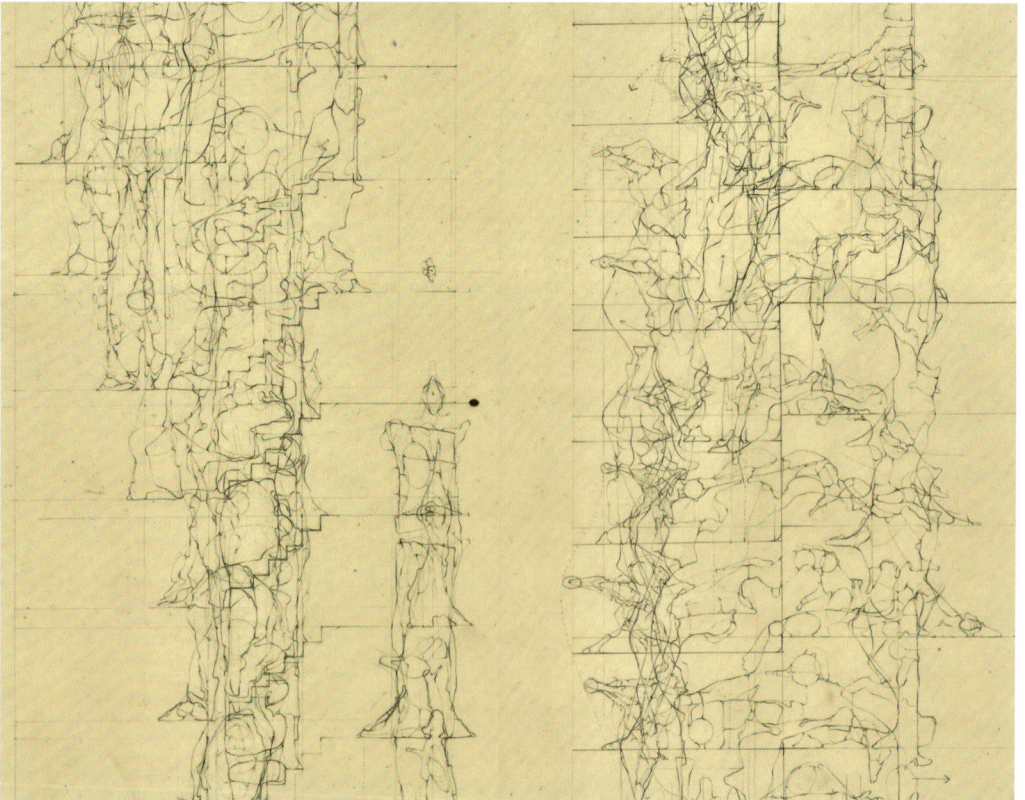

21.8

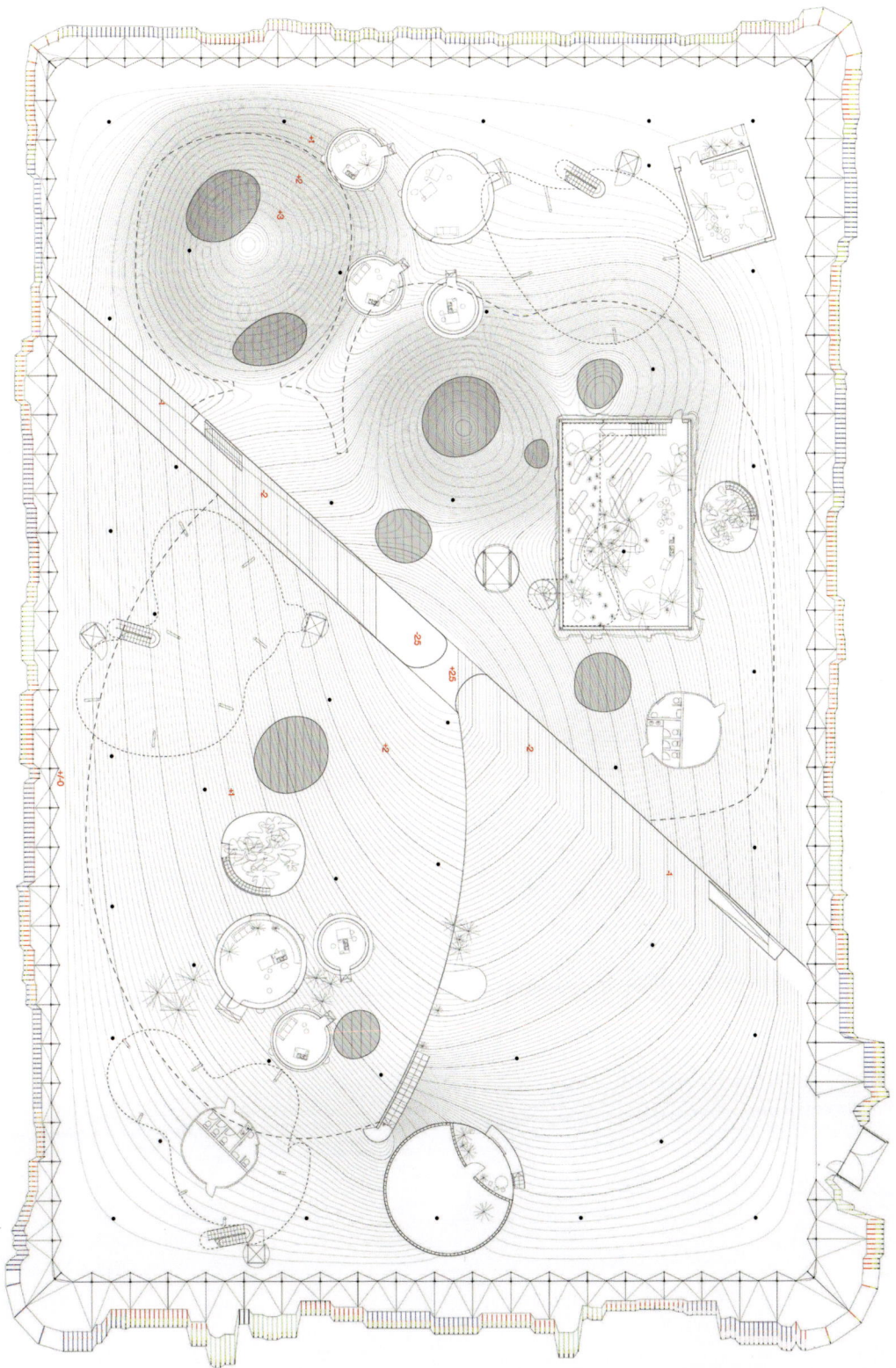

21.9

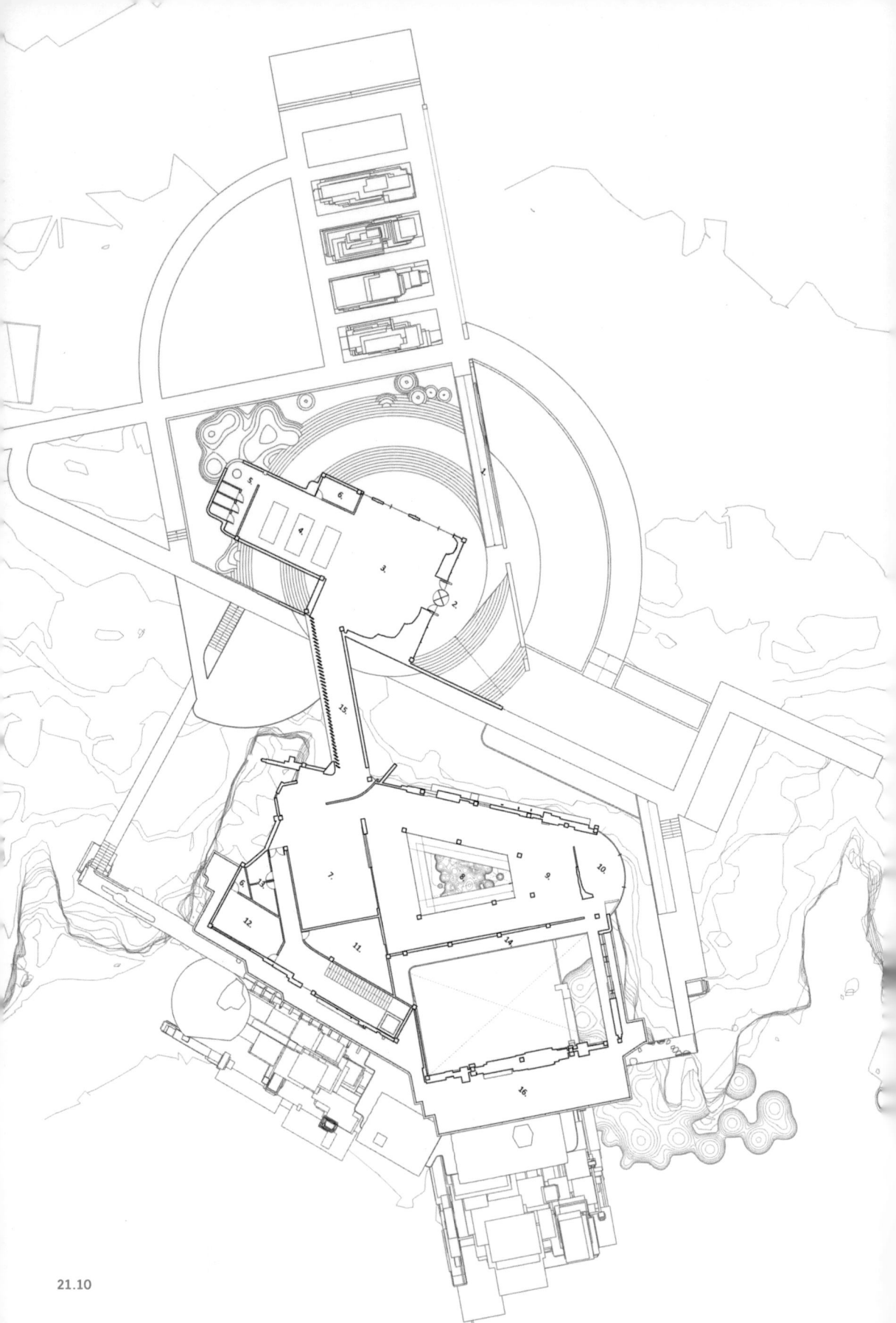

21.11

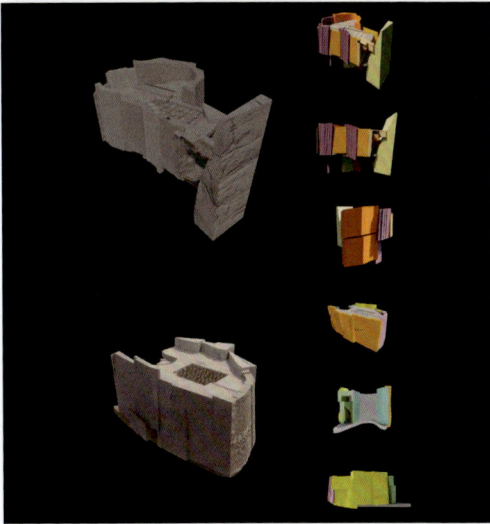

21.12

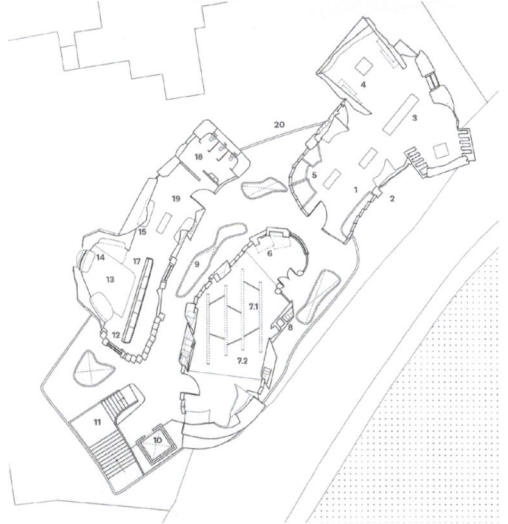

21.13

21.14

21.15

21.16

21.17

21.18

21.19

21.20

21.21

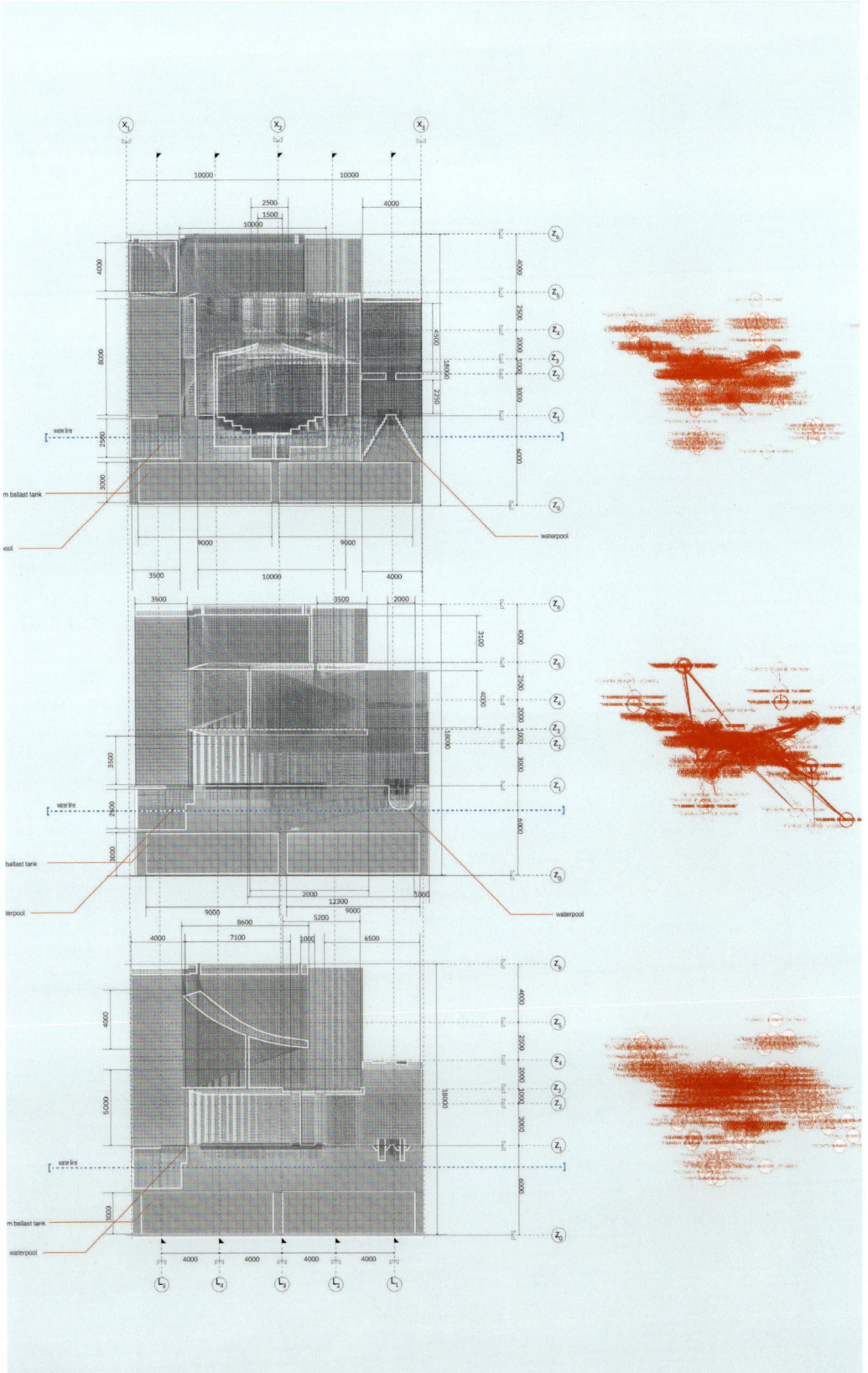

21.22

Architectural & Interdisciplinary Studies BSc

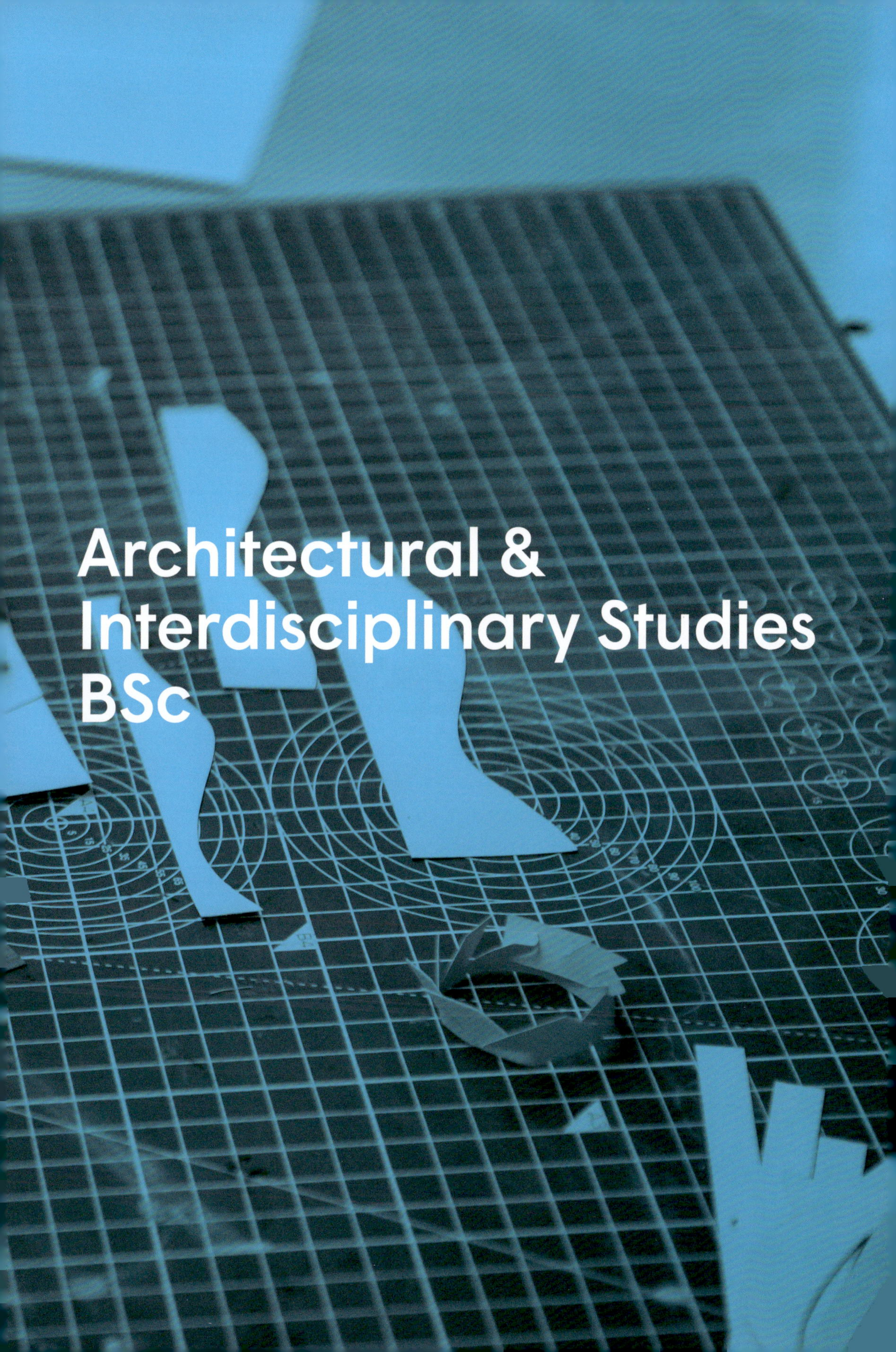

Architectural & Interdisciplinary Studies BSc

Programme Director: Elizabeth Dow

Architectural & Interdisciplinary Studies BSc is a degree that is unique not only within UCL but also in the UK, as it allows students to select their own modules and tailor their studies to their wider interests. By combining architectural research with design and creative practice and complementing these subjects with modules from across UCL, our students are able to demonstrate that architectural culture is not singularly centred around the accredited profession. They are able to recognise and benefit from the fact that there are many other people working in related fields – film, media, public engagement, policy, conservation, curation, design and creative practice – who shape debates and ideas around architecture in significant and important ways and are actively participating in these conversations through their studies and beyond.

The greatest strength of the programme is its interdisciplinary nature. We encourage our students to navigate their studies in a focused manner, while choosing from a diverse range of modules from across UCL alongside their architectural studies. They develop a range of skills and build a unique knowledge set tailored to their interests, empowering them to go on to apply themselves to careers such as journalism, art, design policy, activism and environmental and urban studies.

There are two specially tailored modules for Architectural & Interdisciplinary Studies students: Design & Creative Practice and Architectural Research. Images from the resulting design projects and an excerpt of work produced for this year's Architectural Research III essay-based module can be found on the following pages.

Architectural Research
Tutors and PGTA: Sabina Andron, Brent Carnell, Kirti Durelle, Stelios Giamarelos, Tom Keeley, Sophie Read, David Roberts, María Venegas Rabá

Design & Creative
Practice tutors and PGTA: Faraz Alian, Kirsty Badenoch, James Green, Kevin Green, Tom Kendall, Ifigeneia Liangi, Freddy Tuppen, Gabriel Warshafsky, Henri Williams

Technical tutor and consultant: Henri Williams

Critics: Siufan Adey, Jos Boys, Amy Butt, William Victor Camilleri, Lucinda Chua, Charlie Clemoes, Stephanie Farmer, Simon Gleave, Polly Gould, Niamh Grace, Lola Haines, Anthony Julius, Marcy Kahan, Alex Lăcătuşu, Ben Lee, Eloise Maltby Maland, Lo Marshall, Andrew Merritt, Chi Nguyen, John Philip Sage, Anete Salmane, Suzi Sendama, Amy Spencer, Jack Tan, Nathaniel Télémaque, Colin Thom, Manijeh Verghese, Tom Wilkinson

Greening Cities
Tutor and PGTA: Blanche Cameron, Jakub Plewik

Computing for Design & Creative Practice
Tutor: Bill Hodgson

Programme Administrators
Beth Barnett-Sanders, Pani Fanai-Danesh

Architectural Research III

Module Coordinator: Brent Carnell

Architectural Research III is an advanced module allowing students to work on an interdisciplinary architectural subject of their own choosing, undertaking rigorous primary research and writing an 8,000-word essay. Concurrent to individual research projects, students also work collaboratively on the production of a group output for dissemination in June. This year, this component took the form of a book and website. The website adds to the work of previous Architecture Research III student work. The themes this year focuses on scale, from the small to the extra-large – domestic, communal, institutional, national and international. Tags include Architecture & Health, Gender, Memory, Pedagogy, Perspectives, Inclusiveness, Safety, Utility, Community, Sustainability, Capitalism, Regeneration, Gentrification and Globalisation. The website can be accessed at **archresearch3.com**.

Over the year, students hone their research methods, while distilling the fruits of their own unique interdisciplinary education gained at The Bartlett and other departments across UCL, developing unique understandings of the multifarious ways in which architecture interrelates with society and the world.

This year's projects are truly interdisciplinary. They offer an impressive range of built environment investigations that demonstrate the strengths of the module and the diversity of the programme. The teaching team is profoundly impressed with the rigour, commitment and development of each study.

Students
Isobel Binnie, Anya Blanchfield, Richard Hardy, Shiori Kanazawa, Haobo Li, Jiying Luo, Clara Lyckeus, Laurence Milton-Jefferies, Siobhan Rothery, Leyao (Vesper) Wang

Module Tutors
Stelios Giamarelos, Sophie Read, David Roberts

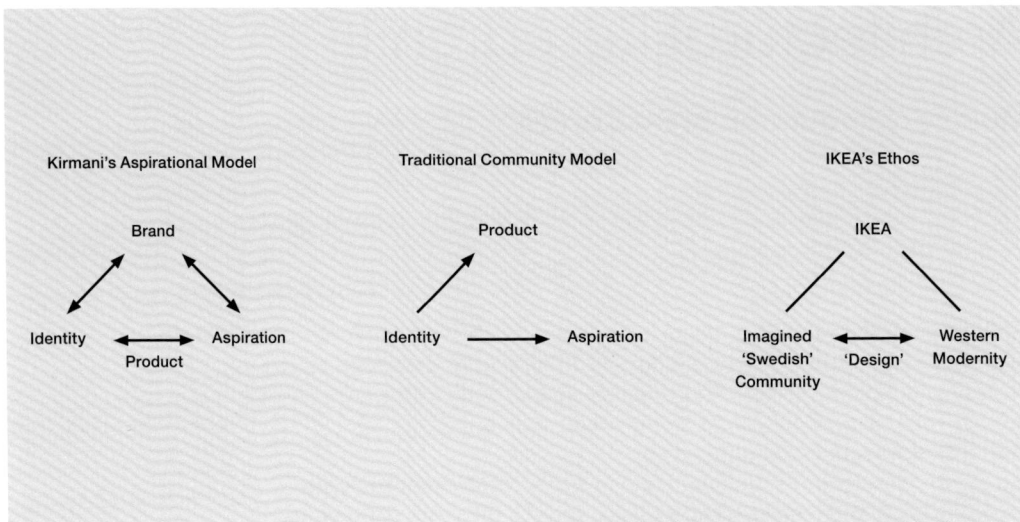

Kirmani's Aspirational Model   Traditional Community Model   IKEA's Ethos

Brand   Product   IKEA

Identity — Product — Aspiration   Identity → Aspiration   Imagined 'Swedish' Community ← 'Design' → Western Modernity

IKEA in India: The Colonial Power of International Retail
Isobel Rose Binnie

A trip to IKEA has become a rite of passage for many of us, with the shop providing homewares for every stage of our lives. Designs such as the BILLY bookcase have become so universal that we see the same models almost everywhere. Our environment may change, but the furniture remains the same. IKEA's takeover of the furniture industry has grown across 52 countries using the same product range. In doing so, the retailer has created a universal aesthetic for interiors. By encouraging the complete refurnishing of interiors based on IKEA design, local furniture and craft are marginalised and negatively associated with high prices and heritage.

IKEA's products are organised under the IKEA brand. It is as representations of the IKEA brand that products benefit from its unique signification. Products in their distinct style and construction have the IKEA look, but the signification of this look is the result of its positioning and elevation. This dissertation focuses on the construction of this signification and how it interacts with previous colonial value systems. IKEA does not recreate colonialism, but rather presents an altered and renewed form of cultural domination through the 'soft power' implicit in design and branding[1] and the separation of this power from political responsibility.

IKEA's relegation of craft is consistent with globalisation and the neutrality of goods in international economic trade flows. It is also consistent with the practices of colonialism. Even IKEA's assertion of a unique capacity to define and rationalise itself – the characteristic of its brand – establishes a connection with the colonial world. Colonial regimes had the ability to set the terms of their interaction and mythologise themselves in order to define their power. The formidable network of signification that IKEA brings to its expansion in India strongly resembles the autonomy and self-sufficiency of colonial regimes. In this case however, the state and its institutions are not the main objects of takeover. The object of takeover is the consumer, the individual whose identity provides the key to the success of the brand. It is through the conversion of individuals and their aspirations to its brand that IKEA replicates the authority of colonial power.

Image: Visual representation of IKEA's aspirational consumer model to Kirmani's conceptualisation of aspirational consumer identity and Trentmann's theorisation of demand in traditional communities. Image by the author.

1. Nye, J. (2004). *Soft Power. The Means to Success in World Politics*. New York: Perseus Books.

Design & Creative Practice 1, 2 & 3

Design & Creative Practice is a 15-, 30- and 45-credit module that is taught across Years 1, 2 and 3 of Architectural & Interdisciplinary Studies BSc, and is taken by Bartlett students, affiliate students and those from other departments. This year's Year 1 students speculated on the design and making of tools. Considering tools to be devices which mediate, filter or amplify the body's interactions with its environment, our students imagined the constellation of gestures, strokes and materials that make up a craft. These crafts emerged from personal and shared necessities, sometimes practical in their nature, at other times poetic and wondrous. Working intuitively between making, drawing, performance and writing, students elaborated on new material environments shaped by their tools, before going on to consider how their emerging new crafts could be imparted to others to effect ambitious spatial or cultural change. In the process, students investigated the limitations of their tools, while developing techniques of instruction, persuasion and demonstration to amplify their impact on the city around them.

Year 2 is a year of experimentation. In the context of the Anthropocene, we explored the role of 'process' within design, architecture and landscape, as well as our responsibility as designers to embrace materials and scenarios in and out of our control. This year interrogated two themes – horizons and tectonics. The horizon provided us with a datum through which to gauge the changing world around us, and tectonics asked us to work materially with environmental politics. As our experiments took us from the laboratory to the workshop and out into the city, we curated a series of public exhibitions and group performances, engaging with artists, makers and scientists along the way. Together we ran an auction of Gordon Square, embarked on a witch-hunt and froze and melted sections of the River Thames. Individually we collected, dug, kneaded, stretched and censored our way into entirely new modes of creative play.

In Year 3 we experiment with strategies for creative practice that are sustainable within a wide cultural context, looking outside of the institution and promoting public-facing, socially engaged projects, while collectively exploring a theme relating to architecture and the built environment. This year we explored the theme of 'communication'. We have been living through a time in which humans have shown incredible ingenuity in adapting and evolving the way we communicate. In this context we sought to explore how architecture can learn from new and unexpected modes of communication. The year centred around an ambitious public event, The Karaoke Court, inspired by song duel practices from indigenous communities as a dispute resolution process. Developed in collaboration with artist Jack Tan the event centred voices less frequently heard from both inside and outside The Bartlett, while proposing a new space of communication.

Year 1
Marie-Lou Absous, Arin Issa, Sofia Alvarez Manilla Hernandez, Grace Bonham, Nathalie Chieveley-Williams, Maria Corti, Adam Dalton, Imogen Dawe-Lane, Ioanna Fragaki, Ying (Amy) Gao, Ipek Hakki, Freya Leonard, Jiahong (Kingsley) Luo, Iona McVean, Yaya (Ernest) Mfor Mpecassah, Nicole Onstad, Noah Ponte, Ema Pop, Tian (Tina) Qi, Samuel Quaille, Ruby Ray, Harang Seo, Xinran (Paula) Shen, Marius Sidaravicius, Catrin Sinclair, Tom Skoulding, Charles Stone, Alexia Vela Akasaka, Yezhen (Enid) Zhang, Yiwen Zhao

Year 2
Emilia Bryce, Chongyu Chen, Eric Castellarnau Feitoza, Katharina de Mel, Maia Dubois, Henry Galano, Mahika Gautam, Stela Kostomaj, Yuyang (Sunny) Li, Cecelia Liu, Qiqi Liu, Christa Lockyer, Katherine McClintock, Nadoln Narongdej, Merle Nunneley, Muinot (Angel) Quandry, Ning (Cristina) Su, Ionela Mihaela Suciu, Javas Tan, Yifan Wang, Xiaoyan (Ivanka) Zhao

Year 3
Yasmina Alhaddad, Isobel Binnie, Anya Blanchfield, Margaret Chao, Zahra Chatha, Gurmukh Dhanjal, Richard Hardy, Shiori Kanazawa, Haobo Li, Jiying Luo, Clara Lyckeus, Daniel McCarthy, Laurie Milton-Jeffries, Mungeh Ndzi, Olivia Niklasson, Anna Orbanic, Siobhan Rothery, Alexandra Savova, Leyao (Vesper) Wang

DCP.1 Katharina de Mel, Merle Nunneley, Y2
'The Auction of Gordon Square'. Confronted by the dark realities of our environment, we find ourselves in a changing relationship with the natural world. Human rights are no longer granted simply to humans. Through the staging of a public auction of Gordon Square, the project explores plant and animal legal rights; alternative currencies and promises of exchange; the perceived valuation of nature; and a re-evaluation of ownership. How many years would you sacrifice not buying clothes for, for the sake of Camden's squirrels?

DCP.2 Freya Leonard, Y1 'Streams of Consciousness'. This project challenges preconceived ideas of cleanliness through the redesign of the squeegee. Transitioning from the collection of water to the facilitation of the journey of a single droplet, this new craft celebrates the impurities of the built environment instead of washing them away. Bringing together theatre, painting, cleaning and photography, the craft reflects on the dreamlike state of drawing.

DCP.3 Marie-Lou Absous, Maria Corti, Nicole Onstad, Xinran (Paula) Shen, Tom Skoulding, Y1 'To Fall Asleep'. This group project is about the moment of falling asleep: a hat changes the colour and intensity of light while protecting the skin, a duvet stitches sunlight and turns it into an embroidery, a cocoon made of paper blooms with water droplets, a layered dress curls around the body, a pen becomes an extension of our fingers, and a curtain unfolds according to the moonlight.

DCP.4 Nicole Onstad, Y1 'Soporific Cocoon'. This project uses water, paper and thread to create spaces that induce sleep. The subtle movements and curling of paper absorbing water are observed through photography in the design of a craft that helps put us to sleep. The proposal is an enclosure of paper sculptures that can be activated and moved when sprayed with water.

DCP.5 Xinran (Paula) Shen, Y1 'Me'. This project explores cultural identity through the design of a craft and the creation of armour. The craft is an exploration of making sculptural fabrics by combining personal objects such as hair curlers with everyday actions such as baking. The proposal is an armour composed of four flowers, an allegory of four cultural identities. The wearable armour questions what home can be.

DCP.6 Marius Sidaravicius, Y1 'Finding Form and More'.This project uses string, slip and gravity to make large-scale structures. The process of making string structural with slip is a time-consuming and laborious craft, best enjoyed in good company. This new craft recognises the importance of collaboration and considers this in its process. It needs two to four people to stand upright, while it has the average height of the people who operate it.

DCP.7 Stela Kostomaj, Y2 'Stretch/Censor'. The project embarks on a performative dialogue between actor and audience, controller and the controlled. Engaging in physical tension between human bodies in relation to themselves and one another, we stretch, survey, expose and antagonise.

DCP.8 Ning (Cristina) Su, Cecelia Liu, Y2 'Dissolved, Decayed, Discovered'. Exploring the cyclical process of material growth and decay, a series of bioresponsive material installations are salvaged from and slowly relinquished back to the earth from which they came.

DCP.9 Christa Lockyer, Y2 'Silky Catch'. Inspired by the intricacy and effectiveness of spider webs, the project treads a fragile line between the natural and curated worlds of Gordon Square. Living woven sculptures merge into the gaps in the garden, as the surrounding environment blossoms and blooms through springtime.

DCP.10 Emilia Bryce, Ionela Mihaela Suciu, Y2 'The Bubbles that Hold Us Together'. The gentlest of stereotomic acts expand space and prompt growth. A participatory yeast-based installation invites a revolt against productivity, through intimate acts of co-creation and conversation around breadmaking. It is in the seemingly empty bubbles that the self grows.

DCP.11 Yuyang (Sunny) Li, Xiaoyan (Ivanka) Zhao, Y2 'Knots of the Ground'. Our historical understanding of the world is based on blocks, yet it is our relationships that define us. What if a house becomes a knot in the fabric of the ground? The installation imagines an entirely woven, interconnected world, an anti-monument shaped and reshaped by the wind, the trees and the conversations between us.

DCP.12 Clara Lyckeus, Y3 'Sean and Jane Examine Pins Found on the Foreshore'. This investigation was guided by an interest in identifying 'other' spaces in the city. The potential freedom embedded in empty, wasteland sites led to the project being centred on the foreshore of the River Thames at low tide. Through the practice of mudlarking on the river banks, the project explores how this distinct topography allows city dwellers to engage in a therapeutic practice that disrupts one's understanding of society. The project defines the idiosyncratic 'topia' instigated by its public engagement element, whereby a close understanding of the community of mudlarkers is formed and the varying motivations behind the practice are examined.

DCP.13 Isobel Binnie, Y3 'Implosion'. The design of the chair responds to the psychophysical laws that connect mental and physical events within a virtual reality. These opposing realities merge through the attempt to emulate the movement, structure and feel of the virtual seating. Standardised objects and mass-produced furniture contradict the bespoke, boundless nature of the design of the digital realm. These do not need to be truthful but connect in a manner cohesive to our conscience and our rational or causal understanding of the functioning of the physical realm.

DCP.14 Anna Orbanic, Y3 'Self-feeding Root Structure'. The project encourages root and mycelium growth and sees the entangling of natural and human-made structures as highly beneficial. The weave is a starting point, creating a base structure for the substrate and the seeds (or mycelium) to be combined. Over time and through the process of self-feeding, the roots grow stronger and reinforce the woven network. These structural elements initially serve as green habitats and flood absorbers but gradually transform into a source of material for a new urban fabric.

DCP.15 Alexandra Savova, Y3 'Relighting the Lost'. The installation offers a different perspective on reading historic landscapes. The latex casts inside the installation resemble exploration sites as they capture traces of dirt, dust and rust found on the surface. The casts are placed on lightboxes and rendered onto a gallery wall so that observers can view the natural matter trapped inside the material. The final stage of the practice touches on the theme of preservation, offering alternative ways of reading the landscape by shedding light on the overlooked objects found on historical sites.

DCP.16 Mungeh Ndzi, Y3 'Dreamscape Scene'. The project explores the representations of architecture in dreamscapes by transcribing the work of Heinrich von Kleist, the author of the play *Der Prinz von Homburg,* into a series of sets designed for the Deutsches SchauSpielHaus in Hamburg. The sets respond to the themes of mistrust and uncertainty that are central to the play.

DCP.1

DCP.2

DCP.3

DCP.4

DCP.5

DCP.6

DCP.7

DCP.8

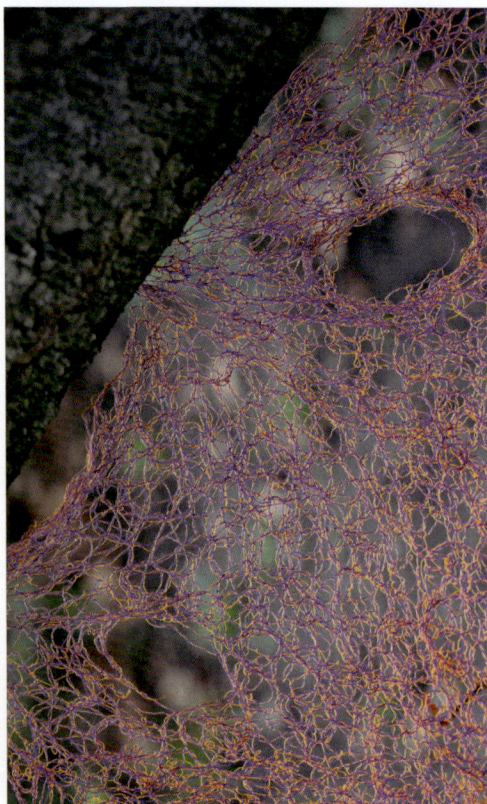

DCP.9

DCP.10

DCP.11

DCP.12

DCP.13

DCP.14

DCP.15

DCP.16

First-year Engineering & Architectural Design MEng students, 2022
Photo: Sarah Lever.

Engineering & Architectural Design MEng

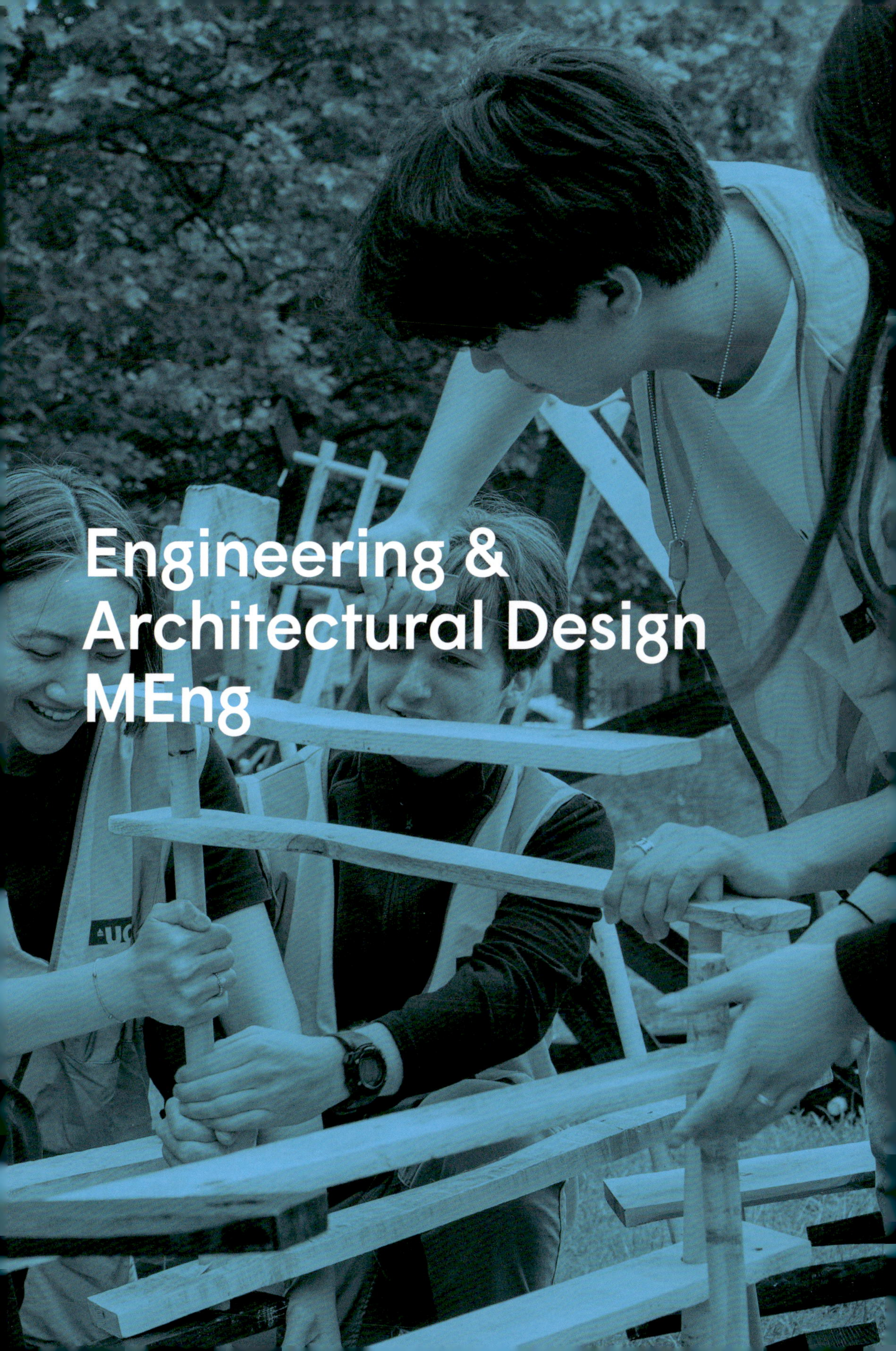

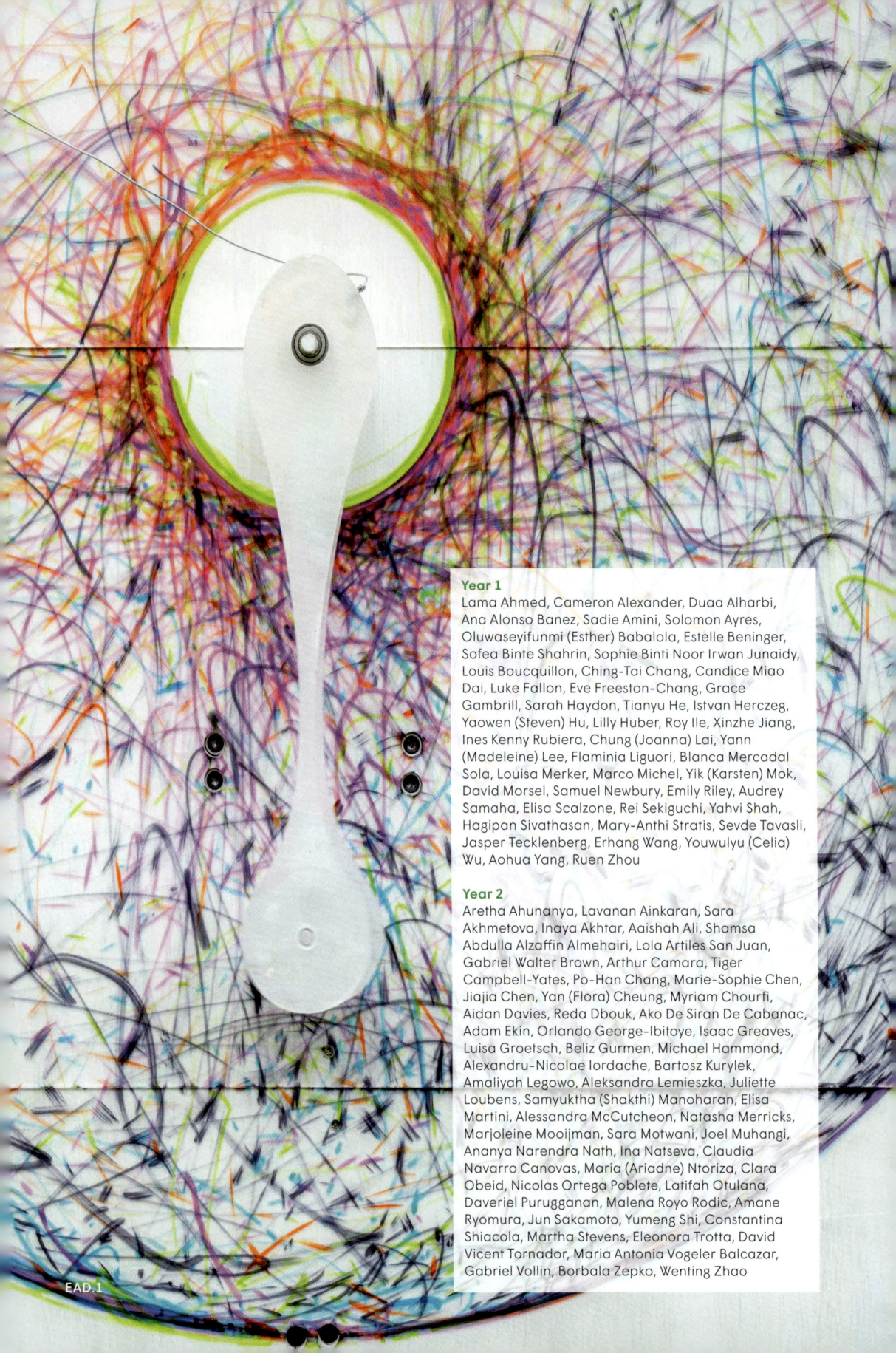

Year 1

Lama Ahmed, Cameron Alexander, Duaa Alharbi, Ana Alonso Banez, Sadie Amini, Solomon Ayres, Oluwaseyifunmi (Esther) Babalola, Estelle Beninger, Sofea Binte Shahrin, Sophie Binti Noor Irwan Junaidy, Louis Boucquillon, Ching-Tai Chang, Candice Miao Dai, Luke Fallon, Eve Freeston-Chang, Grace Gambrill, Sarah Haydon, Tianyu He, Istvan Herczeg, Yaowen (Steven) Hu, Lilly Huber, Roy Ile, Xinzhe Jiang, Ines Kenny Rubiera, Chung (Joanna) Lai, Yann (Madeleine) Lee, Flaminia Liguori, Blanca Mercadal Sola, Louisa Merker, Marco Michel, Yik (Karsten) Mok, David Morsel, Samuel Newbury, Emily Riley, Audrey Samaha, Elisa Scalzone, Rei Sekiguchi, Yahvi Shah, Hagipan Sivathasan, Mary-Anthi Stratis, Sevde Tavasli, Jasper Tecklenberg, Erhang Wang, Youwulyu (Celia) Wu, Aohua Yang, Ruen Zhou

Year 2

Aretha Ahunanya, Lavanan Ainkaran, Sara Akhmetova, Inaya Akhtar, Aaishah Ali, Shamsa Abdulla Alzaffin Almehairi, Lola Artiles San Juan, Gabriel Walter Brown, Arthur Camara, Tiger Campbell-Yates, Po-Han Chang, Marie-Sophie Chen, Jiajia Chen, Yan (Flora) Cheung, Myriam Chourfi, Aidan Davies, Reda Dbouk, Ako De Siran De Cabanac, Adam Ekin, Orlando George-Ibitoye, Isaac Greaves, Luisa Groetsch, Beliz Gurmen, Michael Hammond, Alexandru-Nicolae Iordache, Bartosz Kurylek, Amaliyah Legowo, Aleksandra Lemieszka, Juliette Loubens, Samyuktha (Shakthi) Manoharan, Elisa Martini, Alessandra McCutcheon, Natasha Merricks, Marjoleine Mooijman, Sara Motwani, Joel Muhangi, Ananya Narendra Nath, Ina Natseva, Claudia Navarro Canovas, Maria (Ariadne) Ntoriza, Clara Obeid, Nicolas Ortega Poblete, Latifah Otulana, Daveriel Purugganan, Malena Royo Rodic, Amane Ryomura, Jun Sakamoto, Yumeng Shi, Constantina Shiacola, Martha Stevens, Eleonora Trotta, David Vicent Tornador, Maria Antonia Vogeler Balcazar, Gabriel Vollin, Borbala Zepko, Wenting Zhao

Engineering & Architectural Design MEng

Programme Director: Luke Olsen

Engineering & Architectural Design MEng is a multi-disciplinary, award-winning and pioneering programme. It spans the professional, pedagogic and cultural boundaries of all three major disciplines who design the built environment, namely architecture, civil engineering and building service engineering.

Hosted by The Bartlett School of Architecture, the programme is designed, developed and taught by architects, engineers and designers from three leading UCL departments: The Bartlett School of Architecture, the Institute for Environmental Design and Engineering and the Department of Civil, Environmental and Geomatic Engineering.

At the heart of the programme is the three-tutor design studio forming a progressive laboratory of speculation, creativity and analysis. Students bring maths, physics, computing, enterprise, art, culture, history, theory and enterprise into every cutting-edge project.

Our Year 1 students operate within the reality of 1:1 design and making alongside the unlimited creative realm of the drawing. Operating within one of four design studios specialising in craft, digital fabrication, interactivity and art practice respectively. This year's 1:1 pavilions responded to the brief of '2012 Olympic Games: 10 Years On'. The pavilions are open to the public in the Queen Elizabeth Olympic Park, London as part of the New London Architecture (NLA) and Platinum Jubilee celebrations.

Our Year 2 students design within one of five design studios. They follow a shared brief to develop integrated building designs as spaces of environmental and structural mutability. This year's projects are situated in the forest surrounding Flimwell Park with 1:1 interventions leading to propositions that dissect along the Camden Highline as sites for collective context of community.

Programme Administrators
Dan Carter, Alice Whewell

Staff
Sabina Andron, Salam Al-Saegh, Dimitris Argyros, Simon Beames, Vasileios Bakas, Bedir Bekar, Harry Betts, Santosh Bhattarai, Andrea Botti, Esfandiar Burman, Haden Charbel, Matthew Coop, Daniel Ovalle Costal, Pippa Cowles, Ben Croxford, Satyajit Das, Dina D'Ayala, Klaas de Rycke, Simon Dickens, Yasmin Didem Aktas, Jan Dierckx, Phillipe Dufour, Shyamala Duraisingam, Dave Edwards, Sam Esses, Alberto Fernández González, Fabio Freddi, Mark Garcia, Laura Gaskell, Agnieszka Glowacka, Daniel Shinzu Godoy, Virginia Gori, Timo Haedrich, Laura Hannigan, Jack Hardy, Mina Hasan, Matthew Heywood, Mark Hines, Del Hossain, Oliver Houchell, Anderson Inge, Aurore Julien, Judit Kimpian, Vasiliki Kourgiozou, Mangesh Kurund, Déborah López Lobato, Luke Lowings, Liora Malki-Epshtein, Valentina Marincioni, Dejan Mumovic, Shaun Murray, Sahar Navabakhsh, Olivia Riddle, Yair Schwartz, Andrew Scoones, Sandra Smith, Michael Stacey, Sam Stamp, Tom Svilans, Iga Świercz, Farhang Tahmasebi, Jerry Tate, José Torero Cullen, Melis Van Den Berg, Martha Voulakidou, Michael Wagner, Andrew Walker, Alice Whewell, Isabel Why, Graeme Williamson, Michael Woodrow, Yi Zhang, Barbara Zandavali, Marek Ziebart, Stamatis Zografos

EAD.1 Louis Boucquillon, Magda Kolarska, Emily Riley, Yahvi Shah, Jasper Tecklenberg, Y2 'Chaos-Release'. The group has invented a public place of sonic and visual disturbance: a single, repeatable module in the form of a non-compliant panel comprising a self-actuating double pendulum triggered at will by passers-by. Layers of sound are created by the panels' action, building to a cacophony of motion and noise, only to cease through the chance combination of the pendulum movements in an instant of improbability. This strange drawing and noise-making device creates an intentional resonance with the experience of a burst of activity during a tennis match at the Olympic Games, the source of inspiration for this year's work. As the double pendulum gyrates and stalls in unpredictable fits, a pen at its extremity records this ungainly motion by drawing onto the panel in a continuous line. Like staring at clouds in the sky, this trace of a physical phenomenon reveals nothing, yet at the same time suggests forms and hints at near-repetitive behaviours, an all-at-once device of never-the-same-ness.

EAD.2 Ana Alonso Banez, Even Freeston-Chang, Tianyu He, Roy Ile, Blanca Mercadal Sola, Youwulyu (Celia) Wu, Aohua Yang, Y1 'Control-Grip'. To reflect the antagonism and cooperation witnessed within so many disciplines of the Olympic Games, the group has invented two diametrically opposed and interrelated spatial experiences on either side of a self-supporting partition which members of the public may experience and influence either individually, in pairs or in groups, on their own terms. The opaque partition prevents eye contact and is perforated by horizontal poles which can be pushed or pulled. On one side interconnections can be made between poles, resulting in a delayed but connected response which is impossible to predict on the other, while the other side displays pole ends painted in the five colours of the Olympic Rings, a subtle but direct reference to the source of research which has culminated in such an unusual device. People can collaborate through discussion, or wilfully resist collaboration, resulting in an openness of signification in an ever-changing but unresolvable spatial device that exists for play, contemplation and exploration.

EAD.3–EAD.4 Lama Ahmed, Sadie Amini, Estelle Beninger, Istvan Herczeg, Hagipan Sivathasan, Ruen Zhou, Y1 'Embrace, Cherish and Esteem'. The team's name is *Amplexum*, a Latin word chosen for its association with being embraced, cherished and esteemed. These qualities appear to be missing from the Paralympics, which are often seen as an afterthought to the 'main event', but which should be seen as a display of true Olympic spirit. The mutual support and interdependence of the structural elements (developed from folded and bent paper studies), the design and construction team itself (which grew more solid over time) and the symbolic resemblance to a tree all combined to make a powerful statement of mutual support and shelter. The codes on each leaf to help assembly are written in braille and reinforce the idea of inclusion. The structure is a shell made entirely of 4mm-thick birch ply, developed from a toroidal geometry. Curved vertices to a simple triangular subdivision of the torus produce stiffened bent surfaces in leaf shapes. Drawn digitally and then transferred directly to cutting machines, the leaf components incorporated etched images of the design and construction process as a drawn record on the structure itself.

EAD.5–EAD.6 Aleksandra Lemieszka, Y2 'Treaty of Mannequins: The Ectypal Book of Genesis'. In Bruno Schulz's *Street of Crocodiles*, an act of kindness is presented as a battle between dehumanisation, exclusion and the insurmountable imagination of a child who uses their pure innate power of metamorphosis to fight the difficulties of the world and redefine the act

of giving. The project is focused on helping people who are experiencing homelessness and who have been deprived of their basic needs. By creating residential spaces and providing job opportunities, the project shows that improvements to quality of life are achievable. Kindness can also help protect the Earth from environmental damage. Our planet can be nurtured through pioneering manufacturing methods with the use of mycelium as a building material. By curtailing climate disasters and avoiding the resulting social and political unrest, it is projected that the rate of homelessness will decline.

EAD.7 Tiger Campbell-Yates Y2 'Camden Conversations'. The proposal is for a public space that encourages discussion and involvement at all levels of Camden policy-making, in addition to gathering suggestions from the public through interaction. This will be done by tackling all three key components of the various current public engagement projects – engagement, understanding and action – to help improve Camden in a manner that suits all of its communities. The proposal is designed to incorporate the use of virtual and augmented reality to aid the presentation and understanding of ideas. Public speaking spaces are included to further encourage locals to have a say in the future of the borough.

EAD.8 Juliette Loubens, Y2 'Camden's Friendly Giants: The Wandering Puppet Troupe'. This project embarks on a journey of playful mischief and satirical theatrics, retelling the art of puppetry as it reclaims its place in Camden's rich history of performance culture. For centuries, the puppet has been used as a tool to drive social change. The project calls for a reimagining of buildings as characters that inhabit our cities with evolving temperaments, stories and relationships that grow and evolve beyond mere materiality. The friendly giants have temporarily settled in Camden Gardens with a mission to accommodate a touring puppet troupe while they share their craft throughout the local community.

EAD.9–EAD.10 Maria-Antonia Vogeler Balcazar, Y2 'Market 7'. The project follows the motif of the old Camden Lock Market and offers artists and craftspeople private and common workshops in addition to exhibition spaces where their work can be viewed. The building addresses the detrimental effects of gentrification by engaging with Camden's urban culture and increasing exposure for its local creatives. The Camden Highline is transformed into a public exhibition space for graffiti artists. The project synthesises the Highline's industrial theme and the historical brick architecture to represent Camden's eclectic atmosphere.

EAD.11 Gabriel Brown, Y2 'Pot, Fire and Bath'. The project combines relaxation, creativity and communication through a public bathhouse, pottery studio and shared living spaces. It provides moments of connection for Camden residents experiencing social isolation. Unclothed companionship facilitates friendly conversation in the bathhouse, while new skills and confidence are cultivated in the pottery studio. The kiln symbolises the heart of the project, providing passive heat for bathwater and firing architectural ceramics for interior finishes across all the spaces. A fibre-optic daylighting cable system is used to distribute natural light deep into the existing Highline arches. A staggered construction process is utilised where the façade bricks and rammed earth walls are manufactured on-site from the excavated soil. Different forms of brick arch reflect the different amenities in the building programme while responding sensitively to the existing environment.

EAD.2

EAD.3

EAD.4

EAD.5

EAD.6

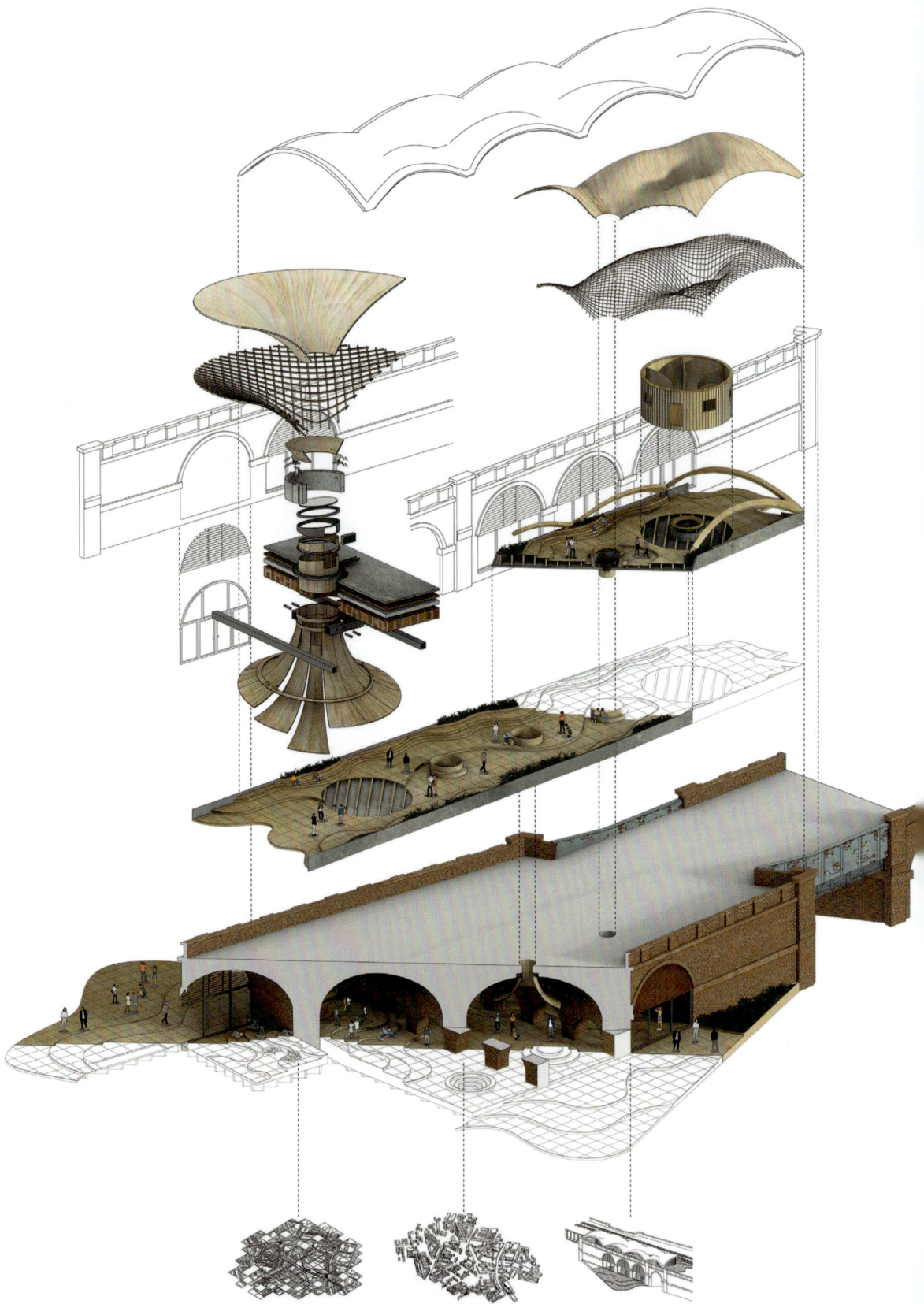

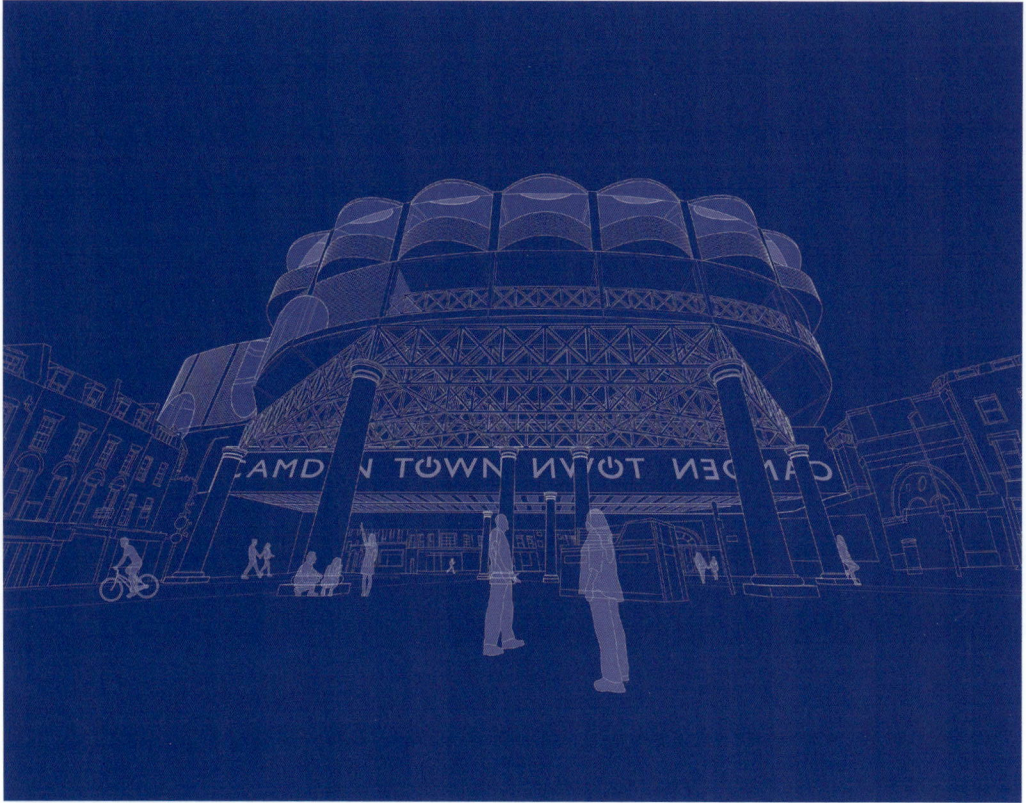

EAD.9

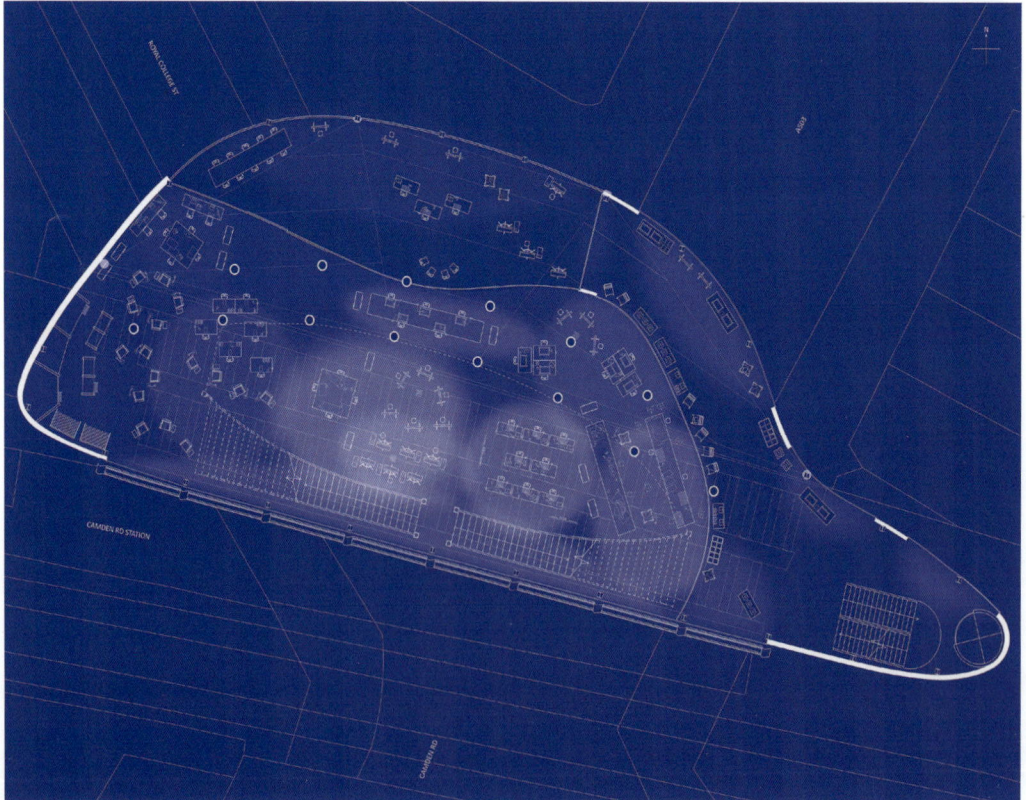

EAD.10

Years 3 & 4

Third and fourth-year Engineering & Architectural Design MEng students work within one of six vertical progressive integrated design units. Developing their unique individual vision as integrated designers, students harness robust knowledge in evidence-based engineering principles and analysis with open-ended integrated design to tackle complex near-future issues such as sustainability, climate change, zero carbon, inequality, food logistics, free clean energy and ecological, social and cultural regeneration.

Speculating on the future of the Tate in 'Tate Wapping', Unit 1 explored the adaptive reuse of the former power station, reigniting its vast engine rooms and its wider site to reimagine what it means to be a leading arts and culture institution during a time of unprecedented crisis.

Unit 2's project brief 'The Gate in the Hedge' synthesised architecture and engineering, with students designing ecologies as sutures for buildings in Highgate. Students explored city-making in the curious void between politicians and project managers where new roles need to be formed. Projects ranged from rethinking a walking library to encouraging sleep while descending a staircase.

Unit 3 hacked London's architecture and food supply chain in 'Tomorrow's Harvest' to redefine systems of value and attitudes associated with the logistics, production, consumption and waste of food and buildings.

In 'Zero Carbon Croydon', Unit 4 took a holistic and critical position relative to both the 1960s 'city of the future' ideal and Croydon's current urban regeneration projects. The resulting proposal was a zero-carbon alternative future.

Unit 5 collaborated with the Norman Foster Foundation (NFF) and the Advanced Nuclear and Production Experts Group (ANPEG) on 'An Atlas of Nuclear Islands'. Students researched and designed buildings in a cooperative, zero-carbon microgrid for future communities on Lundy, powered by one 10 MW nuclear battery. Projects ranged from carbon counting moai to a nuclear happiness spa.

Unit 6 investigated landscapes and society through collaboration. 'Graft / Seeding Cities' saw students work with growable, metamorphic material sited in the forest of Flimwell Park and London's urban landscape. Students explored the adaptive reuse of buildings nearing the end of their design life, extending their use by 125 years while strengthening symbiotic ecologies.

Jamila Aboueita, Azman Azhari Rizal, Bianca Bodo, Cheuk (Chester) Cham, Paraskevi (Vivian) Chatira, Tatyana Cheung, Regina Dufu Muller-Uri, Victoria Ewert, Masaki Hattori, Phoebe Hensley, Liana Hoque, Young Choel Moses (Bogeum) Jeon, Eddie Jones, Andreina Kostka, Joshua Labarraque, Jing (Jason) Li, Ekaterina Lopatina, Cynthia (Marjorie) Luque Escalante, Pedro (Antonio) Merino Ramon, Bihi Mohamed, Maxime Ostroverhy, John (Daniel) Perski, Sanara Piensuparp, Logan Scott, Sara Sesma Costales, Aya Souleimani, James Standing, Sheung (Emily) Tse, Ciying Wang, Yueyao Wang, Haoming (Isaac) Wang, Emily Wang, Hetian Zhang

Year 4

Tamanna Abul Kashem, Yuval Ben-Giat, Wenhui Cao, Yi Chen, Yuzhe Chen, Ruiyi (Rennae) Du, Andreea Dumitrescu, James Grimmond, Panagiota Grivea, Sarah Hassan M Alsomly, Iman Jemitola, Hans Kei Käppeler, Leo Kauntz Moderini, Victor Noorani, Sarina Kalpan Patel, Franca Pilchner, Jakub Plewik, Jahnina Queddeng, Mateo Rossi Rolando, Kimberley Rubio Ugalde, Ralf Saade, Samuel Seymour-Blackburn, Xi Shen, Nikie (Rosa) Siabishahrivar, Allegra Simpson, Johanna Stenhols, Harry Sumner, Emma Temm, Yile (Aloe) Wu, Zhuofan Wu

EAD.12 Leo Kauntz Moderini, Y4 'Iterated Wardian Case – Physical Model'. The first iteration of the Wardian case was taken from Here East, London, to Flimwell Park in East Sussex, where the birch saplings were collected.

EAD.13 Leo Kauntz Moderini, Y4 'The Baron in the Trees – Single Bay Section'. The two rooms contain one furniture unit each to swap between bedrooms and nursery rooms. Occupant-controlled natural ventilation, a shaded façade, underfloor heating, phase-changing plasterboard and highly insulated slabs aid occupant comfort and reduce active systems loads.

EAD.14–EAD.15 James Grimmond, Y4 'Inno-Tate: A New Home for Tate Research'. This project proposes a spiritual home for Tate's research, centring around its doctoral students. The project provides them with a permanent workspace and access to dedicated conservation facilities as well as a central meeting point to collaborate with other research staff. For one week of the year, the new Tate Wapping will throw open its doors and invite thinkers from the arts for a week-long celebration of creative research. The building will transform, deploying a roof and creating a unique semi-indoor auditorium. Tate Wapping is a celebration of art research and stands in defence of culture against the ever-present threat of funding cuts.

EAD.16 Yuzhe Chen, Y4 'Tate Wapping'. The project invites visitors to rethink plastic waste by reusing it as an art material, with the resulting work being exhibited on-site. The new intervention has been elevated from the ground to create a more permeable ground plane and to keep the original machinery in place. Landscaping in and around the building has been mindfully planned to weave the building into the surrounding urban context.

EAD.17 Harry Sumner, Y4 'YOI Tate Wapping'. Questioning the role, requirement and current performance of the UK's young offender institutes, the project is an arts-led social rehabilitation retreat for dysfunctional teens who are due to re-enter society. Each month the building is inhabited by 20 young offenders for a 30-day, three-phase creative rehabilitation programme, with a range of art workshops.

EAD.18 Yi Chen, Y4 'The Walking Library, Internal View of Space F (Fairy Tale Theme)'. An interior view of Space F – an experimental reading space for children and adults reflecting the atmosphere that the famous publisher Frederick Warne pioneered in his colourful children's books.

EAD.19 Yi Chen, Y4 'The Walking Library, Internal View of Space L (Zen Theme)'. An interior view of Space L – an experimental reading space that showcases the poetic mood of the famous Zen poet, Lucien Stryk.

EAD.20 Yi Chen, Y4 'The Walking Library, External View of Walking Library'. An exterior view of the building as seen from the pedestrian bridge, looking into the exhibition space.

EAD.21 Yi Chen, Y4 'The Walking Library, Internal View of Space D (Sci-Fi Theme)'. The interior of Space D – an experimental reading space that adopts the technological ambience of a spaceship interior and references the science-fiction writer Douglas Adams's fantasy of the future.

EAD.22–EAD.25 Panagiota Grivea, Y4 'Beauty Will Either Be Edible, or Not at All'. The project consists of the reimagination of Varvakeios Agora as a synthetic meat market and production hub, where the material of Athens' classical disused buildings is reused to construct the additive cannibalistic architecture of a market within a market. Set in the heart of traditional Greek culture, this project challenges our perception of tradition and origin in the context of food and raises questions on the related issues of globalisation and cultural internationalism.

EAD.26–EAD.27 Tamanna Abul Kashem, Y4 '(Un)Guided Living'. Britain's housing stock fails to reflect its diversity of cultures and lifestyles. By critiquing housing design codes and examining the domesticity of multigenerational families, a 'Rebel Architect' manifesto is crafted. The manifesto proposes unconventionally large and small residential units. The apartments support each other in a building-wide sharing economy of spaces and services.

EAD.28 Emma Temm, Y4 'A Tapestry of Recovery'. Reframing the process of recovery for victims of domestic abuse. The design creates layers of protection around key spaces and uses the image of a village to domesticate the shelter typology. Traditionally feminine crafts are put at the core by creating a multistorey shared atrium structurally supported by a large-scale cross-stitch.

EAD.29 Sarina Kalpan Patel, Y4 'Growing Green'. A design critique of the consented scheme for a residential development in Croydon to minimise demolition. The project speculates on the idea of biophilic-led regeneration to improve air quality in response to Croydon's 2040 vision. The existing building will be retrofitted to offer a farm-to-table restaurant, market and biophilic community workspaces.

EAD.30 Bianca Bodo, Y3 'Water Treatment Garden'. A 10MW Nuclear Battery (NB) is used to power a water treatment centre on the toxic abandoned former chemical works on Channelsea Island in the borough of Newham. Over a period of ten years the building, nearly entirely made of pipes and vats, cleans the water and land of hazardous toxins and remains open to the public throughout as a vertical garden for walking and cycling.

EAD.31 Bianca Bodo, Y3 'Water Treatment Garden'. The NB provides zero-carbon energy as a micro-grid which Newham Council can sell back to the national grid as democratised energy. This not only provides free zero-carbon energy from the garden in the sky but also clean water, thus improving the health, economy, green spaces and social benefits for the local community.

EAD.32 Hans Kei Käppeler, Y4 'Nuclear Biorock Pre-Fab-Lab'. A 10MW NB provides electricity to create biorock (calcium carbonate) through the process of electrolysis on rebar immersed in the sea. This process not only captures carbon dioxide from the atmosphere but also creates a building material as an alternative to concrete. Every week, 163 tonnes of CO_2 can be sequestered while construction components are built to order using biorock in the fabrication laboratory (this includes operational energy use).

EAD.33 Hans Kei Käppeler, Y4 'Nuclear Biorock Pre-Fab Lab'. Sited in a no-catch zone, the NB creates biorock in the Bristol Channel and increases North Sea coral for the sea life around Lundy. The bespoke integrated biorock building components can be made to order in the pre-fab lab, where clients can dive and quite literally watch their building grow. Components with integrated heating, ventilation and air conditioning (HVAC), mechanical and electrical (M&E) and structural services are then shipped to their destination and assembled on-site.

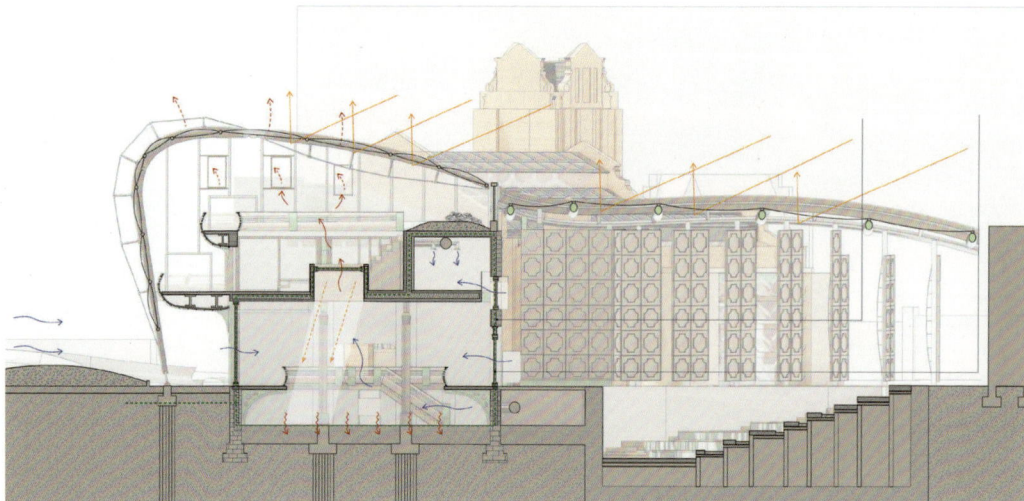

EAD.14

EAD.15

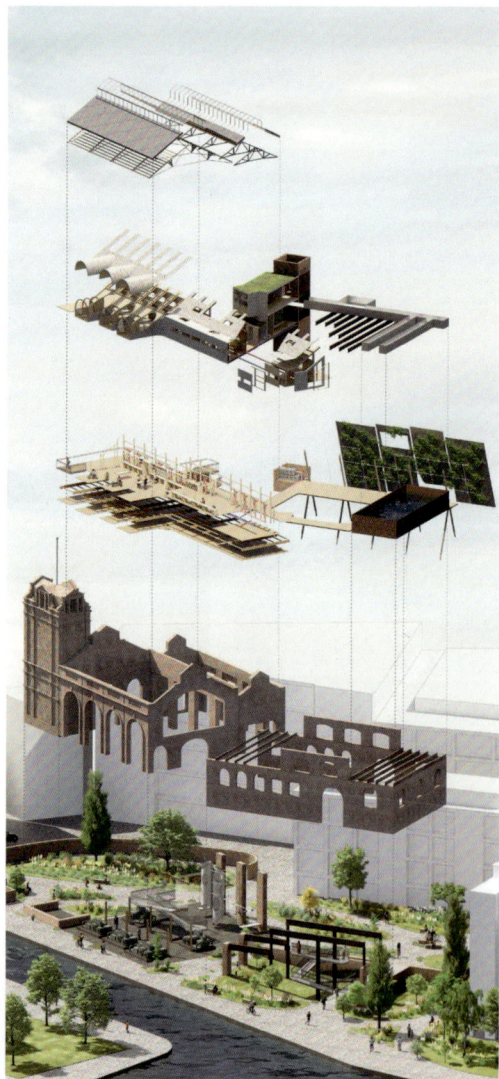

EAD.16

EAD.18

EAD.19

EAD.20

EAD.21

EAD.22

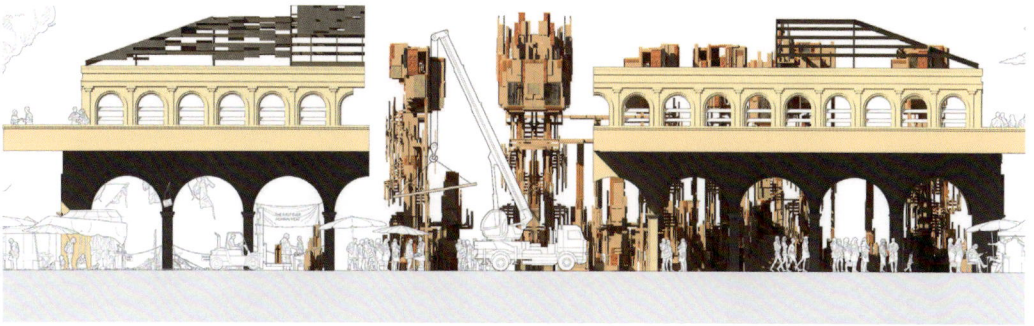

EAD.23

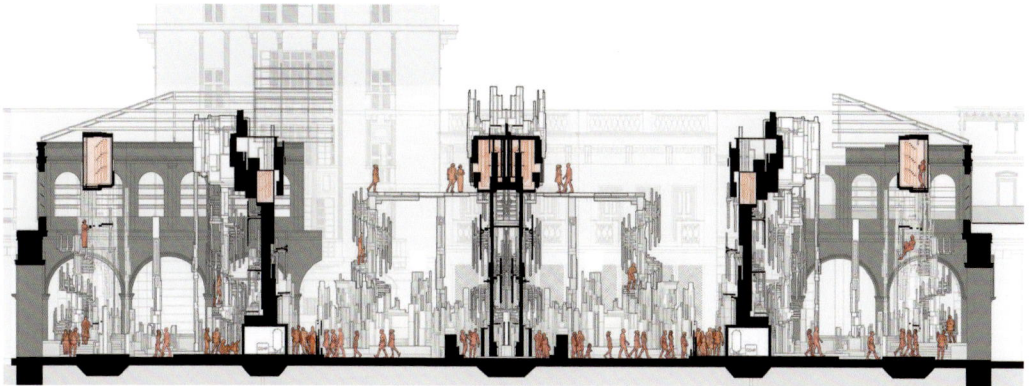

EAD.24

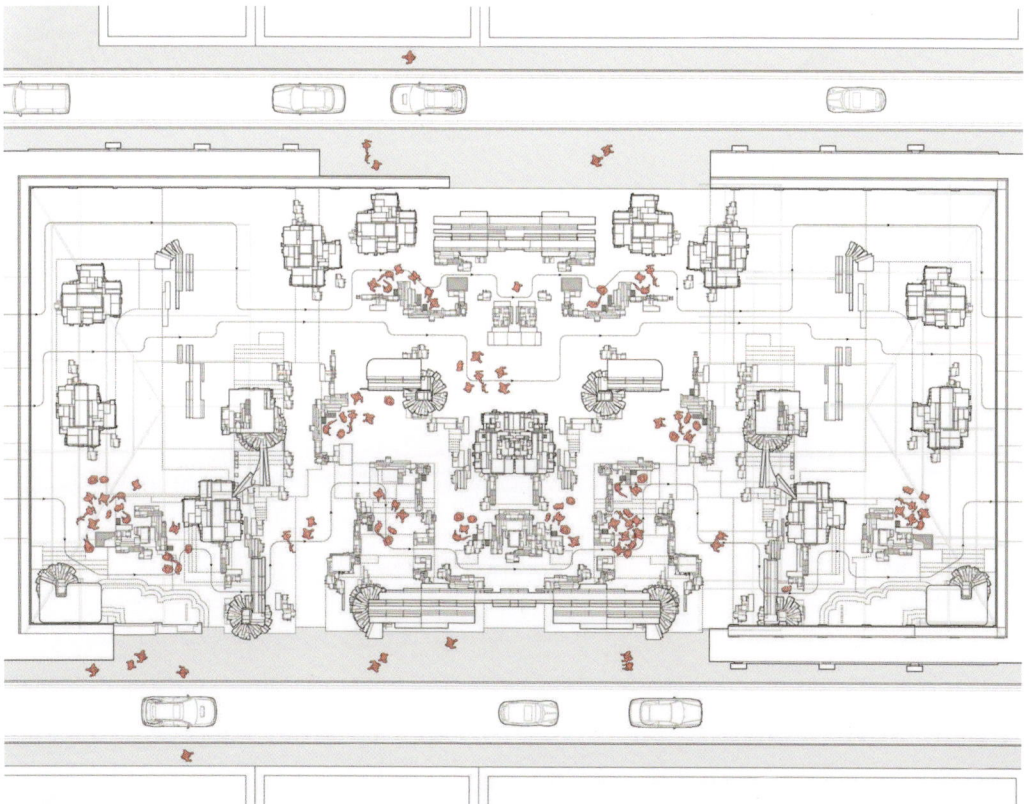

EAD.25

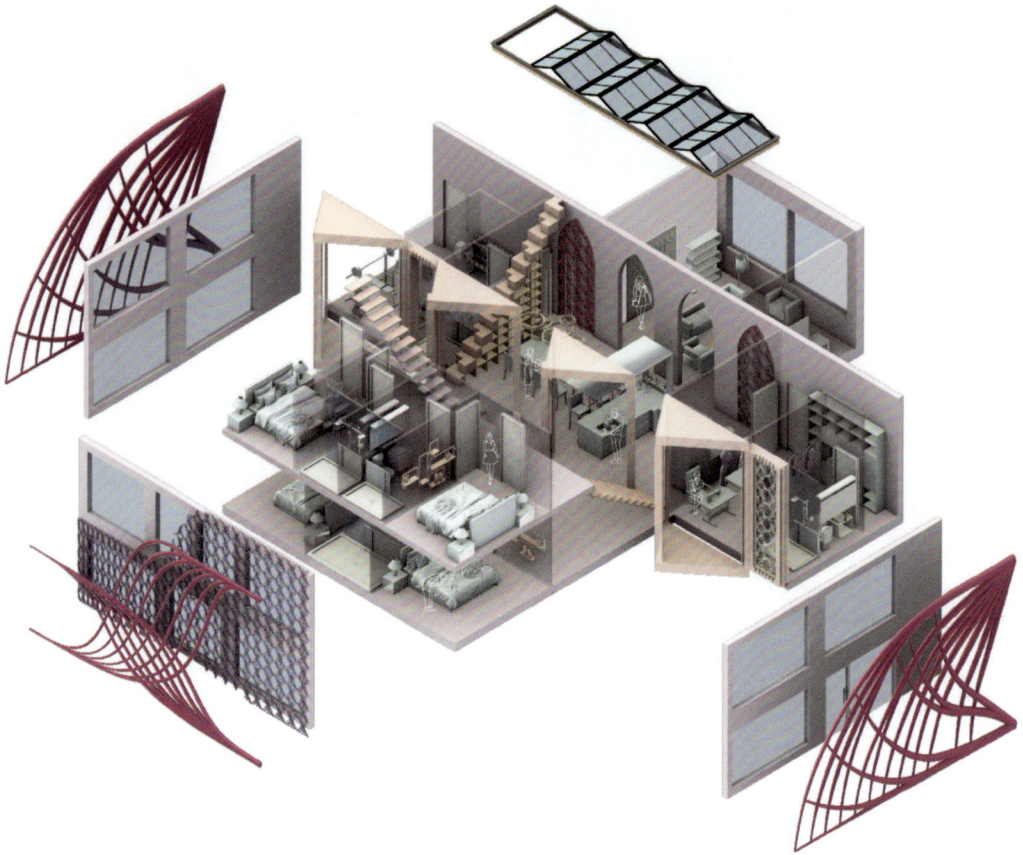

EAD.26

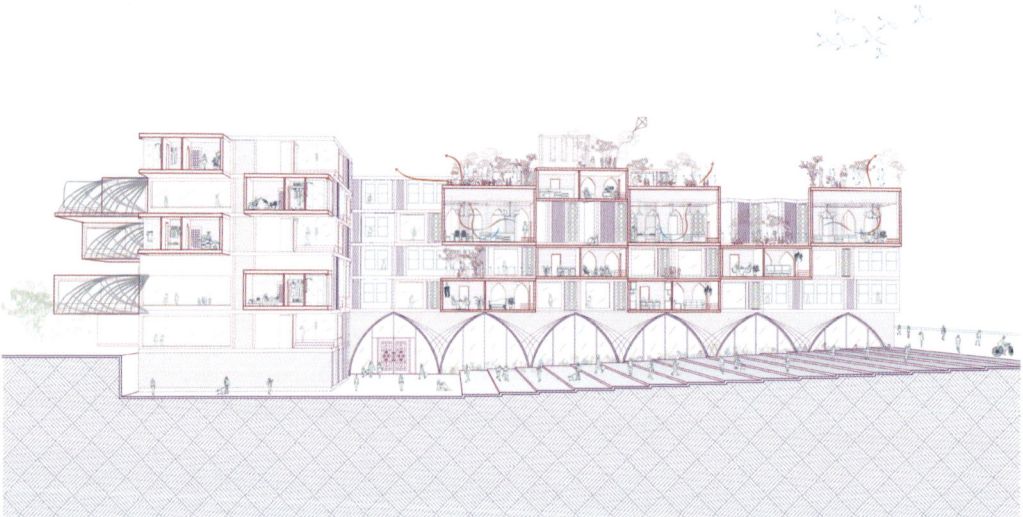

EAD.27

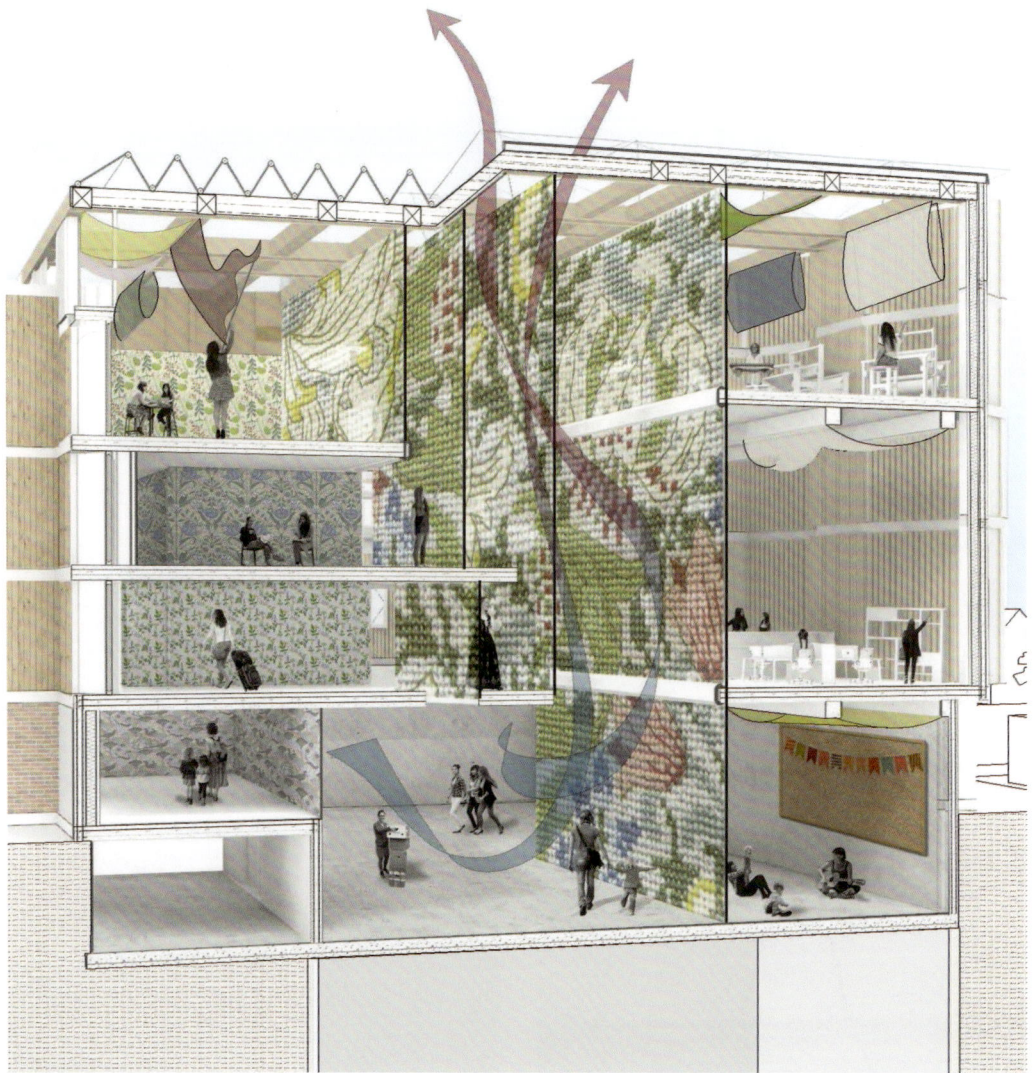

EAD.28

EAD.29

EAD.30

EAD.31

EAD.32

EAD.33

Architecture MSci
(ARB Part 1 and Part 2)

Architecture MSci (ARB Part 1 and Part 2)

Programme Director: Sara Shafiei

Architecture MSci is a new five-year programme that integrates the undergraduate and postgraduate study of architecture and includes a final year on placement at an architectural practice. During the first four years of study, students explore the design and construction challenges faced by the future of the built environment and learn how to incorporate specialist disciplinary information into creative, sophisticated design. Students examine relevant world issues through an annual theme that consists of broad architectural and social issues this year Health and Wellbeing. This theme, which extend across the years and modules, was examined from a local and global perspective that encompassed historical, current and future challenges.

As well as defining the relationship between students' learning and their participation in research, the programme offers a holistic approach to education. It encourages connections between disciplines, years of study, staff (practice-based and academic) and students. The programme promotes interdisciplinary questions and challenges, encouraging both staff and students to interrogate critically the nature of evidence and knowledge production across different subject fields in our digitally mediated world.

This year saw the second cohort of Architecture MSci students welcomed to the school. For both students and staff, it has been an opportunity to start something new and to break with traditions often considered fixed. The programme continues to challenge preconceived ideas of what architecture is and how we use and inhabit space. It encourages a culture of individual research, through testing and re-examining the fundamental elements of architecture. Students are asked to embark on a journey into the unknown and to embrace the experimental and forward thinking, as well as the mundane.

This year's work explores the theme of 'Health and Wellbeing'. The programme fosters a creative dialogue between design, digital and analogue representation, technology, history and theory to enable students to make informed yet creative decisions that are grounded in a real-life context.

Year 1 students explored architectural interventions along the (lost) course of the River Fleet from its source at the Vale of Health to Camden and the Regents Canal. Students were asked to respond creatively to complex site conditions, addressing the social, historical, technological, political and cultural narratives of the area. Students investigated the life cycle of materials used in the construction process to make sensitive yet ambitious design proposals, examining the impact of the annual theme of Health and Wellbeing through multiple lenses.

Year 1 Students
Rebeca Allen Tejerina, Temilola Animashaun, Jihoon Baek, Maria Balanuca, Jia Qi Chan, Jenny Cheng, Pauline Comte, Alice Coverton, Ilia Dynkin, Abdelrahman Eladawi, Anda Guinea, Charles Hayles, Divine-Dione Ifeobu-Zubis, Mohammed Jivanjee, James Kennedy, Tate Kiveal, Phoenix Koo, Yan (Charisse) Kwong, Jayne Lee, Ryan Long, Laura Lui, Ming (Leroy) Ma, Nan (Esther) Mei, Karin Metz, Matan Michaels, Sara Mir, May Parkes-Young, Katie Pitcher, Joseff Rowlands, Aiala Samula Lopez, Jasmine Shek, Matilda Sinclair, Gini Smart, Raihan Syed, Charles Timms, Thaleia Tsoutsos, Janssen Wong, Forrest Xie, Jennifer Yang, Yifei Yu, Lizhe (Enrique) Zhang Zhuo

Year 1 Staff
Sabina Andron, Matthew Barnett Howland, Megha Chand Inglis, Krina Christopoulou, Sam Coulton, Ruth Cuenca, Christina Dahdaleh, Stelios Giamarelos, Kostas Grigoriadis, Jessica In, Matthew Lucraft, Sara Martinez Zamora, Matei Mitrache, Giles Nartey, Danae Polyviou, Guang Yu Ren, Sara Shafiei, Alistair Shaw, Sabine Storp, Barry Wark, Patrick Weber, Andrew Whiting, Sal Wilson, Stamatios Zografos

Programme Administrator
Alice Whewell

1.1 Toby Prest, Anna Williams, Y2 'Repopulating Iffley Meadows: Community Housing on the Canal'. The scheme proposes a new rural typology for community housing that regenerates the landscape of Iffley Meadows through a model of environmental stewardship. The project responds to Oxford's housing crisis by increasing the value of flooded sites, otherwise deemed unusable by developers. This contemporary typology utilises buoyant structures, a modular thatching system and prefabricated cross-laminated timber (CLT) to provide a feasible strategy to inhabit Iffley Lock. In this way, the scheme facilitates the exchange between existing canal boaters and land-based communities through the provision of recreational space and amenities on the waterway. This culminates in an end-of-life strategy whereby the site is returned to the Oxford Green Belt, fully restored.

1.2 Ilia Dynkin, Y1 'Into the Earth'. This proposal explores the ritual of burial and its implications for the built form, questioning current practices while proposing a new approach to dealing with the passing of loved ones. The scheme explores the architectural translation of the sense of ritual and emotions involved in coping with death. Constructing elaborate performances for the living, its purpose is to continuously reinstate faith in the continuity of life. The proposal honours the dead, creating an ever-changing environment as a result of the burial process – a 'forest of memories' that glorifies and celebrates our passage through life.

1.3 Jia Qi Chan, Y1 'The Regenerative Refectory'. A community kitchen and garden located in the heart of the Wendling Estate in Camden. The project celebrates decay and the lifecycle of food through the experience of harvesting, cooking, eating and composting. Spaces are designed with a focus on cooking and eating as social acts. Visitors follow a curated culinary journey surrounding sycamore trees found on-site, picking herbs and vegetables grown along and within the façade of the building. The proposal functions as a self-sufficient system, with fallen leaves and food waste used to create compost which brings on the next lifecycle.

1.4 Janssen Wong, Y1 'Under the Surface'. A proposal for a water-quality monitoring station and museum along the intersection of Royal College Street and Baynes Street in Camden. The building is designed for the occupancy of two inhabitants, humans and water, with the purpose of providing a better understanding of water beyond its essential role in everyday life. Visitors follow the flow of the water in, out and around the building as the architecture exhibits the water in its different forms: drip, trickle, stream, sheet and cascade. At the same time, the building measures local water quality and its roof quills create a dynamic tectonic based on the data of a nearby monitoring station.

1.5 Jayne Lee, Y1 'Sensory Bakehouse'. The project proposes a breadmaking workshop and bakery in Fleet Road, Camden, to cater for bread lovers in the surrounding community. The building invites a sensory experience through an exploration of the natural and manual processes of breadmaking. A sensory journey for both the baker and the dough is emphasised through distinct spaces of varying internal climates and proportions. Roofs of varied heights, vaulted ceilings, rooflights, adjustable windows and building orientation facilitate the necessary temperatures, humidity levels and specific baking environments needed in each part of the process.

1.6 Forrest Xie, Y1 'Curious Building'. The project proposes to provide a workshop for Camden's local makers. In response to the visual interest – or rather, lack thereof – in the area immediately surrounding the site, a curious structure is conceived. Its skin serves as its outer layer of defence, carefully impeding while still allowing visual access into the building's inner layer. Its skeleton acts as a structure and allows the skin to be perceived as a rigid protective covering while maintaining its fluidity and softness. Carved spaces exist within the organs of the building – its most protected area – and act as a safe haven for the public and makers reclaiming Camden's craft community to gather, discuss, think and exhibit.

1.7 Yan (Charisse) Kwong, Y1 'Follow the Light'. A summer pre-school for young children in Woodland Walk, Camden. The project explores the 3D qualities of light borrowing from Barragán and Holl's spatial lighting techniques. Spaces in the building are organised so as to achieve specific lighting effects at precise times: a light 'crosswalk' appears across the foyer space at arrival and dismissal times, a gradient light corridor allows students' eyes to adjust and walls are spotlit at the start of scheduled class periods.

1.8 Jihoon Baek, Y1 'Hide-Out to Seek-Out'. A playground and teahouse for children and their parents sited on the Wendling Estate, Camden. Centred around the three sycamore trees on-site, key spaces such as play areas, workshops and tea stations are designed with the game of 'hide-and-seek' in mind, enhanced with light and sound. Partial blindspots and vantage points are created through viewing corridors, with diffused or reflective material to hide and reveal occupants from and to each other both within the building and out on the site.

1.9 All Students, Y1 'Making Architecture'. Photograph of the first-year cohort proposals.

1.2

1.3

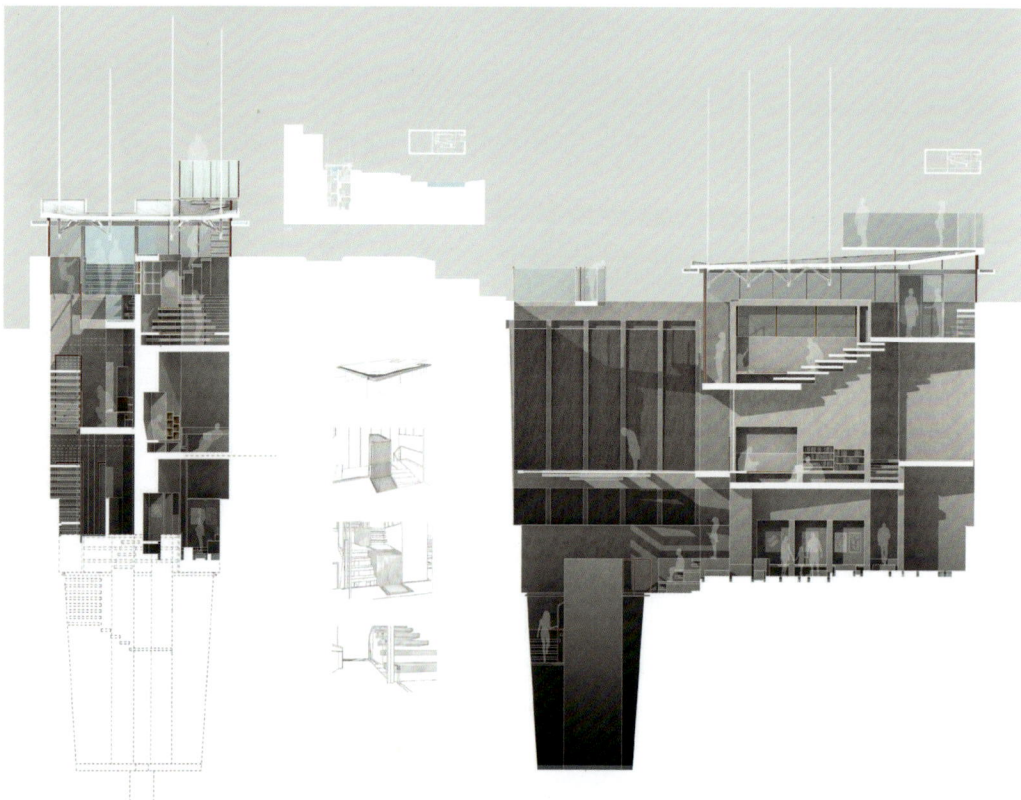

1.4

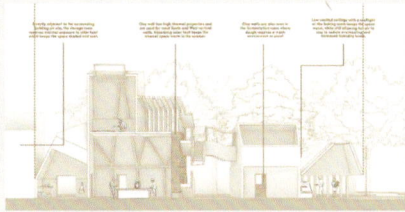

1.5

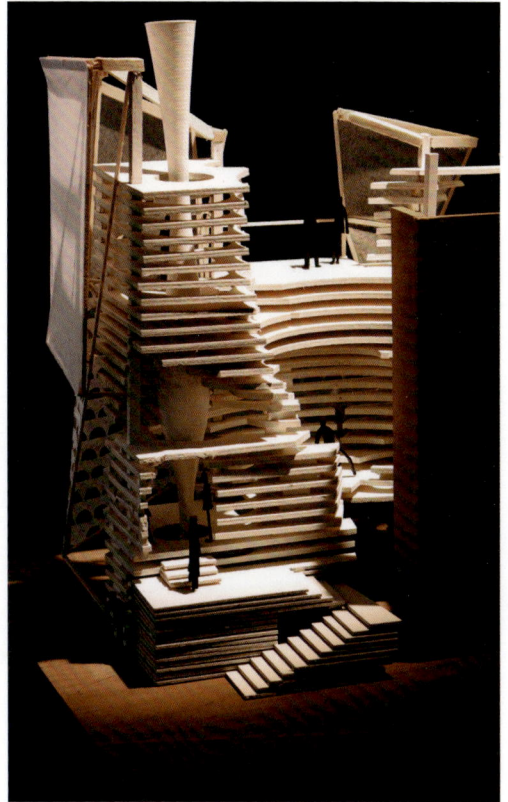

1.6

1.7

1.8

Studio 2A: Exchange

This year's work explores the sub theme 'Exchange' within the programme's annual theme of 'Health and Wellbeing'.

Has the urban and rural split become narrower now that digital communication has, for many, become normalised for work and social life? For certain privileged groups in the UK we see signs of a city-living exodus; work and home no longer need to be linked in close physical proximity. Our work-life balance has been challenged for better and worse as the Covid-19 pandemic and Brexit have created a mixture of opportunity and uncertainty. Contrary to this we see many in our society trapped and disenfranchised in urban and rural communities, with little opportunity for exchange or for gaining experience of the other. This lack of shared belonging is leading to entrenched polarisation in our communities. How can architecture challenge these divides and bring communities together? What might a new architecture of rural/urban exchange and belonging look like? Can we really 'build back better'?

Architecture MSci Year 2 students explored the architecture of exchange and belonging. They investigated these notions both physically and intellectually, relating the findings to past, present and future scenarios. Students examined places of trade, transaction and commerce, as well as buildings/land for learning and social/cultural exchange; they carefully curated spaces at urban/rural thresholds, with the intention of relating a new exchange architecture to both its local and broader social/political context.

Proposals were situated on the outskirts of Oxford. Here they investigated the relationship between a historically layered city, known for intellectual and commercial exchange, and the contrasting boundaries and hinterlands, interrogating the thresholds between rural and urban land.

Students were asked to consider current and future ideas of 'town and gown'. In so doing they explored how the urban and rural context – and the communities which exist within them – can come together in buildings of exchange and belonging. They also reflected on the ways in which we as designers can create an architecture that is inclusive and a natural place of sharing.

Proposals critically evaluated the programme's annual theme, considering the possibility for architecture to transform the lives of the diverse communities in Oxford through spaces that, directly and indirectly, improve the health and wellbeing of those they bring together, both human and non-human.

Year 2 Students
Maria Paola Barreca, Tabathu Crook, Hanna Eriksson Södergren, Xan Goetzee-Barral, Salyme Gunsaya, Samuel Jackson, Ismail Mir, Alannah Nethercott, Dominic Nunn, Toby Prest, Yutong Tang, Shuhan (Hansen) Wang, Anna Williams, Jun Zhang

Year 2 Design Unit Lead
Johan Hybschmann, Matthew Springett

Year 2 Staff
Matthew Barnett Howland, Megha Chand Inglis, Kevin Gray, Alice Hardy, Stefan Lengen, Tim Lucas, Matei Mitrache, Guang Yu Ren, Sara Shafiei, Alistair Shaw, Sabine Storp, Saptarshi Sanyal, Kathryn Timmins, Nina Vollenbroker, Barry Wark

Programme Administrator
Alice Whewell

2.1, 2.5 Toby Prest, Anna Williams, Y2 'Repopulating Iffley Meadows: Community Housing on the Canal'. The scheme proposes a new rural typology for community housing that regenerates the landscape of Iffley Meadows through a model of environmental stewardship. The project responds to Oxford's housing crisis by increasing the value of flooded sites, otherwise deemed unusable by developers. This contemporary typology utilises buoyant structures, a modular thatching system and prefabricated CLT to provide a feasible strategy to inhabit Iffley Lock. In this way, the scheme facilitates the exchange between existing canal boaters and land-based communities through the provision of recreational space and amenities on the waterway. This culminates in an end-of-life strategy whereby the site is returned to the Oxford Green Belt, fully restored.

2.2 Maria Paola Barreca, Xan Goetzee-Barral, Y2 'Gateway to the Hinterland'. Lying within the hinterland between Oxford and the surrounding flood-prone countryside, a food education centre is proposed to promote exchange through food's many facets: growing, collecting, serving, eating and disposing. The centre is embedded within the city's logistical food network and homeless community, acting as social infrastructure that provides spaces to improve health and wellbeing outcomes through food education. A modular construction system allows the building to adapt to Oxford's ever-changing social and environmental needs and to propose a replicable prototype. Water is collected by an extensive roof canopy, promoting a sensorial experience of the landscape and establishing the site as a gateway to the hinterland.

2.3 Tabatha Crook, Samuel Jackson, Y2 'Fabricating Safety'. The project strives for an architecture that modernises the current model of foster care for mothers and babies. The programme will improve the chances of mothers maintaining custody of their children through nurturing healthy relationships and providing a holistic education. These concepts are connected through an exchange between the public and those using the residential facilities. Screens and apertures play with the concept of visual porosity to ensure that there is a consistent connection between the foster carer, baby and mother. The scheme allows mothers to become more confident and independent and at the same time educates the community on the foster care system. This new model of care is the driving factor behind the architecture, unifying public and private, city and suburb, mother and child.

2.4 Hanna Eriksson Södergren, Jun Zhang, Y2 'Barton Portal'. Oxford is a city growing against a rural edge, with new developments forming vast residential areas and the need for public space for residents often ignored. The project proposes to create portals for interaction across Barton, currently an underdeveloped area. It creates a range of public spaces to increase social wellbeing, encouraging interaction and exchange between residents, including parts of the community that have been excluded through a box-ticking approach to Section 106 agreements.

2.6 Ismail Mir, Y2 'The Oxford Comm[Union]'. The project imagines a meeting space and visitor centre in the ecologically protected wetland meadows of Oxford. Why are crucial deliberations on climate typically held in the austere world of corporate architecture? The Comm[Union] is designed to merge harmoniously with its natural environment by considering both materials and spatial design. A series of transitional thresholds are curated between the human architecture and the natural architecture of hedgerows and grass. Visitors can immerse themselves in the natural richness of the site.

As such the architecture hopes to offer a new environment for vital deliberations on the climate where nature is both psychologically and physically brought to the fore, a pervasive reminder of the Earth's ecological rights.

2.7–2.8 Salyme Gunsaya, Alannah Nethercott, Y2 'Peasemoore Library: Carving a Place for New Marston'. Located on the University of Oxford's sports grounds, the low-lying library is composed of two principal strands which encourage collegiate and individual pursuits, respectively. Five periphery follies further mark local claim over the land. Given its social value, the existing pavilion façade is preserved within the auditorium at the heart of the scheme, becoming the central gathering point between the local and university communities. The subtractive use of local limestone ensures that Marston's democratic space of learning has the integrity and longevity typically only afforded to Oxford's exclusionary institutions. Strategic cuts in the stone walls focus views between both strands across a seasonal waterscape, creating a shared sense of motivation through watching others work.

2.9 Dominic Nunn, Shuhan (Hansen) Wang, Y2 'Reconciliation Landscapes'. The proposal is an experimental hydrology testing device which conserves Oxford's precious flood meadows by demonstrating their importance. The ancient plough-scarred meadows are augmented by a grid of plots bounded by water-channelling apparatus. Artificial flooding can be initiated and its impact on architecture and ecology trialled and adapted. The scheme serves as a research and education hub where studies are done against and in collaboration with the natural landscape and its cycles. The tests and their findings can be used as points of interest to bring the scientific community and the general public of Oxford together, while at the same time bringing them closer to nature and the opportunities it can provide.

2.3

2.4

2.5

2.6

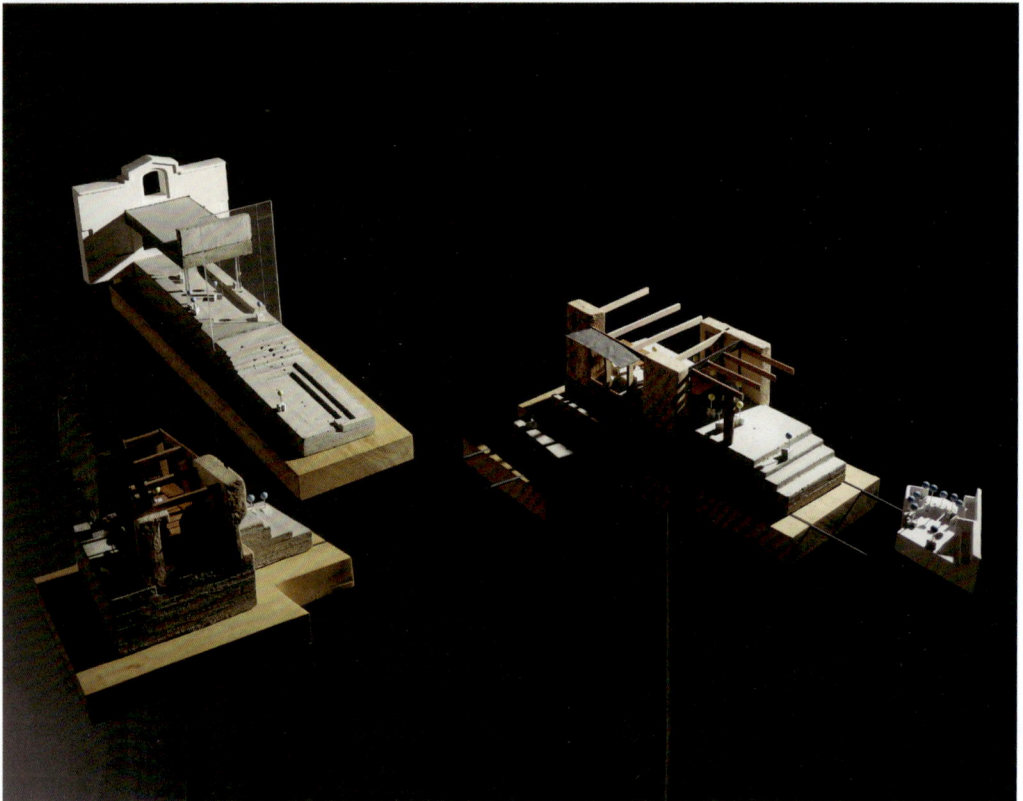

2.7

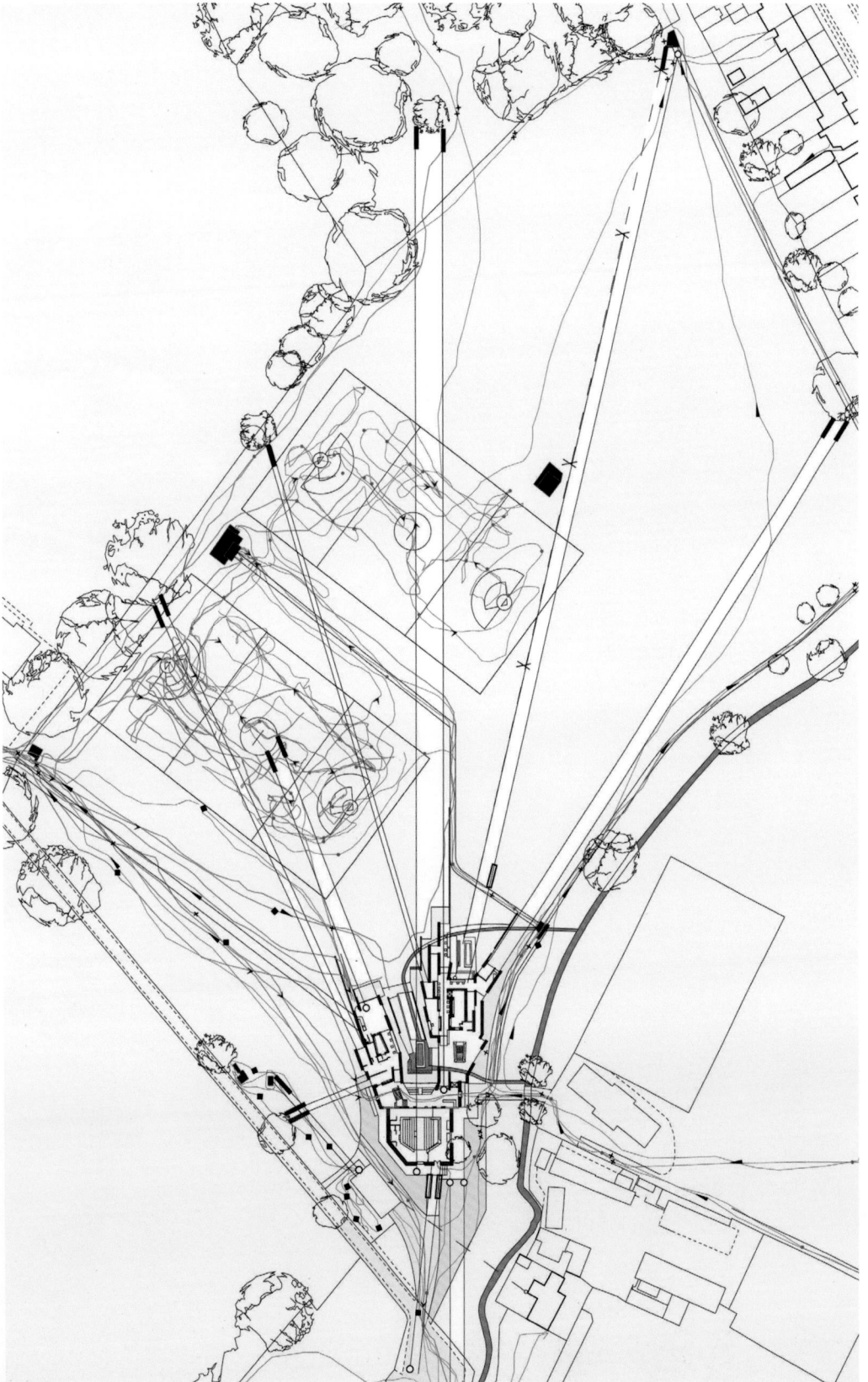

2.8

Architecture MArch
(ARB/RIBA Part 2)

Architecture MArch (ARB/RIBA Part 2)

Programme Directors:
Julia Backhaus, Marjan Colletti, Kostas Grigoriadis

Words, Works, Worth

Architecture MArch students provide content and context to their academic efforts by writing about architecture, designing architecture and scrutinising architecture – as a discipline, practice, culture and career choice.

Words

Architecture is bursting with technical jargon, acronyms and keywords that might appear puzzling to new students, only to gradually become assimilated into the everyday language of architectural students and professionals alike. Think of GAs (General Arrangement Drawings), BIM (Building Information Modelling), CAD (Computer-Aided Design), CNC (Computer Numerical Control), CFD (Computational Fluid Dynamics), HVAC (Heating Ventilation and Air Conditioning), LCA (Lifecycle Analysis), MDF (Medium-Density Fibreboard), LVL (Laminated Veneer Lumber), VR (Virtual Reality), ML (Machine Learning), AI (Artificial Intelligence), GA (Genetic Algorithms), GAN (Generative Adversarial Network), LWC (Light-Weight Concrete) and FRC (Fibre-Reinforced Concrete) to name but a few.

Architects also often use open, philosophical, scientific and sometimes metaphysical terms to talk about design, design processes and buildings – terms like becoming, emergence, morphogenesis, experimentation, iteration, seriality, metaphor, hybridity, adjacency and materiality.

This may not come as a surprise, since, as educators and designers, we so highly value the process of exploring, testing and researching ideas, sites, cultures, forms, functions, materials and solutions for architectural purposes. These terms acquire an altogether different meaning when used in an architectural context. Architectural vocabulary is constantly enriched with language derived from critical contemporary issues, such as the climate emergency or the passage of architecture into the information age.

Works

Attempting to author a thought-provoking essay, draw a complex detail or be inventive and innovative about a problem can be challenging at the best of times, with or without the implications of a pandemic. There is so much hard work and intelligence on display in this year's projects that words alone cannot suffice. As architects, we not only rely on words to strengthen our arguments but also engage with a multitude of visual examples, drawing styles and illustration techniques. These can be two-dimensional, or more often three-dimensional, four-dimensional and increasingly multi-dimensional, thanks to technologies that enable immersive and interactive works of architectural design to be experienced first-hand.

The images reproduced in this catalogue cannot do justice
to the complex and multi-layered projects developed throughout
a whole academic year, but they are proof of an incredible amount
of intuition, diligence and enthusiasm nurtured in the school.

Worth

Architecture is an ever-changing discipline that needs to survey, adopt
and adapt to societal developments. Change is difficult but necessary.
Business as usual is not a valid option when it comes to architecture's
plea towards equality, diversity and inclusivity for its makers and users;
its response to climate, ecology and sustainabilit; or its obligation to
improve the health, wealth and wellbeing of communities.

We believe that architecture can make a key contribution to
solving some of the most urgent problems of our times, with disciplinary
boundaries being broken; alternative socio-political, ecological and
material system-driven ideas being proposed; and new technological
advances being made to better both the built and natural environment
we all rely upon.

Let us look forward over the following pages and discover how
ethical and driven this cohort of future practitioners, academics and
scholars promise to be in terms of understanding their position in
architecture and society.

We hope that you will share the students' and tutors' enthusiasm
and optimism to make this world a better place. As programme
directors, we are privileged to work with passionate, conscientious
and insightful individuals who constitute the complex human ecology
this programme thrives in. Many of them are documented in this
catalogue. We would like to thank all our students, academics,
administrative staff, guests and visitors for their dedication and for
sharing their views.

Idiosyncrasy

Simon Dickens, CJ Lim

Idiosyncrasy in architecture and urbanism assumes many forms. The projects that fly in the face of reason are modern-day *wunderkammern* – crammed with randomly juxtaposed curiosity and with varying degrees of validity, they could empower the disenfranchised by embracing equality, diversity and identity.

From the metaphoric *Delirious New York* of Rem Koolhaas to the make-believe constructs of *The Truman Show's* Seahaven, Wes Anderson's *The Grand Budapest Hotel* and Gary Ross's *Pleasantville*, idiosyncrasy offers liminal conditions of being in a space somewhere between lived experience and fairytale possibility. The telling architectural-cultural episodes from Koolhaas proved, above all, the city's dedication to the most rational, efficient and utilitarian pursuit of idiosyncrasy.

Idiosyncrasy also comes in the form of micro-nations: the Vatican City inside Rome, the Principality of Sealand and the Danish island of Elleore, for example. Established as a gentle satire of the government structure and royal traditions of Denmark, Elleore has its own idiosyncratic traditions including a ban on the novel *Robinson Crusoe* (1719) and the use of 'Elleore Standard Time', which runs 12 minutes behind national Danish time. Locations of cities and communities can be equally eccentric and illogical. Tehran, Los Angeles, Kolkata, Tokyo, Jakarta and New Orleans all face a constant threat of potential calamity from earthquakes, monsoons, floods or tsunamis.

Our idiosyncratic weather and seasons can also be treated as resources. In the case of Jukkasjärvii's IceHotel in Sweden, ice is harvested for construction in late November from the frozen Tome river. By April the sun's rays have begun to melt the building and during June the IceHotel eventually dissolves completely into water. No two hotels are the same. From the river the ice came and to the river it shall return; all that remains are memories. In Djenné, Mali the immense undertaking of the epic one-day event known as the *crépissage* (plastering) ensures that the Great Mosque survives the brief but brutal rainy season. The shape of the mosque, along with the town's traditional adobe homes, alters ever so slightly each year.

Whether by bold environmental gestures or by subtle entrepreneurial spirit, our love affair with the city and its architecture is constantly rewritten. In the process, we build a fundamentally different idea of society at different times and in different places.

Year 4
Jasper Choi, Christopher Collyer, James Eaton-Hennah, Kin (Anson) Hau, Hanna Hendrickson-Rebizant, Francis Magalhaes Heath, Joseph Singleton, Kwan Yau Soo, Chuzhengnan (Bill) Xu

Year 5
Luke Angers, Yang Di, Shuwei Du, Tsun (Xavier) Lee, Shaunee Tan, Roman Tay, Rebeca Thomas

Technical tutors and consultants: Xiaoliang Deng, Philip Guthrie, David Roberts, Edmund Tan, Vilius Vizgaudis, Matthew Wells, Eric Wong

Critics: Peter Bishop, Andy Bow, Brian Girard, Simon Herron, David Roberts

10.1 James Eaton-Hennah, Y4 'Remaining Grounded: The Great British Staycation'. Idiosyncrasy is the interruption and provocation of everyday lives and routines through imaginative redefinitions of caution and logic. In partnership with Amazon, Flyme and the UK government, the proposal sees a reimagined Southampton Airport embrace the Covid-19 pandemic to redefine current notions of travel and retail for those choosing to remain grounded within the UK. During lockdown, airports – particularly domestic airports – sat disused and empty. At the same time, there was a rapid growth in 'staycations', with parts of the UK becoming overrun with British tourists. While addressing the environmental impact of air travel on the planet, the project harks back to the golden age of Victorian British seaside holidays and our yearning for Mediterranean landscapes.

10.2 Roman Tay, Y5 'The Un-forgetful Nature'. Idiosyncrasy is when forgetfulness erodes time, offering the wonder of the unfamiliar and new to disseminate origin stories. Colonisation has forced native communities to assimilate, losing both their culture and rights to their land. Situated on the salt flats of the Great Salt Lake Desert, the proposal starts by returning ownership of the sacred land to Native Americans to bring back its original identity. The uninhabitable landscape is infused with mythologies and beliefs to cultivate fresh water through the use of sea asparagus (samphire). Engagement with nature brings awareness of how changes in the forgotten communities could empower a country, while salt is a new resource for building climate resilience.

10.3 Shaunee Tan, Y5 'The Island of Water'. Idiosyncrasy is seeking refuge from the inhospitable, allowing us to yearn for what we often take for granted. Without human colonisation of the local ecology, how can the landscape provide all the resources required for living? Situated on Christmas Island, the project challenges the notion of yearning and critiques consumerist human behaviours. In a slow-paced development choreographed by nature, the new inhabitable landscape acts as an interface for the symbiotic relationship between ecology and humans, striking a balance between nature and the built form. This education and research community provides a radical repositioning of what constitutes 'living within our means', suggesting that for humans to be saved from themselves, they must first protect nature.

10.4 Shuwei Du, Y5 'Freetown'. Idiosyncrasy is the ability to embrace climate malfunction, offering the potential to balance inequalities and foresee social and environmental metamorphosis. Subject to devastating flooding and uneven development, Jaywick, a coastal village in Essex, has been named one of the most deprived areas in Britain. Adopting the philosophy of the Freetown movement, Jaywick respects nature and harnesses the inexhaustible free resources of sea-level rises to liberate its citizens from the economic burden, material limitation, spiritual bondage and political restriction of a capitalist and consumerist society. In an exploration of the opportunities at the threshold of an equal society, waste mountains, wind farms, swallows' nests, Cypress forests, vineyards and amphibious housing replace infertile land, planning restrictions, administrative inaction, poverty, unemployment, food insecurity and even health crises.

10.5 Christopher Collyer, Y4 'The House of Wisdom'. Idiosyncrasy is found in the in-between world, a superimposed refuge made from what was stolen and where forbidden knowledge of one's own reality is discovered. Located at the border between Egypt and Sudan, an arid, rocky desert at the intersection of disputed colonial borderlines, the architecture is a place of temporary settlement and pilgrimage for Egyptian and Sudanese women who have been denied an education. Alongside their studies, they work among light gardens, which harvest solar energy and nurture the newly greened land. The women subvert the traditional notion of male wisdom with ancient Earth-wisdom, utilising the ground, water, wind and sun to cultivate shelter and sustainable peace across borders, with shade being the key protagonist.

10.6 Yang Di, Y5 'Mount Epistle'. Idiosyncrasy is the attempt to engage human interactions in order to alter time, space and convention to attain self-consistency without reliance on technology. The civic infrastructure explores the potential of paper, namely through handmade paper-crafting during the day and a public letter-writing hub at night, reclaiming lost crafts and tactility with our surroundings and humanity. Renamed Mount Epistle, the old Mount Pleasant Mail Centre is an alternative public space that offers opportunities for human interaction and provides Londoners with a refuge from digital technologies. The shape of the mountainous truss beams and the plans are derived from the love letters of Henry VIII, who is believed to be the founder of the Royal Mail.

10.7 Tsun (Xavier) Lee, Y5 'The City: Falling/Fallen'. Idiosyncrasy is a scar from hell, sprinkled with love. Like society's outcasts, the Kowloon Walled City has been a scar on governance and misunderstood by the rest of Hong Kong. The project is a social commentary on the current situation in Hong Kong. Light, water, air and sound are brought together in a vast and complex urban development as a metaphor for empowerment. Each protagonist responds to their specific functional calling and is no longer frowned upon but is a true saviour of the city. By this twist of fate, the reimagined Kowloon Walled City – once believed to be hell – is a love letter to the lost freedom and independence of old Hong Kong.

10.8 Rebeca Thomas, Y5 'Mr Murakami's Place'. Idiosyncrasy is repeatedly carrying out the futile Sisyphean tasks that are unlikely to offer answers to the questions of climate change. Told through the nine lives of Haruki Murakami's cat, the nine protagonists (from nine of Murakami's novels) travel to the very 'end of the world' in search of the author-cum-agony uncle for answers. Instead of meeting the author, they are met with nine futile tasks, which they must endure for nine days. Within the extreme climatic context, the metaphor of the feline forms the architectural constructs on unresolved, uncertain and curious islands. By the ninth day, just like the endings in Murakami's novels, the protagonists leave without answers, with only memories of hope to help them reflect on their personal impact on the environment.

10.9 Luke Angers, Y5 'The United Natures of Yestermorrow'. Idiosyncrasy is the expression of unexplainable, unpredictable and unaccountable phenomena, perceived through the anomalies of chance. Under the guise of environmental protection, preventing sea-level rise and cooling the Arctic, the United States performs a covert land reclamation of the ice floes in the Bering Strait. The Americans surreptitiously salvage drifting ice to grow the footprint of Little Diomede year-round, creating a landmass ever closer to the surface area of Russia's Big Diomede. The 'gift' of world diplomacy in the form of the UN headquarters is akin to a Trojan horse, disguising the export of American nuclear waste to the farthest corner of their territory. The new American architectural espionage is offered as a model of sustainable environmental design, generating warmth for the delegates' accommodations and diplomacy at the speakers' tables.

10.3

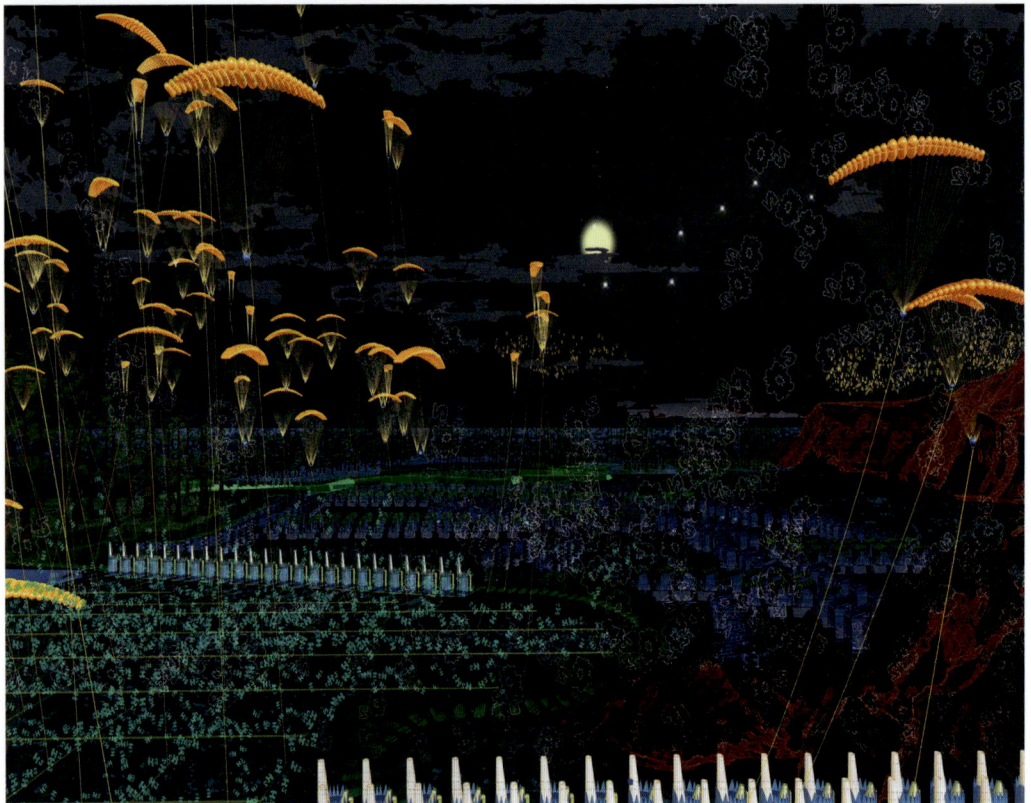

10.4

MOUNT EPISTLE
10.6

11.1

The Progress Paradox

Laura Allen, Mark Smout

PG11 continues to challenge the paradoxes of preservation versus progress and wilderness versus culture. We examined the radical, even revolutionary ideas that stitch together the past, present and future, revealing the cultural and political complexity of the built environment. In a world more dangerous yet more open to opportunity than ever, these notions are also affected by 'the progress paradox' – the more forward progress is made, the more problems are created.

Our interest in environments that exhibit displacement, restoration, redundancy, progress, dormancy and future living is exemplified by the UK's National Parks. Initiated by the 19th-century 'Freedom to Roam' movement, large areas of land are now protected by law for the benefit of the nation. This is due to their special and particular qualities of countryside, wildlife and cultural heritage.

Until relatively recently little acknowledgement was given to thinking about nature as a system. Boundaries were laid out according to convenient political or economic interests rather than to reflect ecological realities. As keystone institutions of environmental conservation, the parks are operated as managed systems: 'interactive ecologies' of people, nature, landscape and infrastructure. Charged with protecting fragile ecosystems and vulnerable regional identities, they also – more now than ever – act as outdoor playgrounds.

The National Parks, themselves often cultural paradoxes, are also influenced by political activities and decisions. Changes taking place outside their boundaries can have a tremendous impact on preservation efforts within. This can result in damage to local economies and environments, overloaded rural infrastructure and even threats to their conservation goals and nature reserve status, particularly where the weight of tourism is unsustainable.

This year students looked at temporal and spatial cultural scenarios to reveal underlying processes that continue to affect our built and natural environment, our societal institutions and the fascinating consequences of adapting the cultural imaginary. They asked how legislated territories should accommodate cultural and environmental changes and how future transformations in society and the natural environment could be reflected in the built environment. Students also explored the role of architecture in a complex 'interactive ecology'. Finally they considered what might be the implications – and, more importantly, the opportunities – of designing architecture for uncertainty and alternative futures.

Year 4
Harry Andrews, Chia-Yi Chou, Yu (Pearl) Chow, Ka Chun (Mark) Ng, Charles Pye

Year 5
Theo Clarke, Michael Holland, Justin Lau, Kit Lee-Smith, Rory Martin, Iga Świercz, Yun (Kenny) Tam, Annabelle Tan, Zifeng Ye

Technical tutors and consultants: Rhys Cannon (Gruff Architects Ltd), Stephen Foster (Foster Structures), Ioannis Risoz, (Atelier Ten)

Thesis supervisors: Gillian Darley, Kelly Doran, Murray Fraser, Daisy Froud, Elise Hunchuck, David Rudlin, Tania Sengupta, Oliver Wilton

Critics: Barbara-Ann Campbell-Lange, Doug John Miller, Aisling O'Carroll, Alicia Pivaro, Tim Waterman

11.1 Zifeng Ye, Y5 'Anxious Nostalgia'. This project is a study into Shanghai's waning living space, combining typological research into the city's disappearing *lilong* neighbourhoods with speculative reimaginings of modern domestic space. The project seeks to reinvigorate old communities and encourage ad-hoc spatial appropriation in the otherwise regimented cosmopolis.

11.2 Chia-Yi Chou, Y4 'Foreston Keynes: Carbon Capture in a Progressive Town'. Milton Keynes has always been an experimental city that leads bold future-proofing schemes. Responding to the city's ambition of becoming carbon-neutral, the building captures carbon dioxide and generates carbon credits. It also erects a new image that celebrates and reshapes the modernist town.

11.3 Harry Andrews, Y4 'The Park Ascending'. The project provides protective measures against the physical pressures and impacts of tourism by amplifying the sense of place. By restoring an emotional connection with the landscape, the proposal reveals the undiscovered networks of lost navigational methods in the national parks.

11.4 Ka Chun (Mark) Ng, Y4 'Casting Redcar'. In response to the demolition of the Redcar Steelworks complex, the project envisages a landscape archive and research centre where Redcar's industrial heritage will be celebrated and remediation of soilscapes will be carried out over a 50-year span. Sited in the unique slag region of South Gare, the design explores both landscape casting and tilt-up construction as ways of revealing the industrial scars of the contaminated site and as an opportunity for phytoremediation of the polluted landscape.

11.5 Yun (Kenny) Tam, Y5 'Keystone Architecture: A Wilding Experiment'. The project challenges architecture's role in nature by mimicking ecological interaction with endangered species. The proposal stitches together five keystone architectures along the Ledge Route to the summit of Ben Nevis. It encourages visitors to participate in a wilding experiment, while at the same time generating empathy for these fragile spaces.

11.6–11.7 Justin Lau, Y5 'Simulating National Parks'. In the age of ecological emergency, is it time for our capital to become Britain's newest national park to safeguard our agriculture, water, energy and people? Roughly 47% of London is made up of green space. This green space is a vital asset in building a climate-resilient city that can combat rising temperatures and flash floods. The project reverses the traditional notion of national parks in rural settings and uses ecology as a form of architectural construction for London's industrial landscapes.

11.8 Annabelle Tan, Y5 'Past, Present and Post-Tropicality'. Colonial spectres and contemporary evolutions of tropicality continue to shape Singapore. Framing tropicality in terms of scarcity and affordance, the proposal unmakes neo-colonial vestiges of tropical solutions and remakes a 'nature-ficial' landscape of affordance. By linking a threatened forest to a nationally recognised nature reserve, the scheme dissects social and physical ideas of scarcity, creating a new set of values around productive and performative dwelling practices that synthesise nature and culture and lead towards a nascent monument of post-tropicality.

11.9 Iga Świerc, Y5 'Moving Upwards: Mimicking Mersea's Resilient Relocation'. The diverse ecosystem and community of Mersea Island, Essex, are under threat of extensive coastal erosion and flooding. To address this issue, a new managed retreat is proposed. The self-made Mersea Commons design plan supports the community in creating a common methodology for the relocation. Designed with the input of the community, local and bioregional scales allow for multiple futures for the new Mersea Commons. The participatory citizen science model recognises and addresses the needs of the residents of Mersea Island while enabling the renewal and preservation of its ecosystem.

11.10 Michael Holland, Y5 'A Peat Protopia'. This research and restoration facility is dedicated to furthering our understanding of peatland habitats through an architecture in constant conversation with the landscape. The building systematically restores damaged peat through a cyclical process of saturation, while simultaneously questioning wider discussions of land ownership, sustainable land management and rewilding.

11.11 Theo Clarke, Y5 'Hijacking the Elan Valley'. The project leverages the existing rich hydrological landscape of the Elan Valley reservoir system in Wales to impose an infrastructural energy-buffering stratum across the valley's vast watershed. The carefully orchestrated pumped hydro system creates the framework for a 'buffering town', a quasi-bulwark/communal housing development where one can experience the extremes of whitewater rapids passing underfoot, while tending an allotment, before a game of lawn tennis.

11.12–11.13 Rory Martin, Y5 'Tales from the Flood'. As the people of Morfa Borth, Wales, discover their town will no longer receive the necessary sea wall defence funding to protect them from rising sea levels, the residents band together to preserve the soul of their community by mobilising to start their journey to higher ground and safety.

11.14–11.15 Kit Lee-Smith, Y5 'Transboundary Massif'. The project questions the need for Portland cement in the Albertine Rift in Africa, and instead explores the potential of geopolymer cement from mine tailings in north Burera, Rwanda. The project integrates community construction within Rwanda's extraction policy, minimising building footprints in this densely populated area. It proposes a 'construction-arium' to express, explore and educate inhabitants, utilising and stabilising past industrial scarring through geopolymeric lateritic soil blends and techniques.

11.16 Charles Pye, Y4 'Ruining the Road'. The project encourages the abandonment of motor vehicles within the city, while simultaneously saving the UK's national parks from increased environmental damage. City roads also undergo reform, nurturing new national park typologies within the urban fabric.

11.17 Yu (Pearl) Chow, Y4 'Snowdonia Plant-nation'. A paper mill for the e-commerce giant Amazon within a carbon-offsetting tree plantation in Wales. The project tackles themes of exploitation and codependency between the urban and the natural, and explores the power dynamic between the money-hungry and the carbon-hungry. It serves as a pioneering project through its use of locally sourced timber from the surrounding forest and its derivatives produced as by-products during the cardboard-making process.

11.2

11.3

11.4

11.6

11.7

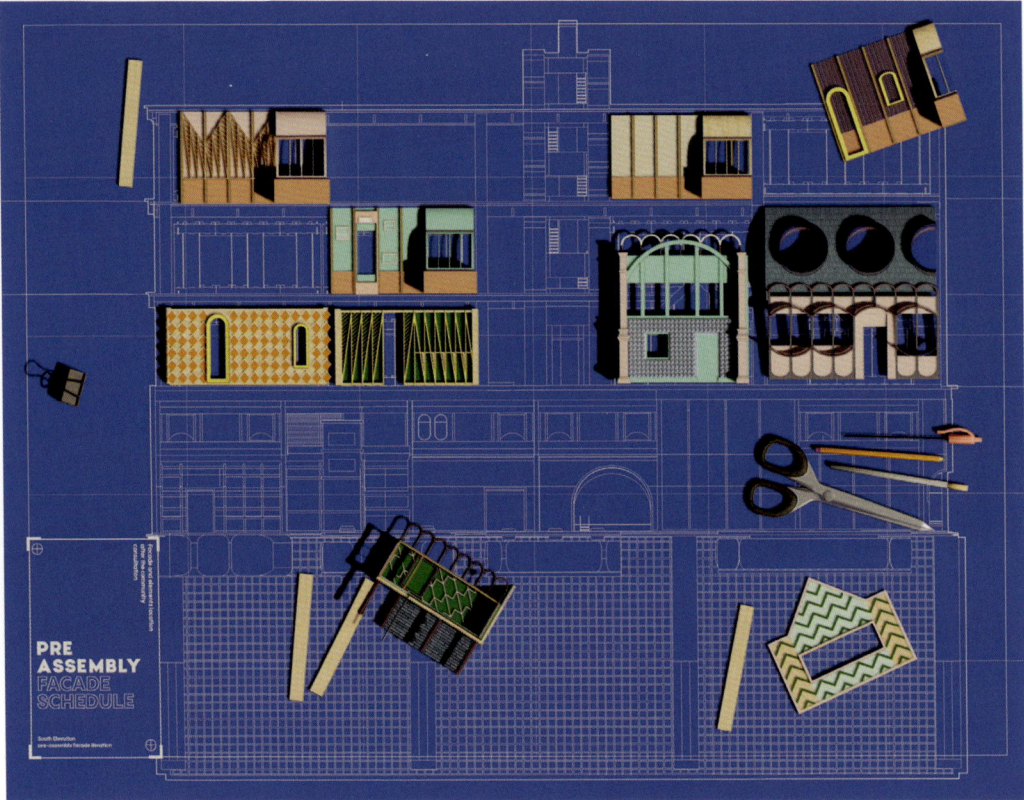

11.9

11.10

11.12

11.13

11.14

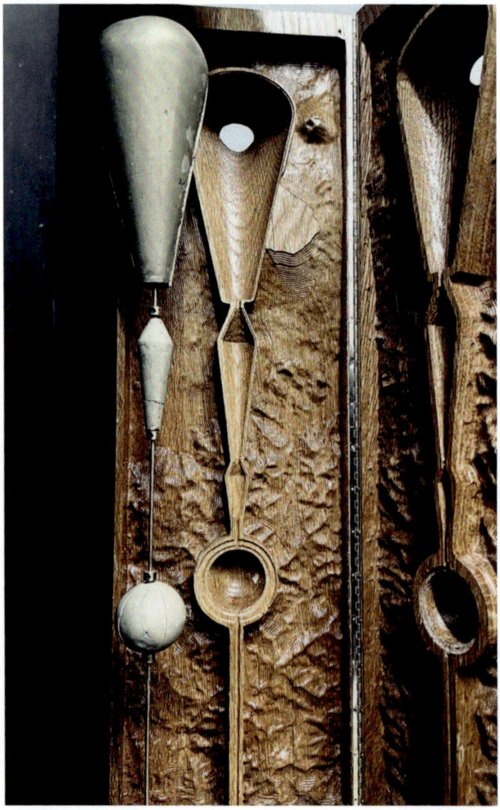

11.15

11.16

11.17

12.1

Architect as Storyteller: Forest City

Elizabeth Dow, Jonathan Hill

We expect a story to be written in words, but it can also be delineated in drawing, cast in concrete or sown in soil. Such tales have special significance when they resonate back and forth between private inspiration and public narrative. Conceiving the architect as a storyteller places architecture at the centre of cultural production, stimulating ideas, strategies and emotions. Exceptional architects are also exceptional storytellers.

While a prospect of the future is implicit in many novels, it is explicit in many designs. Some architects conceive for the present; others imagine for a mythical past, while yet others design for a future time and place. Alternatively, an architect can envisage all three in a single structure. To understand what is new, we need to consider the present, the past and the future: we need to think historically. Our concern is the relevance of the past – recent or distant – to the present and future, even as we speculate on the question: how and why might this happen now?

As well as history in its broader sense, we are interested in personal history. PG12 encourages students to develop a personal collection of ideas, values and techniques that reflects their unique outlook.

Our project brief for the year was the Forest City. We considered the city as a place of nature and growth, and the forest as a state that connects air to earth, climate to geology. We observed how each forest, city or building is a complex ecosystem, teeming with creatures and subject to their rhythms, intertwined in a network of relations with other life forms, including humanity.

The Forest City, being analogous to an ever-changing ecosystem, should be more temporally aware than other architectures. It requires constant re-evaluation, encouraging and questioning the creative relations between objects, spaces and occupants at varied dimensions, scales and times. Multiple iterations of the Forest City were designed and redesigned, both literally and allegorically. With the forest journey acting as a metaphor of the imagination, each project was founded upon the stories that students conceived, the research that they undertook and the architectural languages that they developed and honed across the year.

Year 4
Theodosia (Ted) Bosy-Maury, Giorgos Christofi, Silvia Galoforo, Pierson Hopgood, James (Kai) McLaughlin, Joe Watton

Year 5
Caitlin Davies, Lola Haines, Theodore Lawless Jones, Jaqlin Lyon, Sijie Lyu, James Robinson, Felix Sagar, Gabrielle Wellon, Tianzhou Yang, Yunshu (Chloe) Ye

Technical tutors and consultants: James Hampton, Chloe Hurley, James Nevin

Thesis supervisors: Gillian Darley, Stephen Gage, Christophe Gérard, Stelios Giamarelos, Polly Gould, Elise Hunchuck, Thomas Pearce, Guang Yu Ren, Oliver Wilton, Stamatios Zografos

Critics: Alessandro Ayuso, David Buck, Carolyn Butterworth, Barbara-Ann Campbell-Lange, Kate Cheyne, James Hampton, Penelope Haralambidou, Jessica In, Chee-Kit Lai, Constance Lau, Thandi Loewenson, Artemis Papachristou, Barbara Penner, Rahesh Ram, Elin Söderberg, Jonathan Tyrrell, María Venegas Raba, Dominic Walker, Dan Wilkinson, Fiona Zisch

12.1 James Robinson, Y5 'Martian Migrators: The Non-Essential Essentials of Thriving on Mars'. The project examines how humans might flourish on Mars. The notion of thriving is explored through the development and success of humans and architecture in the inhospitable environment of Mars. Components of Martian thriving are questioned through individual and large-scale studies.

12.2, 12.3 Caitlin Davies, Y5 'For Peat's Sake: A DEFRA Institute of Agricultural & Architectural Research'. Proposed as the new seventh division of the Department for Environment, Food and Rural Affairs (DEFRA), the institute acts as a site where agricultural and architectural research can be developed in tandem. By moving government offices to the remote peat bogs of the Yorkshire Dales, the project reframes nature as the building's primary occupant and explores how architecture can be an active participant in the conservation of these damaged landscapes.

12.4, 12.5 Tianzhou Yang, Y5 'A Sanctuary for Chinese Calligraphy in the Desert'. This project explores ways to preserve the art of calligraphy and its spirit of independence in an ever-changing political and cultural environment. Located in the harsh environment of the Gobi Desert in north-west China, the sanctuary is far from the political and urban madding crowd, in the hope that unwanted hands are kept away from the masterpieces of calligraphy. The centre allows calligraphers to study these masterpieces in peace, so that recognisable versions can continually contribute to the preservation of cultural heritage.

12.6, 12.7 Felix Sagar, Y5 'The Chalk Works: Chalk-Based Renovation, Remediation and Regeneration'. Through establishing wider systems of material industrial symbiosis and methods of tailored chalk-based renovation, this project proposes the use of waste chalk 'filter cake' to renovate, remediate and regenerate the derelict Shoreham Cement Works, converting it into a 'Chalk Works' – a construction school which offers an alternative material-driven curriculum.

12.8 James (Kai) McLaughlin, Y4 'Staging Liminality'. The project explores ways in which effective cultural hybridisation can mobilise direct forms of productive ecological and societal change. It proposes the construction of a Japanese Noh theatre on the site of a recently demolished lighthouse on the shingle spit of Orford Ness. The scheme uses reconstruction as a ritually resilient practice to act alongside this dynamic landscape of coastal erosion. These rituals of construction are superimposed onto a wider shingle restoration scheme, blurring the boundaries between performance, restoration, participation and construction.

12.9–12.11 Lola Haines, Y5 'A Debate in the Dark'. How can we have more accessible ways of seeing and sharing our riverscapes? This project provides an alternative way of engaging with our riverscapes. An eco-political initiative of dark sky river corridors addresses distinct yet overlapping subjects: water and light pollution, climate change and flooding, and social and economic migration.

12.12 Jaqlin Lyon, Y5 'Cold Comforts and Savoury Air: A Hospital for Bodies and Buildings'. Through the dialectic of illness and repair, the project explores notions of care at the scales of body and building. Treating an array of illnesses which at times overlap in surreal and theatrical operations, the hospital conflates past, present and future narratives within the crumbling city of Kiruna in northern Sweden.

12.13, 12.15 Theodore Lawless Jones, Y5 'A Weird Pub in the Middle of Nowhere'. Bizarre carvings on the King Stone monolith on Stanton Moor posit a pictorial and literary conundrum in which Charles Dickens's imaginary realm enters the actual. Both the real and fictitious worlds exist as vignettes in an inverted presentation of the mundane to deliver a body of junctures and phenomena celebrating the mystery.

12.14 Joe Watton, Y4 'Of Sheep, Stone & Hedgerows'. The project responds to the recent developer-led expansion of Axminster, a historic agricultural market town in East Devon. The current masterplan is used as a testbed to develop a more socially and ecologically responsive vernacular derived from the centuries-old network of Devon hedgerows which currently occupy the site.

12.16–12.18 Sijie Lyu, Y5 'Getting Lost in the Woods'. We are obsessed with the undistorted quality of glass but overlook its magical potential. The project challenges the limited range of applications glass is currently afforded within the built environment. Material choices in the proposal often counter building conventions, demonstrating the performative and theatrical side to a new architecture located in the Black Forest, Germany.

12.19 Giorgos Christofi, Y4 'Re-Fertilising Gaia'. The Temple of Gaia (goddess of the Earth) is located between the city of Kalambaka and the Meteora forest in Greece. The Ancient Greek ritual of Thesmophoria is revived in the temple in an effort to encourage the regrowth of the forest in exchange for human fertility.

12.20 Pierson Hopgood, Y4 'Lore of the Land'. The New Epping Commune, an evolving school of craft and construction, explores the long-lasting metaphorical connection between storytelling and craft. The project focuses on the importance of using one's hands and building a deeper spiritual connection with the process of making.

12.21 Theodosia (Ted) Bosy Maury, Y4 'Spinning Ruins'. This is an alternative history in which the Crescent Wool Warehouse in Wapping is adapted and added to by two artists in alternation. Over the course of several decades, the pair make an accretive theatre, constructed of salvaged materials, castings, rubble aggregates and wool, which filters and stores storm surge water.

12.22 Silvia Galofaro, Y4 'San Siro: Destroying and (Re)building an Icon'. The project reimagines the iconic San Siro Stadium in Milan, scheduled for demolition in 2026, by reanalysing the contemporary notion of iconoclasm. By referencing the Duomo Cathedral of Milan and the Veneranda Fabbrica del Duomo guild, the project explores the process of reverse quarrying through the Roman technique of *spolia*.

12.23 Gabrielle Wellon, Y5 'Freedom to Roam'. The project presents a proposal for a more progressive right to roam in England that encourages greater inclusivity and access to open space. By extending the right to a wider variety of landscapes and designated open-access buildings, the proposal intends to encourage roaming, both internally and externally. Situated in the context of Wiltshire's private estates, the constructed spatial narrative is based on the allegorical Wiltshire 'everywoman', Ruby.

12.2

12.3

12.4

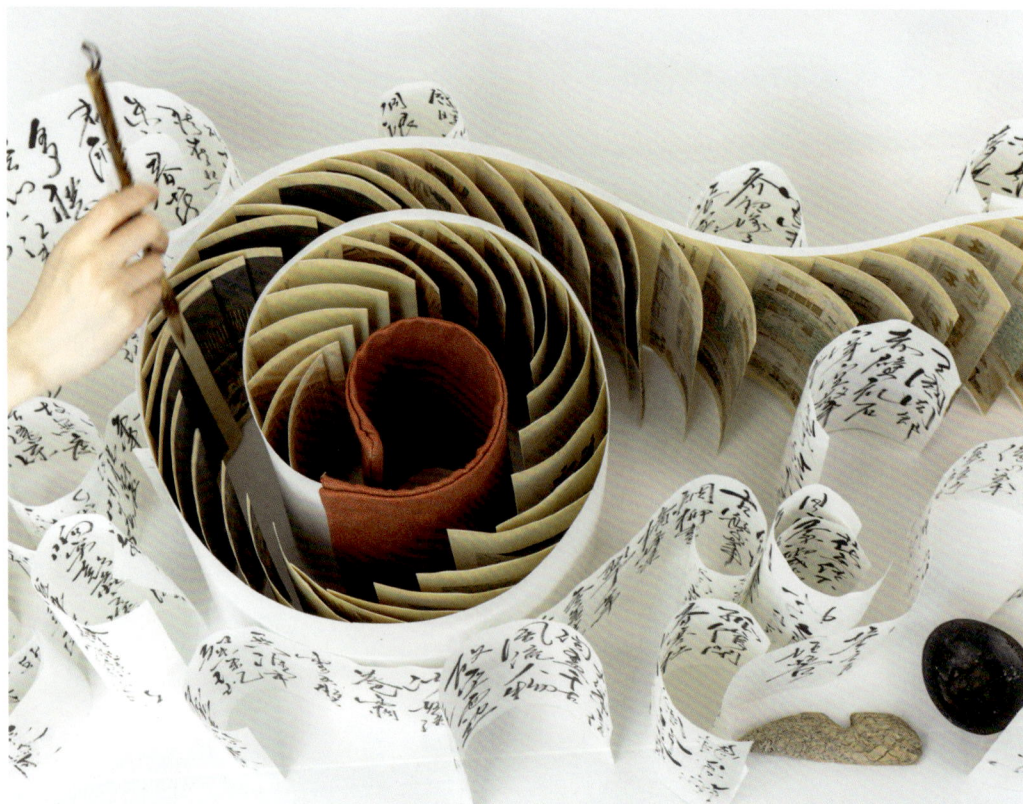

12.5

12.6

12.7

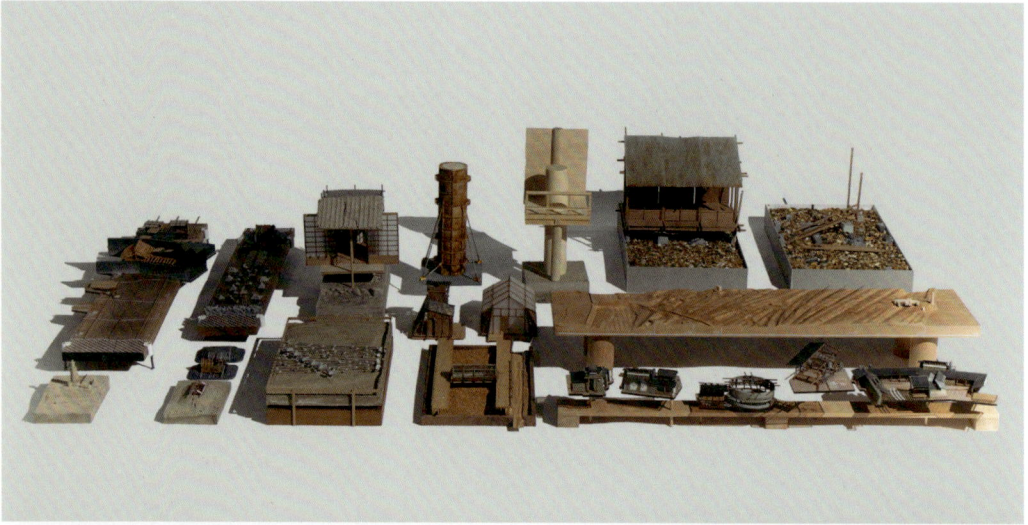

12.8

12.9

12.10

12.11

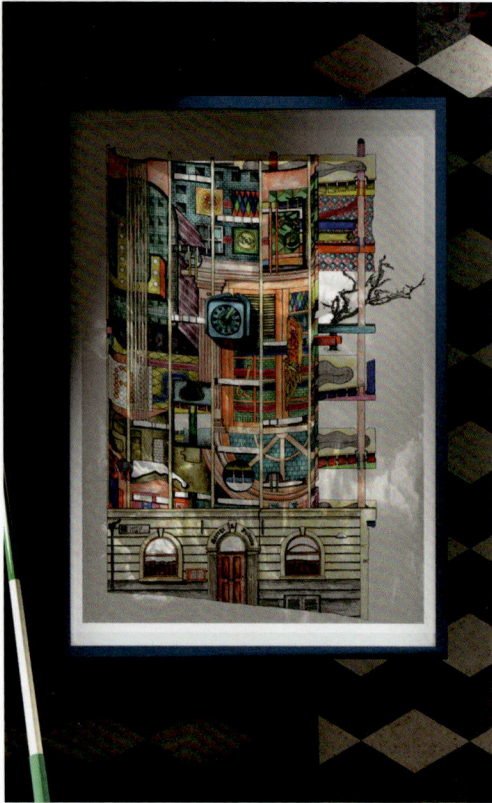

12.13

12.14

12.15

12.16

12.17

12.18

12.19

12.20

12.21

12.22

13.1

A Festival of the Mundane PG13

Sabine Storp, Patrick Weber

The Everyday 01

Most of us have been locked in the cycle of the everyday for the last two years of lockdowns and quarantines: stuck in the same space, the same rooms and the same routines. The monotony of the everyday has become a mental health issue, with little to no chance to break out of the vicious cycle.

Everyday life is an amorphous concept. We all seem to refer to it as a universal state, but on close inspection each of us occupies a very particular and very personal 'solo-verse'. At the same time, the extraordinary situation that Covid-19 produced suddenly put the spotlight on the simple things that have become important to us. The pandemic forced us to reset our relationship with how, where and why we inhabit; challenging our habits has been an interesting experience.

The Everyday 02

During his lifetime, it is estimated the Dutch painter Johannes Vermeer (1632–1675) completed around 50 paintings, of which 35 clearly attributed works survive today. Most depict domestic scenes celebrating the lives of ordinary people. It is remarkable that of these 35 paintings at least 19 were painted in the same room, often using the same subjects. Vermeer was not very successful during his lifetime and after his death was largely forgotten. Painting the everyday did not bring him any fame.

The scenes he portrayed may seem mundane, yet each painting is constructed using a precise array of props – pieces of furniture, domestic items and garments. Each element has been carefully chosen, playing a predetermined part in an everyday story. The real subjects of Vermeer's paintings are not the characters depicted; they are rather the everyday space, the light and the materiality of the objects painted.

This year PG13 explored the 'everyday'. We looked in detail at how we live together, how we inhabit space and the routines that inform architectures. We investigated common materials and traditional fabrication methods to challenge ourselves. The everyday does not need to be boring; it is the responsibility of the individual to elevate it to greatness.

The everyday is the measure of all things. Guy Debord

Year 4
Patricia Bob, Ernest Chin, Dilshod Perkins, Malgorzata Rutkowska, Hester Tollit, Maya Whitfield

Year 5
Nikhil (Isaac) Cherian, Agata Malinowska, Thabiso Nyezi, Jolanta Piotrowska, Muyun Qiu, Callum Richardson, Thomas Smith, Chloe Woodhead, Chenwei Ye

Technical tutors and consultants: James Hampton, Chloe Hurley, James Nevin

Thank you to Jenna de Leon, Edoardo Tibuzzi (Structural Engineer, AKT II), Tom Greenhill (Environmental Engineer, Max Fordham)

Thesis supervisors: Paul Dobraszczyk, Jane Hall, Claire McAndrew, Guang Yu Ren, Oliver Wilton

Critics: Barbara-Ann Campbell-Lange, Doville Ciapaite, Luke Draper, Sahra Hersi, Marjut Lisco, Inigo Minns, Maxwell Mutanda, Zahira el Nazer, Paolo Zaide

13.1, 13.17 Callum Richardson, Y5 'Ministry of the Inevitable'. Our climates are fragile and ever-changing. Since the dawn of the Anthropocene, our effect on the landscape has increased exponentially, yet governments across the globe remain fractured and unwilling to form a unified response to the climate emergency. The project contributes to a collective urban memory of experience and knowledge. One of the barriers to change is the lack of willpower necessary from those in power; the ministry aims to challenge this.

13.2–13.3 Chenwei Ye, Y5 'Tea Parliament'. The project questions current non-interventionist models of forest preservation triggered by the Chinese government's propagandistic intentions in Longjing, Hangzhou. The architecture forms part of a new community forest, which aims to empower residents to participate in forest administration and ecological preservation. In centuries to come, the architecture and people will be gone, but the forest will remain and thrive.

13.4 Nikhil (Isaac) Cherian, Y5 'Anthropomorphic Patina'. Care is essential not only in sustaining vulnerable members of society, but also in maintaining our everyday lives. How can this relationship exist as a two-way street? The project focuses on the now demolished Brook House in Hackney, initiating an exploration into the layered nature of memories and exploring the landscape of care as a sensory environment. It is a speculation on an alternative future for the existing Georgian health infrastructure that also examines the methods of care and the messy assemblages of memory.

13.5–13.6 Muyun Qiu, Y5 '(Don't) Dwell on the Past: The Rebirth of Yuanming Yuan'. Sited in Yuanming Yuan, Beijing's former Summer Palace destroyed in the Second Opium War, the project seeks to realise the potential of heritage through actively reusing the ruins instead of monumentalising them for nationalist propaganda. It proposes to return the ruins to the local population so that they can reconcile with a dark chapter of national history through the formation of a symbiotic relationship between the people themselves, their interventions and the ruins.

13.7 Chloe Woodhead, Y5 'Fabric Waste Depository'. Textile waste is a huge contributor to global environmental pollution. The Institute of Positive Fashion states that community, environment and craftsmanship are the key pillars in reducing the damage caused by textile waste. This project utilises these principles to create a space for waste that allows the community of Deptford to consider waste as part of their environmental experience. The dichotomy of material, movement and space is essential to the discussion of the waste experience.

13.8 Thomas Smith, Y5 'Water Descending'. Wild bathing is a necessity. It provides an escape from the city and water's ephemeral properties awaken the senses as we purge ourselves of trivial woes, soothing a mind and body that yearns for untamed nature. With our tribal uniforms removed, we expose ourselves, releasing the barriers between us and nature. Only in this raw state can we truly tap into our primal and physiological needs. The project improves access to this cultural activity in London.

13.9 Agata Malinowska, Y5 'Polish Wonderland'. Our lives need some escapism. We often go about our everyday mundane tasks seeking something that will give us relief. This project explores escapism through Polish forests, envisioning them as enchanted places where anything can happen. Through storytelling, fairy tales and imagination, the project examines the way that narrative can help us interact with space.

13.10 Jolanta Piotrowska, Y5 'Reinventing the Longhouse'. Everyday life would look very different if it weren't for the invisible work carried out by women. This 'reproductive labour', as Silvia Federici describes it, is 'work we do that is sustaining, work that you have to do over and over again, work that seems to erase itself'. This project brings about change and highlights the wealth and wisdom of invisible labour by focusing on developing the cultural identity of Wolin, an island off the coast of Poland. The design adapts the invisible labour principles of care, value and community in order to form a relationship between the people and the land and create a building suited to their needs.

13.11–13.12 Ernest Chin, Y4 'Margate Placeholder'. The project asks: 'What if regeneration strategies prioritised locals?' The scheme, a self-build community centre, utilises the abundant chalk beneath Margate as a catalyst to suggest an alternative approach. The process of neighbourhood involvement, material use and collective building provides the platform for a bottom-up, intrinsically local regeneration strategy that empowers the community to reclaim Margate and improve it on their terms.

13.13 Maya Whitfield, Y4 'Constructing Play Store'. The project examines increasing child poverty, homelessness and inequality within Margate and Cliftonville. It challenges the existing environment, while facilitating a new procurement route for delivery and completion of a self-build scheme organised by the community. By allowing participation within the design process, the act of collective building as a pedagogical tool encourages community members to explore their everyday, while improving independence and common understanding.

13.14 Hester Tollit, Y4 'Curtain Call'. The project questions how under-represented voices can gain confidence to speak out and be heard. By exploring the characteristics and opportunities within degrees of transparency, the proposal investigates the relationship between internal and external activity, creating an open and creative dialogue in and around a community theatre. The dynamics of perspective and light interact to enable layered and evolving relationships between wider socio-economic communities and provide a beacon with which to 're-light' Margate.

13.15–13.16 Thabiso Nyezi, Y5 'The Promised Land'. The project examines the different vernaculars that redefine relationships with community, landscape and living in the city of Milton Keynes. By reimagining the 1970s vision of a 'City in the Forest' in rural Buckinghamshire, the project explores how different cultures could be celebrated by the built environment while addressing the town's urban ambitions. The result is a town that celebrates rather than resists transcultural exchanges and sees them as vital to its own evolution.

13.2

13.3

13.4

13.5

13.6

13.7

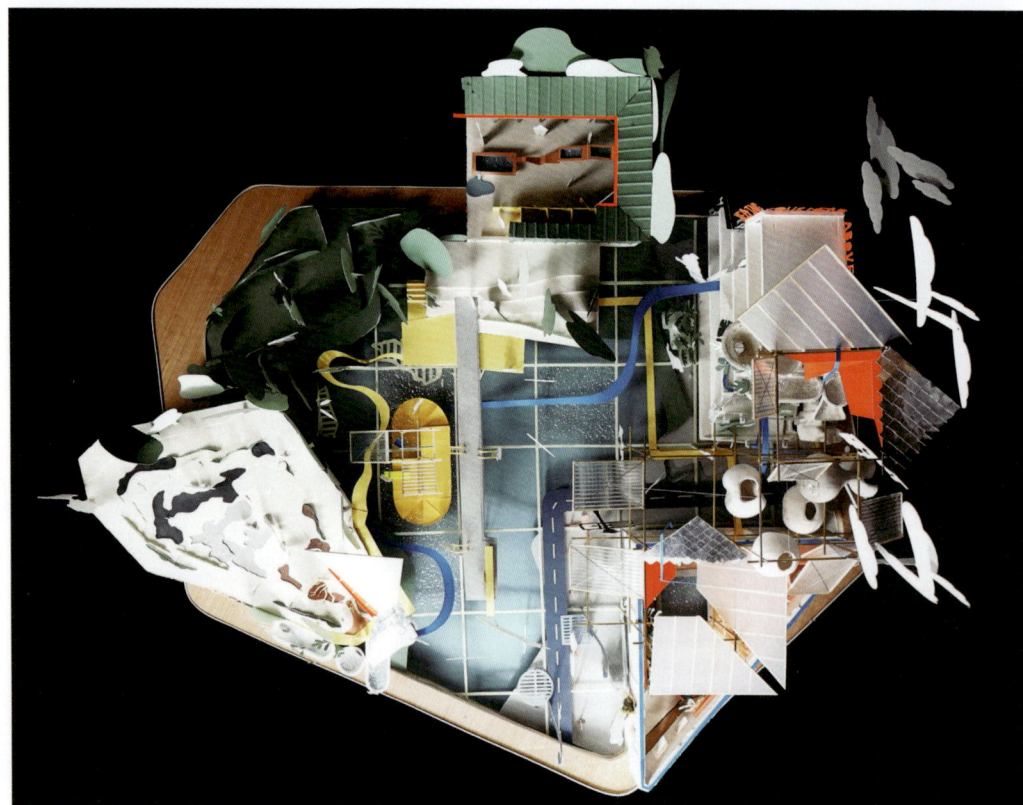

13.8

...and they lived happily ever after

13.9

13.10

13.11

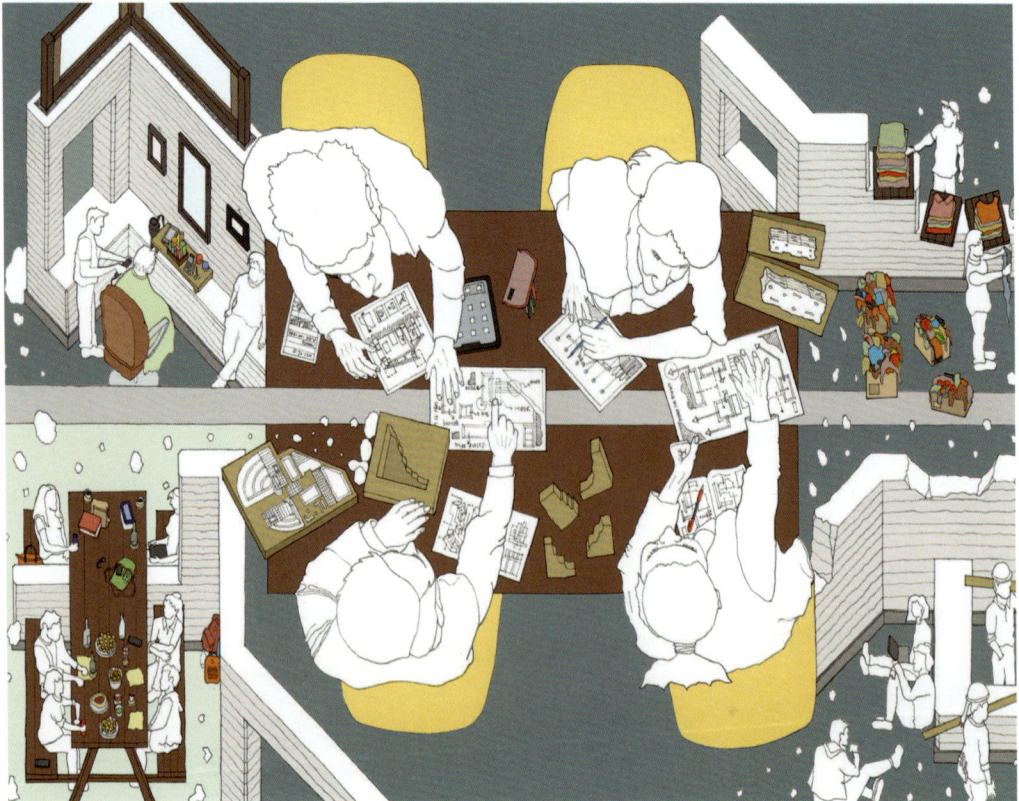

13.12

13.13

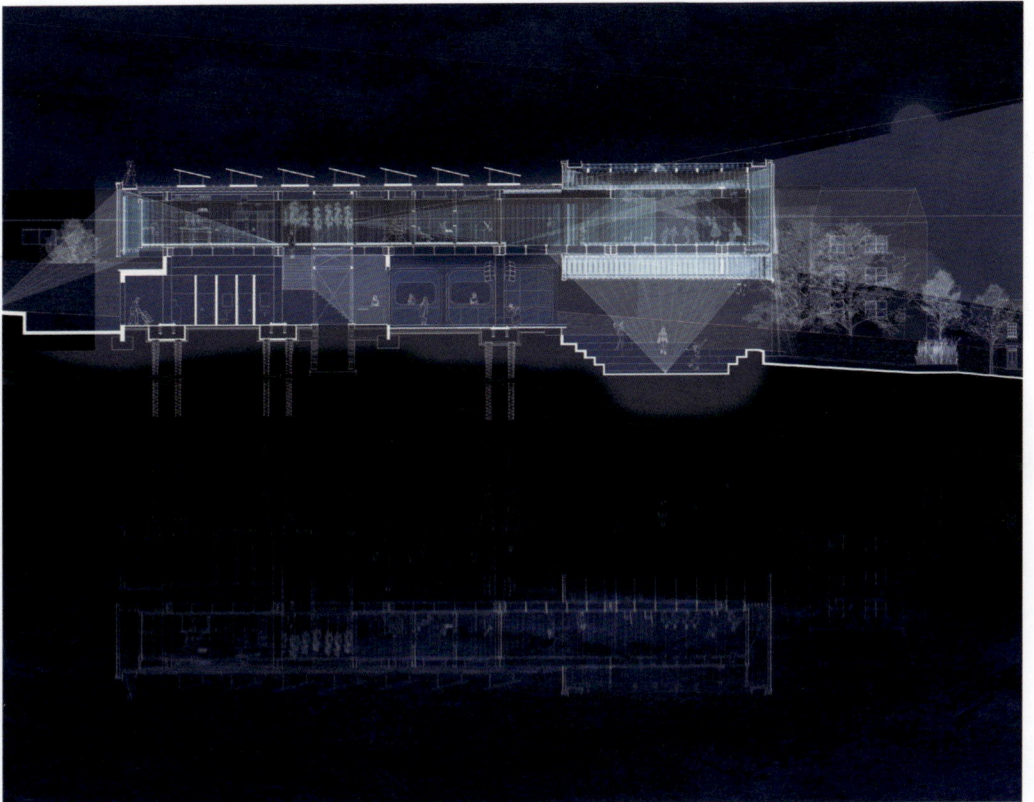

13.14

13.15

13.16

13.17

Spatial Tectonic PG14

Jakub Klaska, Dirk Krolikowski

PG14 is a testbed for exploration and innovation, examining the role of the architect in an environment of continuous change. We are in search of the new: leveraging technologies, workflows and modes of production seen in disciplines outside our own. We test ideas systematically by means of digital as well as physical drawings, models and prototypes. Our work evolves around technological speculation with a research-driven core, generating momentum through the astute synthesis of both.

Our propositions are ultimately made through the design of buildings and in-depth consideration of structural formation and tectonic constituents. This, coupled with a strong research ethos, generates new and unprecedented, viable and spectacular proposals. They are beautiful because of their intelligence, their extraordinary findings and the artful integration of these into architecture.

The focus of this year's work evolved around the concept of 'spatial tectonic'. This term describes architectural space as a result of the highest degree of synthesis of all underlying principles.

Constructional logic, spatial innovation, typological organisation and environmental and structural performance are all negotiated in an iterative process driven by architectural investigation. These inherent principles of organisational intelligence can be observed in both biotic and abiotic systems, in all spatial arrangements where it is critical for the overall performance of any developed order. Ultimately such principles suggest that the arrangement of constituents provides intelligence as well as advantage to the whole.

Through a deep understanding of architectural ingredients, students generated highly developed architectural systems in which spatial organisation arose as a result of sets of mutual interactions. These interactions were understood through targeted iterations of spatial models, uncovering logical links while generating ambitious and speculative arrangements. Sequential testing and the enriching of abstract yet architectural systems were the basis of architectural form – communicating the relationship of all logical dependencies, roles and performances within the system.

Year 4
Alysia Arnold, Muhammad (Fazeel) Babur, Dominic Benzecry, Sebastian Birch, Joel Jones, Kishan Mulji, Matthew Needham

Year 5
Teodor Andonov, Vegard Elseth, Holly Hearne, Ryan Moss, Benjamin Norris, Kacper Pach, Svenja Siever, Chen-Ru Sung

Technical tutors and consultants: Damian Eley, Florian Gauss

Thesis supervisors: Hector Altamirano, Andrew Barnett, Tim Lucas, Michael Stacey, Oliver Wilton

Critics: Andrew Abdulezer, Barbara-Ann Campbell-Lange, Xavier De Kestelier, Damian Eley, Charlie Harris, Ho-Yin Ng, Ricardo Carvalho De Ostos, Saman Saffarian, Dan Wright

Sponsors: HASSELL (main sponsor), RSHP, ALA, DKFS, Expedition Engineering, knippershelbig, Seth Stein Architects, ZHA

14.1, 14.23 Ryan Moss, Y5 'Power for London'.
As Transport for London searches for new localised
electricity sources, the project attempts to civilise nuclear
power production with a small modular reactor sited in
a new underground station entrance at Bank Junction.
The building takes inspiration from the Gothic innovation
of masonry construction, with mass timber sheet material
taking on new forms through folding and pleating.

14.2, 14.21 Kacper Pach, Y5 'Train Station Katowice
Główne'. The project explores a novel timber structural
system for a new train station in Katowice, Poland.
Through its materiality, dense vegetation and wider
pedestrianised public space, the station redefines
a new open and green image of the city, embodied
within sustainable public transport infrastructure.

14.3, 14.12 Vegard Elseth, Y5 'Fjordbyen City'.
Located at the fjord of Oslo's old port line below
Akershus Fortress, the project proposes an extension
of the city's tramline, and the embedment of this within
cultural infrastructure in order to activate Oslo's 'Fjord
City'. Based on nautical technological investigations,
stepped profiles evolve into a sweeping roof span, which
is formed of block lamination derived directly from the
material's production possibilities.

14.4, 14.9 Teodor Andonov, Y5 'Tech-Folk New Urban
Vernacular'. The project proposes an independent town
hall for Plovdiv, Bulgaria, where technocratic innovation
and vernacular lifestyle fuse in a new civic model. The
developed structural system synthesises the character of
the local vernacular with material innovation, through a
new design-to-fabrication computational methodology
for freeform timber frames based on 2D CNC milling.

14.5 Chen-Ru Sung, Y5 'Sumo_X'. The project explores
the structural potential of a folding oriented strand
board (OSB) plate system to design a robotic sumo arena
in Tokyo. A layering strategy is adopted to maximise
structural efficiency and reduce material waste. The
proposal provides novel entertaining experiences for the
audience and explores a new typology for arenas after
the pandemic to counter the challenges of an ageing
society and social isolation that Japan currently faces.

14.6, 14.22 Sebastian Birch, Y4 'The Carpenter's
Guildhouse'. The project imagines a future guild house
for timber framers, sited in the German city of Lübeck,
building on the history of this obsolete but formerly
valuable typology. The project speculates on the
development of glued laminated timber (glulam)
fabrication technologies with a focus on nodal
connections. By leveraging the expressive possibilities
of the system, the project draws on the traditions of
craftsperson organisation in Germany and a future
typology influenced by digital possibilities.

14.7, 14.19 Svenja Siever, Y5 'The Lindworm Festival'.
The project examines the optimisation of large-span
glulam structures in Munich, Germany. The brief
investigates the economic and cultural ties between
Germany and China within the Bavarian context.
Taking the concept of the diverse 'Volksgarten', the
project helps to facilitate international exchange while
bringing back greenery to a site that was once lush
grassland. Spatial qualities are investigated through
subdivision surface modelling (SubD). A glulam frame
structure is projected onto the typology, while material
is saved using a Lindenmayer system.

14.8, 14.18 Holly Hearne, Y5 'Cycle Line'. Consisting
of two branches, the High Line and the Under Line, the
new Cycle Line is a solution to the rapid post-pandemic
cycling boom. The High Line proposes a new elevated
cycling network, while the Under Line will regenerate
London's disused underground tunnels into cycle paths.
This new network culminates in a central interchange,
allowing cyclists to move seamlessly from an elevated

network to a subterranean network, and out to the
ground level and the city beyond.

14.10 Muhammad (Fazeel) Babur, Y4 'Reimagining
the Manchester Piccadilly Entertainment District'.
Reinvigorating Piccadilly Gardens for public leisure,
the project reimagines it as a series of accessible
performance venues for use by under-represented
artists in the city, who can capitalise on the passing
public as their audience. Architecturally it takes its
precedent from the Piccadilly Entertainment District,
a 1960s scheme proposed for the site which never
came to fruition.

14.11 Kishan Mulji, Y4 'Lhuentse School of Crafts'.
The proposal brings together the Himalayan construction
technique of Kath Khuni – characterised by the systematic
layering of bands of timber and dry stone – with a hybrid
user group of foreign exchange students and native
craftspeople. Through the introduction of a crafts-based
educational programme in eastern Bhutan, the scheme
celebrates the region's historical infrastructure, reframing
the heavily spiritualised lens through which the Himalayas
is normally viewed.

14.13 Benjamin Norris, Y5 'Freedom Valley'. The project
proposes the systemic reuse of the under-utilised
Los Angeles River for varying clusters of community-
led public infrastructure that play host to cultural
production in a coming age of mass technological
unemployment. In response to the increasing
gentrification of creative districts within the city,
makers' spaces, workshops and garages cantilever
over and cut into the disused concrete embankment
that is reimagined as a national park for creatives
from the city and beyond to connect and create.

14.14, 14.17 Dominic Benzecry, Y4 'Gammur
Sviðslistamiðstöð'. The project introduces cultural
infrastructure to a remote northern region of Iceland in
the form of a performing arts centre which responds to a
centralised economy, a growing music industry and rich
landscape folklore. The architecture sits in harmony with
and in contrast to the landscape, with a stone pedestal
created from milled basalt blocks and a prefabricated
steel semi-monocoque structure sitting above. The
central space is carved into the landscape, with a
performance hall surrounded by a gallery, workshops,
geothermal pools and accommodation for both staff
and visitors.

14.15 Joel Jones, Y4 'Thistle and the Burr'. In response
to the Scottish independence movement, the project
proposes a new British Embassy located in Edinburgh.
Designed in a Neo-Tudor style, the project acts as a
physical manifestation of 'Britishness', helping to create
a new partnership with an autonomous, sovereign
Scotland following the dissolution of the union.

14.16 Alysia Arnold, Y4 'New Nordic Federation'.
The project speculates on the formation of a new
federal union between the Scandinavian countries
to form a single socio-economic development area.
Situated on the western Danish hinterland, the project
proposes a new transport node embedded within cultural
infrastructure, which will provide rapid connectivity
between the hinterlands and the wider Scandinavian cities.

14.20 Matthew Needham, Y4 'The Liverpool Docks'.
Situated in the historical Salisbury Dock in Liverpool,
the project proposes an entrepreneurial trade hub
embedded within a robotic greyhound racing stadium.
The proposal regenerates the docking area that has
come to ruin, with the stadium being crafted around
the procession of the race day events.

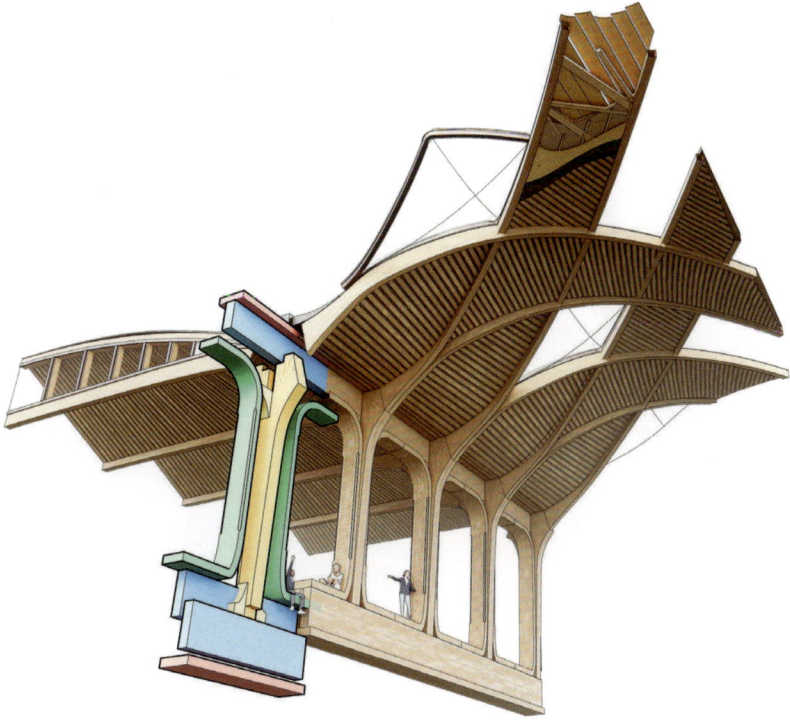

14.2

14.3

14.4

14.5

14.6

14.7

14.8

14.9

14.10

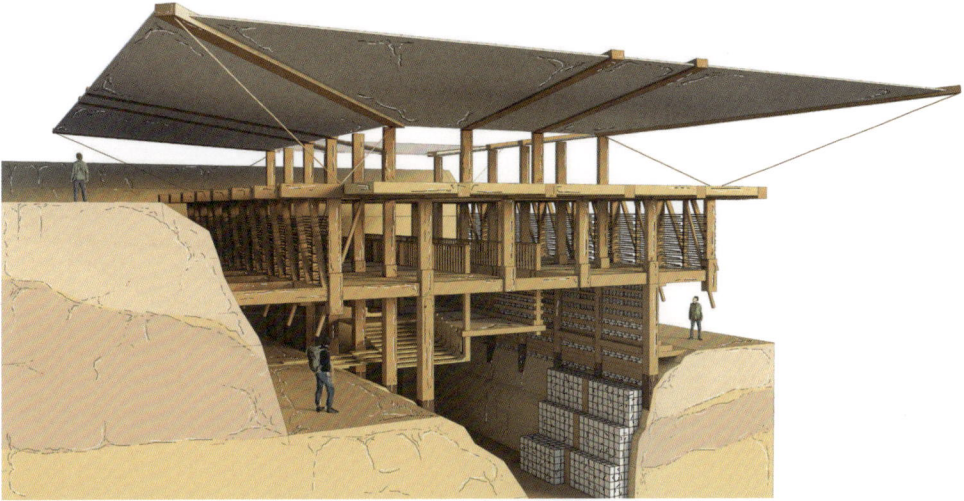

14.11

14.12

14.13

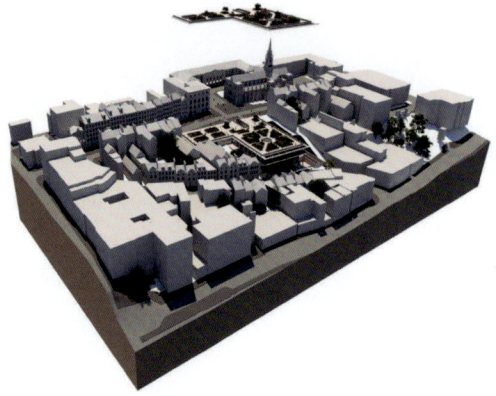

14.14

14.15

14.16

14.17

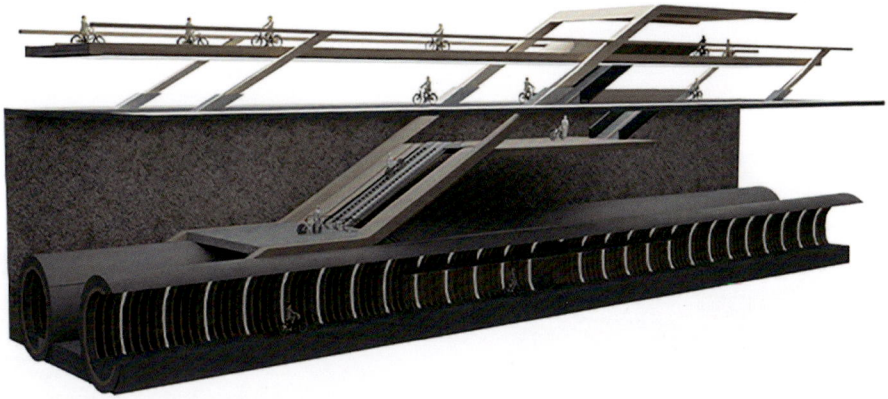

14.18

14.19

14.20

14.21

14.22

14.23

16.1

Forms of Collision Where the Earth Meets the Sky

Matthew Butcher, Ana Monrabal-Cook

PG16 is focused on the exploration of an architecture that re-emphasises the need for us to have a physical engagement with, and a relationship to, the environments we choose to inhabit.

This year we focused our interest in explorations of particular environments, specifically by engaging with the ground (the Critical Zone) and architecture's inherent relationship to it in three ways. Firstly as geology, to appreciate how deep time has formed the materials that give character to the places we live in, as well as providing evidence of the way in which ecologies are adjusting in the face of climate change; secondly, to understand architecture as primarily a material inference in the ground – and subsequently to seek to justify this inference as a means to reconnect us physically to the places we inhabit; and thirdly as tenure, to question how centuries-old forms of land ownership can inform contemporary sustainable forms of habitation.

The site of our enquiries and our field trip this year was the remote Highlands of Scotland. Here the relationship with the ground and the land has a rich, and at times fraught, history. We reflected on the matter beneath our feet by looking at the unique and historically unappreciated peatland that is intrinsic to the identity of this region. In focusing on this territory, we sought to engage recent international recognition of the environmental importance of this type of wetland as an extremely efficient carbon sink that can be found across the UK.[1]

Our research also focused on forms of land occupation and ownership, in particular the crofting model. This form of land tenure, unique to Scotland, has contributed to the retention of communities in the most remote parts of the United Kingdom. Through our study of the Scottish croft, we developed creative approaches to the diversification of rural activities as a way to support rural communities, biodiversity and the sustainable use of land.

Year 4
James Della Valle, Amy Kempa, Olga Korolkova, Kyle Mcguinness, Julia Remington, Alasdair Sheldon, Long (Ron) Tse

Year 5
Jack Barnett, Lauren Childs, Danny Dimbleby, Zachariah Harper-Le Petevin Dit Le Roux, Tudor Jitariu, Aleksandra Kugacka, Maria (Tea) Marta, Elliot Pick, Rupert Woods

Technical tutors and consultants: Will Jefferies, Ollie Wildman, Sal Wilson

Thesis supervisors: Alessandro Ayuso, Carolina Bartram, Stephen Gage, Polly Gould, Elise Hunchuck, Robin Wilson

Critics: Graham Burn, Tamsin Hanke, Johan Hybschman, Alex Kitching, Matthew Springett, Sabine Storp, Dimitar Stoynev, Patrick Weber

Partners: Emilia Leese (Natural Capital Laboratory), Richard Lindsay (UEL), Chris White (AECOM)

1. 'Peatland Pavilion will feature at UN Climate Change Conference (COP26)', IUCN: National Committee United Kingdom, 2021.

341

16.1, 16.22 Elliot Pick, Y5 'Tales of Isolation and Cultivation in Northern Scotland'. Set off the coast of Loch Hourn, Scotland, the project narrates the unique practices of three isolated cultivators. As atonement for past unsustainable practices, each cultivator wears a ritualised suit that causes discomfort to the body. The suits scale into tailored dwellings, navigating relationships between humans and nature.

16.2 Julia Remington, Y4 'Persistent Memories'. A new archive addresses the threatened cultural heritage of Pyramiden, an abandoned Soviet mining town in the High Arctic. Current conservation practices are challenged through the proposal of different strategies to archive, preserve and curate its forgotten paraphernalia. Developed strategies address conflicts between exploitative owners, dark tourism and a constantly changing environment.

16.3 Jack Barnett, Y5 'Peatland Proprioception: Vernaculars between People, Plants and Places'. The Ord Crofting Inn choreographs a series of environmental balancing acts on Skye and takes on the form of three dwellings. Each facilitates a unique experience of its surroundings and engages guests' physicality and proprioceptive sense to build awareness and physical relationships between people, plants and places.

16.4–16.5 Olga Korolkova, Y4 'Reimagining Siberia: Byas Kuel Firefighters' Village'. Dedicated to Siberia's devastating wildfires, the scheme comprises a hybrid typology of fire station and biofuel production facility, which reuses wood from the burnt forests. Multiple fields and forest structures facilitate a new sustainable economy and celebrate Yakutian culture with architecture that rethinks centuries-old fire-resilient construction and local spiritual rituals.

16.6 Kyle McGuinness, Y4 'A New Peatland Paradigm'. This project proposes the restoration of degraded Scottish peatland and its conversion to productive wetland to produce common reed. To reverse misconceptions about land use, the architecture embraces and celebrates the landscape's deficiencies while actively restoring the ground's water table to healthy conditions.

16.7 Alasdair Sheldon, Y4 'A Place between the Crofts'. The project proposes a new codependent crofting system on the island of Benbecula through two experimental houses and an intermediate building. The architecture attempts to mitigate the effects of coastal encroachment and increased flooding and in this way protects crofters from a threat to local land security.

16.8 Lauren Childs, Y5 'Caring for a Scarred Landscape'. The project is a response to the degraded state of the Scottish peatlands. It proposes a dam alongside workshops and bothies that will contribute to the remediation of the Strathy South Plantation, a landscape currently dominated by non-native Sitka spruce trees.

16.9 Aleksandra Kugacka, Y5 'Warp, Weft and the Wetlands'. The project examines the craft of willow weaving as a means of peatland rehabilitation in Scotland's Flow Country. A proposal for a COP36 Convention Centre celebrates weaving and functions as a vessel for the Scottish crofting identity, engaging visitors with the condition of the unstable ground.

16.10–16.11 Tudor Jitariu, Y5 'The Space below Ground'. Located within the geological context of the Highland Boundary Fault, this project investigates structural, formal and spatial approaches to creating underground spaces to research the region's geological diversity. A decentralised institution serves to question existing attitudes towards the image and the perception of the subterranean condition.

16.12–16.13 Zachariah Harper-Le Petevin Dit Le Roux, Y5 'Contested Ground'. Sited on the exposed coastal peat of Kentra, the project sets out a proposal for the conservation of the region's eccentric bog system, looking to the antecedent practices of Highland Games to develop strategies that will defend their history and the landscapes on which they are performed.

16.14–16.15 Maria (Tea) Marta, Y5 'Acts of Resistance: Place and Policy in the Danube Delta, Romania'. Situated in the Danube Delta, Romania, the project investigates the possibility of using architecture as a catalyst for political and environmental debate. It is an architecture of protest that accompanies existing local resistance acts and hosts localised deliberation spaces, where international, national and local authorities engage with the context they affect.

16.16–16.17, 16.19 Amy Kempa, Y4 'Cultivating a Collective – Landscape as Timeshare'. Located within a degraded blanket bog, interventions of varying temperance serve both croft and crofter. The dwellings remediate the poor ground condition by proposing primitivist domestic spaces that value the cycle of nature.

16.18 Rupert Woods, Y5 'Erdkunde – Earth Tidings'. The literal translation of the German word *erdkunde* is 'messages brought by the earth'. Two avatars have been developed on the Scottish peatlands that will listen to these messages by measuring environmental components. The avatars will then personify these results as emotions of celebration or distress.

16.20 James Della Valle, Y4 'The Mark of Man'. A collection of *taigh* (Gaelic for home) upholds the preservation of the crofting model through the construction of a contemporary crofting vernacular. An architectural proclamation declares the revival of centuries-old forms of Scottish craft while espousing novel forms of autonomous tooling.

16.21 Long (Ron) Tse, Y4 'Sheep Dyke Reimagined: Towards an Architecture of Wellbeing'. The project proposes living within a 13-mile-long dry-stone structure surrounding North Ronaldsay, Orkney Isles. The scheme explores a primitive relationship between domestic space and the island's agricultural context.

16.2

16.3

16.4

16.5

16.6

16.7

16.8

16.9

16.10

16.11

16.12

16.13

16.14

16.15

16.16

16.17

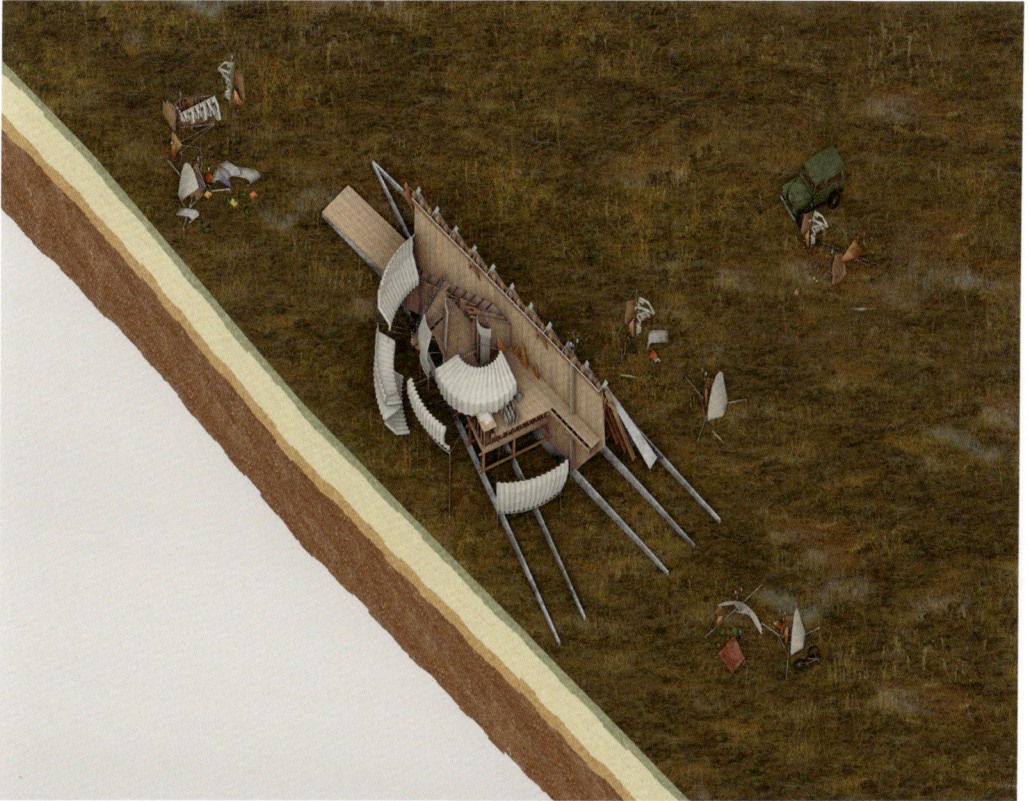

16.18

16.19

16.20

16.21

17.1

Between

Yeoryia Manolopoulou, Thomas Parker

Architecture connects. It makes myriad interconnections between physical matter, systems of knowledge, cultures and experiences – entities that are never fixed but in constant dialogue. Architecture also separates. Yet neat oppositions no longer exist, so our concept of 'between' aims to challenge common dichotomies maintained in our discipline: nature and things, local and global, the individual and the collective, the settler and the nomad. To produce a sustainable, fairer and more inclusive architecture, we need to rethink such distinctions.

'Between' suggests a spatial and temporal transition, as well as liminality. What happens at thresholds, on borders, in the interval between before and after? An in-between situation can cause friction and discontinuity, but can also be the source of enormous creative potential for new kinds of architecture and new kinds of connection.

We are interested in intermediate structures, hybrid objects and processes. We understand buildings as environments that entangle human conditions, as well as components and services that are themselves in flux. Buildings are physical continuities of matter changing at different rates. What exists beneath them is multifaceted, so our foundations are both literally and metaphorically compromised. Lands, oceans and communities are in transformation. Migration, social health and environmental ethics concern us urgently.

Our projects are always works of adaptation. Learning to design with the material and conceptual remains of situations will prepare us for working sensitively with residues of conditions in the future.

We started the year by living and making at Grymsdyke Farm. This collaborative work required scaffolding the size of our team configurations from two to four and ultimately to 16 students. We drew on and collectively glazed more than 360 ceramic tiles. Together we built a large-scale landscape installation involving found materials on the site and the spatial unravelling of three kilometres of rope. Drawing upon this initial performative work, we then developed individual design proposals on sites of our choice in Milton Keynes. In addition, all fourth year students assembled the *Milton Keynes Collective*, a collaborative manifesto with pilot design projects, expertise and ideas for the future of a sustainable and dynamic city.

Year 4
Ceren Erton, Matthew King, Desire Lubwama, Karin (Kei) Nagano, Vilius Petraitis, Anton Schwingen, Tia-Angelie Vijh

Year 5
Zhongliang Huang, Rebecca Lim, Polina Morova, Kaye Song, Negar Taatizadeh, Ella Thorns, Alexander Venditti, Janet Vutcheva, Qingyuan (Rubin) Zhou

Technical tutors and consultants: James Daykin, Lidia Guerra, Guan Lee, Jessie Lee, Rachel Pattison

Critics: Barbara-Ann Campbell-Lange, Nat Chard, Hannah Corlett, Murray Fraser, Kostas Grigoriadis, Perry Kulper, Chee-Kit Lai, Constance Lau, Guan Lee, Anna Liu, Petra Marko, Emma-Kate Matthews, Michiko Sumi, Jonathan Tyrrell, Oliver Wilton, Simon Withers

17.1 Group Project, Y4&5 'Sixteen'. Collaborative installation and performance carried out in the first term with materials found at Grymsdyke Farm, Buckinghamshire.

17.2 Group Work, Y4&5 'An Archaeology of Making'. This assemblage gathers some of the physical work produced by PG17 during this academic year, highlighting a studio ethos that is based on coexistence and the supportive experience of making and doing.

17.3 Ceren Erten, Y4 'Waste + Value'. The project proposes a new residential expansion strategy for Milton Keynes using a recycled plastic-block construction system. Critiquing the current cultural misuse of plastic – an extremely long-lasting material – as throwaway, the project explores tensions between disposability and permanence.

17.4 Qingyuan (Rubin) Zhou, Y5 'Land Graffiti'. Located at a Roman archaeological site at Stantonbury, a small village in Milton Keynes, the project challenges the public to understand the past as having multiple narratives by designing methods of excavation and reinterpretation. This proposal responds to the authorised heritage discourse that cements the area's rich archaeological significance and invites the local community to manifest and craft the multiplicity of their history.

17.5 Karin Kei Nagano, Y4 'Finding Counterpoint'. This project offers a counternarrative to the initial 1960s plan of Milton Keynes which, by muffling urban noise, resulted in the absence of interaction between its different communities. Reclaiming rare remaining pockets of public space, the project brings sound to the forefront and envisions its function as an instrument, giving the community a voice and enabling it to evolve.

17.6 Negar Taatizadeh, Y5 'Housing Reciprocity'. The project anchors itself in three thematic subjects: rebuilding, reconnecting and revealing. It proposes a systematic approach towards rebuilding to reconnect the community across generations while revealing the clay material context of this location. The project is fascinated with the liminality of materials and celebrates their impermanence. A transitory architecture is formed, one that promotes connection, reciprocity and care above all.

17.7 Kaye Song, Y5 'Double Edged'. A design for a porous and accessible edge to Milton Keynes emphasises its position as a thoroughfare city. A proposal for a green, populated and community-owned distribution park bridges the utilitarian and industrial with the wild and organic, welcoming hybridity and fluidity as essential to the contemporary experience of the English landscape.

17.8 Anton Schwingen, Y4 'Theatre of Matters'. The construction industry is responsible for a large proportion of global CO2 emissions, necessitating a radical change in the way we build. The theatre is a storage and inventory facilitating the shift to reusing building components. It also becomes a space to debate, observe juxtaposition and negotiate the city of the past and the future.

17.9 Zhongliang Huang, Y5 'Wayward Growth'. This proposal reinvigorates the industrial ruins of the Wolverton railway works by adapting and reusing the derelict building material while growing a new communal garden. The proposal also contains a workshop and accommodation units for lifelong learning in the arts and sciences.

17.10 Vilius Petraitis, Y4 'Between Estate'. The project establishes a shared playing field, which lays the groundwork for a temporary cohousing scheme, weaving communities together while their homes undergo vital repairs. With doubt and delight as design parameters, the project looks at creating an architecture where the building is not an end in itself. Instead, the constructions encourage the continual need for change.

17.11 Matthew King, Polina Morova, Anton Schwingen, Ella Thorns, Y4&5 'Quartet'. A device that connects four people by joining couples through an interdependent junction.

17.12 Alexander Venditti, Y5 'A Point in Time'. The Point cinema multiplex has been slated for demolition. Rejecting a *tabula rasa* restart, an alternative future inspired by its cinematic history is proposed, which sees the iconic site transformed into an open-air film stage. The oscillating states of set demolition and reconstruction strip back the veil of cinema and reveal the secrets behind its production, all while filling a gap of cultural identity within the city.

17.13–17.14 Polina Morova, Y5 'Softening Milton Keynes'. The centre of Milton Keynes offers an experiential example of rigid living where urban components of the city feel solitary and separate, and where life becomes a series of discrete experiences, clear-cut roles and identities. Within this context, the proposed park becomes a respite from daily life, offering a change of scene where the alienation one feels in the city becomes the poetic alienation one feels in nature.

17.15 Ella Thorns, Y5 'Consequential Cognition'. This project designs and interrogates a new food-based masterplan for the neighbourhood of Oldbrook, Milton Keynes. Criticising the dissonance of our current food system, the architecture processes food and consumption by-products around its users, resulting in consequential awareness.

17.16 Janet Vutcheva, Y5 'Quarrying Fluidity'. The project investigates river valley quarrying and proposes a new quarrying technique through which an inhabited hydro-common is constructed over time. The project offers a new model for inhabiting wet environments, which brings human and 'more-than-human' inhabitants together.

17.17 Desire Lubwama, Y4 'The Wedding House'. Addressing issues of cultural, historical and ecological sustainability, the proposal is an adaptive space that explores applications of waste plastic, earth and clay to create temporally stable structures in the Tree Cathedral, Milton Keynes. The value of ritual is combined with material processing to re-engage the public and influence the design of these spaces.

17.18 Tia-Angelie Vijh, Y4 'MUR MUR'. Set within Bletchley Park, Milton Keynes, the project proposes to retrofit and restore the abandoned Block D – once home to the original codebreakers of World War II – into a quantum computer laboratory with exposed dilapidated courtyards. Through the use of historical and fictional text in relation to Block D and Alan Turing, the project proposes a series of adaptations, with the insertion of new courtyards and chambers.

17.19 Rebecca Lim, Y5 'Tempered and Timed Minimum Dwellings for Maximum Social Living'. Minimum dwellings, anchored by kilns and ovens for heating, making and sharing, extend Cosgrove Lakes holiday park in Milton Keynes. The post-digital architectural practice of drawing and machine learning critically reconfigures the notion of the conventional dwelling by seeing time and temperature as agents of social interaction. The dwelling is minimised through multiplicities of space but maximised for social exchange.

17.20 Matthew King, Y4 'Traces of Rhythm'. The scheme nestles where techno, Neolithic tradition and woodland management converge. By exploring these themes through the notation of cyclical processes, the scheme looks to uncover natural rhythms that bind us to the landscape. By cross-programming a timber yard with a rave site, the architecture becomes a vessel for reassociating young people in Milton Keynes with the landscape, instilling a sense of care.

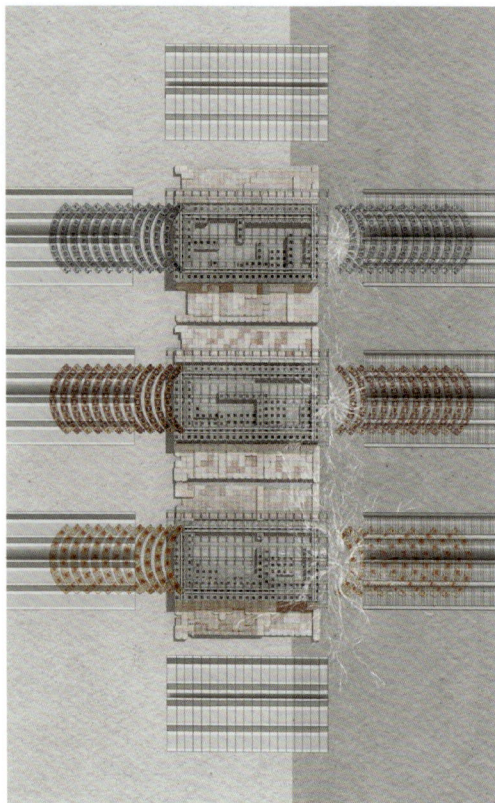

17.3

17.4

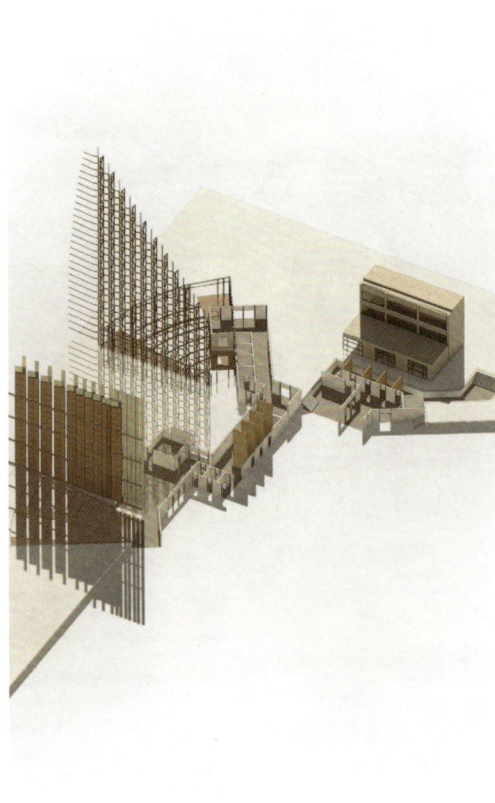

17.5

17.6

17.7

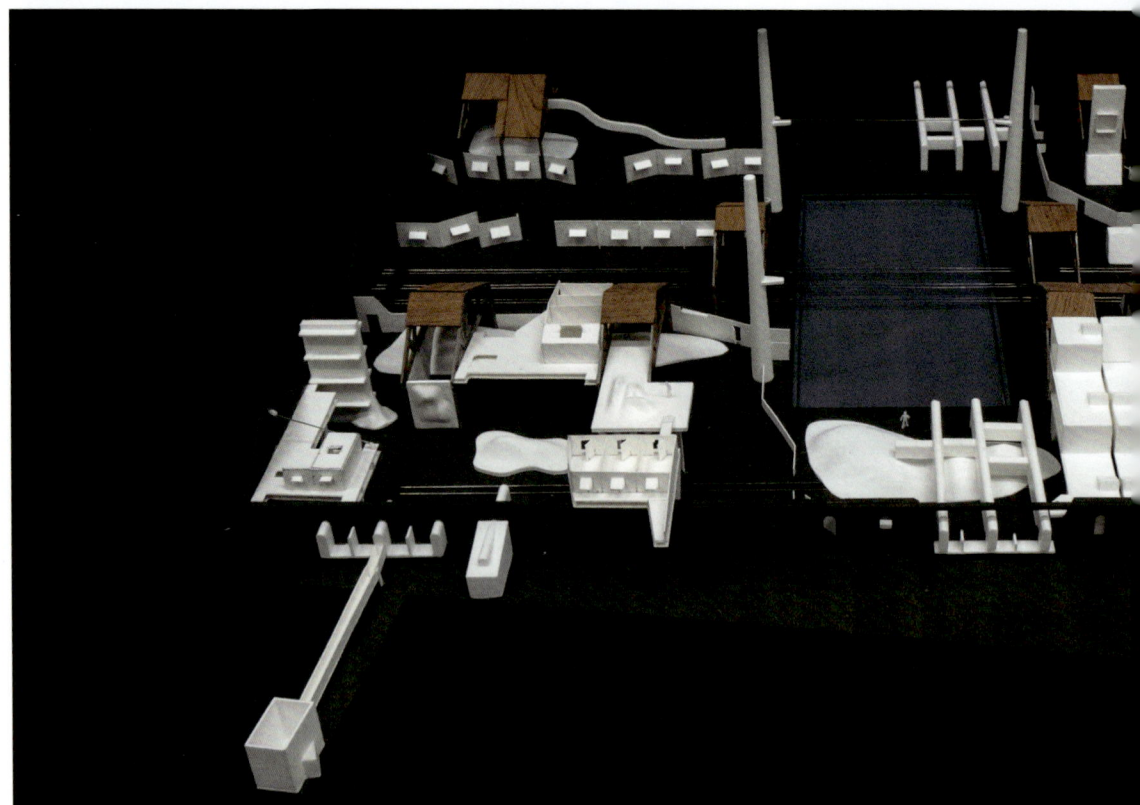

17.9

17.8

17.10

17.11

17.12

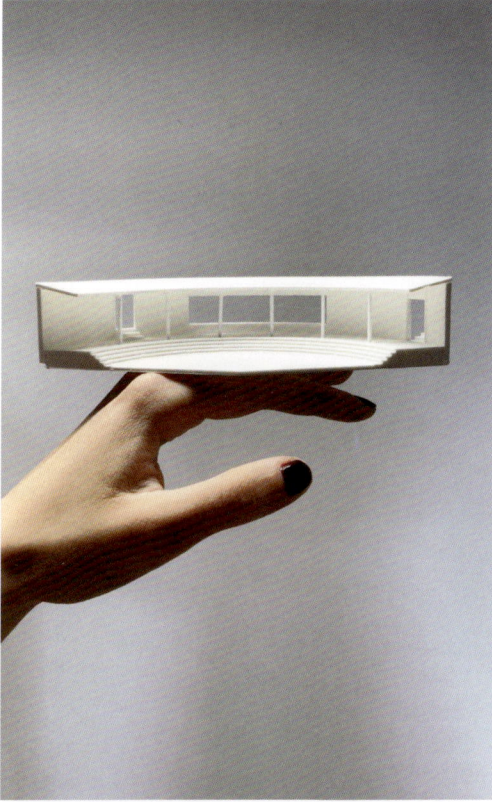

17.13

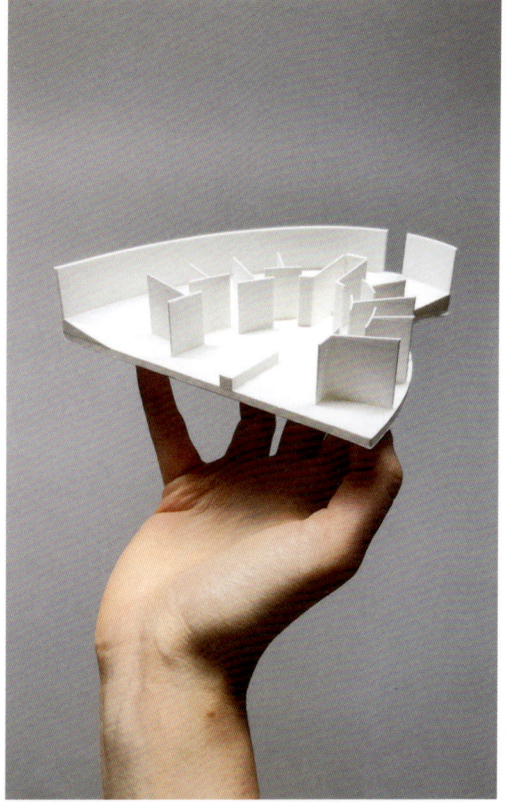

17.14

17.15

17.16

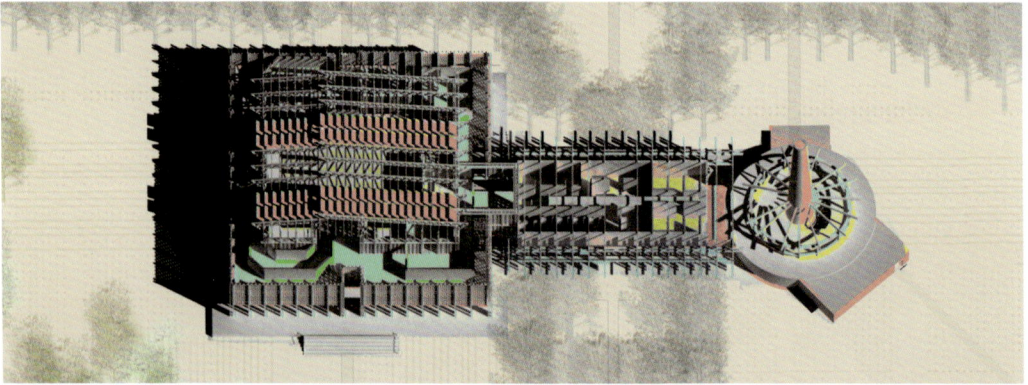

17.17

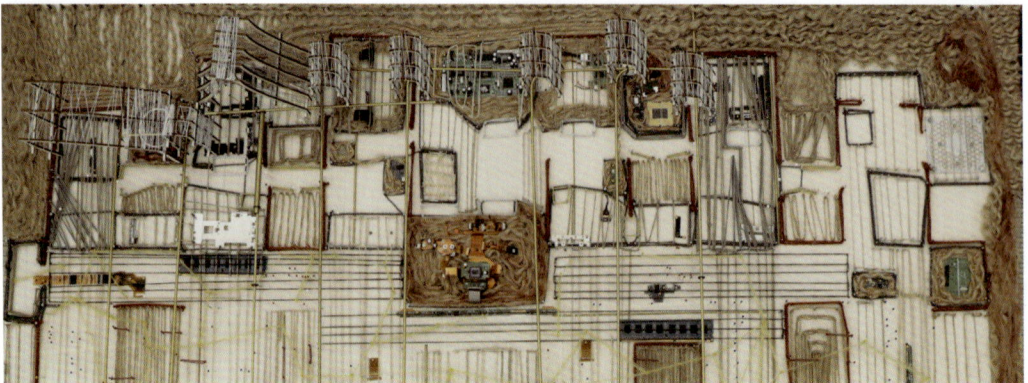

17.18

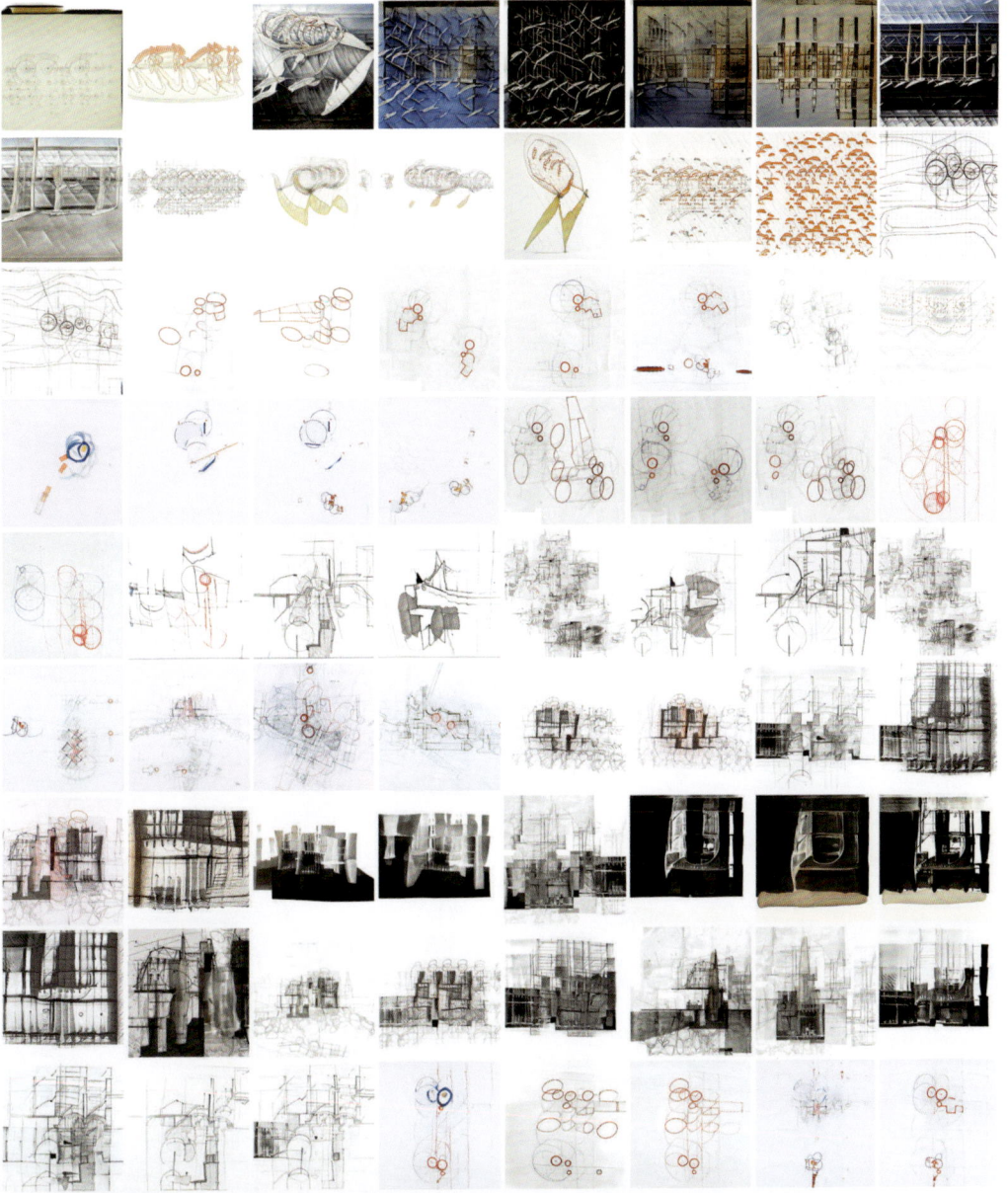

17.19

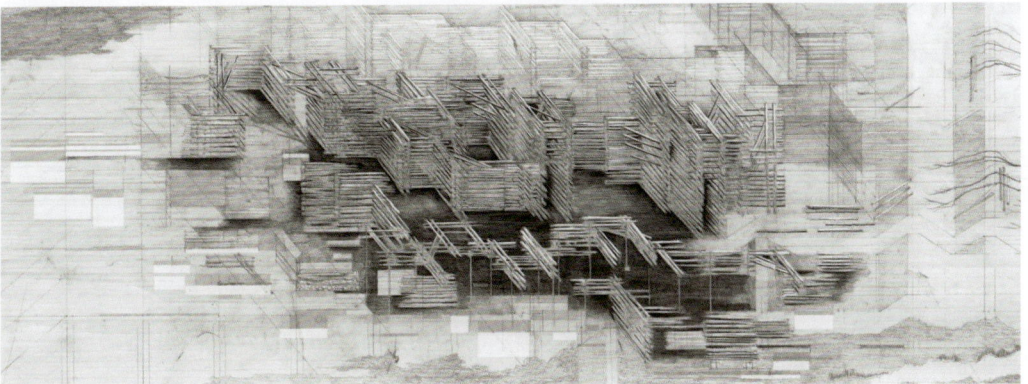

17.20

Generational Phantoms / WE 2.0

Isaïe Bloch, Ricardo Carvalho De Ostos

The longer people live, the more they tend to question the three sequential stages of 20th-century life: education, work and retirement. Inspired by the challenge of increasing life expectancy in the 21st century, PG18 researched and designed educational institutions for a new life structure. Over a spectrum of classical, digital or alternative learning systems, students considered current political and economic pressures; from the impact of Web 2.0 social networks and ecological uncertainty to the massive ongoing transformation of learning environments. PG18 offered a series of seminars alongside digital workshops stimulating agile conversations between anthropological concepts and design experiments.

Ideas of longevity for young university students may sound unusual, but concepts of financial literacy, multiple career paths, non-formal continuous learning, healthier lifestyles and sustainable practice are relevant to their lives. Research into education models is less an abstract idea and more about shaping aspirations for a different educational process, one to which students will want to belong. Themes from economics, biology, forestry, disappearing coasts, crypto and NFTs became topics to fertilise architectural ideas. PG18 is a place that enables students to bring their own interests to the foreground of their work, while at the same time offering critical and constructive debate about the role of individuals in society.

Heather Black's fourth-year project illustrates the merger of crypto economies to revitalise a forest in Scotland. Utilising tokens and the early ideas of ownership present in crypto space, the project proposes a building to attract both forest enthusiasts and investors, creating bridges between preservation and collective stewardship. Ecological education becomes linked to practices of care, maintenance of trees and the overall tokenisation of the landscape's arboreal coverage.

Fifth year student Pablo Wheldon investigated how an abandoned mining site could be recreated as a sustainable forestry complex, uniting a diverse group of workers. Focusing on the intersection of congregational spaces and timber processing, the project addresses local industrial history, shifting it to a more sustainable landscape. Instead of ignoring the past, the proposed architecture encourages coexistence, productive conflict and future forest economies.

Inspired by our passion for culture and its expression in architecture tectonics, PG18 shows how rich, non-dogmatic and innovative the future of educational institutions can be.

Heather Black, Ma Patricia Castelo, Neelkanth Depala, Noah Robinson-Stanier, Olivia Shiu, Joshua Snell, Biyi Sogbesan

Year 5
Victoria Bocchiotti, Tu-Ann Dao, Sara Eldeib Leo Francois-Serafin, Grégoire Gagneux, Tobias Himawan, Alvin Lim, Sophie Peterson, Raul Rutnam, Pablo Wheldon

Technical tutors and consultants: Rob Haworth, Nick Ling, Hareth Pochee

Critics: Oliver Domeisen, Christina Grytten, Jack Moreton, Jez Ralph, Alisa Silanteva, Tul Srisompun, Paulo Waisberg, Yeena Yoon

18.1 Pablo Wheldon, Y5 'The Timber Colliery'. The proposed building is a timber-processing facility in the Forest of Dean on top of a former colliery. The proposal repurposes the fragments of the area's coal-mining infrastructure into the timber process, from transport and milling to drying.

18.2 Tobias Himawan, Y5 'The Sacred Guardians of the Coast'. Situated in Fairbourne, a Welsh coastal village planned to be decommissioned by 2054 due to its failing sea defences, the project reviews the rich heritage of Christian pilgrimage in Wales and proposes three pilgrimage structures across three sites within the village.

18.3–18.4 Pablo Wheldon, Y5 'The Timber Colliery'. The new journey of timber is mapped across the old route of coal, with the material approach and architecture of the building reflecting these transitions from above ground to below ground.

18.5–18.6 Tobias Himawan, Y5 'The Sacred Guardians of the Coast'. Utilising geological narration, time, coastal dynamics, eroding earth materiality and the changing climate as architectural resources and design drivers, each proposed structure uncovers the varying struggles of the village against the future coastal climate. The architecture ultimately serves as a place where the villagers and the pilgrims interact, exchanging their knowledge as both are confronted with the transient reality of man-made habitation.

18.7 Alvin Lim, Y5 'Dreaming with Scales in My Eyes'. The project's surreal, reimagined realities propose an architectural position and expression that intends to safeguard the region's fishing heritage amid a changing nature and culture. An illustrated narrative forms a cultural education that shifts between optimism and uncertainty, revealing architecture's capacity to be emotionally compelling. The project moves below the sea's surface and beyond the land's edge, to where all eyes in Cornwall cannot help but turn – the ocean.

18.8 Raul Rutnam, Y5 'London Craft Studies & Research Centre'. The project speculates on the future of transference and distribution of education in London through knowledge of accomplished craftsmanship, materiality and architectural tradition. The workshops explore the mass customisation of bespoke architectural components and objects of industrial design by exploring future tooling methods and fabrication, combining both digital processes and handcrafts.

18.9 Joshua Snell, Y4 'Insect Monitoring Centre'. The proposal establishes a cultural landmark which creates the habitat and spatial opportunity for interactions with insects, while also hosting an interactive data exhibit for displaying data captured by the community.

18.10–18.11 Grégoire Gagneux, Y5 'Elastogenesis Flexible Institution'. Elastogenesis explores the potential of flexible spaces to increase the performance of physical interactions, in a context in which longevity and technology generate new methods of working, teaching and living together. Creating a hybrid between virtual and physical space, the scheme facilitates observation, experience and sharing. The digital translation of natural growing models is proposed to deal with the notion of flexibility, articulating semi-virtual spaces within the architectural massing.

18.12 Leo Francois-Serafin, Y5 'The Library of Babel'. As the city of London aims to become net zero by 2050, the project proposes the creation of a centre for reskilling dedicated to workers of the High Speed Two (HS2) line. Open to workers and visitors alike, the building's permeability and layout become a catalyst for education and socialisation.

18.13 Victoria Bocchiotti, Y5 'Hydrotherapy Centre or How to Live Longer'. Hydrotherapy has been present across cultures and has long been used to aid people both physically and mentally. Steam bathing, for example, was recognised by both the Greeks and Romans for its many benefits. Through its architecture, the hydrotherapy centre brings people into a space that can educate them about how water can benefit the body and mind.

18.14 Olivia Shiu, Y4 'Navigating a New Zero: Natural Disaster Education Centre'. Warping wood model study. Located in London, the project provides a physical space for disaster management education as we adapt to changing water levels. The project investigates timber as the principal material and explores the hygroscopic qualities of wood in reaction to natural weathering.

18.15 Raul Rutnam, Y5 'London Craft Studies & Research Centre'. Milled, steam-bent and hand-finished parts of an interior model. Ornamental surfaces are designed by the architect in collaboration with craftspeople.

18.16 Grégoire Gagneux, Y5 'Elastogenesis Flexible Institution'. Model exploring interlocking spaces. The stretching, intersecting and interlocking of spaces not only mixes spatial perception associated with textures, but also extends architectural functions to multiple areas.

18.17 Sophie Peterson, Y5 'The Pharos Centre: Migration Community Centre'. Material model experiment exploring physical qualities and atmosphere. Set in the year 2051, the project is a training centre for individuals who have migrated from different climates, as well as being a base for learning new skills and languages, acquiring mental health services and finding safety, stillness and connection.

18.18 Olubiyi Sogbesan, Y4 'Rites of Passage'. Set in 2080, the project proposes a non-profit training facility that help build resilient and equitable communities that are sustainably integrated within the natural world. Through ongoing experimentation with earth-based additive manufacturing, trainees are entrusted to personalise their units while providing innovative solutions to environmental issues.

18.19–18.20 Patricia Castelo, Y4 'The Merry Hill Agroecological Centre'. The project looks at how architecture can facilitate education in agroecological farming and growing while fostering a mutual relationship with the natural world. This is explored through the inclusion of non-human life forms in the built environment, focusing on a phenomenological approach towards learning and design, and challenging the relationship we have with how buildings are inhabited and the materials that are used.

18.21 Heather Carole Black, Y4 'Trading Boundaries'. The scheme taps into the psychology of ownership and possession to incentivise people to take responsibility for forestry in Scotland, where the forestry is largely commercial and owned by a few wealthy elite. The project allows community members and investors to purchase plots of land in the form of non-fungible tokens (NFTs) and to collectively own the forest. The architectural response to the tokenised forest takes the form of a new-age investor's centre.

18.3

18.4

18.5

18.6

18.7

18.8

18.9

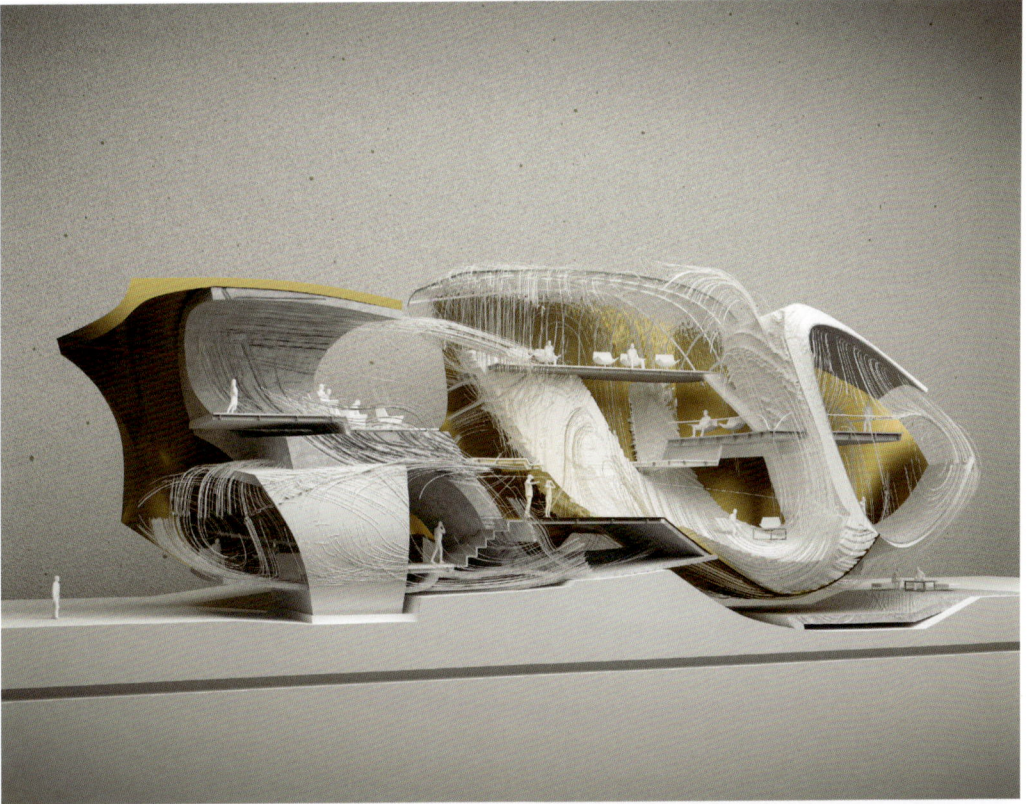

18.10

18.11

18.12

18.13

18.14

18.15

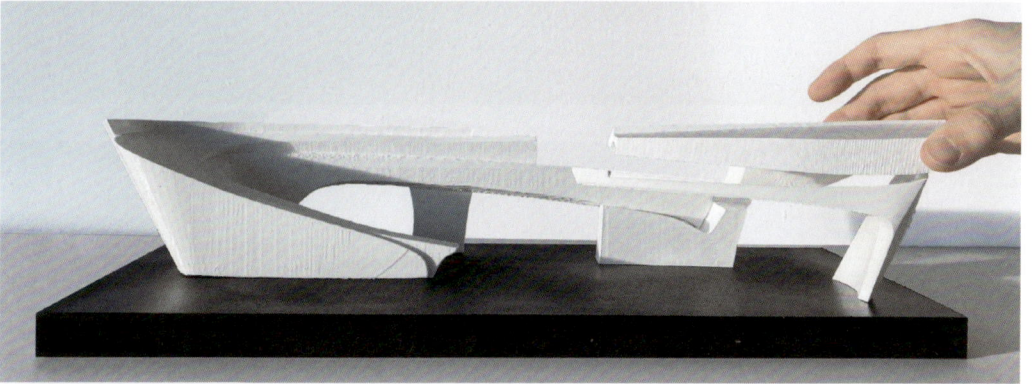

18.16

18.17

18.18

18.19

18.20

PG20 - 82%

PERSON - 61%

VASE - 52%

TREE - 36%

TV - 20%

LANDSCAPE - 39%

MARJAN - 8%

JAVIER - 8%

DAVE - 5%

20.1

Post-Digital Practices: Decentralised City 2.0

PG20

Marjan Colletti, Javier Ruiz Rodriguez

Centralised society as we know it is a relatively recent phenomenon. The invention of agriculture allowed people to settle and build larger communities which broke away from the smaller, self-organised tribal society standards of the past. These new societal systems grew much larger than the cognitive limit suggested by the anthropologist Robin Dunbar. He proposed that humans can maintain around 100 to 250 stable relationships (the so-called 'Dunbar number'), beyond which people-based trust systems cannot scale up. Nowadays, as technology-based trust systems scale virtually without limit, we are experiencing a new decentralised trust system that promises to play a large part in the upcoming radical changes of the Fourth Industrial Revolution.

Cities of the 20th century sought to bring citizens relief from traffic, pollution and congestion by proposing a non-hierarchical, growth-based system of urban densification in a closer correlation with nature and the countryside. Understood as a place of production (Fordian Industry 2.0), the city was formed of distinct and discrete parts: infrastructure, buildings and the natural landscape. In hindsight, the modernist design manifestations of this decentralised city appear outdated, unequal and not sufficiently diverse or inclusive. In fact, postmodern cities in the late 20th century provided a critique of such grand utopian visions of total planning and total design, reintegrating tradition, bricolage and iconoclasm within the scope of architecture. From today's point of view these also failed, however, remaining too static and introverted to fit today's dynamic societies. Digital cities in the 2000s attempted elastically to parametrise them. Here, too, the vision of urbanity became too self-similar and monolithic, rejecting collaging and noise, but failing to address environmental and human-centric aspects.

PG20 researched what post-digital decentralised cities might look like, learning from past strategies and suggesting alternative solutions. The projects resulted in complex hybrids, where technology and tradition, artifice and nature are equal: not put into binary (modernist), collage (postmodern) or parametric (geometric) relationships, but into a complex, feedback-driven exchange. Here such concepts are decentralised, fragmented yet connected, and ready for the radical changes for which architecture must be prepared.

We understood the city as a trans-scalar entity that requires designing on multiple scales, from the micro (biology, material, technology) to the macro (nature, cities, infrastructure).

Year 4
Wojciech Karnowka, Paul Kohlhaussen, Isaac Palmiere-Szabo, Luke Topping

Year 5
Nadya Angelova, James Ballentyne, Michael Brewster, Paul Brooke, Yuqi (Kenneth) Cai, Paul Kohlhaussen, Kar Bo (Thomas) Leung, Carolina Mondragon-Bayarri, Shenton Morgan, Luke Parkhurst, Michaella Tafalla, Abigail Yeboah, Zhong Zheng

Technical tutors and consultants: Tom Clewlow, David Edwards, Alistair Shaw, Michael Woodrow

Thesis supervisors: Camillo Boano, Amica Dall, Stephen Gage, Abel Maciel, Claire McAndrew, Rokia Raslan, Guang Yu Ren, Michael Stacey, Robin Wilson, Oliver Wilton, Fiona Zisch

20.1, 20.19 Yuqi (Kenneth) Cai, Y5 'The Second Border'. With the rise of AI-enhanced surveillance, the need for an architecture that exposes and counters these mechanical gazes is clear. Designed with a bespoke architectural system, the glitched data-scape on the Hong Kong border encrypts our multidimensional spaces and faces. The project raises questions not just about privacy, but also about the equilibrium between humans, machines and nature.

20.2–20.3 Kar Bo (Thomas) Leung, Y5 'Post-Mined Mongolia'. By analysing the tension between Mongolia's urbanisation and its traditionally nomadic culture, the proposal focuses on the spatio-temporal rehabilitation of a decommissioned Oyu Tolgoi copper mine through scientific (agent-based) and intuitive (physical and digital) processes of experimentation. This imagines a decentralised urban settlement prototype that serves both mining and herder communities, alleviating the existing pressures of rural-urban migration.

20.4, 20.16 Paul Kohlhaussen, Y4 'Isle of Tides'. The project focuses on the phased construction of a flood defence strategy for Canary Wharf on a decentralised, per-building basis. By harnessing the naturally occurring biological processes of the intertidal zone, the infrastructural intervention becomes encrusted with a synthetically biomineralised architecture that hosts a hybrid programme of aquacultural production, seafood trade and a new raised public streetscape.

20.5 Nadya Angelova, Y5 'BioMorph'. The project envisions interplanetary biogenerative architecture as the final frontier for the survival of carbon life. A symbiotic relationship between humans and plants is fundamental for securing long-term existence. By exploring how algorithmic simulations of the natural processes moulding organic growth can be modified to the context of outer space, a generative spatial system is imagined that adopts and supports vegetative matter in an extraterrestrial environment.

20.6 Carolina Mondragon-Bayarri, Y5 'Cognisant Landscapes'. Advances in technology have resulted in buildings being reliant on heating, ventilation and air conditioning (HVAC) systems and becoming increasingly detached from the external environment. The energy fields around us are alive, mutable and transient. Computational fluid dynamics and solar radiation simulations are incorporated into the design process to generate climate-driven morphologies, reflecting the aspiration for a symbiotic relationship between buildings and the external world.

20.7, 20.18 Michaella Tafalla, Y5 'Coastal Modding'. The project explores a decentralised fabrication method for the micro-town of Sitio Pariahan in the Philippines and speculates on how the coastal community will adapt to its changing material ecology. Experimentation is carried out through a computational process. Fabrication methods using salvaged synthetic waste as building material combine with traditional vernacular systems to create a new 'Anthropocene' coastal construction method.

20.8, 20.20 Isaac Palmiere-Szabo, Y4 'The Barbican Digester'. Anaerobic digestion is integrated into a dense mixed-use building to metabolise the surrounding neighbourhood's waste and give its residents decentralised free energy with no carbon cost. It tests the integration of heavy infrastructure with architecture to create a productive ecosystem whose outputs feed into its inputs. Beginning life as a bodysuit, the system evolves into a building.

20.9, 20.11 Wojciech Karnowka, Y4 'Saxa Fractionis'. The project explores analogies between the rapidly evolving digital realm and the City of London – a highly centralised enclave that has failed to adapt to the changes in our work-life environment. The proposal challenges the paradigm of how buildings are designed, constructed and managed through new systems of ownership.

20.10 Luke Topping, Y4 'Coalescence'. A new crafts quarter in the City of London that decentralises the trade, training, production, inhabitation and storing associated with the creation of craft goods. Looking to medieval working topologies as decentralised autonomous systems of production, the project investigates the relationship between the master and apprentice, guild systems and their contemporary translation.

20.12 Zhong Zheng, Y5 'Fortress Besieged'. The urban village is a unique alternative urban typology, an economic and social ecosystem formed because of failures in urban governance and economic greed. The spontaneous nature of the urban village puts it in a position to become the space that can resist the complete commodification of urban space and total urbanisation.

20.13 Paul Brooke, Y5 'Post-Industrial Ephemera'. Sited within the post-industrial scarred landscapes of the UK, this project reconsiders the decentralised infrastructural wasteland as a site of rich material opportunity. Through the development and data-driven deployment of novel symbiotic post-waste composite materials, a functionally graded infrastructural network remediates the toxic biome, establishing a new era of carbon-negative industrial production.

20.14 Michael Brewster, Y5 'VRAM'. In the age of big data, every memory captured by a digital photograph is forever stored online via cloud services. Virtual Reality Augmented Memories (VRAM) is a real-time experience designed to leverage these cloud archives and enable an individual to explore their digital memories and arrange these within a dreamlike architectural encapsulation of subjective experience.

20.15 James Ballentyne, Y5 'Terr[Air]Forma'. The project envisages the 'city of the future' in a world where the population is expected to reach 9.8 billion by 2050. With the overcrowding of urban areas, the possibilities of building in areas we have previously deemed too extreme to build on are investigated, to relieve the strain on the ever-growing urban environment.

20.17 Abigail Yeboah, Y5 'Lagos: An Amphibious City'. The growth of cities often increases the economic disparities contained within them. People in informal settlements live in areas with poor-quality housing. This project proposes a regeneration of Makoko by improving living conditions through incremental changes. It sets out to decentralise the construction industry in Nigeria and increase access to potable water by harvesting water from individual buildings.

20.21–20.22 Shenton Morgan, Y5 'Exogenesis'. The project develops off-world architectures capable of evolving to endure the extreme environments of outer space. It navigates cultural identity through juxtaposing domesticity with robotics, archiving vernacular architectures of Earth using machine learning and reimagining historical typologies through deep-learning methodologies. The project's goal is to create a new, adaptive architectural system for human inhabitation, informed by the diverse vernaculars of Earth.

20.23–20.24 Luke Parkhurst, Y5 'Augmented Space Station'. The project provides inflatable spaces for the current International Space Station (ISS) and develops novel ways to address the confinement and isolation experienced by astronauts. Virtual reality headsets work in conjunction with the interior fabric of the proposal to free astronauts from the confines of the ISS and enable reconnection with the Earth's natural environments.

20.2

20.3

20.4

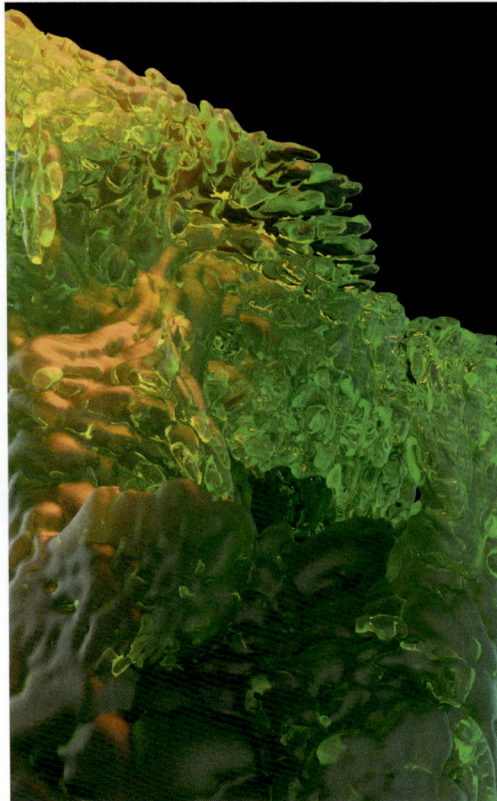

20.5

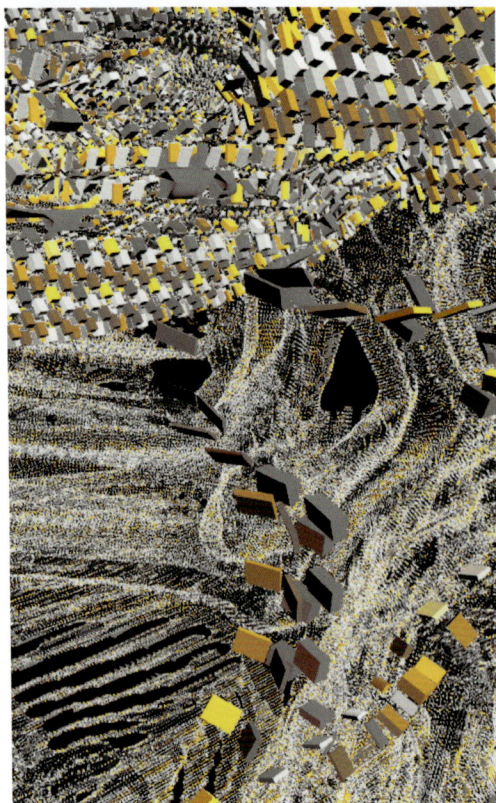

20.6

20.7

20.8

20.9

20.10

20.11

20.12

20.13

20.14

20.15

20.16

20.17

20.18

20.19

20.20

20.21

20.23

20.24

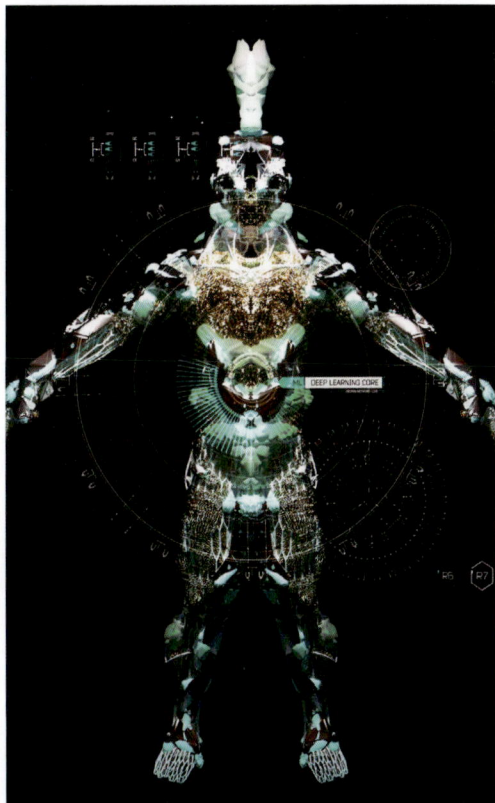

20.22

Finite

Abigail Ashton, Tom Holberton, Andrew Porter

This year PG21 considered the finite.

The past 18 months of accelerated digital development have tested what can be achieved with less material consumption and physical movement. As we return to a supposed 'normality', urgent questions remain unanswered. As of 2014, humanity's global ecological consumption is 1.7 times the Earth's capacity. Apocalyptic deadlines suggest the world will be running out of sand (20 years), fresh water (28 years), food (18 years) and iron (64 years). Architecture increasingly looks beyond one moment of design to influence material supply chains and consider the entire lifespan of a space.

PG21 were asked to consider different aspects of the finite and the infinite. Can we create inventive architecture by imposing a strict limit on a material, a boundary, on time or perception? When do we use infinite digital space and infinite change to augment the fixed and finite? When do society's rules create artificial limits and change the ways in which we design?

Architecture that values the finite needs to be created within time. Many systems around us operate as infinite games, with no ultimate outcome, measuring their value through incremental changes. New ways of drawing, modelling and filmmaking can consider architecture as a dynamic process of near infinite change and feedback. The Poincaré disk model, used by M. C. Escher, draws infinite space in a simple circle using hyperbolic geometry. Computer simulations and calculus quantify infinitesimal changes to provide certain predictions from many tiny moments of uncertainty. Fractal shapes contain never-ending patterns that resemble one another across different scales.

The students' research this year straddled the material and immaterial, the physical and the infinite. They developed inventive design processes that not only followed strict rules of resources, materials and making but also provided architecture that was dynamic, reflective and thoughtful – and made best use of the digital infinite.

We travelled to the Isle of Portland on the south coast of the UK, an area described by Jonathan Meades as a 'bulky chunk of geological, social, topographical and demographic weirdness'. Here students developed their own highly individual design processes and architectures.

Year 4
Shou-Hui Chen, Emily Child, Sebastian Coupe, Migena Hadzui, Hugo Loydell, Oscar Maguire

Year 5
Alp Amasya, Kiren Kaur Basi, Lewis Brown, Carmen Kong, Rolandas Markevicius, Ajay Mohan, Maria Eleni Petalidou, Samuel Pierce, Zhi (Zoe) Tam, Yat Shun Tang

Technical tutors and consultants: Tom Holberton, Brian Eckersley (Eckersley O'Callaghan), Ali Shaw (Max Fordham) with additional support from Julian Besems, Steve Webb

Critics: Julian Besems, Roberto Bottazzi, Naomi Gibson, Kostas Grigoriadis, Bethan Ring, Jasmin Sohi

21.1–21.3 Rolandas Markevicius, Y5 'Synthetic Synaesthesia'. The developments in deep neural networks force us to reconsider the role of references. The project frames this statement through the challenge of establishing synaesthetic links between architecture and music, suggesting that the new instruments offered by machine learning allow designers to play with abstract features systematically. The project proposes the practical implementation of a Pix2Pix general adversarial network, creating common maps between architectural drawings and audio spectrograms and shaping methodologies for formalising relationships between sets of data. Personalised software and data augmentation procedures are developed throughout the project to aid the design of a music school in Portland in Dorset, UK.

21.4–21.5 Alp Amasya, Y5 'How to Draw a Hyperobject'. Taking Timothy Morton's theory of hyperobjects as a starting point, the project creates a drawing system that translates hyperobject principles into architecture. This philosophical approach to high-dimensional systems is spatialised through digital simulations, focusing on the Jurassic Coast of England. The project creates a drawing method performed by the fossils embedded in Portland stone. Looking at the intangible qualities of architecture as a hyperobject, building clusters alternate between multiple options, offering ambiguous boundaries and ever-changing design outcomes.

21.6 Maria Eleni Petalidou, Y5 'Unwrapping Heritage: A Garden of Artefacts'. If all the artefacts in the British Museum were returned to their home countries, what would happen to its Bloomsbury building? The project proposes a thematic garden of unwrapped artefacts where one can experience their aura through architecture. The design is based on 3D scans of artefacts taken from the museum. The scanned models are cut, unwrapped and rewrapped to create new spatial forms that generate a landscape that reflects not only the qualities of the artefacts themselves but also the stories behind them. In an era where the digital is merging with the physical, the information behind cultural heritage is a starting point to create a modern pleasure garden of artefacts.

21.7 Oscar Maguire, Y4 'Transposing the Courtyard'. Since the 1850s, the Courtyard Societies had been accommodated rent-free in Burlington House in London, a grand neoclassical edifice built from Portland stone. Recently, however, the UK government has decided to start charging rent on the property. This has been increasing yearly at an unsustainable rate so that the tenants must either negotiate a deal, find a new home or perish. This project proposes an architectural solution to their problem, whereby all five societies occupy a Portland stone quarry that is being restored to a natural environment, reversing the historical extraction of material, capital and culture from the area.

21.8–21.9 Kiran Kaur Basi, Y5 'A Non-Extractivist University'. Countering the idea of the Isle of Portland as a sacrifice zone, a non-extractivist mindset is adopted to refill a disused quarry with value and contribute to the sustainable development of the island. This is designed using a combination of recursive algorithms and topographic data to generate a highly contextual scheme which is bold in its design, which celebrates the legacy of the island's stone industry while inspiring its students and promoting mindful extraction.

21.10 Carmen Kong, Y5 'Archiving the Jurassic Coast'. Sited on the Jurassic Coast, this project highlights the paradox of conserving an eroding coastline. The coast, the only natural heritage site in the UK, is a geomorphological landscape that encompasses 180 million years of geological history, acting as a natural archive. This project documents the coast through speculative fossil data; this data is then used as a positive volume, allowing the architecture to mould into the negative space mimicking the coastal processes. As the coastline recedes, the Jurassic Coast is fossilised into the architecture.

21.11 Ajay Mohan, Y5 'Between the Line and the Land'. The project speculates upon the spatial polarity between the City of London and the Isle of Portland, developing into an insurgent distortion of a formless landscape via a series of physical navigations undertaken in the City. Once an unwitting product of an exploratory process, the navigational line now emerges as the spatial protagonist of the cliffside site, negotiating between the medium of land, air and sea; the architecture that emerges is alien in nature, a geodetic artefact that dances between the line and the land.

21.12 Yat Shun Tang, Y5 'Coastline Infinity'. The project focuses on the World Heritage coastline in southern England and examines its hundred-million-year-old geomorphology. The design of the new Jurassic Coast Fund Centre employs a series of algorithms that represent the dynamic forces of the Isle of Portland.

21.13 Hugo Loydell, Y4 'Defining the Architectural Foveal'. Within the scarred landscape of Portland, a proposed climbing research centre explores the agency of the eye's gaze within space. Through experiments in spatialising foveated level of detail, the fixations and saccades of the eye are utilised to encode spatial narratives and develop new climbing typologies. This serves to reduce the dissonance between the imagined and experienced architecture, the climber and the wall.

21.14–21.15 Samuel Pierce, Y5 'YOI Portland: Rehabilitative Landscapes'. Augmented and virtual reality technologies make the world of information visually immediate. The transformative effects of virtual environments are applied to a proposed young offender's institute on the Isle of Portland whose history is deeply intertwined with the development of the modern carceral system. The project strives for a compassionate, adaptive and therapeutic architecture by providing a wide range of physical spatial conditions which address the specific requirements of the user while further moderating their progression through digital environments. Landscape and architectural devices provide the necessary boundaries between spaces while maintaining a visual connection further articulated through digital augmentation. Agency over their social, educational and visual environment allows individuals to take control of their pathway back into society, cultivating new levels of self-awareness.

21.16–21.17 Sebastian Coupe, Y4 'The Stone Organ: A Concert Hall for a Lunar Landscape'. The idea of an environmentally positive stone renaissance runs contrary to an island that continues to suffer environmental degradation at the hands of the quarrying industry. Many within Portland see the preservation of its natural beauty as a crucial element in generating future tourism to the island and condemn the impact of quarrying, while others regard quarrying as fundamental to Portland's identity. It is within the context of this dialogue that this project utilises the quarrying and stonecutting processes that have defined the island for centuries to create a place of cultural and social significance.

21.18–21.21 Lewis Brown, Y5 'Printed Morphologies'. The project elevates desktop 3D printing to a performative art, through iterative feedback systems and reactive drawing practices. The dynamic printer bed acts as a flux terrain that can shift seamlessly between scales, existing in a dualistic state that spans both the geological landscape of Portland and the printed topography of the generative physical model.

21.2

21.3

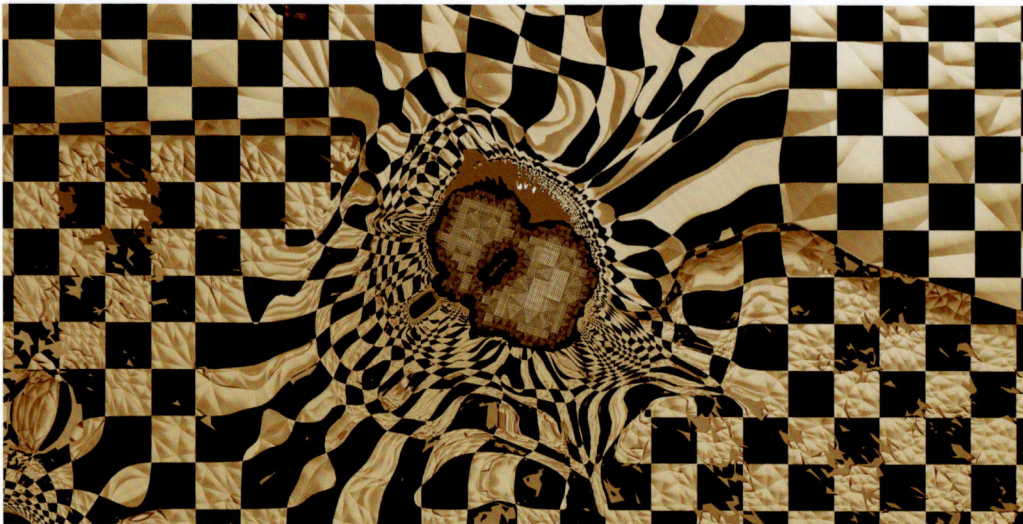

21.4

21.5

21.7

21.8

21.9

21.10

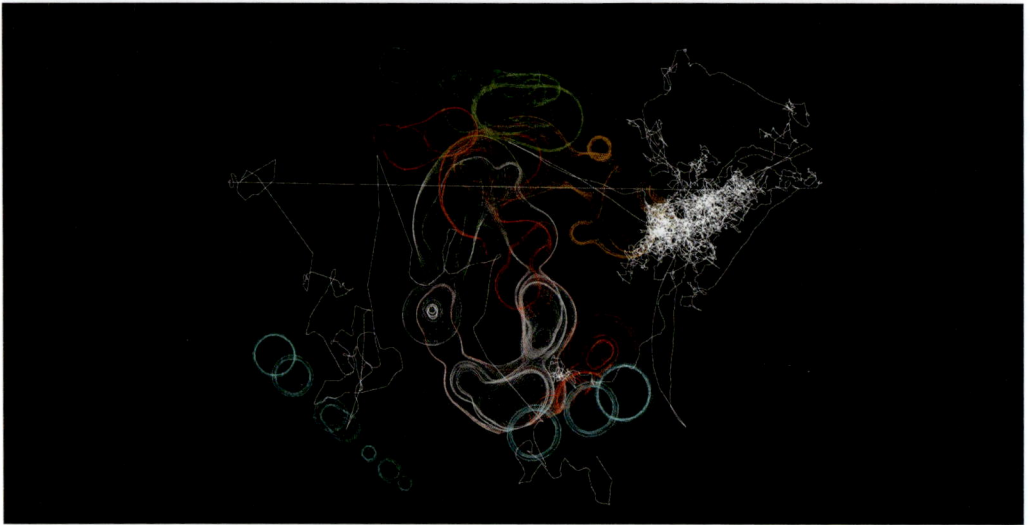

21.11

21.12

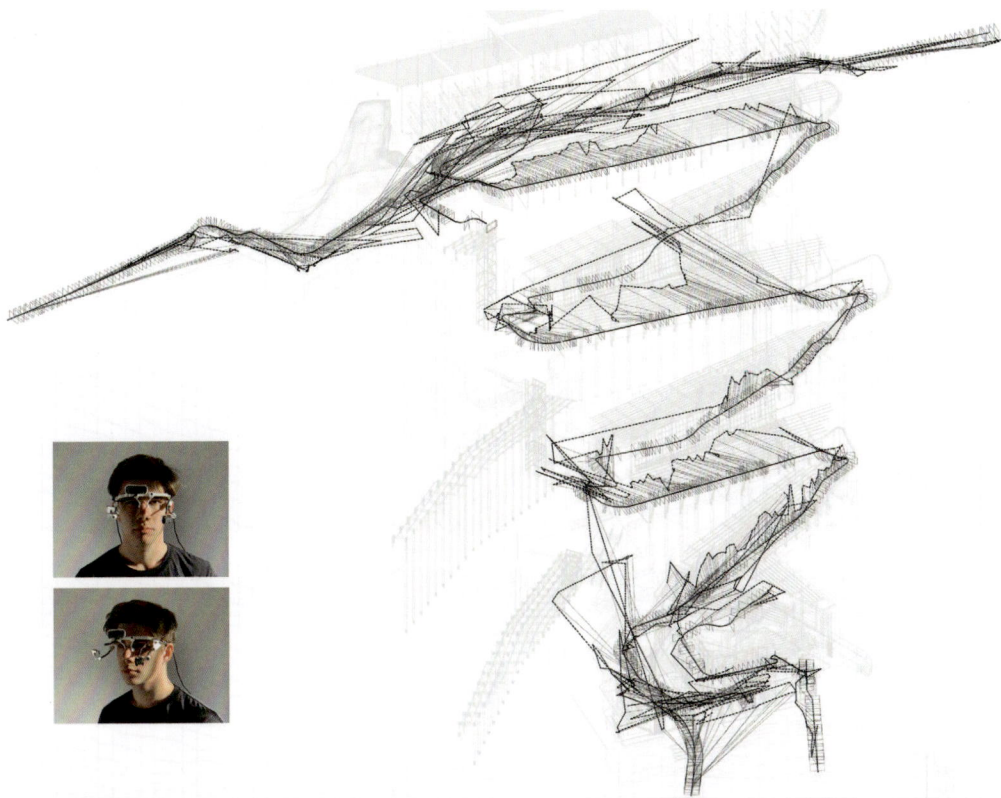

21.13

21.14

21.15

21.16

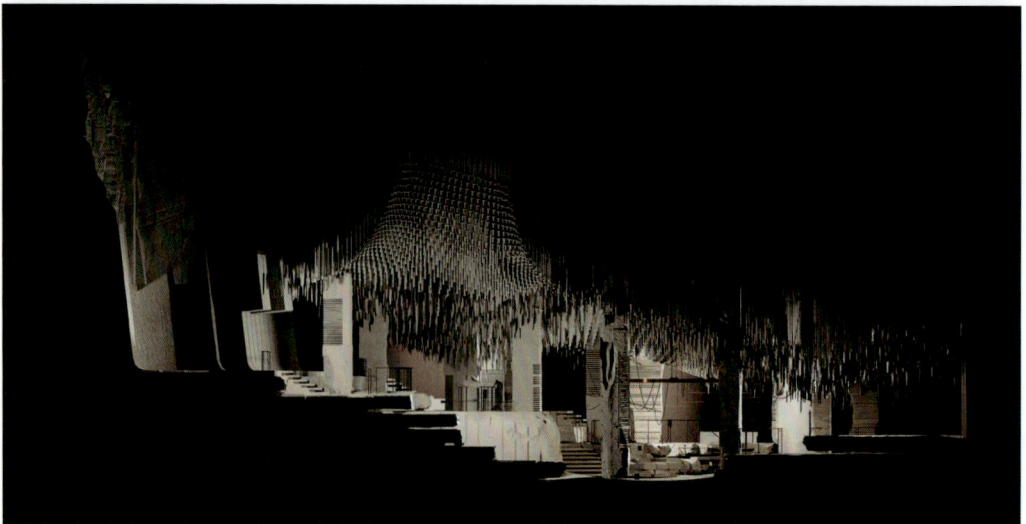

21.17

21.18

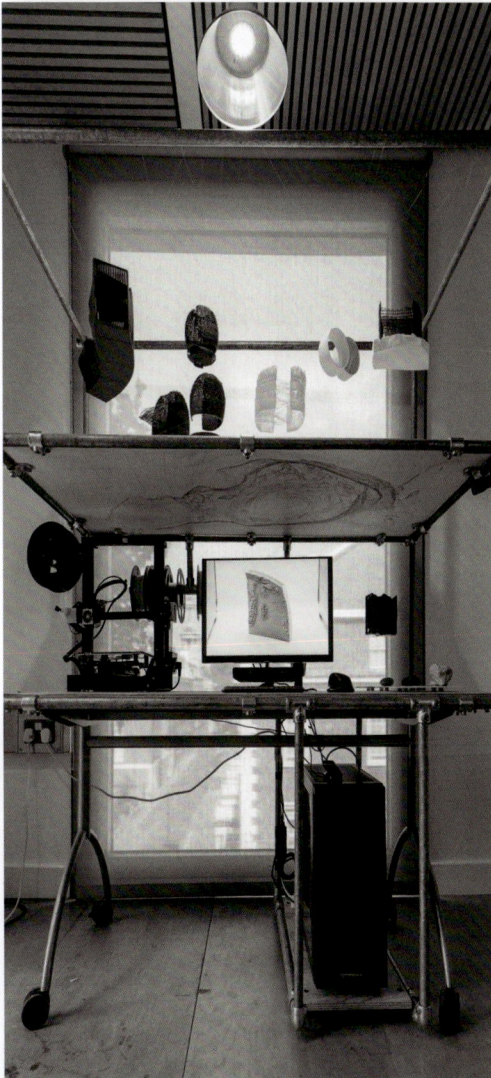

21.19

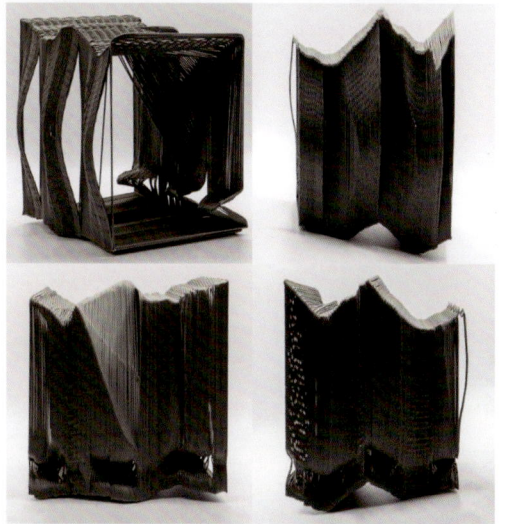

21.20

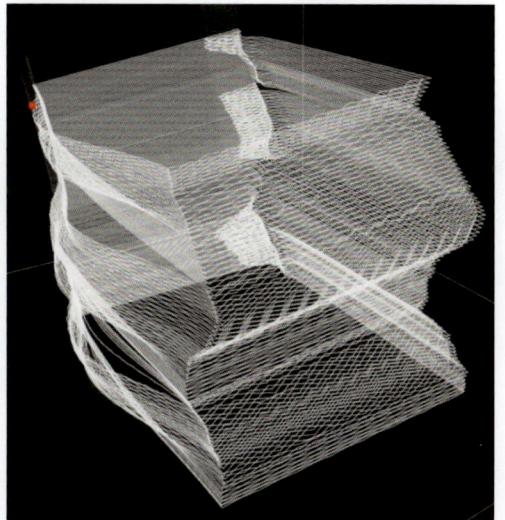

21.21

Dollhouse, Bingo and Ring PG22

Izaskun Chinchilla Moreno, Jan Kattein, Daniel Ovalle Costal

This year PG22 students were invited to develop a design critique of mass-produced austerity in architecture, uncovering the politics behind it and proposing alternatives.

The ethos of the Arts and Crafts movement, born in mid-19th century Britain under the auspices of figures such as William Morris, John Ruskin and Augustus Pugin, was suggested as an example of socially conscious anti-austerity. The title of the brief refers to three games, mostly played by women of that era, which inspired the three design exercises proposed.

Sociologist Richard Sennett highlights the importance of craftsmanship in books such as *The Craftsman* and *Together*. He argues that the 'enduring basic human pulse' that comes from perfecting a craft creates deep inner satisfaction. For Sennet, allowing principles of craftsmanship to guide an individual's life at their own pace can provide benefits for both individuals and society. His writing on craftmanship provides an alternative reading of the Arts and Crafts as one of the most socially desirable architectural movements in history.

The movement did not merely propose a style or a visual repertoire; it rather offered an idyllic lifestyle in which people could work in quasi-domestic workshops, caring about the origin of materials, the choice of crafting techniques and the quality of the result.

In retrospect, it is reasonable to question why 20th-century architects abandoned the Arts and Crafts philosophy *en masse*, instead embracing the Modern Movement principles of industry and standardised mass production with great enthusiasm. The austerity inherent to mass produced design was introduced by the proponents of the Modern Movement to distinguish revolutionary new architecture from old 19th-century traditions. They dedicated far more effort to fighting ornament than to critically assessing the living conditions and lifestyle that mass production imposed upon workers who fabricated these new designs.

From today's perspective, there is something perverse in the proposition that to democratise design it must be stripped of variation and visual and material richness. A century on, we should critically reconsider whether mass-produced austerity has satisfied its initial aspirations of supporting and empowering the working class, fostering intellectual honesty and cultural progress.

Year 4
Long Yin Au, Deluo Chen, Ayla Hemou El Mardini, Monika Kolarz, Jack Nash, Hei Tung Michael Ng, Sonakshi Pandit

Year 5
Asli Aktu, Annabelle Blyton, James Ford, Luba Kuziw, Verena Leung, Jignesh Pithadia, Cheuk Ying Sharon So, Olivia Trinder, Simon Wong

Technical tutors and consultants: Gonzalo Coello de Portugal, Roberto Coraci, Roberto Marín Sampalo

Thesis supervisors: Hector Altamirano, Sabina Andron, Carolina Bartram, Jan Birksted, Amica Dall, Paul Dobraszczyk, Murray Fraser, Joshua Mardell

Critics: Lluis Alexandre Casanovas, Sarina da Costa Gómez, Pepe la Cruz, Naomi Gibson, Faye Greenwood, Kyriakos Katsaros, Matthieu Mereau, Ana Mayoral Moratilla, Adam Peacock, Pedro Pitarch, Guillermo Sánchez Sotés, Chrysanthe Staikopoulou, Joshua Thomas, Jonathan Tyrrell, Kate Woodcock-Fowles

22.1 Luba Kuziw, Y5 'The Modern Tradition'. An exploration of the use of straw as a modern building material, turning the industry inwards and developing a world of cyclical craft between communities. The project is situated in London's Robin Hood Gardens and proposes the gradual replacement of the estate's poorly performing façades with prefabricated biodegradable panels developed by craftspeople from the community using locally grown wheat.

22.2 Simon Wong, Y5 'The Maiden's Tale'. The project introduces a different method of acquiring new skills while continuing to develop a sense of community for the low-income families that live in the Maiden Lane Estate in Camden. Conceived as a bottom-up initiative, the project proposes a retrofit academy to upskill residents and upgrade the estate. The academy will provide retrofitting not just for Maiden Lane, but for the entirety of the borough as well.

22.3–22.4 Asli Aktu, Y5 'The Social Stair'. This project is the continuation of the Dawson's Heights estate in East Dulwich, establishing a new design agenda from a 2022 perspective, influenced by and in response to its architect, Kate Macintosh. The proposal combines social ambitions for the estate with a centralised stairwell which provides a new point of access alongside a variety of social amenities for residents of the estate and the wider community across 12 levels.

22.5 Ayla Hamou El Mardini, Y4 'Hideaway Gardens: Redefining Private Gradients'. A redesign of the traditional neighbourhood framework using a precedent from historical Islamic Mamluk architecture – the Qalawun complex in Cairo, Egypt. The project is a mixed-use building with residential units, carpet refurbishment workshops, a carpet-weaving academy and retail spaces. These programmes are configured around a sequence of semi-public courtyards.

22.6 James Ford, Y5 'Low Speed One'. A design critique of the High Speed Two (HS2) railway. The project challenges the benefits of a new high-speed rail service across England by instead proposing the reversal of the 'Beeching cuts' of the 1960s and 70s. Low Speed One speculates on whether the implementation of a slow transport network could have a greater impact on more communities, while helping to implement the government's 'levelling up' agenda.

22.7 Sonakshi Pandit, Y4 'The Rewilding Hub: Remediation through Reciprocity'. Situated in the car-centric area of South Croydon, the proposal seeks to repurpose obsolete gas works, transforming them into hubs that support seed and soil preservation, as well as providing infrastructure to facilitate seed dispersal in a radical rewilding of road infrastructure.

22.8 Long Yin Au, Y4 'Tottenham Hale Cycletopia'. An alternative masterplan based on the principles of the 15-minute city, which proposes a cycling infrastructure to encourage more people to shift from cars to bicycles. At the centre of the masterplan is the headquarters of Pashley Bicycles, made up of workshops, BMX training grounds, offices and a bike-through kitchen. The building exemplifies how bicycle culture extends beyond cycling and into forms of creative expression, campaigning, performing and gathering.

22.9 Deluo Chen, Y4 'UCL Urban Agriculture Faculty'. The project proposes transforming Vauxhall City Farm into a mixed-use urban farm with in-residence research in the form of the UCL Urban Agriculture Faculty. This project reimagines the city farm and goes beyond its current form to create a living, breathing and thriving community for humans and animals alike, a place where coexistence between species is the driving force.

22.10–22.11 Verena Leung, Y5 'Urban Living Rooms'. An alternative regeneration of the Brownfield Estate in Poplar, East London, that reactivates its domestic streets by dissolving private and public boundaries and creating a new urban living room. In view of the fashion industry's revival in East London, the project introduces slow fashion programmes to transform the underused street into a collective live-work space.

22.12 Hei Tung Michael Ng, Y4 'The Bright Kitchen'. Reimagining cooking spaces as new agents of social sustainability, local empowerment and circularity. The project introduces a community-led food cooperative as an alternative urban regeneration scheme for a post-war estate. The proposal creates a bright, transparent and accessible food-sharing network that connects domestic and urban realms.

22.13–22.14 Annabelle Blyton, Y5 'The Walthamstow Water Collective'. The project collects water in the literal sense, while also bringing people together over the positive potential of water. New studies reveal that proximity to water has a similar positive impact to closeness to green space, with an added 'psychologically restorative effect'. The project promotes a greater understanding of these therapeutic blue spaces and improves access to them.

22.15 Jack Nash, Y4 'Mixing Up Making in Clerkenwell'. The project puts forward a mixed-use strategy with a combination of live-work spaces for single crafters and makers. Concerned with reviving Clerkenwell's historic reputation for making and crafting, it hopes to offer an updated form of the guilds for the 21st century.

22.16 Olivia Trinder, Y5 'Wasted Space: De-Growth of Tottenham Hale'. The design proposal is set in the not-too-distant future, where complications surrounding the current development of Tottenham Hale have led to its construction being halted. The local community has been able to buy up the abandoned site in pursuit of creating a shared living space. Utilising both traditional and modern construction methods and materials, inhabitation occurs close to the ground plane in this pastoral, slow-living high-rise.

22.2

22.3

22.4

22.5

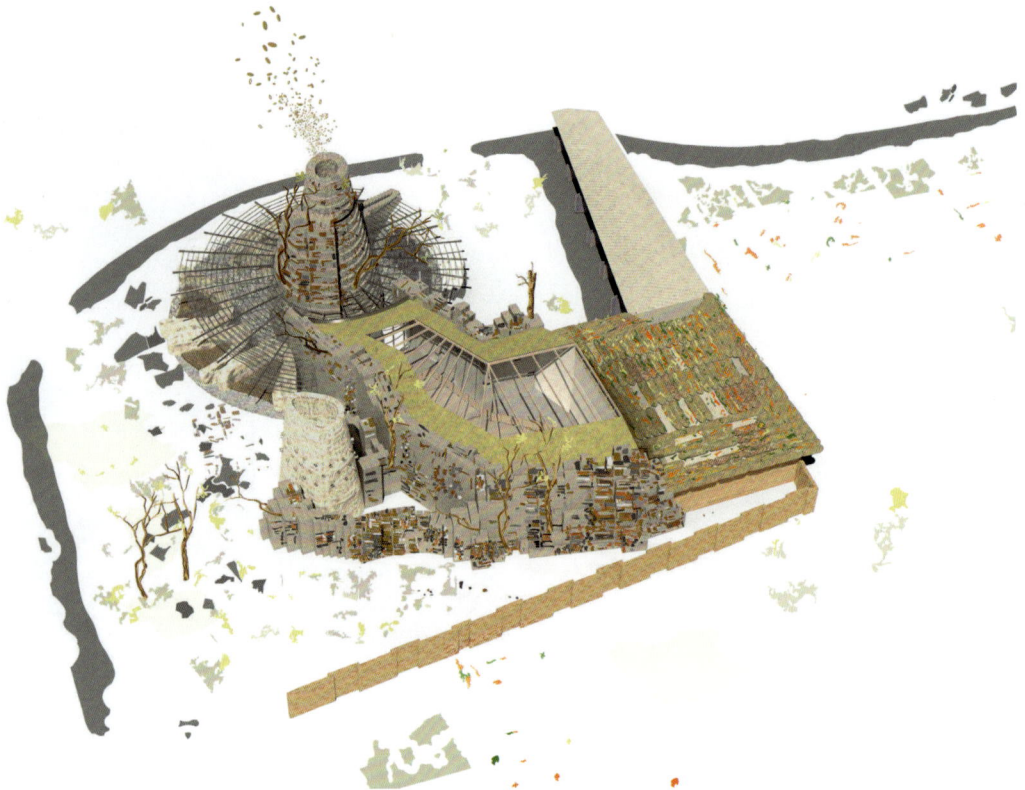

22.7

22.8

Urban Agriculture

Vauxhall Pleas

22.10

22.11

22.12

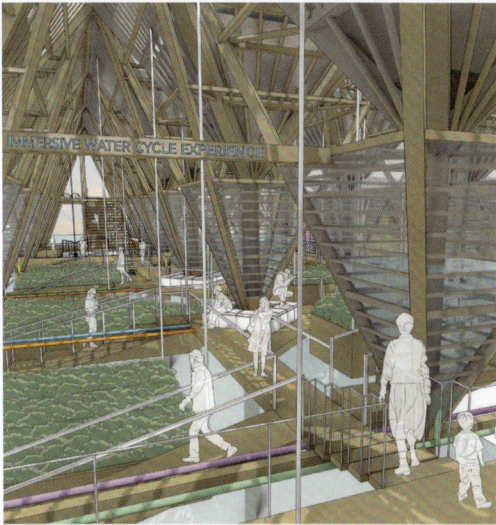

22.13

22.14

22.15

24.1

Vibrant Matter

Penelope Haralambidou, Michael Tite

PG24 is a group of architectural storytellers who employ film, animation, VR/AR and physical modelling techniques to help make sense of the complexity of today's world. Inspired by philosophy, this year we questioned our relationship with matter.

In *Vibrant Matter*, political philosopher Jane Bennett theorises a vital materiality that runs through and across human and non-human entities. Furthermore, thinkers such as Graham Harman and Timothy Morton propose an 'object-oriented ontology' that perceives material things as alive and multi-scaled, sentient even. They insist that we are made of, and are surrounded by, a vibrant world of correlated habitats and non-human conscience: a steel column, a hurricane, a cup of tea, a microbe – all belong to a universal material sameness that created us.

The climate emergency is seen as the result of human activity. Solutions often use the same technological thinking that has led to the crisis in the first place. But what if we firstly (and urgently) reconsider our understanding of the world of things? Instead of shaping matter, can we allow matter to shape our sensibility as designers?

We considered these ideas like sculptors obsessing over raw materials or philosophers engaging intellectually with the concept of matter itself. How is time embedded in matter? How do we define value in materials? What about edible matter and architecture's relationship to food? When does material become waste?

In the process we invented new types of physical and digital hybrid matter, tethering ethereal new behaviours to tangible material. We reflected on how this new hybrid matter can influence not only our manufacturing, design and entertainment industries, but also our everyday, helping to form new local and global communities. To support this material awakening we explored the historical, social and industrial heritage of diverse sites, portraying the stories embedded in the life of their material resources and the communities that these create. In so doing we moved towards an architecture of vibrant matter.

Year 4
Loukis Menelaou, Cira Oller Tovar, Joshua Richardson, Matthew Semião Carmo Simpson, Chak (Anthony) Tai

Year 5
Vitika Agarwal, Jatiphak Boonmun, Kalliopi Bosini, Paris Gazzola, Gabriele Grassi, Holly Harbour, Daniel Johnston, Carlota Nuñez-Barranco Vallejo, Tom Ushakov, David Wood

Technical tutor and consultant: Matthew Lucraft

Thesis supervisors: Camilo Boano, Amica Dall, Oliver Domeisen, Claire McAndrew, Harry Parr, Tania Sengupta, Robin Wilson, Oliver Wilton, Fiona Zisch, Stamatis Zografos

Critics: Laura Allen, Mark Breeze, Rhys Cannon, Barbara-Ann Campbell-Lange, Marjan Colletti, John Cruwys, Claude Dutson, Pedro Gil-Quintero, Matt Lucraft, Matei Mitrache, Caireen O'Hagan, George Proud, Javier Ruiz Rodriguez, Mark Smout, Jasper Stevens, Jonathan Tyrrell

24.1 Paris Gazzola, Y5 'My Land, Mine Land'. The project is an investigation into the gold-mining towns of Western Australia. It critiques imported colonial knowledge and imagines a new future for the settlement of Leonora. The settlement is composed of an archipelago of residential islands on the surface that extend into social, commercial and industrial spaces underground. A new kind of desert living is proposed that sits in contrast to the resource-hungry models of the recent past – one based on local resources and knowledge, remediation and the coexistence of different societies. The film explores this interconnected underground realm as a cinematic love letter playing backwards – a hopeful, resilient and optimistic future for a once-scorched Earth.

24.2 Kalliopi Bosini, Y5 'Mani Stone Kneaded'. The Greek peninsula of Mani is facing increasingly difficult environmental and social challenges as younger generations move to bigger cities. This internal migration is leading to the gradual abandonment of the region, resulting in the loss of equilibrium between heritage, identity and socio-economic growth. The new settlement in the village of Kardamyli traces the timeless reciprocal relationship between the land, extracted materials and the shaped architecture. A rebirth of the families' domestic and labour needs is enabled through the exclusive production of olive oil and soap. A new socially, economically and environmentally sustainable Maniotian vernacular is imagined, matching the village's origins and its true historic identity.

24.3–24.5 Carlota Nuñez-Barranco Vallejo, Y5 'Queens of the Desert Age'. Located in southern Spain at a point in the near future, a female-led settlement survives in an incredibly hostile environment. Three primary technological powers (wind, solar and organic matter) are harnessed and sit alongside residential dwellings. Research into the science-fiction genre generated a positive future vision, where climate change is a force for active development. Three mystical 'queens' emerge from the desert terrain, each responsible for controlling and channelling their regions' power, each with an amorphous identity that translates into their respective architectures. Building on utopian visions of agrarian societies, the project comments on the uneven city-centric population distribution in Spanish society.

24.6 Gabriele Grassi, Y5 'Wast\ed'. The project explores food production, consumption and waste systems. An unconventional material palette is proposed, fusing traditional building materials with food: an architecture of chocolate, milk, vegetables, plastic, cardboard and wood. A storytelling dining table capable of blurring scales and material conditions, morphs between the fictional and the informational, the real and the virtual. The final film borrows narrative elements of Lewis Carroll's *Alice in Wonderland* to tell a contemporary story of consumption and waste. The result is a surreal communal dining hall with a sobering wake-up call to our contemporary state of gluttony.

24.7–24.9 Tom Ushakov, Y5 'Gatekeepers of Memory'. The project translates idiosyncratic metaphysical concepts into space and takes the form of pavilions nestled in a speculative landscape. Readings of Pallasmaa, Yates and Plutchik's 'Wheel of Emotion' underpin the layout of this imaginary realm, depicted in a large-scale model/table/mindscape masterplan. Each pavilion is assigned an emotion and a memory which, when combined, create a central edifice – the 'House of Emotion'. A semi-autobiographical protagonist sets out on a hero's journey to explore these internal monochromatic landscapes, reflecting on past experience and searching out new forms. Upon his return to reality, he builds the table as a cathartic act, to give an external grounding to his internal world.

24.10 Jatiphak Boonmun, Y5 'Performances of Authenticity'. A series of performative architectures reveal the indigenous truths of the Republic of Formosa. Reacting to the fictitious histories presented to the West by George Psalmanazar in the 1740s, the project foregrounds the islanders' true heritage while also forging new spatial possibilities. Exploring how aboriginal performativity navigates architecture against the backdrop of nuclear waste storage, this filmic architecture exposes and critiques various forms of cadastral land interpretation. The proposal is a quasi-theatre nuclear waste facility that follows a crafted itinerary. It describes a surreal world that sits between performance, theatre and historical storytelling.

24.11–24.13 Holly Harbour, Y5 'The Beautiful and the Dammed'. In the mountains of Guatemala, mega-infrastructure projects lead to the forced displacement of local Mayan farming communities, with protestations claiming the lives of indigenous activists. The project imagines a new future for a hydroelectric dam that is reclaimed by local people as a site of pilgrimage and a memorial to lives lost. The structure provides a stage for the performance of rituals and festivities whose degree of transience relates to the Mayan calendar, taking inspiration from ancient mythology and the magic realist writings of Miguel Ángel Asturias. The building is shaped by time, water and human activity in a manner that contrasts the traditionally immutable structure of a dam.

24.14 Daniel Johnston, Y5 'The Para-Nominal (e)State'. The project explores contemporary ideas of value, which have become eroded as technology has progressed. It asks whether an alternative digital valuation system can create new commodities, typologies and emergent programmes, and how it might alter everyday physical spaces. Responding to London's housing crisis, a new kind of dwelling is prototyped within the Barking Riverside masterplan, including 19 residential units, a corner shop, bin store and courtyard. Unrestricted by screens, the form and content of the home become warped and twisted. A universal digital overlay is designed within the estate, offering residents the chance to customise their homes and link to the wider community.

24.15–24.17 David Wood, Y5 'Capturing the Arctic'. The project describes an expedition, a yearly ritual of capturing, transporting and reconfiguring Arctic ice. Arriving in London, an ice harvester is met by a small flotilla that journeys down the Thames, transforming the ice into a water fountain, an ice rink and an Arctic temple. Mirroring the otherworldliness of remote, extreme landscapes, the film explores the fragility between preservation and loss on a human scale through a part-drawn, part-digital architecture. The ceremonial proposal addresses the overwhelming enormity of shifts that are occurring in the Arctic and the memory of landscapes that are disappearing from sight.

24.18 Vitika Agarwal, Y5 'Inhabiting Hybridity'. The project responds to the postcolonial theory of cultural hybridity through a combination of British and Indian culture. The film depicts the migrant experience of being rooted in many places at once. Located at the prime meridian line in Greenwich Park, the proposal obscures the symbolic division between East and West, creating a fertile third space. Stone, a material used in both cultures as a signifier of permanence, is imagined as an amorphous, transcendental material. Through a digital time-based refiguring, it carries the potential to be constantly reshaped by addition and subtraction. The resulting architecture is a hybrid reforming of Britain and India, the past and present, the real and imagined.

24.3

24.4

24.5

871452

5629

24.6

24.7

24.8

24.9

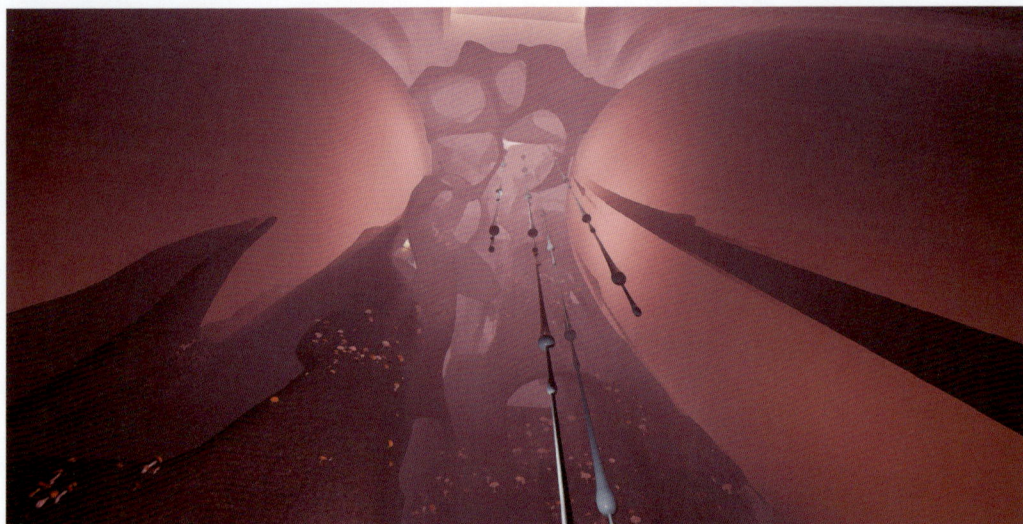

24.11

24.12

24.13

24.15

24.16

24.17

An Ecology of Architectural Knowledge

Nat Chard, Emma-Kate Matthews

This year PG25 is running architectural research and creative practice in parallel. We asked what constitutes an ecology of architectural knowledge, with a particular emphasis on each student's underlying practice. The unit helps students develop a practice that is individual to their fascinations, with an emphasis on the processes, material and media that can carry a particular form of speculation. Research and practice are developed simultaneously, both through experimentation and careful reflection. Although the academic year typically places emphasis on the final project, this year we acknowledged that most practitioners have a practice that constantly evolves and transcends an individual project.

One of the pleasures of architecture is that it first gathers many ideas and interests, then makes sense of them through an assembly that is richer and more telling than the parts. Where does the knowledge enabling us to do this come from and how do we further that knowledge? We have investigated how new architectural knowledge is generated while also learning from the past. We also explored the ongoing studies of architects and artists in other fields, examining ideas and acts of practise to develop skills and sensibilities. We were specifically interested in how spatial networks equate to ecological networks across disciplines, and the ways in which architectural knowledge exists within larger networks.

Our site this year was the Isle of Portland, Dorset. Unimaginable volumes of stone have been extracted from the island to build London's monuments (one million cubic feet for St Paul's Cathedral alone). The combination of the given geology and subtractive quarrying have created a captivating landscape. As stone is having a renaissance as a sustainable material and a more economically viable material to work with due to CNC tools, Portland provides an opportunity to study the rich history of stone construction and to speculate on its future possibilities.

Year 4
Theo Brader-Tan, Florence Hemmings, Yu-Wen (Yvonne) Huang, Joe Johnson, Ziwei Liu, Olivia O'Callaghan

Year 5
Hannah Anderson, George Barnes, Samuel Beattie, Grant Beaumont, George Brazier, Conor Clarke, Eleanor Evason, Bessie Holloway Davies, Simona Moneva, Sindija Skilta, Adam West

Technical tutors and consultants: Bedir Bekar, Ioannis Rizos, Jerry Tate

Thesis supervisors: Alessandro Ayuso, Oliver Domeisen, Christophe Gérard, Polly Gould, Joshua Mardell, Elise Misao Hunchuck, Shaun Murray, Thomas Pearce, Stamatis Zografos

Critics: Alessandro Ayuso, Barbara-Ann Campbell-Lange, Perry Kulper, Ben McDonnell, Alex Pillen, Mark Ruthven, Gill Scampton, Justin Sayer

Partners: Emmanuel Vercruysse and Frederik Petersen (Hooke Park)

25.1–25.2 Hannah Anderson, Y5 'Nightwalking the Highlands'. The project explores our relationship with the night and landscapes of darkness. Darkness is an everyday phenomenon that could easily be overlooked due to its apparent simplicity: a lack of light. But what if darkness is not as simple as it seems? How might we see more when we see less? Could the night reveal rather than conceal?

25.3 Adam West, Y5 'Infra-Sculpting Portland'. How could architecture make relationships between different speeds of change? The research began with examining events too fast or slow for us to usually notice. In an abandoned gulley in Tout Quarry, Portland, an existing sculpting infrastructure is extended, providing opportunities for local students to develop artistic practices and reconnect with traditional local crafts.

25.4–25.5 Samuel Beattie, Y5 'An Isle of Excavation – A Guildhall for Stonemasons'. The project adopts a decommissioned Admiralty mine as the site for a stonemason's guild and supplementary workshop. The question of temporality is a key element explored throughout the project. A series of conversations between landscape and occupant evolve through the development of the architecture.

25.6 Yu-Wen (Yvonne) Huang, Y4 'Once upon a Tide'. This project explores the architecture of choreography, using physical and digital garments as drawing instruments to transpose the body's tacit knowledge of Portland Bill's coastal landscape into built spaces across a magnitude of scales.

25.7–25.9 George Brazier, Y5 'Body and Rock'. The body primarily relates to space through furniture and architectural details such as handrails. Furthermore, the act of climbing shifts a largely horizontal usage of space to a vertical one. The work culminates in the design and manufacture of a dining table/climbing wall/site model/drawing board that allows the body to be used as a design tool and questions how the body relates to architecture.

25.10 Grant Beaumont, Y5 'Don't Mention Rabbits'. The Isle of Portland Falconers' Lodge is an experiment in pre-emption, anticipation and finding home. Using the operations of a falconry lodge, the architecture explores how to position itself on the site in the most meaningful way possible, while holding itself in a state of apprehension, waiting for its next requirement. As it does this, it allows for new conditions and spaces to emerge, and with them, the potential for new ecological discoveries.

25.11 Olivia O'Callaghan, Y4 'Somewhere I Have Never Travelled'. After years of producing successful books, a group of authors are running out of ideas and are looking for new ways to write. One of the authors particularly enjoys long walks to develop their ideas. On one of these walks, they overhear a couple animatedly discussing a strange story about the surrounding area.

25.12 George Barnes, Y5 'Regenerative Pressure Points: The Portland Archive at Durdle Pier'. The term 'regenerative pressure points' highlights the use of the old to influence the new. Through the inclusion of our past, whether recent or distant, we are able to imagine an architectural framework where old and new can contribute to an architectural totality.

25.13 Ziwei Liu, Y4 'Untitled'. The project explores the body as a site of transformation and reinvention, while questioning the conventions between body and architecture. If the body is changed, how does architecture change? Conjoined bodies investigate how multiple bodies might come together and ask 'what are the terms of their engagement both with the architecture and with each other?'

25.14–25.15 Simona Moneva, Y5 'Satellite House'. The project is sited on the coastline of the Isle of Portland and is a two-studio residency in which artists and researchers can live and work, providing temporary accommodation, shared spaces and private studies. The architecture is an exploration of spatial connections between physically disconnected fragments (satellite structures) which are bound by a conceptual framework, lines of sight and methods of communication.

25.16–25.17 Eleanor Evason, Y5 'Of Nips & Nits'. The work teases the idea of artefacts 'not-in-place' through an exploration of fossilisation – that strange transformation of something alive and soft into something porous and bone dry. The results of anthropocentric fossilisations are fascinating: shoals of pint glasses partially digested in the trunk of a Volkswagen Beetle.

25.18–25.19 Theo Brader-Tan, Y4 'The Sweep, the Cut and the Lay Up'. This project is an investigation into the relationship between drawing and making, a relationship that is taken for granted in architecture, with its established drawing conventions such as the section and two-point perspective. The topic is enlivened, however, by peering into the historical means of drawing-to-make by shipwrights (the loft) and stonemasons (the trait).

25.20 Florence Hemmings, Y4 'Between the Grains and Gaps – An Object-Led Conditions Forecaster'. Enabling the perception and prediction of the near and far, through the inspection of washed-up objects gifted to the reconfigurable littoral site by the tide, the programme operates within the realms of a 'lost and found' concept, but with projective capacity.

25.21 Bessie Holloway Davies, Y5 'Of the Body, of the Earth: Portland Crematorium'. The project provides a space for mourners to celebrate the lives of their deceased loved ones, allowing memorialisation and remembrance to take precedence via the rituals that take place. Themes of transformation and containment are particularly present. The relationship between the body and ceramics will facilitate the containment of the physical and metaphysical body and soul, allowing for the immortalisation of an embodied memory.

25.22–25.23 Joe Johnson, Y4 'Linkage Lamination – Carving a Festival in Portland, UK'. Stemming from a close study of Michihiro Matsuda's recycled guitar No.125A, this project is concerned with minimising material waste and developing fabrication strategies that extract the maximum potential from timber and local materials. The project explores two methods of fabrication – earth casting and timber lamination. Initial studies in casting concrete in carved earth reveal the scope for fluid, highly intricate geometries to be achieved without the need for complex formwork.

25.24–25.25 Sindija Skilta, Y5 'In Search of the Ordinary and Forgotten'. This exploration of nature pursues a transdiscursive approach. In so doing, it extends the discourse of architectural knowledge. Formed from various readings of nature, studies reveal the entanglement of natural phenomena as their materiality, forces and modes of generation overlap and affect each other.

25.26 Conor Clarke, Y5 'A School For Trespassing'. The project explores the viscosity of space and the fluidity of bodies through cutting metal and textiles. There are two stages to forming sheet metal: cutting and folding and stretching and shrinking. When using the wheeling machine, the process happens within arm's reach – the form is determined between the capacities of the machine and the body and becomes a metaphor for making architecture.

25.2

25.3

25.4

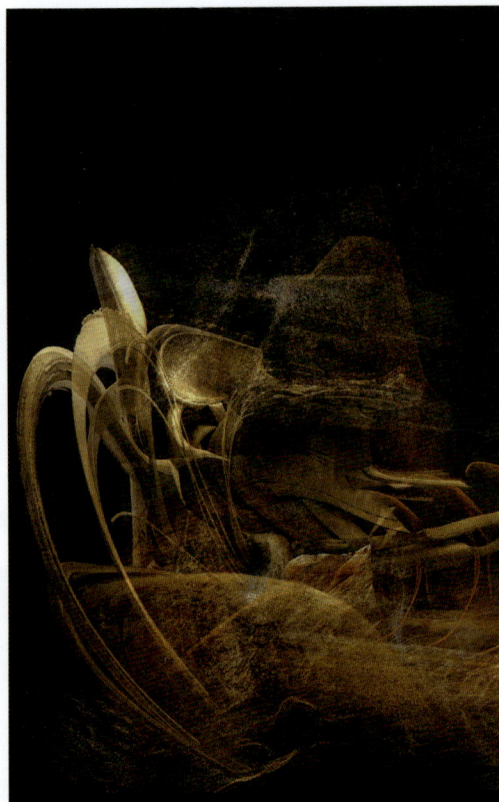

25.5

25.6

25.7

25.8

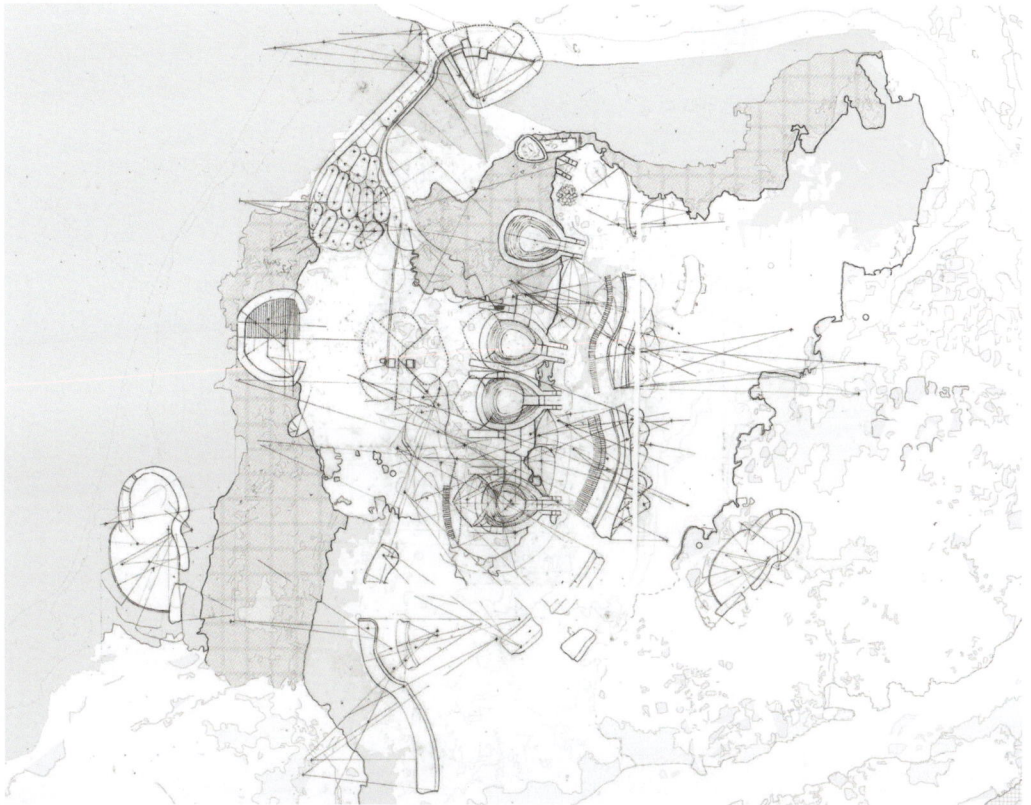

25.9

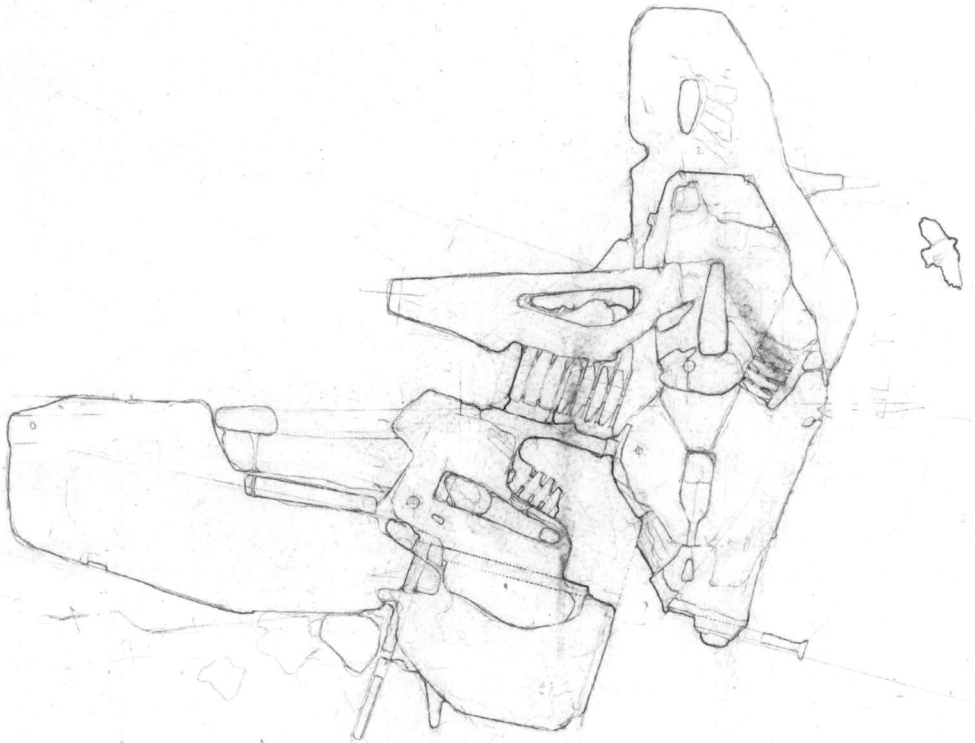

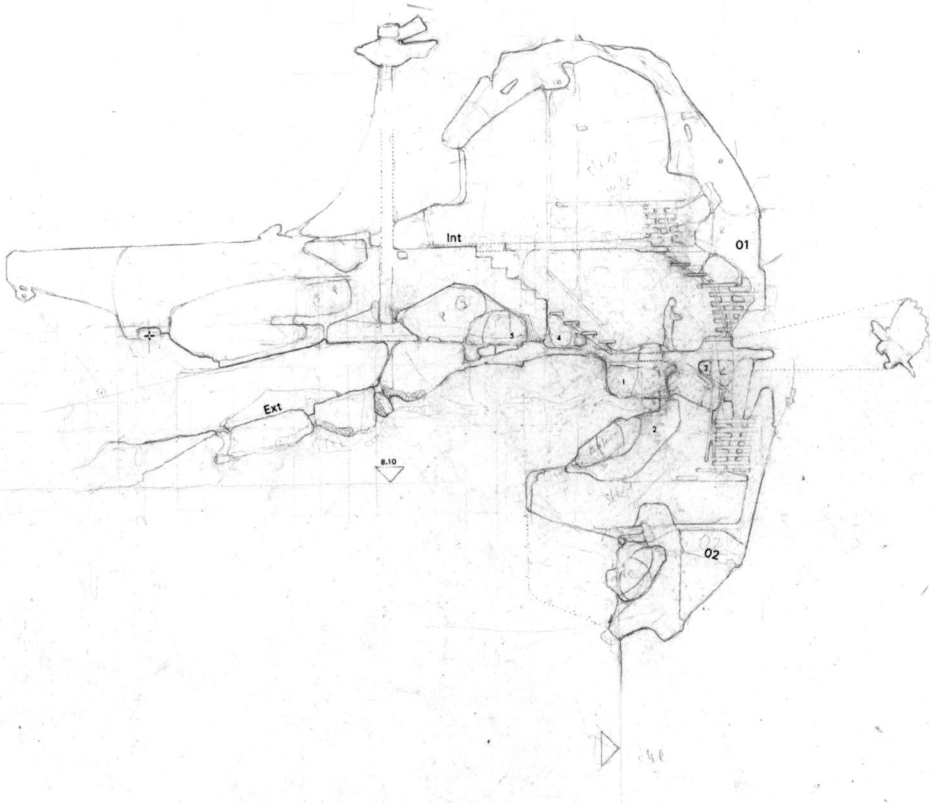

25.11

25.12

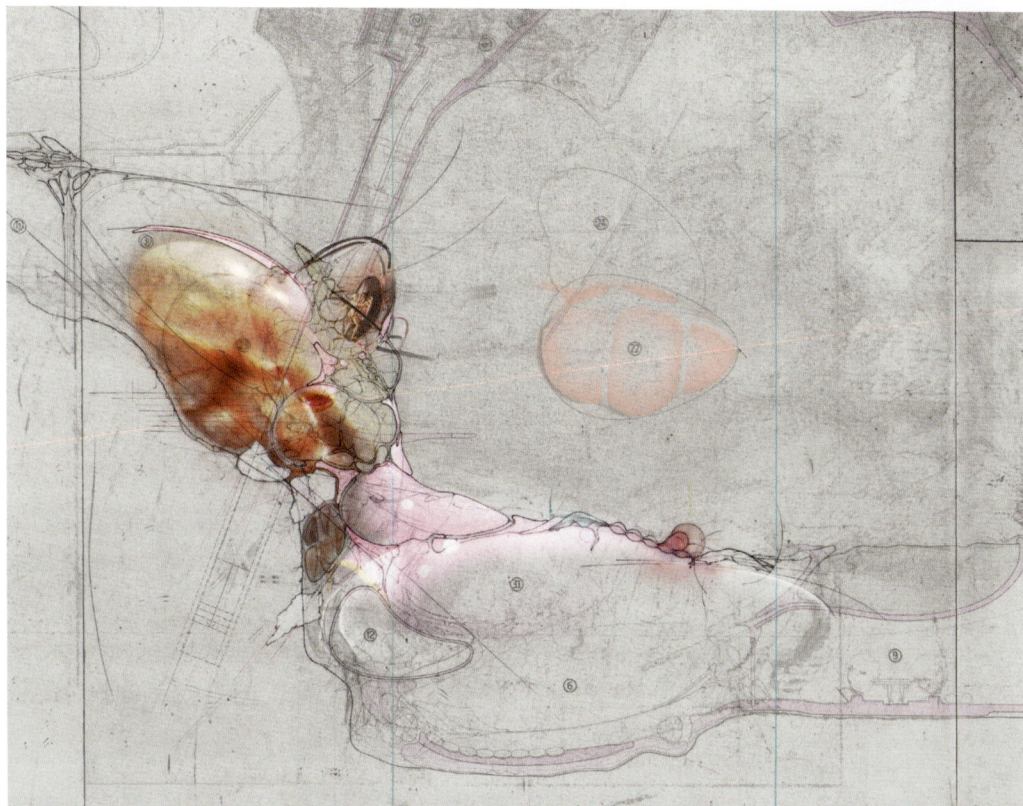

25.13

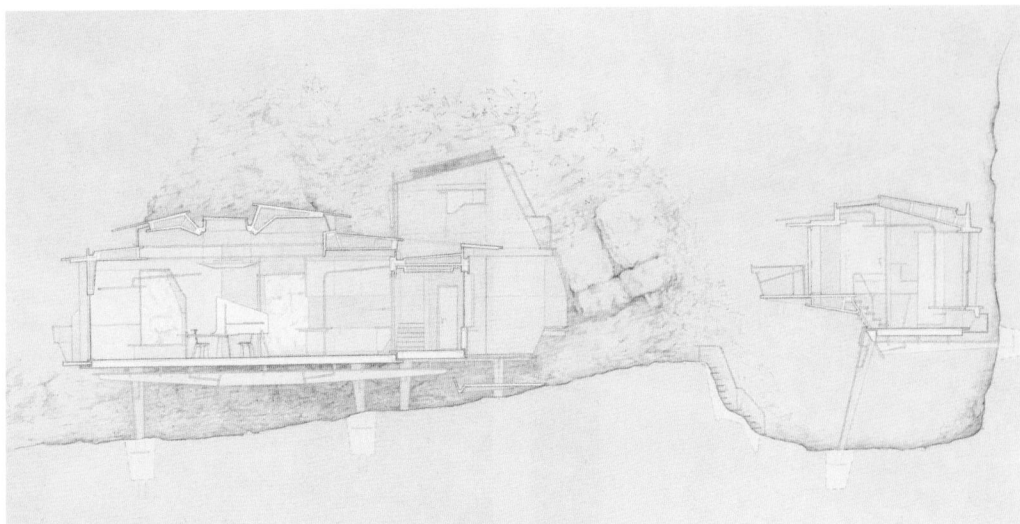

25.14

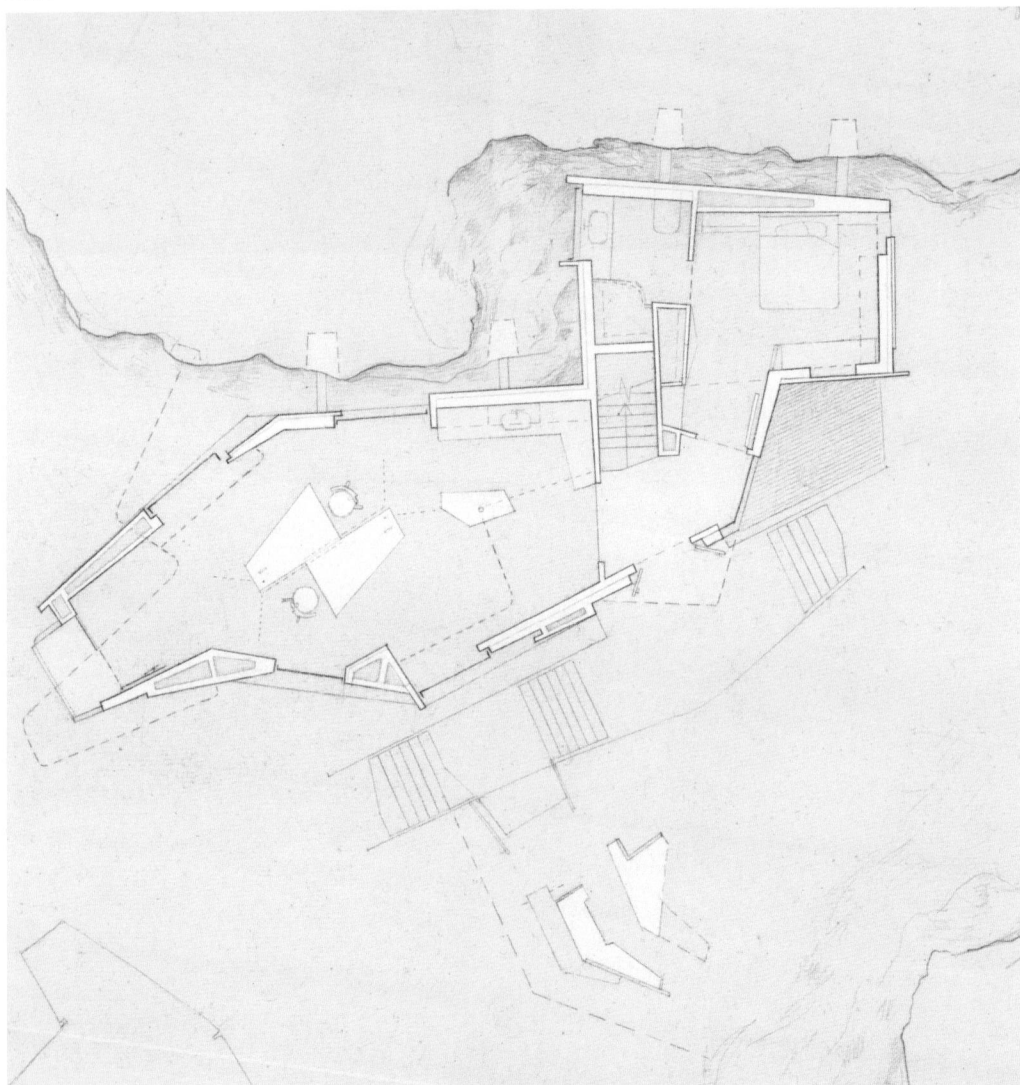

25.15

25.16

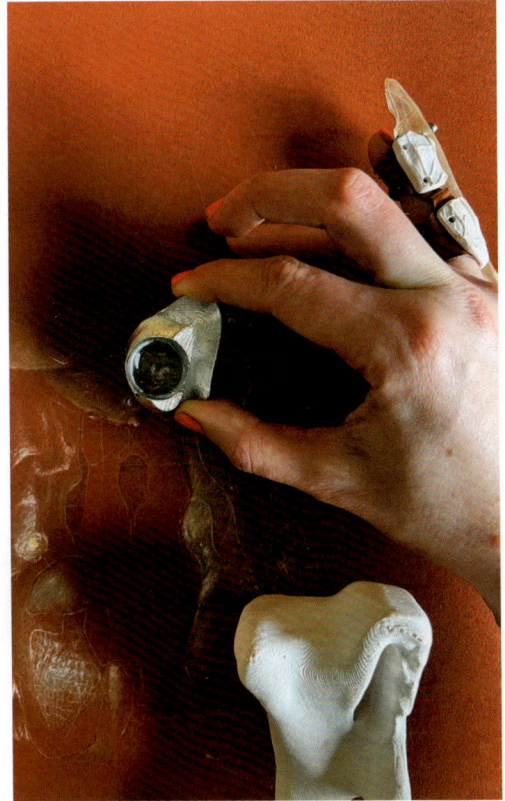

25.17

25.18

25.19

25.20

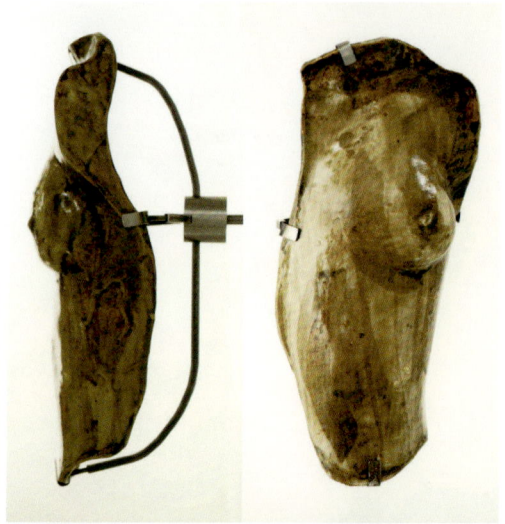

25.21

25.22

25.23

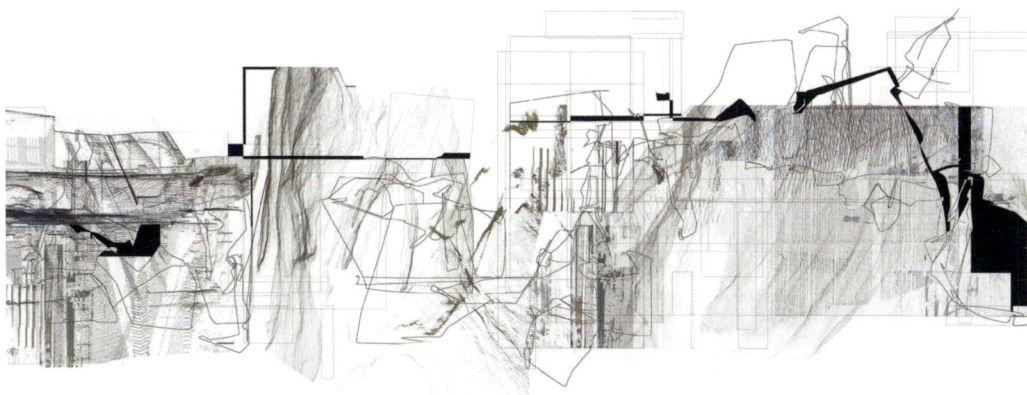

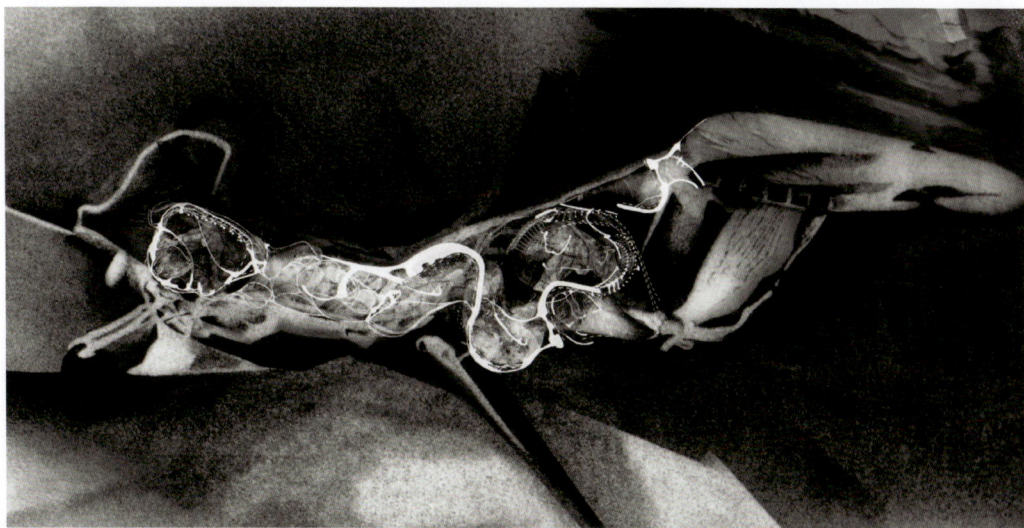

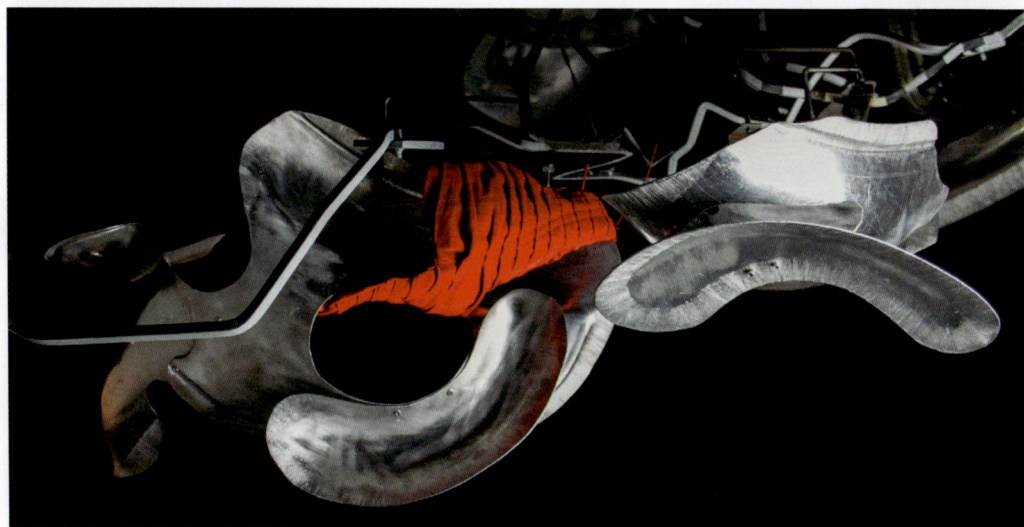

Design Realisation

Year 4

Module Coordinators:
Pedro Gil-Quintero, Stefan Lengen

Design Realisation provides an opportunity for all Year 4 Architecture MArch students to consider how buildings are designed, constructed and delivered within the temporal context of the building life cycle. It provides a framework to facilitate experimentation through the design of buildings, and encourages the interrogation and disruption of technical ideas and principles. Students propose their ideas at a variety of scales and represent them using drawings, diagrams, animations, physical models and 3D digital models. They are encouraged to take risks in their design thinking and strategy.

The module bridges the worlds of academia and practice, engaging with many renowned design practices and consultancies. A dedicated practice-based architect, structural engineer and environmental engineer support each design unit, working individually with students to develop their work throughout the module.

This year generated a wonderful array of projects that test, explore and innovate across a wide spectrum of principles and mediums. Students developed typologies that push the boundaries of technical and professional practice disciplines. Projects include inventive structural systems, environmental strategies, buildings for challenging sites, community engagement proposals, infrastructural projects and entrepreneurial proposals, to name but a few.

Thanks to all the structural consultants who have worked with individual students to realise their projects; to Atelier Ten, Max Fordham and Sal Wilson, environmental consultants to all design units; to our practice tutors for their remarkable commitment and dedication; and to Oliver Wilton, Director of Technology for his continual support and guidance.

Image: Isaac Palmiere-Szabo, PG20, 'The Barbican Digester'. Anaerobic digestion is integrated into a dense mixed-use building to metabolise the surrounding neighbourhood's waste and give its residents decentralised free energy with no carbon cost. It tests the integration of heavy infrastructure with architecture to create a productive ecosystem whose outputs feed into its inputs. Beginning life as a bodysuit, the system evolves into a building.

Lecturers
Nat Chard (The Bartlett), Izaskun Chinchilla Moreno (The Bartlett), Jenna de Leon (Cook Hafner Architecture Platform), Maria Fulford (Picture Plane Architects), Pedro Gil-Quintero (The Bartlett), Kirsten Haggart (Waugh Thistleton Architects), Laura Hannigan (Simple Works Structural Engineers), Tanvir Hasan (Donald Insall Associates), Stefan Lengen (The Bartlett), Anna Liu (Tonkin Liu Architects), Yeoryia Manolopoulou (The Bartlett), Hareth Pochee (Max Fordham Engineers), Alistair Shaw (Max Fordham Engineers), José Torero Cullen (UCL), Emanuel Vercruysse (Hooke Park, AA Design + Make), Rae Whittow-Williams (GLA London), Rachel Yehezkel (XCO2 MEP Engineering)

Practice Tutors
PG10 Matthew Wells (Techniker Ltd), **PG11** Rhys Cannon (Gruff Limited), **PG12** James Hampton (New Makers Bureau), **PG13** Jenna de Leon (Cook Haffner Architecture Platform), **PG14** Jakub Klaska (The Bartlett), **PG16** Will Jefferies (Rogers Stirk Harbour + Partners), **PG17** James Daykin (Daykin Marshall Studio), **PG18** Robert Haworth (Lineworks Architects), **PG20** David Edwards (Dave Edwards Design Ltd), **PG21** Tom Holberton (The Bartlett), **PG22** Gonzalo Coello de Portugal (Binom Architects), **PG24** Matthew Lucraft (Studio Jenny Jones), **PG25** Jerry Tate (Tate + Co)

Module Administrator
Kelly Van Hecke

PGTA Assistants
Farbod Afsar Bakeshloo, Hamish Muir, Yuki Tong, Conny Yingchin Yuen

Advanced Architectural Studies

Year 4

Module Coordinator: Brent Carnell

The Advanced Architectural Studies module in the first year of the MArch Architecture programme focuses on architectural histories and theories. Here we reflect on architecture within a broader, critical, intellectual and contextual field – simultaneously producing and being produced by it. We look at architecture's interfaces with other knowledge fields – from the scientific and technological to the social sciences and the humanities. We straddle empirics and theory, design and history, the iconic and the everyday.

The module seeks to engage students with architectural history and theory as a critical approach to augment design, as a parallel domain to test out approaches or as a discrete or autonomous domain of architectural engagement. It focuses on three key aspects: first, a reflective, critical and analytical approach; second, research instinct and exploratory methods and research as a form of practice; and third, skills of synthesis, writing and articulation. It also acts as foundational ground for the students' final year thesis.

Our lecture series, entitled 'Critical Frames', covered the following themes this year: 'Learning from 'Disorder', 'Architecture, Language, Medium', 'The City as Memory', 'Two Readings of Materiality' and 'In Other Voices'. These lectures were accompanied by the heart of the module, which is a set of themed seminars. The seminars straddle, geographically, the architectural histories and theories of multiple global contexts, and, thematically, buildings, urbanism, landscapes, design, art, film, ecology and climate crisis, politics, activism, technology, production, representation, spatial and material cultures, public participation and urban regeneration. At the end, drawing upon the seminars and lectures, the students formulate a critical enquiry around a topic of their choice and produce a 4,500-word essay.

2021–22 Seminars
Insurgent Cities, Sabina Andron
Architecture On & Off Screen, Christophe Gérard
Architecture and The People, Daisy Froud
The Ecological Calculus Seminar: Green New Dialogues, Jon Goodbun
Architecture, Art and the City, Eva Branscome
Architectural Splendour: The History and Theory of Ornament 1750–2021, Oliver Domeisen
Architecture and the Image of Decay, Paul Dobraszczyk
Good Things: Ethical Sociality and Materiality in the Architectures, Tim Waterman

Teaching Assistant
Farbod Afshar Bakeshloo

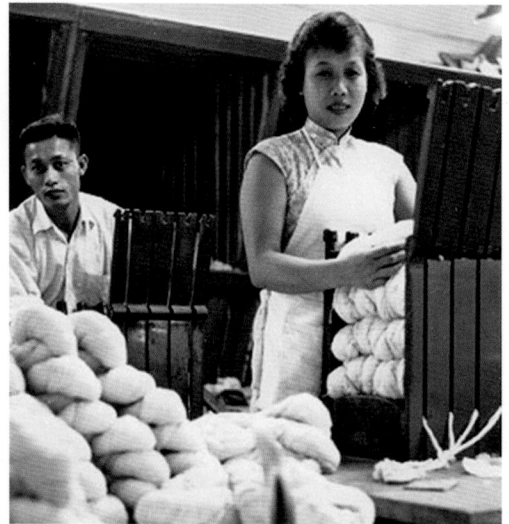

The Mills: Fabricated Heritage
Long Yin Au
Tutor: Eva Branscome

Abstract: Hong Kong has attempted to reconcile its urban identity as a metropolis straddling East and West since the colonial handover in 1997. This is particularly true of heritage discourse regarding the city's metamorphosis from an *entrepôt* industrial centre to the global city it is today. However, industrial heritage within the city remains underrepresented, although these architectural relics present a fragment of a bygone era, enabling individuals to relate collective past experiences.

As such, the site now rebranded as The Mills poses a unique heritage situation manifested through the political and capital forces which have informed its revitalisation. Originally known as Nan Fung Textile Mills, the building is located in Tsuen Wan, a district with a rich fabric manufacturing history. Given the role of the historic urban environment in interpreting and representing our past, as well as the ideologies it reinforces, this brings into question the extent to which The Mills memorialises the lives of the forgotten industrial workforce in Hong Kong.

This research argues that the existing renovation project neglects to critically address the location's contested past as an industrial site for female migrant workers. Instead, it has been reinvented as a form of 'fabricated heritage' which focuses on its marketability and industrial aesthetic and manifests itself through the commercialisation of urban redevelopment.

Redressing this, the essay seeks to provide an alternative nuanced understanding of The Mills as heritage, evidenced by migration, gendered experiences and working-class narratives, thereby generating a new understanding of Hong Kong's urban history. Based on first-hand accounts and employing an anthropological approach to help understand this architecture through its previous modes of inhabitation, this work seeks to rectify and prioritise important yet sidelined layers of the past. By allowing the spatial narratives of the female workforce to re-emerge, the study hopes to celebrate the often marginalised collectives which have shaped Hong Kong's contemporary built environment.

Images: Left – Author's grandmother Chan Lin Hing worked as a roving and spinning worker at Nan Fung Textile Mills between 1954 and 1976. Image author's own. Right – Mill6 CHAT, Yarn Packing in Mill 1, 1950s.

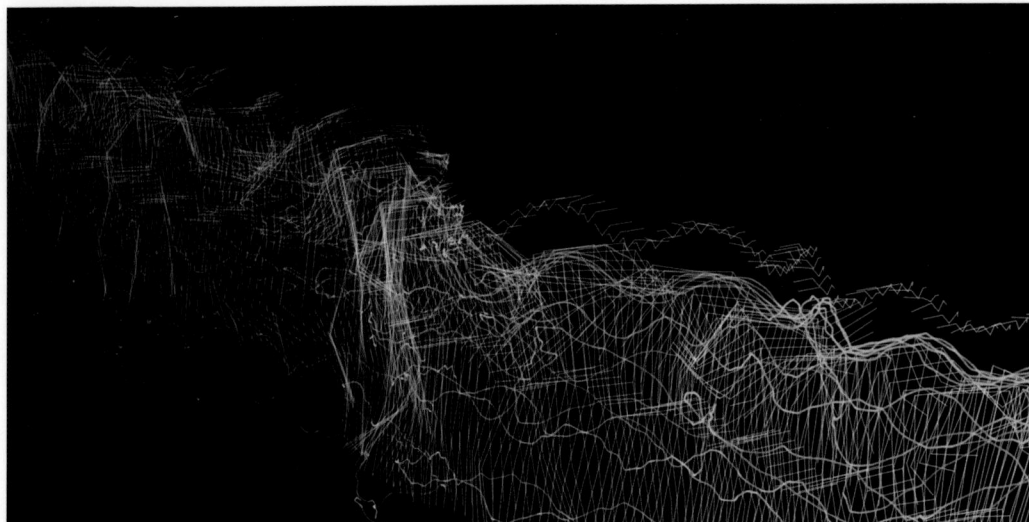

Four on the Floor: Autopoiesis and Rave
Matthew King
Tutor: Tim Waterman

Abstract: Through vibration, music facilitates interactions between bodies and matter, coupling us to our environment. Four-on-the-floor rhythms are one such manifestation and have powerful transcultural implications. From funk to techno, they lay the groundwork for hypnotic grooves that drive rituals and parties into the early hours. Through a collective dance, these rhythms and frequencies bind us to the landscape and each other.

Autopoietic in nature, the act of raving is sustained by a layering of complex sub-systems interacting as a network. Much like the autopoiesis of the human cell, the act of raving creates the parts that define the system and its boundary. After breaking away from existing notions of the floor as an architectural element, we can understand it as a boundary-defining, shifting phenomenon that is enacted and controlled by the processes that occur on it. The dance floor delineates the threshold between raving as a system and its environment.

The manifestation of the dance floor is dialectically coupled with the system of dancing. By engaging with an individual's creative dance process, the flow of information within the rave can be expressed as a symbiosis of interpretation and interaction between autonomous bodies. These interacting systems create a dense network of meaning.

Through the rave, the essay begins to investigate how meaning within a social system relates to space, architecture and rhythmic vibration. Applying sociocybernetic theory provides a greater understanding of the rave and its formation relative to its spatial context and environment. How does the phenomenon of the floor and four-on-the-floor rhythms relate to this autopoiesis, allowing the act of raving to unfold?

Image: The Four-on-the-Floor Raver. Image by author, 2022.

Un-Binding Boundaries: Architecture of an Altered Consciousness – Enter the Void by Gaspar Noé

Yu-Wen (Yvonne) Huang
Tutor: Christophe Gérard

Abstract: *Enter The Void* (2009) by Gaspar Noé is a cinematic interpretation of an altered perception of Tokyo under the effects of N,N-Dimethyltryptamine (DMT). It is the most accurate representation of a psychedelic experience to date, and from where it differs one can speculate on the architecture at play, which seems to unexpectedly reveal itself.

The aim of this essay is not to encourage drug consumption but to tentatively unbind the visceral boundaries in traditional architectural understandings in biological, psychological and phenomenological terms through the filmic construct of altered consciousness.

The first part of this essay dissects the architecture in the self by analysing the protagonist's transitional state of consciousness in the opening sequence. The mental dissolution of spatial relativity and the altered translation of objective reality highlight the process of perceptual binding,[1] which relies on prior knowledge and experiences to convert spatial information into neural representations and ultimately perceptions, interrogating the architecture when all rules are shifted.

The second part of this essay investigates the role of the self in architecture through the protagonist's out-of-body experience and the filmic interpretation of ego dissolution. When the representational process ceases to exist both externally and internally, the assimilation of self and architecture seems to transgress the architectural reality that otherwise only exists in its ontological form, framing the architecture as something more symbiotic than we ever imagined.

In conclusion, the internal, time-based architecture parallels Tschumi's discourse[2] and uncovers the hedonism in its amorality. By transgressing the rationality we impose on our architectural perceptions, we can unearth the pleasure in our experiences that are also ourselves.

Image: Still from *Enter the Void*, Fidélité Films, 2009.

1. Stevenson RA, Zemtsov RK, Wallace MT (2012), Individual Differences in the Multisensory Temporal Binding Window Predict Susceptibility to Audiovisual Illusions. *Journal of Experimental Psychology: Human Perception and Performance*, 38(6), 1517–1529.
2. Tschumi Bernard (1975), *Questions of Space: The Pyramid and the Labyrinth (or the Architectural Paradox)*. Studio International; 190: 136-142.

Thesis

Robin Wilson, Oliver Wilton

The thesis enables Year 5 Architecture MArch students to research, develop and define the basis for their work, addressing architecture and relevant related disciplines such as environmental design, humanities, engineering, cultural theory, manufacturing, anthropology, computation, the visual arts, physical or social sciences and urbanism.

The year starts with a short research methods study. Students then develop individual research proposals which are reviewed and discussed with module coordinators and design tutors. Following review, students proceed to undertake their research in depth, supported by specialist tutors who are individually allocated based on each student's stated research question and proposed methodology. The result is a study of 9,000 words or equivalent, that documents relevant research questions, contexts, activities and outcomes.

The thesis is an inventive, critical and directed research activity that augments the work students undertake in the design studio. The symbiotic relationship between thesis and design varies from evident and explicit to being situated more broadly in a wider sphere of intellectual interest. The thesis typically includes one or more propositional elements such as discursive argumentation, the development of a design hypothesis or strategy, or the development and testing of a series of design components and assemblies in relation to a specific line of inquiry or interest.

We anticipate that a number of theses from this year's academic cohort will be developed into external publications or projects.

Thesis Tutors
Hector Altamirano, Alessandro Ayuso, Andy Barnett, Matthew Barnett Howland, Carolina Bartram, Paul Bavister, Jan Birksted, Roberto Bottazzi, Eva Branscome, Brent Carnell, Mollie Claypool, Amica Dall, Gillian Darley, Edward Denison, Paul Dobraszczyk, Oliver Domeisen, Murray Fraser, Daisy Froud, Stephen Gage, Christophe Gérard, Stelios Giamarelos, Polly Gould, Gary Grant, Elain Harwood, Elise Hunchuck, Jan Kattein, Zoe Laughlin, Luke Lowings, Abel Maciel, Richard Martin, Anna Mavrogianni, Claire McAndrew, Níall McLaughlin, Shaun Murray, Thomas Pearce, Guang Yu Ren, David Rudlin, Tania Sengupta, Michael Stacey, Iulia Statica, Robin Wilson, Oliver Wilton, Simon Withers, Stamatis Zografos

Panlam: Rethinking Freeform Timber
Teodor Andonov
Tutor: Michael Stacey

This research focuses on the development of the Panlam system, a design-to-fabrication computational methodology for freeform timber (FFT) frames based on the use of three-axis CNC milling tables and timber panel lamination. Is it possible to rethink current FFT frame design and fabrication methodologies and achieve a structural system for the digital age which is flexible, customisable, automated and open? Current FFT practices produce efficient and evocative structures, but they can also be seen as exclusive, materially wasteful and inefficient in terms of fabrication. Manufacturing know-how is preserved in a few centres and hardly disseminated. On a planet in environmental crisis, an open and inclusive FFT methodology can help develop timber industries in new and prospective regions.

The context for this thesis is the European timber industry; the Panlam system targets forested regions and economies with the potential to develop local innovations in FFT, specifically the Balkans and Bulgaria. The thesis commences with a review of timber and its history, and an analysis of current FFT design and fabrication practices. It then sets out the intention to develop an alternative FFT methodology as well as exploring relevant case studies. It outlines the computational experiments undertaken as part of the project, as well as the digital models and physical prototypes created. This informs the development of the design-to-fabrication Panlam computational system and algorithm.

The final section of the thesis provides the context of a small masterplan project in Plovdiv, Bulgaria, set up with the aim of testing the Panlam methodology through several specific architectural designs. Two structural elements from the project are developed into large-scale physical prototypes which further explore the Panlam fabrication and assembly processes. The key outcome of the research is a new FFT frame system which eliminates the need for bending. Instead, flat panel lamination and multi-element assemblies are utilised to approximate curvature. A computational system for rapid and optimised design of Panlam structures based on simple line-and-curve 3D networks is presented. This work lays the foundational principles and strategies for freeform panel-laminated structures and presents the opportunities and potential benefits of further research in the field.

Image: Panlam Prototype 5: From panel lamellas to freeform timber parts and assembly. Image by the author.

My Land, Mine Land
Paris Gazzola
Thesis Tutor: Camillo Boano

This thesis creates a conversation between two societies that occupy the same land: the Indigenous and non-Indigenous peoples of the Western Australian desert. These groups have contrasting relationships with the land, which results in profoundly different, often divergent ontologies and ecological consequences. Through decolonial theory supported by forensic analysis of archival photos, videos and maps, the thesis reveals how even the most fundamental aspects of Australia's spatial organisation and land use are geared towards impetuous colonial-capitalist regimes of power, appropriation and accumulation. The non-Indigenous society views land as a financial commodity to be exploited in pursuit of economic gain, modernity and the agrarian-capitalist definition of progression. This imported colonial knowledge and mentality has hindered Australia's ability to peacefully inhabit the land, ultimately resulting in its destruction.

'Desert' was a label used to describe a place that could not be occupied using colonial knowledge – but all that is needed is a different kind of knowledge. Indigenous Australians developed sustainable land management practices over a period of 60,000 years, yet they have been silenced and sidelined. What they learned over this time is invaluable. Excavating submerged Indigenous relationships between land and care exposes an alternative practice through which Australians can occupy, cultivate and relearn sustainable land management praxis, becoming a vessel for which a new ontology can be created. We must question how valuable the land is: is it simply a commodity, or is it as much alive as you or I? If it is alive, the domination over the land is not just the exploitation of resources but the destruction of life. Despite the differences between Indigenous and Western communities, the one factor that unites them is the land and, more importantly, how to survive in a land in constant peril. The thesis concludes with a 'Provocation Atlas of Common Land' which suggests ways in which we can rebuild relationships between care, community and land by adapting Indigenous knowledge and practices to fit within the modern world. Methods of computational design, experimental form-making and speculation shape a provocative spatial reimagining that remains open-ended.

Image: Diptych depicting the same landscape two centuries apart. Different interpretations of what a full and prosperous landscape looks like. Image by the author.

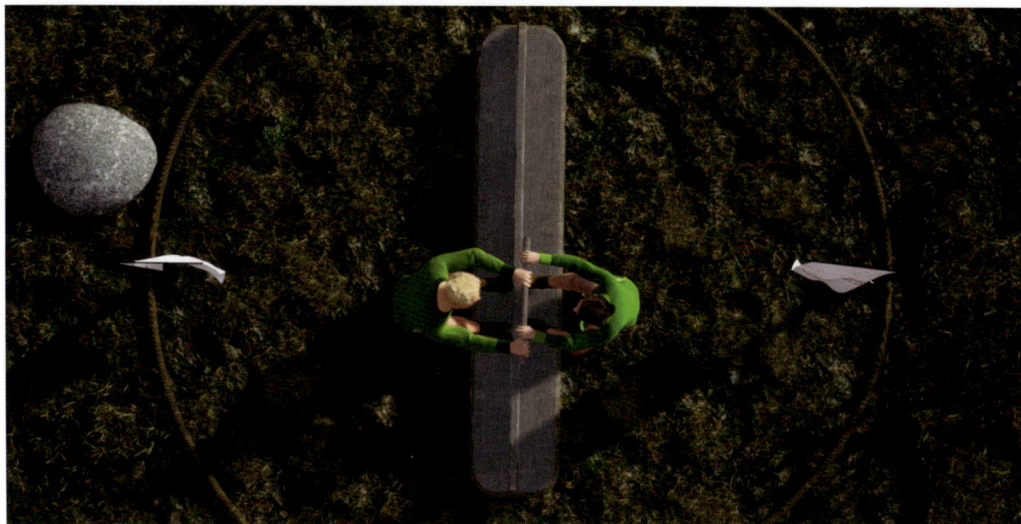

Contested Ground: Cultural Politics, Game Space and Identity in Scottish Highland Games
Zachariah Harper-Le Petevin Dit Le Roux
Thesis Tutor: Polly Gould

In asking if Scottish Highland Games are a practised form of architectural space, this thesis used the architectonics of game spaces and virtual worlds as tools to explore the complex cultural markers and performances of Scottishness that communicate national identity.

'Contested Ground' reflects on the Highland Games as an act of social construction that draws together bodies, landscapes and artefacts to rehearse and perform a non-representational form of Scottish history drawn from historical labour practices, construction processes and the agricultural enclosure of the region. It asks whether we might think of these games as forms of architectural space that are played and contested. By playing with national identity, the ruination of architectural heritage, agricultural traditions and clan affiliations has been reconciled and reconstituted as a set of game spaces that – through practice – are used to embody and revise ideas about self, region and nation.

As part of the methodology, the Highland Games was digitally reproduced in a game engine. This constructed a played form of architecture that seeks to defend what remains of Highland material culture from Scotland's own legacies of historical revision and policies of agrarian land reform, which have eroded regional cultural and spatial practices. This digital reconstruction of bodily action, artefact and Scottish landscape in the major contests that form the Highland Games – such as the caber toss, stone put and hill race – helped to examine the spatial aspect of the practices, myths and historical trajectories that led to the formation of each event.

The archive of digital assets, animations and images this process created then served as a useful tool for speculating on how the ephemeral and practised qualities of architectural space that these games create are informed by Scotland's history and contemporary politics, and the performance of bodies on the ground.

An argument for perceiving Highland Games as architecture not only contributes to specific ideas about Scottish architectural history and alternative modes of architectural production, but also calls into question the discipline's relationship with a politicised study of cultural history by highlighting spaces that are played and performed – open to continual practice, revision and erasure.

Image: Still extracted from virtual game engine development of the maide-leisg (Scots Gaelic meaning 'lazy stick'). Image by the author, 2022.

445

Right to Roam: A Spatial Investigation into the Freedom to Roam in the English Landscape
Gabrielle Wellon
Thesis Tutor: Gillian Darley

Although national taxes provide landowners with billions of pounds in subsidy payments each year, the public are denied access to 92% of the land in England. With walkers confined to designated pathways or areas of 'open-access land', the right to roam remains limited. Multiple lockdowns caused by the Covid-19 pandemic not only highlighted disparities in the ability to access open space but also emphasised the importance of exercising our fundamental human right to free movement. Despite the partial 'right to roam' granted by the Countryside and Rights of Way (CRoW) Act 2000, it is evident that a further extension to existing legislation could assist in providing equal accessibility to the English landscape.

By investigating the inception, influences and implications of exclusion from the English landscape, this thesis aims to provide a contemporary spatial argument in favour of an extended right to roam. As property rights remain a source of contention, this study has required engagement with a wide range of audiences and academic fields. Positioned within the context of England's history, socio-politics and legislation, this thesis interrogates theoretical concepts of power, propriety and place in connection to restricted accessibility rights. To explicate this critique, it investigates a paradigm of autocratic landownership in England in the form of Lord Richard Benyon (Parliamentary Under-Secretary of State for Rural Affairs, Access to Nature and Biosecurity), who is the proprietor of the Englefield Estate in West Berkshire.

Crucially, this thesis has been researched and written during an epoch of English land reform. Subsequent to the UK's departure from the European Union in 2020, the Department for Environment, Food & Rural Affairs (DEFRA) has committed to replacing the EU Common Agricultural Policy's Basic Payment Scheme with a more progressive approach by 2028. Despite pledging to use "public money, for public goods", the government is yet to announce any plans to direct any public funding for public accessibility to open spaces under the new Environmental Land Management Scheme (ELMS). As the future of accessibility rights remains uncertain, this timely academic critique aims to explicate current political theory as well as compiling circumstantial evidence in favour of a liberal right to roam.

Image: Private property signs erected in the private gardens of Englefield House, Berkshire. The public are granted partial access to the estate courtesy of Lord Richard Benyon, the current Parliamentary Under-Secretary of State for Rural Affairs, Access to Nature and Biosecurity). Drawn by author.

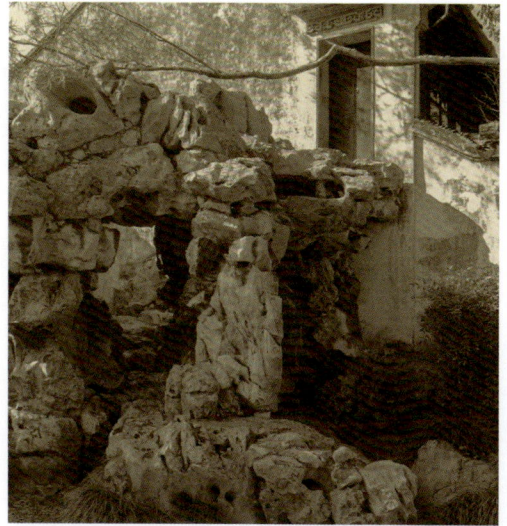

Spatialised Poetry: A Study on the Role of Calligraphy in the Space Making of the Chinese Literati Garden
Tianzhou Yang
Thesis Tutor: Guang Yu Ren

Literati gardens have been a main topic of inquiry in architectural studies in China since the 1950s. However, researchers tend to focus on the physical space itself, paying very limited attention to the contribution of traditional art forms such as calligraphy to space-making. This study therefore aims to examine the interaction between the tangible space of literati gardens and the intangible forms of traditional art, with a particular emphasis on the the role played by calligraphy inscription. It starts with how calligraphy, poetry and literati paintings were integrated with traditional garden-making. Contrary to the imperial garden, which highlighted the authority of the emperor/empress, the literati garden emphasised independent expression. Given that the literati in pre-modern China were all well-recognised masters of calligraphy, poetry and painting – the primary media for personal expression at the time – their gardens turned out to be spatial extensions of these three closely integrated art forms.

The key method of literati garden space-making is *Zaojing*, or scenery-making. The scenery designs were often inspired by well-known poems, with calligraphy inscriptions given as clues to the original poem, thus taking the visitors into the artistic realm beyond the physical scenery.

The inscriptions are always implicit and allusive and therefore cannot be fully understood without a deep knowledge of history and cultural traditions. Based on the data collected from five classical gardens in the city of Suzhou, China, the study identifies the active role calligraphy inscriptions play in space-making. They are able to define a flexible spatial boundary and shape the spatial organisation; in some instances, they are good references for the design of architectural details, and they even actively engage with visitors, guiding their exploration into the gardens and thus affecting their perception and experience of the garden space. The findings have confirmed the integral role of calligraphy art in space-making, offering a new perspective on the understanding of diverse cultural contexts of space-making.

Image: Left – The stairways throughout the rock mountain serve as a 'cloud ladder' in the courtyard in front of *Tiyun shi*. Right – The artistic realm generated by the inscription through its poetic allusion. The physical 'cloud ladder' in the courtyard acts as a precise response to this, contributing to the physical creation of an artistic realm. Photography and collage by the author.

Shoreditch Village Phase 2, London
Photography by Timothy Soar

Allford Hall Monaghan Morris supports the students' Summer Show

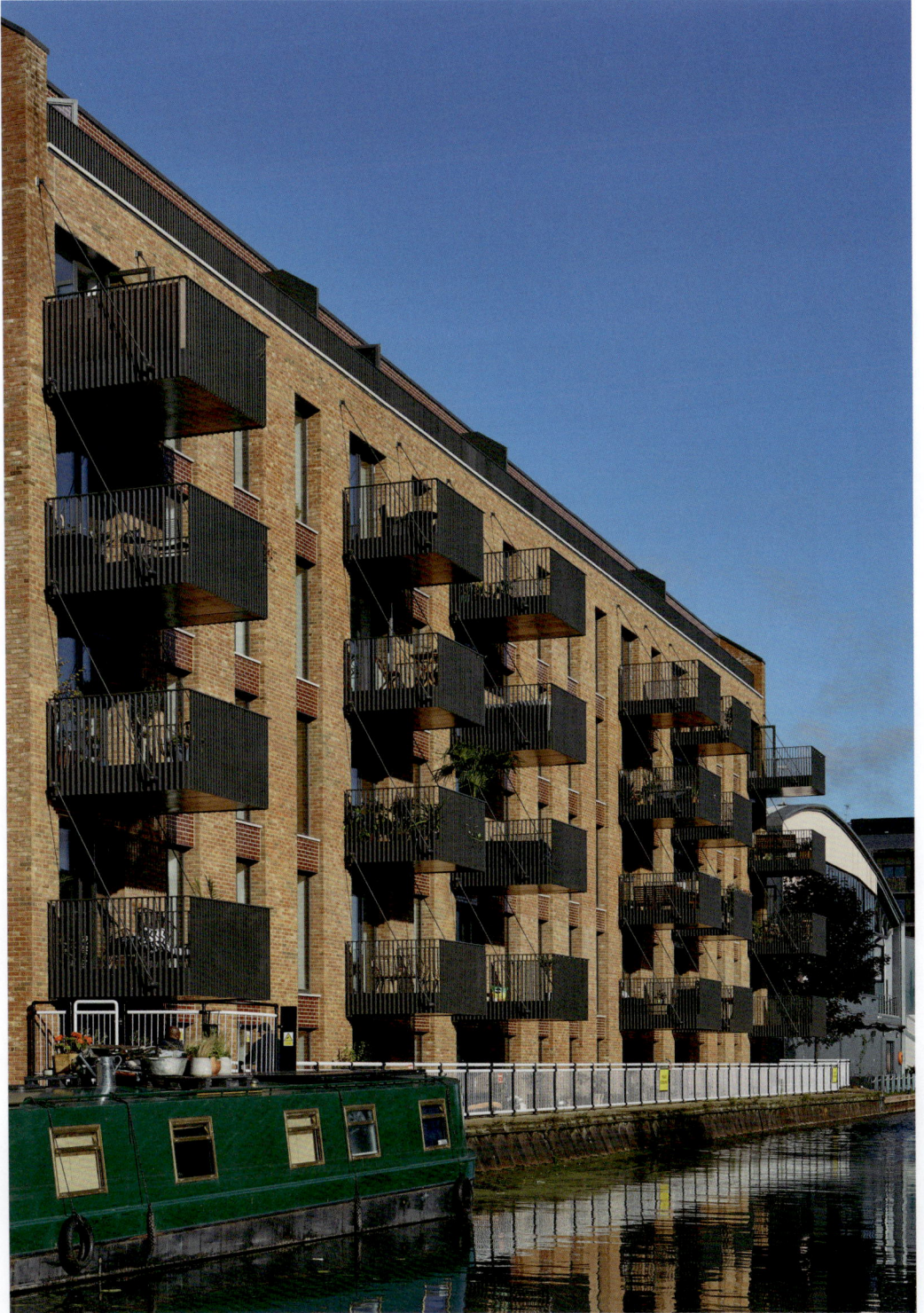

Bream Street, London
Photography by Rob Parrish

Foster + Partners
fosterandpartners.com

Our Programmes

The Bartlett School of Architecture currently teaches undergraduate and graduate students across 28 programmes of study and one professional course.

Across the school's portfolio of teaching, research and professional programmes, our rigorous, creative and innovative approach to architecture remains integral. You will find below a list of our current programmes, their duration when taken full time (typical for MPhil/PhDs) and the directors. More information, including details on open days, is available on our website.

Undergraduate

Architecture BSc (ARB/RIBA Part 1)
Three-year programme, directed by Ana Monrabal-Cook & Dr Luke Pearson
Architecture MSci (ARB Part 1 &2)
Five-year programme, directed by Sara Shafiei
Architectural & Interdisciplinary Studies BSc
Three or four-year programme, directed by Elizabeth Dow
Engineering & Architectural Design MEng
Four-year programme, directed by Luke Olsen

Postgraduate

Architecture MArch (ARB/RIBA Part 2)
Two-year programme, directed by Julia Backhaus, Professor Marjan Colletti & Kostas Grigoriadis
Architectural Computation MSc/MRes
12-month programmes, directed by Manuel Jiménez Garcia
Architectural Design MArch
12-month programme, directed by Gilles Retsin
Architectural History MA
One-year programme, directed by Professor Peg Rawes
Architecture & Digital Theory MRes
One-year programme, directed by Professor Mario Carpo & Professor Frédéric Migayrou
Architecture & Historic Urban Environments MA
One-year programme, directed by Professor Edward Denison
Bio-Integrated Design MSc/MArch
Two-year programmes, directed by Professor Marcos Cruz & Dr Brenda Parker (MSc only)

Design for Manufacture MArch
15-month programme, directed by Peter Scully
Design for Performance & Interaction MArch
15-month programme, directed by Dr Ruairi Glynn
Landscape Architecture MA/MLA
One (MA) and two-year (MLA) programmes, directed by Professor Laura Allen & Professor Mark Smout
Situated Practice MA
15-month programme, directed by James O'Leary
Space Syntax: Architecture & Cities MSc/MRes
One-year programmes, directed by Dr Kayvan Karimi (MRes) & Prof Kerstin Sailer (MSc)
Urban Design MArch
12-month programme, directed by Roberto Bottazzi

Advanced Architectural Research PG Cert
Six-month programme, directed by Professor Nat Chard

Architectural Design MPhil/PhD
Three to four-year programme, directed by Professor Jonathan Hill
Architectural & Urban History & Theory MPhil/PhD
Three to four-year programme, directed by Professor Sophia Psarra
Architectural Space & Computation MPhil/PhD
Three to four-year programme, directed by Ava Fatah gen Schieck
Architecture & Digital Theory MPhil/PhD
Three to four-year programme, directed by Professor Mario Carpo & Professor Frédéric Migayrou
Architectural Practice MPhil/PhD
Three to four-year programme, directed by Professor Murray Fraser

Professional

Architecture (ARB/RIBA Part 3)
10 to 23-month course, directed by Professor Felicity Atekpe

Public Lectures

Visit our Vimeo channel to watch this year's recorded lectures – search 'Bartlett School of Architecture' to find us.

The Bartlett International Lecture Series
Attracting guests from across the world, our International Lecture Series has featured over 500 distinguished speakers since its inception in 1996. Lectures in this series are open to the public and free to attend.

This autumn and spring, the series was curated as an index of the school's programmes and broadcast live on YouTube. Each lecture was curated by a programme to inspire, invent, imagine and provoke and co-hosted by students with tutors. The series aimed to expose different modes and methodologies of design and design thinking to embrace urgencies, subtleties and complexities of social, spatial and environmental justice.

Lectures this year featured:

— **Contingent**
M. Casey Rehm (Sci-Arc)
— **The Landscape Model**
Luis Callejas (LCLA Office)
— **Solidarity in Everyday Space**
Jos Boys (LEEDIC) and Nina Tame
— **Engineering Carbon –
A Small Practice Perspective**
Peter Laidler (Structure Workshop)
— **What is the Future of Chinese Architecture?**
Jianxiang He & Ying Jiang
(O-Office Architects)
— **How to Talk About the Weather**
Astrida Neimanis (University of British Columbia Okanagan)
— **Poikilohydric Design**
Professor Marcos Cruz Inaugural Lecture
— **Building Integrated Environments:
A Cognitive Framework**
N. Katherine Hayles
(University of California)
— **Rethinking Urban Materiality:
Time as a Resource**
Anupama Kundoo
(Anupama Kundoo Architects)

— **The Making of Making (Architecture)**
Josep Miàs (MiAS Architects)
— **Direct Urbanism**
Barbara Holub (transparadiso)
— **What Can We Learn from One Billion Images?**
Lev Manovich (City University New York)
— **Scale**
Mari Hvattum (Oslo School of Architecture and Design), Federica Goffi (Azrieli School of Architecture and Urbanism), Igor Marjanović (Rice Architecture) and Eunice Seng (The University of Hong Kong)
— **Difference and Design**
Justin Garrett Moore
(Andrew W. Mellon Foundation)
— **Building Beyond**
Dr Sonya Dyer and Dr Barbara Imhof
(LIQUIFER Vienna-Bremen)
— **Queer Infrastructures**
Professor Ben Campkin Inaugural Lecture
— **Innovation at the Urban Scale**
Laura Narvaez Zertuche and Martha Tsigkari (Foster + Partners)
— **Return**
Mae-ling Lokko (Center for Ecosystems in Architecture, Yale University)

Prospectives
The Bartlett's B-Pro history and theory lecture series continued to offer a platform for the presentation, discussion and theoretical reflection on the links between digital thought, architecture and urban design. Speakers included:

— **Emmanuelle Chiappone-Piriou**
— **Kyle Steinfield**
— **Daniel Cardoso Llach,
Carnegie Mellon University**

Work in Progress
A public lecture series from Landscape Architecture programmes, the series comprised curated but informal talks from practitioners and academics. Speakers were invited from a range of disciplines, to reflect on their work in progress, working methods and the process of working with landscape. Speakers included:

- Ed Wall, University of Greenwich
- Jala Makhzoumi, American University of Beirut
- Herb Sweene, Michael Van Valkenburgh Associates
- Felicity Steers, erz Studio

Bartlett Research Conversations

The Bartlett Research Conversations series featured presentations of research from students undertaking the Architectural Design or Architectural and Urban History and Theory MPhil/PhD programmes. Students were joined by senior academics from across the school, including PhD programme directors and supervisors, alongside members of the wider Bartlett and UCL community. This year research was presented by:

- Olivier Bellflamme
- Jhono Bennett
- Paola Camasso
- Nikoletta Karastathi
- Alexandra Lăcătuşu
- Xiuzheng Li
- Ana Mayoral Moratilla
- Petra Seitz

Space Syntax Laboratory Research Seminars

This academic seminar series featured researchers sharing their findings, discussing their ideas and showing work in progress from The Bartlett's Space Syntax Laboratory. Seminars were moderated by Dr Kimon Krenz. They were open to the public and attended by Bartlett's staff and students. Guests to the series included:

- Lars Marcus, Chalmers University of Technology
- Francesca Froy, The Bartlett School of Planning, UCL
- Ha Minh Hai Thai, RMIT School of Architecture and Urban Design
- Constance Desenfant, Weston Williamson + Partners
- Ahmed Tarek Zaky Fouad
- Gareth Simons, The Bartlett Energy Institute, UCL
- Martin Bielik, Bauhaus University Weimar

- Isabelle Soares, Leibniz University
- Paolo Santi, MIT Senseable City Lab
- David Fredrick & Rhodora G. Vennarucci, University of Arkansas
- Lingzhu Zhang, Tongi University & Alain Chiaradia, University of Hong Kong

Bartlett Screening Rooms

The Bartlett Screening Room addresses questions around critical urbanism through the screening of short films and moving images, followed by discussion. It is a collaboration between Henrietta Williams, an artist/researcher based at The Bartlett School of Architecture, and Oliver Wright, programmer of the Open City Documentary Festival. Guests to the series included:

- Forensic Architecture
- Kiran Kaur Brar
- Mike Revereza
- Simon Liu
- Sasha Litvintseva
- Sindhu Thirumalaisamy
- Bedwyr Williams
- Riar Rizaldi
- Audrey & Maxime Jean-Baptiste
- Suneil Sanzgiri

Queering Urbanism Lecture Series

Queering Urbanism is a new online event series initiated by B.Queer, The Bartlett Faculty of the Built Environment's network for lesbian, gay, bisexual, trans, queer, intersex, asexual (LGBTQIA+) students, staff and allies. Organised by Claire Tunnacliffe, Jordana Ramalho and Ben Campkin, the series connects queer and trans studies to urban studies and practices of urbanism, foregrounding issues of equity, diversity and inclusion in the built environment. Guests to the series included:

- Petra Doan, Florida State University
- Dhiren Borisa, Jindal Global Law School
- Sarah Ensor and Tim Waterman, The Bartlett School of Architecture, UCL

Conferences & Events

As we emerged from the Covid-19 pandemic, a diverse programme of events was held in hybrid formats at our Bloomsbury and Here East campuses exploring innovative ideas and current issues, with inspiring speakers from across the globe. Students were able to exhibit their work physically for the first time in two years at exhibitions both on and off-campus.

Polysocial Realities, 10 September 2021 took place as part of Ars Electronica Festival. Students from Design for Performance & Interaction MArch participated in their first physical group exhibition in two years, at fold.ldn in East London.

Architects! Climate Action Network (ACAN) held an **Education Toolkit Workshop, 28 September 2021** with ideas, guidance and resources for use by students, tutors and others who want to take immediate, ongoing and meaningful action towards a new climate education for architecture.

Supported by the UCL-Wits Strategic Partnership fund, **Unfinished Symphonies: Transformational Decolonial Urbanism, 14-15 October 2021** saw Professor Achille Mbembe give a public lecture followed by a PhD workshop to share and discuss work-in-progress on transformational decolonial urbanism.

The student-led symposium **Common Threads: Intersectional Methodologies of Architectural History Symposium, 18 November 2021** responded to notions of historical narrative, unacknowledged histories and modes of representation.

The sixteenth annual **PhD Research Projects Conference, 22 and 24 February 2022** included two days of intense debate and discussion between students, staff, invited guests, critics and the public, discussing doctoral work in development and drawing to conclusion.

Eight temporary pavilions were exhibited at UCL Here East for **The Olympic Games – 10 Years On, 24 March 2022** by 50 first-year Engineering & Architectural Design MEng students.

Filmed just months before the invasion of Ukraine, **What Shall We Do with These Buildings?, 4 May 2022** was previewed at a fundraising event in support of the country. The screening was followed by a discussion with members of the film production, academics and invited guests from the Ukrainian architecture community.

Book Launches
Landscape Citizenships, 30 November 2021
Dr Tim Waterman, lecturer at The Bartlett School of Architecture, UCL, Jane Wolff, University of Toronto and Ed Wall, University of Greenwich discussed their latest book, Landscape Citizenships in a hybrid event between UCL and Toronto.

Dreaming the Impossible to Build the Extraordinary: The Formative First Year of Architectural Education, 1 March 2022
An informal launch of a new Bartlett publication by Frosso Pimenides, Director of Architecture BSc Year 1, with Jeremy Melvin.

Designs on History: The Architect as Physical Historian, 3 March 2022
Professor Jonathan Hill held a lively online discussion with the contributors of his book looking to understand design as a visible and physical history.

A Landscape Utopia: A double book launch with Tim Waterman and Cannon Ivers, 4 May 2022
The launch of two new books from the Landscape Architecture programme at The Bartlett School of Architecture: *250 Things a Landscape Architect Should Know* by Cannon Ivers and *The Landscape of Utopia: Writings on Everyday Life, Taste, Democracy and Design* by Tim Waterman.

Bartlett Shows Website

In September 2020, the school launched its bespoke digital exhibition environment, presenting The Summer Show 2020. Since then, eight further student shows have been shared digitally, including The Summer Show 2021 and The B-Pro Show 2021. Each digital exhibition has attracted thousands of online visitors from across the globe, with the Summer Show 2021 content viewed over 200,000 times.

The digital exhibition space was designed by creative agency Hello Monday, working together with the school's exhibitions and communications teams, to create a unique online experience for the visitor. Hello Monday delivered a virtual show space that allows the user to explore the work spatially, within exhibition rooms, and in detail, on student project pages. Students have the opportunity to display their work using video, high-definition imagery and 3D models alongside detailed narratives.

With each exhibition, the digital environment is being refined to improve the visitor experience and to encourage greater engagement with the student work displayed. Projects are now searchable by thematic concern with all previous shows available to browse from a single landing page.

The Bartlett's digital show environment has won web design awards at both the Awwwards and Favourite Website Awards and has been shortlisted for the prestigious Archiboo and D&AD Awards in the Digital Design category. Within the UCL community, the virtual shows team, specifically Chee-Kit Lai, Director of Exhibitions, Professor Penelope Haralambidou, Director of Communications, and David Shanks, Project Manager, have been recognised for their outstanding contribution to the learning experience with a UCL Education Award in the student-staff partnership category.

www.bartlettarchucl.com

The Bartlett
Summer Show 2021

Explore

Screenshot of Summer Show 2021 website.

Alumni

The Bartlett's diverse and vibrant alumni play a vital role in the life of the school, as staff, visiting lecturers, mentors, sponsors, donors and participants.

Each year we organise several alumni events, including an 'R&V' evening, founded by and for alumni as the 'Rogues and Vagabonds' over 60 years ago. After the exceptional circumstances of the past two years, we were delighted to return to in-person gatherings with an R&V drinks reception held at 22 Gordon Street. As well as giving alumni the opportunity to catch up with each other, the event also featured the launch of the new Bartlett publication, *Dreaming the Impossible to Build the Extraordinary* by Architecture BSc Year 1 Director, Frosso Pimenides, written in collaboration with architectural historian Professor Jeremy Melvin. The reception was chaired by Paul Monaghan, Director at Allford Hall Monaghan Morris.

We also invite alumni to join us at The Bartlett Summer Show at an exclusive Alumni Late.

All Bartlett School of Architecture alumni are invited to join UCL's Alumni Online Community to keep in touch with the school and receive benefits including special discounts, UCL's *Portico* magazine and more.

Registered alumni have access to:

— **Thousands of e-journals available through UCL Library**
— **A global network of old and new friends in the worldwide alumni community**
— **Free mentoring and the opportunity to become a mentor yourself**
— **Jobs boards for the exclusive alumni community**

aoc.ucl.ac.uk/alumni

Cover image from *Dreaming the Impossible to Build the Extraordinary.*

The Bartlett Promise

Across higher education and in industry, the built environment sector is not diverse enough. Here at The Bartlett, we promise to do better.

The Bartlett Promise Scholarship was launched in 2019 to enable UK undergraduate students from backgrounds under-represented in The Bartlett Faculty to pursue their studies with us, with the aim of diversifying the student body and ultimately the built environment sector. In 2020, it was widened to include Masters and PhD scholarships, and in 2021, internationally, to Sub-Saharan Africa master's students. We want a Bartlett education to be open to all, regardless of means.

The scholarship covers full tuition fees for the degree programme, plus an annual allowance to cover living and study expenses. All Promise scholars will also receive ongoing academic and career support during their studies. In addition, The Bartlett Promise Sub-Saharan Africa Scholarships provide a comprehensive support package, including travel to and from the UK and study visa costs.

Professor Christoph Lindner, Dean of The Bartlett Faculty of the Built Environment says:

The Bartlett is passionate and serious about creating access for students who face barriers to higher education. Launching The Bartlett Promise Sub-Saharan Africa Scholarship allows us to support students from a region of the world that is significantly under-represented in our faculty and to contribute to realising the potential, and launching the careers, of future leaders in the built environment. This is a long-term commitment and we look forward to seeing the ongoing impact our scholars will have in the UK and the wider world.

To be eligible for a scholarship, candidates must have an offer of a place on a Bartlett degree programme. When selecting scholars, we consider the educational, personal and financial circumstances of the applicant, and how these relate to the eligibility criteria.

Full details of the application process and eligibility criteria can be found on our website.

ucl.ac.uk/bartlett/bartlett-promise

Students at 22 Gordon Street, The Bartlett's Bloomsbury home.

New School Director

The Bartlett School of Architecture is delighted to announce that Professor Amy Kulper will join the school as Director from 01 September 2022, following an international search for a transformative leader.

Amy Catania Kulper is an architectural educator, administrator and innovator, whose teaching and research focus on the intersections of history, theory, criticism and design. Amy joins us from Rhode Island School of Design (RISD), where she has been Head of Architecture for the past five years. She has also taught at the University of Cambridge, the University of California, Los Angeles (UCLA), the Southern California Institute for Architecture (SCI_Arc), and the University of Michigan, where she was an associate professor with tenure and four-time recipient of the Donna M. Salzer Award for teaching excellence.

At RISD, Amy has continued to shape contemporary architectural thought. In 2019 she co-chaired the ACSA national conference Black Box: Articulating Architecture's Core in the Post-Digital Era. As a part of the conference, she co-curated the exhibition, Drawing for the Design Imaginary at the Carnegie-Mellon Museum. More recently she co-curated Drawing Attention: The Digital Culture of Contemporary Architectural Drawings, a group exhibition at Roca Gallery in London.

I am honoured to have been selected as the next Director of The Bartlett School of Architecture and look forward to future collaborations with staff and students. This is a crucial moment for reflection and change as we examine our roles as educators and possible futures for both the discipline and the profession of architecture. The fluency of the architect is expanding to include expertise in racial, social, and environmental justice and decoloniality. I look forward to harnessing the creative innovations of the Bartlett community as we embrace this transformation in the education of the architect.

Professor Amy Kulper

Staff, Visitors & Consultants

A
Ana Abram
Tamanna Abul Kashem
Dr Vasilija Abramovic
Georgios Adamopoulos
Farbod Afshar Bakeshloo
Elena Agafonova
Ava Aghakouchak
Yahia Ahmed
Visiting Prof Robert Aish
Roslyn Aish
Sarah Aljishi
Prof Laura Allen
Carlos Alvarez Doran
Dr Sabina Andron
Arveen Appadoo
Dimitris Argyros
Azadeh Asgharzadeh
   Zaferani
Abigail Ashton
Felicity Atekpe
Edwina Attlee
Joseph Augustin

B
Julia Backhaus
Kirsty Badenoch
Matthew Barnett
   Howland
Beth Barnett-Sanders
Sarah Barry
Paul Bavister
Simon Beames
Richard Beckett
Bedir Bekar
Jonathan Bennett
Julian Besems
Bastian Beyer
Vishu Bhooshan
Prof Peter Bishop
Laurence Blackwell-Thale
Isaïe Bloch
Eleanor Boiling
Jatiphak Boonmun
Prof Iain Borden
Roberto Bottazzi
Visiting Prof Andy Bow
Matt Bowles
Dr Eva Branscome
Albert Brenchat Aguilar
Alastair Browning
Jessica Buckmire
Thomas Budd
Christopher Burman
Mark Burrows
Matthew Butcher

C
Joel Cady
Paola Camasso
Blanche Cameron
William Victor Camilleri
Alberto Campagnoli

Barbara-Ann
   Campbell-Lange
Prof Ben Campkin
Dr Brent Carnell
Prof Mario Carpo
Dan Carter
Martyn Carter
Luciano Caruggi de Faria
Ricardo Carvalho De Ostos
Tomasso Casucci
Dr Megha Chand Inglis
Haden Charbel
Prof Nat Chard
Zahira Chehabeddine
Po Nien Chen
Nikhil Cherian
Prof Izaskun Chinchilla
   Moreno
Tung Ying (Crystal) Chow
Krina Christopoulou
Philia Chua
Sandra Ciampone
Dovile Ciapaite
Mollie Claypool
Prof Marjan Colletti
Michael Collins
Stephannie Contreras-Fell
Emeritus Prof Peter Cook
Hannah Corlett
Samuel Coulton
Prof Marcos Cruz
Rut Cuenca Candel
Nichola Czyz

D
Christina Dahdaleh
Amica Dall
Tiffany Dang
Satyajit Das
Peter Davies
Tom Davies
Klaas de Rycke
Luca Dellatorre
Prof Edward Denison
Pradeep Devadass
Max Dewdney
Dr Ashley Dhanani
Zoi Diakaki
Ilaria Di Carlo
David Di Duca
Simon Dickens
Katerina Dionysopoulou
Thomas Dobbins
Paul Dobraszczyk
Patrick Dobson-Perez
Visiting Prof Elizabeth Diller
Oliver Domeisen
Elizabeth Dow
Sarah Dowding
Andreea Dumitrescu
Shyamala Duraisingam
Kirti Durelle
Thomas Dyckhoff

E
David Edwards
Amr Elhusseiny
Sam Esses
Ruth Evison

F
Pani Fanai-Danesh
Ava Fatah gen Schieck
Alian Faraz
Donat Fatet
Laura Fawcett-Gaskell
Alberto Fernandez
   Gonzalez
Timothy Fielder
Lucy Flanders
Zachary Fluker
Elie Fofana
James Ford
Emeritus Prof
   Adrian Forty
Prof Murray Fraser
Daisy Froud
Maria Fulford

G
Emeritus Prof
   Stephen Gage
Gunther Galligioni
Mark Garcia
Paris Gazzola
Christophe Gérard
Christina Geros
Octavian Gheorghiu
Dr Stelios Giamarelos
Pedro Gil-Quintero
Prof Jacqui Glass
Agnieszka Glowacka
Dr Ruairi Glynn
Alicia Gonzalez-Lafita
   Perez
Dr Jon Goodbun
Dr Polly Gould
Niamh Grace
Gabriele Grassi
Kevin Gray
Emmy Green
James Green
Kevin Green
Sienna Griffin-Shaw
Dr Sam Griffiths
Dr Kostas Grigoriadis
Panagiota Grivea
Eric Guibert
Srijana Gurung
Seth Guy

H
Tamsin Hanke
Prof Sean Hanna
Zachariah Harper-Le
   Petevin Dit Le Roux

Prof Penelope
   Haralambidou
Alice Hardy
Jack Hardy
Wardah Hassan
Sarah Hassan M Alsomly
Ben Hayes
Thea Heintz
Stephen Henderson
Colin Herperger
Simon Herron
Rosie Hervey
Danielle Hewitt
Visiting Prof Neil Heyde
Parker Heyl
Prof Jonathan Hill
Ashley Hinchcliffe
Bill Hodgson
Tom Holberton
Adam Holloway
Tahmineh Hooshyar
   Emami
Tyson Hosmer
Delwar Hossain
Oliver Houchell
Elise Hunchuck
Johan Hybschmann

I
Jessica In
Anderson Inge
Susanne Isa
Cannon Ivers

J
Benjamin James
Clara Jaschke
William Jennings
Manuel Jiménez García
Steve Johnson
Helen Jones
Luke Jones
Nina Jotanovic

K
Melih Kamaoglu
Nikoletta Karastathi
Dr Kayvan Karimi
Dr Jan Kattein
Thomas Keeley
Arnav Kele
Jonathan Kendall
Thomas Kendall
Jakub Klaska
Fergus Knox
Maria Knutsson-Hall
Andreas Korner
Margit Kraft
Dr Kimon Krenz
Anete Krista Salmane
Dirk Krolikowski
Dragana Krsic
Mangesh Kurund

L

Alexandra Lacatusu
Chee-Kit Lai
Lo Lanfear
Ekaterina Larina
Zoe Lau
Ruby Law
Benjamin Lee
Dr Guan Lee
Kit Lee-Smith
Stefan Lengen
Dr Christopher Leung
Thomas Leung
Sarah Lever
Visting Prof Amanda Levete
Tairan Li
Xiuzheng Li
Ifigeneia Liangi
Prof CJ Lim
Enriqueta Llabres-Valls
Visiting Prof Lesley Lokko
Alvaro Lopez
Déborah López Lobato
Luke Lowings
Tim Lucas
Matthew Lucraft
Elin Lund
Abi Luter

M

Alexandru Malaescu
Shneel Malik
Emily Mann
Prof Yeoryia
    Manolopoulou
Vasilis Marcou Ilchuk
Maria Marta
Sara Martinez Zamora
Robin Mather
Emma-Kate Matthews
Billy Mavropoulos
Dr Claire McAndrew
Joseph McGrath
Prof Níall McLaughlin
Visiting Prof Jeremy Melvin
Prof Joseph Miàs
Prof Frédéric Migayrou
Doug Miller
Siraaj Mitha
Matei-Alexandru Mitrache
Tom Mole
Carolina Mondragon-
    Bayarri
Ana Monrabal-Cook
Visiting Prof Philippe Morel
Bongani Muchemwa
Hamish Muir
Dr Shaun Murray
Maxwell Mutanda

N

Tetsuro Nagata
Giles Nartey
Elliot Nash
Filippo Nassetti
Sahar Navabakhsh
Provides Ng
Carlota Núñez-Barranco
    Vallejo

O

Aisling O'Carroll
Toby O'Connor
James O'Leary
Andy O'Reilly
Luke Olsen
Visiting Prof Femi
    Oresanya
Daniel Ovalle Costal
Levent Ozruh

P

Dr Yael Padan
Igor Pantic
Artemis Papachristou
Thomas Parker
Claudia Pasquero
Jane Patterson
Thomas Pearce
Dr Luke Pearson
Prof Alan Penn
Prof Barbara Penner
Drew Pessoa
Samuel Pierce
Frosso Pimenides
Jolanta Piotrowska
Alicia Pivaro
Ruth Plackett
Maj Plemenitas
Jakub Plewik
Danae Polyviou
Lyn Poon
Andrew Porter
Arthur Prior
Prof Sophia Psarra
Stamatios Psarras

R

Dr Lakshmi Priya Rajendran
Robert Randall
Prof Peg Rawes
Dr Sophie Read
Dr Aileen Reid
Guang Yu Ren
Prof Jane Rendell
Gilles Retsin
Charlotte Reynolds
Farlie Reynolds
Callum Richardson
Julie Richardson
Dr David Roberts
Felix Roberts
Gavin Robotham
Daniel Rodriguez Garcia
Javier Ruiz Rodriguez
Mateo Rossi Rolando

S

Ralf Saade
Visiting Prof Jenny Sabin
Kevin Saey
Prof Kerstin Sailer
Rebecca Sainsot-Reynolds
Diana Salazar Morales
Sabrina Samuels
Tan Sapsaman
Ned Scott
Peter Scully
Petra Seitz
Ariha Semontee
Dr Tania Sengupta
Alan Sentongo
Neba Sere
Sara Shafiei
David Shanks
Alistair Shaw
Prof Bob Sheil
Visiting Prof Wang Shu
Naz Siddique
Isaac Simpson
Colin Smith
Paul Smoothy
Prof Mark Smout
Valentina Soana
Joana Carla Soares
    Goncalves
Jasmin Sohi
Jonathan Solly
Amy Spencer
Ben Spong
Matthew Springett
Prof Michael Stacey
Dr Iulia Statica
Johanna Stenhols
Dr Tijana Stevanovic
Rachel Stevenson
Sabine Storp
Greg Storrar
David Storring
Kay Stratton
Sarmad Suhail
Michiko Sumi
Harry Sumner
Lina Sun
Dr Tom Svilans
Iga Swiercz

T

Prantar Tamuli
Emma Temm
Philip Temple
Colin Thom
Kathryn Timmins
Eva Tisnikar
Michael Tite
Claudia Toma
Siyu Tong
Alessandro Toti
Martha Tsigkari
Chan Tsz Long

Freddy Tuppen
Samuel Turner-Baldwin
Jonathan Tyrrell

U

Tom Ushakov

V

Melis Van Den Berg
Kelly Van Hecke
Kim Van Poeteren
Dr Tasos Varoudis
Prof Laura Vaughan
Hamish Veitch
María Venegas Raba
Viktoria Viktorija
Amelia Vilaplana de Miguel
Dr Nina Vollenbroker

W

Michael Wagner
Andrew Walker
Qiong Wang
Prof Susan Ware
Barry Wark
Gabriel Warshafsky
Tim Waterman
Harry Watkins
Patrick Weber
Dingyi Wei
Visiting Prof Lu Wenyu
Paul Weston
Alice Whewell
Andrew Whiting
Alex Whitley
Daniel Widrig
Anna Wild
Daniel Wilkinson
Gen Williams
Henrietta Williams
Graeme Williamson
James Williamson
Dr Robin Wilson
Sal Wilson
Oliver Wilton
Jane Wong
Catherine Wood

Y

Zifeng Ye
Sandra Youkhana
Michelle Young
Ying Ching Yuen

Z

Aikaterini Zacharopoulou
Barbara Zandavali
Emmanouil Zaroukas
Sepehr Zhand
Qingyuan Zhou
Dominik Zisch
Dr Fiona Zisch
Dr Stamatios Zografos

ucl.ac.uk/architecture
bartlettarchucl.com
Find us on f y ⊙ 𝐯

Publisher
The Bartlett School of Architecture, UCL

Editors
Srijana Gurung, Penelope Haralambidou

Proofreaders
Catherine Bradley, Karen Francis

Graphic Design
Patrick Morrissey, Unlimited
weareunlimited.co.uk

ISBN 978-1-8383185-7-4

The Bartlett School of Architecture, UCL
22 Gordon Street
London WC1H 0QB

+44 (0)20 3108 9646
architecture@ucl.ac.uk

The Bartlett
School of
Architecture

UCL

THE BARTLETT

Summer Show Main Title Supporter 2022
AHMM

Sponsors
Foster + Partners
Forterra